40
YEARS OF
ORIGINAL
WRITING

IF THIS IS A MAN
THE TRUCE

Primo Levi

Translated by Stuart Woolf

ABACUS

This combined volume first published in Great Britain by Penguin Books 1979
Published by Abacus 1987
Reprinted 1987 (twice), 1988, 1990 (twice), 1992, 1993 (twice), 1994, 1995 (twice),
1996, 1997, 1998 (twice), 1999, 2000, 2001 (twice), 2002, 2003, 2004,
2005 (twice), 2006, 2007, 2008, 2009 (twice), 2010, 2011 (twice)

This edition published by Abacus in 2013

A CIP catalogue record for this book
is available from the British Library.

ISBN 978-0-349-13901-2

Printed and bound in Great Britain by
Clays Ltd, St Ives plc

Papers used by Abacus are from well-managed forests
and other responsible sources.

MIX
Paper from
responsible sources
FSC
www.fsc.org   FSC® C104740

Abacus
An imprint of
Little, Brown Book Group
100 Victoria Embankment
London EC4Y 0DY

An Hachette UK Company
www.hachette.co.uk

www.littlebrown.co.uk

Contents

Contents

THE TRUCE

Introduction

The danger, as time goes by, is that we will tire of hearing about the Holocaust, grow not only weary but disbelieving, and that out of fatigue and ignorance more than cynicism, we will belittle and by stages finally deny – actively or by default – the horror of the extermination camps and the witness, by then so many fading memories, of those who experienced them. The obligation to remember is inscribed on every Holocaust memorial, but even the words 'Never Forget' become irksome eventually. We don't like being reminded of our obligations, we don't want to go on taking the medicine, especially when we don't accept that we are sick. So it is important that a writer such as Primo Levi is not sold to future generations as being 'good' for them. Again and again Primo Levi's work is described as indispensable, essential, necessary. None of those terms overstates the case: but they do prepare readers new to Levi for a forbiddingly educative experience, making him a writer unlike all others, and the experience of reading him a chore. Which it isn't.

The friendlier language to which enthusiastic publishers and reviewers sometimes have recourse is hardly more appropriate to the case. It means nothing to say of any writer that he is 'readable' or 'a page turner' and Primo Levi is certainly not one you read in a single sitting without pausing for breath. There is much that makes one pause in *If This is a Man*, the record of Primo Levi's eleven-month incarceration in Auschwitz, much one cannot read without needing to lay aside the book and

inhale the breath of common air. But while it would be foolish
to describe him as an entertainer, he nevertheless engages the
reader's interest in a story and an illumination, in character, in
description, et cetera as any other imaginative writer does. His
subject is humanity *in extremis* but it is still humanity. He does
not stand outside the compendious narrative of human life to
which every writer is committed. Nor is he the end of the line.
Things happen in *If This is a Man* that are beyond ordinary
daily experience but it is still us to whom they are happening,
and the understanding Primo Levi seeks is no different in kind
to that sought by Shakespeare in *King Lear*, or Conrad in *The
Heart of Darkness*.

So if we approach *If This is a Man* expecting a historical
investigation of the rise of Nazism and the potency of its appeal
to the German people, or an enquiry into the origins and nature
of evil, we ask both too much and too little of it. Primo Levi is
neither historian nor metaphysician. As a matter of honour, no
less than as a matter of writerly decency – perhaps as a mark of
respect to mankind – he refuses grandiose philosophising or theology. 'We do not believe,' he writes, 'in the most obvious and
facile deduction: that man is fundamentally brutal, egoistic and
stupid in his conduct once every civilised institution is taken
away ... We believe, rather, that the only conclusion to be
drawn is that in the face of driving necessity and physical disabilities many social habits and instincts are reduced to silence.'

The quietness of that 'conclusion', so determinedly rational
and even matter-of-fact, so calm in its rejection of the con-
solations of rage or blame or despair, is characteristically
heart-breaking. 'Reduced to silence' is a humane but terrible
description of man's fate in the camps; it is inevitable, final, an
attrition of spirit of which the beatings and the humiliations are
just the foretaste, and which can only be atoned for, all round,
by the opposite to silence. This is what the book is for. It must

speak of what happened, of what it knows, for the very reason that silence – the removal of the will and wherewithal to speak, and the fear of never being listened to or believed – was the ultimate aim of that system of dehumanisation Nazism embraced, and the proof it had succeeded.

The subject of *If This is a Man* is not how could men do such things, but what was it that they did, how did it fall to some prisoners ('the saved') to endure it and others ('the drowned') not to, what is left when everything but the barest capacity to endure, the power only 'to refuse our consent', is driven out, and by what means are some still able to impress on others the suggestion of a world 'not corrupt, not savage, extraneous to hatred and terror . . . a remote possibility of good'.

From the first pages of the book the essential project of the camps is laid bare: it is, in Levi's words, 'the demolition of a man'. Through small and large acts of deprivation and destruction we follow the process: the removal of hope, of dignity, of luxury, of necessity, of self; the reduction of a man to a hoarder of grey slabs of bread and the scrapings of a soup bowl (wonderfully told all this, with a novelist's gift for detail and sometimes very nearly comic surprise), to the confinement of a narrow bed – in which there is 'not even any room to be afraid' – with a stranger who doesn't speak your language, to the cruel illogicality of hating a fellow victim of oppression more than you hate the oppressor himself – one torment following another, and even the bleak comfort of thinking you might have touched rock bottom denied you as, when the most immediate cause of a particular stress comes to an end, 'you are grievously amazed to see that another one lies behind; and in reality a whole series of others'.

With grievous amazement, never self-pitying but sometimes bordering on a sort of numbed wonderment, Levi records the day to day personal and social history of the camp, noting not only the fine gradations of his own descent, but the capacity of some prisoners to cut a deal and strike a bargain, while others, destined by their age or character for the gas ovens, follow 'the slope down to the bottom, like streams that run down to the sea'.

There are pages where, unexpectedly, amid the horror, a reader feels he has stumbled on a near inconsequential diary entry. 'It is lucky that it is not windy today,' one such passage begins. The incongruity of anything being lucky in such a place strikes the diarist: 'Strange, how in some way one always has the impression of being fortunate, how some chance happening, perhaps infinitesimal, stops us crossing the threshold of despair and allows us to live.' In this way, too, we come to understand how living is possible, how, if it is the small things that demean, it can also be the small things that sustain. Here, perhaps, is the advantage of Levi having written *If This is a Man* so close to his time in Auschwitz. Recollection has not been worn away by years and controversy nor subsumed under the necessity to take a long view of historical events. In much of this book, immediacy does the work of theorising and education.

The anger, also, is too close to the event to feel either tempered or cranked up. Seeing old Kuhn, a religious man, praying aloud and thanking God he has been spared selection for the gas chamber, Levi is furious that Kuhn does not realise it will be his turn next, that 'what has happened today is an abomination, which no propitiatory power, no pardon, no expiation by the guilty, which nothing at all in the power of man can ever clean again ... If I was God, I would spit at Kuhn's prayer.'

It is a bitterly ironic thought, God spitting at a devotee's prayers, as though in such a place, where such crimes have been committed, it is a blasphemy to be religious. A blasphemy, too, even to think of pardon or expiation.

Primo Levi gave his life to considering the full extent of those crimes, for they did not stop at the gates of the camps. They would go on, if the guilty had their way, into the dreams of men like him, mocking them with the promise that they would never be listened to, and even where they did secure a hearing, would never be believed.

In a terrible dream which he discovers he shares with fellow inmates, Levi is back home telling people of his experiences, but they are 'completely indifferent ... speak confusedly of other things among themselves, as if I was not there'. Here is the dread to end dreads – 'the ever-repeated scene of the unlistened-to story'.

And so, of course, in many quarters it has turned out to be. Despite a testament as harrowing as his, and for all its meticulous refusal of melodrama, the Holocaust has become subject to sneering scepticism – now outright denial, now the slower drip of devaluation and diminishment. In later books, as he saw the thing he dreaded becoming a reality, Primo Levi wrote of the 'negators of truth', people who defame not only those who lived to tell the tale, but those for whom they speak as though 'by proxy', the true witnesses of the abomination – that is to say those who did not survive it and so cannot speak for themselves. Thus, in any of its forms, Holocaust denial kills the victims a second time.

Strong though the words of *If This is a Man* are, they are still weak before the will to deny or forget.

Howard Jacobson
April 2013

IF THIS IS A MAN

Author's Preface

It was my good fortune to be deported to Auschwitz only in 1944, that is, after the German Government had decided, owing to the growing scarcity of labour, to lengthen the average life-span of the prisoners destined for elimination; it conceded noticeable improvements in the camp routine and temporarily suspended killings at the whim of individuals.

As an account of atrocities, therefore, this book of mine adds nothing to what is already known to readers throughout the world on the disturbing question of the death camps. It has not been written in order to formulate new accusations; it should be able, rather, to furnish documentation for a quiet study of certain aspects of the human mind. Many people – many nations – can find themselves holding, more or less wittingly, that 'every stranger is an enemy'. For the most part this conviction lies deep down like some latent infection; it betrays itself only in random, disconnected acts, and does not lie at the base of a system of reason. But when this does come about, when the unspoken dogma becomes the major premiss in a syllogism, then, at the end of the chain, there is the Lager. Here is the product of a conception of the world carried rigorously to its logical conclusion; so long as the conception subsists, the conclusion remains to threaten us. The story of the death camps should be understood by everyone as a sinister alarm-signal.

I recognize, and ask indulgence for, the structural defects of the book. Its origins go back, not indeed in practice, but as an

idea, an intention, to the days in the Lager. The need to tell our
story to 'the rest', to make 'the rest' participate in it, had taken
on for us, before our liberation and after, the character of an
immediate and violent impulse, to the point of competing with
our other elementary needs. The book has been written to satisfy this need: first and foremost, therefore, as an interior
liberation. Hence its fragmentary character: the chapters have
been written not in logical succession, but in order of urgency.
The work of tightening up is more studied, and more recent.

It seems to me unnecessary to add that none of the facts are
invented.

PRIMO LEVI

If This is a Man

You who live safe
In your warm houses,
You who find, returning in the evening,
Hot food and friendly faces:
    Consider if this is a man
    Who works in the mud
    Who does not know peace
    Who fights for a scrap of bread
    Who dies because of a yes or a no.
    Consider if this is a woman,
    Without hair and without name
    With no more strength to remember,
    Her eyes empty and her womb cold
    Like a frog in winter.
Meditate that this came about:
I commend these words to you.
Carve them in your hearts
At home, in the street,
Going to bed, rising;
Repeat them to your children,
    Or may your house fall apart,
    May illness impede you,
    May your children turn their faces from you.

1

The Journey

I was captured by the Fascist Militia on 13 December 1943. I was twenty-four, with little wisdom, no experience and a decided tendency – encouraged by the life of segregation forced on me for the previous four years by the racial laws – to live in an unrealistic world of my own, a world inhabited by civilized Cartesian phantoms, by sincere male and bloodless female friendships. I cultivated a moderate and abstract sense of rebellion.

It had been by no means easy to flee into the mountains and to help set up what, both in my opinion and in that of friends little more experienced than myself, should have become a partisan band affiliated with the Resistance movement *Justice and Liberty*. Contacts, arms, money and the experience needed to acquire them were all missing. We lacked capable men, and instead we were swamped by a deluge of outcasts, in good or bad faith, who came from the plain in search of a non-existent military or political organization, of arms, or merely of protection, a hiding place, a fire, a pair of shoes.

At that time I had not yet been taught the doctrine I was later to learn so hurriedly in the Lager: that man is bound to pursue his own ends by all possible means, while he who errs but once pays dearly. So that I can only consider the following sequence of events justified. Three Fascist Militia companies, which had set out in the night to surprise a much more powerful and dangerous band than ours, broke into our refuge one spectral snowy dawn and took me down to the valley as a suspect person.

During the interrogations that followed, I preferred to admit my status of 'Italian citizen of Jewish race'. I felt that otherwise I would be unable to justify my presence in places too secluded even for an evacuee; while I believed (wrongly as was subsequently seen) that the admission of my political activity would have meant torture and certain death. As a Jew, I was sent to Fossoli, near Modena, where a vast detention camp, originally meant for English and American prisoners-of-war, collected all the numerous categories of people not approved of by the newborn Fascist Republic.

At the moment of my arrival, that is, at the end of January 1944, there were about one hundred and fifty Italian Jews in the camp, but within a few weeks their number rose to over six hundred. For the most part they consisted of entire families captured by the Fascists or Nazis through their imprudence or following secret accusations. A few had given themselves up spontaneously, reduced to desperation by the vagabond life, or because they lacked the means to survive, or to avoid separation from a captured relation, or even – absurdly – 'to be in conformity with the law'. There were also about a hundred Yugoslavian military internees and a few other foreigners who were politically suspect.

The arrival of a squad of German SS men should have made even the optimists doubtful; but we still managed to interpret the novelty in various ways without drawing the most obvious conclusions. Thus, despite everything, the announcement of the deportation caught us all unawares.

On 20 February, the Germans had inspected the camp with care and had publicly and loudly upbraided the Italian commissar for the defective organization of the kitchen service and for the scarce amount of wood distribution for heating; they even said that an infirmary would soon be opened. But on the morning of the 21st we learned that on the following day the Jews would be leaving. All the Jews, without exception. Even the children, even the old, even the ill. Our destination? Nobody knew. We should be prepared for a fortnight of travel. For every person missing at the roll-call, ten would be shot.

Only a minority of ingenuous and deluded souls continued to hope; we others had often spoken with the Polish and Croat refugees and we knew what departure meant.

For people condemned to death, tradition prescribes an austere ceremony, calculated to emphasize that all passions and anger have died down, and that the act of justice represents only a sad duty towards society which moves even the executioner to pity for the victim. Thus the condemned man is shielded from all external cares, he is granted solitude and, should he want it, spiritual comfort; in short, care is taken that he should feel around him neither hatred nor arbitrariness, only necessity and justice, and by means of punishment, pardon.

But to us this was not granted, for we were many and time was short. And in any case, what had we to repent, for what crime did we need pardon? The Italian commissar accordingly decreed that all services should continue to function until the final notice: the kitchens remained open, the corvées for cleaning worked as usual, and even the teachers of the little school gave lessons until the evening, as on other days. But that evening the children were given no homework.

And night came, and it was such a night that one knew that human eyes would not witness it and survive. Everyone felt this: not one of the guards, neither Italian nor German, had the courage to come and see what men do when they know they have to die.

All took leave from life in the manner which most suited

them. Some praying, some deliberately drunk, others lustfully intoxicated for the last time. But the mothers stayed up to prepare the food for the journey with tender care, and washed their children and packed the luggage; and at dawn the barbed wire was full of children's washing hung out in the wind to dry. Nor did they forget the diapers, the toys, the cushions and the hundred other small things which mothers remember and which children always need. Would you not do the same? If you and your child were going to be killed tomorrow, would you not give him to eat today?

In hut 6A old Gattegno lived with his wife and numerous children and grandchildren and his sons- and daughters-in-law. All the men were carpenters; they had come from Tripoli after many long journeys, and had always carried with them the tools of their trade, their kitchen utensils and their accordions and violins to play and dance to after the day's work. They were happy and pious folk. Their women were the first to silently and rapidly finish the preparations for the journey in order to have time for mourning. When all was ready, the food cooked, the bundles tied together, they unloosened their hair, took off their shoes, placed the Yahrzeit candles on the ground and lit them according to the customs of their fathers, and sat on the bare soil in a circle for the lamentations, praying and weeping all the night. We collected in a group in front of their door, and we experienced within ourselves a grief that was new for us, the ancient grief of the people that has no land, the grief without hope of the exodus which is renewed every century.

Dawn came on us like a betrayer; it seemed as though the new sun rose as an ally of our enemies to assist in our destruction. The different emotions that overcame us, of resignation, of futile rebellion, of religious abandon, of fear, of despair, now joined together after a sleepless night in a collective, uncontrolled panic. The time for meditation, the time for decision was over, and all reason dissolved into a tumult, across which flashed the happy memories of our homes, still so near in time and space, as painful as the thrusts of a sword.

Many things were then said and done among us; but of these it is better that there remain no memory.

With the absurd precision to which we later had to accustom ourselves, the Germans held the roll-call. At the end the officer asked '*Wieviel Stück?*' The corporal saluted smartly and replied that there were six hundred and fifty 'pieces' and that all was in order. They then loaded us on to the buses and took us to the station of Carpi. Here the train was waiting for us, with our escort for the journey. Here we received the first blows: and it was so new and senseless that we felt no pain, neither in body nor in spirit. Only a profound amazement: how can one hit a man without anger?

There were twelve goods wagons for six hundred and fifty men; in mine we were only forty-five, but it was a small wagon. Here then, before our very eyes, under our very feet, was one of those notorious transport trains, those which never return, and of which, shuddering and always a little incredulous, we had so often heard speak. Exactly like this, detail for detail: goods wagons closed from the outside, with men, women and children pressed together without pity, like cheap merchandise, for a journey towards nothingness, a journey down there, towards the bottom. This time it is us who are inside.

Sooner or later in life everyone discovers that perfect happiness is unrealizable, but there are few who pause to consider the antithesis: that perfect unhappiness is equally unattainable. The obstacles preventing the realization of both these extreme states are of the same nature: they derive from our human condition which is opposed to everything infinite. Our ever-insufficient knowledge of the future opposes it: and this is called, in the one instance, hope, and in the other, uncertainty of the following day. The certainty of death opposes it: for it places a limit on every joy, but also on every grief. The inevitable material cares oppose it: for as they poison every lasting happiness, they equally assiduously distract us from our misfortunes and make our consciousness of them intermittent and hence supportable.

It was the very discomfort, the blows, the cold, the thirst that kept us aloft in the void of bottomless despair, both during the journey and after. It was not the will to live, nor a conscious resignation; for few are the men capable of such resolution, and we were but a common sample of humanity.

The doors had been closed at once, but the train did not move until evening. We had learnt of our destination with relief. Auschwitz: a name without significance for us at that time, but it at least implied some place on this earth.

The train travelled slowly, with long, unnerving halts. Through the slit we saw the tall pale cliffs of the Adige Valley and the names of the last Italian cities disappear behind us. We passed the Brenner at midday of the second day and everyone stood up, but no one said a word. The thought of the return journey stuck in my heart, and I cruelly pictured to myself the inhuman joy of that other journey, with doors open, no one wanting to flee, and the first Italian names ... and I looked around and wondered how many, among that poor human dust, would be struck by fate. Among the forty-five people in my wagon only four saw their homes again; and it was by far the most fortunate wagon.

We suffered from thirst and cold; at every stop we clamoured for water, or even a handful of snow, but we were rarely heard; the soldiers of the escort drove off anybody who tried to approach the convoy. Two young mothers, nursing their children, groaned night and day, begging for water. Our state of nervous tension made the hunger, exhaustion and lack of sleep seem less of a torment. But the hours of darkness were nightmares without end.

There are few men who know how to go to their deaths with dignity, and often they are not those whom one would expect. Few know how to remain silent and respect the silence of others. Our restless sleep was often interrupted by noisy and futile disputes, by curses, by kicks and blows blindly delivered to ward off some encroaching and inevitable contact. Then someone would light a candle, and its mournful flicker would reveal an obscure agitation, a human mass, extended across the floor, confused and continuous, sluggish and aching, rising here and there in sudden convulsions and immediately collapsing again in exhaustion.

Through the slit, known and unknown names of Austrian cities, Salzburg, Vienna, then Czech, finally Polish names. On the evening of the fourth day the cold became intense: the train ran through interminable black pine forests, climbing perceptibly. The snow was high. It must have been a branch line as the stations were small and almost deserted. During the halts, no one tried any more to communicate with the outside world: we felt ourselves by now 'on the other side'. There was a long halt in open country. The train started up with extreme slowness, and the convoy stopped for the last time, in the dead of night, in the middle of a dark silent plain.

On both sides of the track rows of red and white lights appeared as far as the eye could see; but there was none of that confusion of sounds which betrays inhabited places even from a distance. By the wretched light of the last candle, with the rhythm of the wheels, with every human sound now silenced, we awaited what was to happen.

Next to me, crushed against me for the whole journey, there had been a woman. We had known each other for many years, and the misfortune had struck us together, but we knew little of each other. Now, in the hour of decision, we said to each other things that are never said among the living. We said farewell and it was short; everybody said farewell to life through his neighbour. We had no more fear.

The climax came suddenly. The door opened with a crash, and the dark echoed with outlandish orders in that curt, barbaric barking of Germans in command which seems to give vent to a millennial anger. A vast platform appeared before us, lit up by reflectors. A little beyond it, a row of lorries. Then everything was silent again. Someone translated: we had to climb down with our luggage and deposit it alongside the train. In a moment the platform was swarming with shadows. But we were afraid to break that silence: everyone busied himself with his luggage, searched for someone else, called to somebody, but timidly, in a whisper.

A dozen SS men stood around, legs akimbo, with an indifferent air. At a certain moment they moved among us, and in a subdued tone of voice, with faces of stone, began to interrogate us rapidly, one by one, in bad Italian. They did not interrogate everybody, only a few: 'How old? Healthy or ill?' And on the basis of the reply they pointed in two different directions.

Everything was as silent as an aquarium, or as in certain dream sequences. We had expected something more apocalyptic: they seemed simple police agents. It was disconcerting and disarming. Someone dared to ask for his luggage: they replied, 'luggage afterwards'. Someone else did not want to leave his wife: they said, 'together again afterwards'. Many mothers did not want to be separated from their children: they said 'good,

good, stay with child'. They behaved with the calm assurance of people doing their normal duty of every day. But Renzo stayed an instant too long to say good-bye to Francesca, his fiancée, and with a single blow they knocked him to the ground. It was their everyday duty.

In less than ten minutes all the fit men had been collected together in a group. What happened to the others, to the women, to the children, to the old men, we could establish neither then nor later: the night swallowed them up, purely and simply. Today, however, we know that in that rapid and summary choice each one of us had been judged capable or not of working usefully for the Reich; we know that of our convoy no more than ninety-six men and twenty-nine women entered the respective camps of Monowitz-Buna and Birkenau, and that of all the others, more than five hundred in number, not one was living two days later. We also know that not even this tenuous principle of discrimination between fit and unfit was always followed, and that later the simpler method was often adopted of merely opening both the doors of the wagon without warning or instructions to the new arrivals. Those who by chance climbed down on one side of the convoy entered the camp; the others went to the gas chamber.

This is the reason why three-year-old Emilia died: the historical necessity of killing the children of Jews was self-demonstrative to the Germans. Emilia, daughter of Aldo Levi of Milan, was a curious, ambitious, cheerful, intelligent child; her parents had succeeded in washing her during the journey in the packed car in a tub with tepid water which the degenerate German engineer had allowed them to draw from the engine that was dragging us all to death.

Thus, in an instant, our women, our parents, our children disappeared. We saw them for a short while as an obscure mass at the other end of the platform; then we saw nothing more.

Instead, two groups of strange individuals emerged into the light of the lamps. They walked in squads, in rows of three, with an odd, embarrassed step, head dangling in front, arms rigid. On their heads they wore comic berets and were all dressed in long striped overcoats, which even by night and from a distance looked filthy and in rags. They walked in a large circle around us, never drawing near, and in silence began to busy themselves with our luggage and to climb in and out of the empty wagons.

We looked at each other without a word. It was all incomprehensible and mad, but one thing we had understood: this was the metamorphosis that awaited us. Tomorrow we would be like them.

Without knowing how I found myself loaded on to a lorry with thirty others; the lorry sped into the night at full speed. It was covered and we could not see outside, but by the shaking we could tell that the road had many curves and bumps. Are we unguarded? Throw ourselves down? It is too late, too late, we are all 'down'. In any case we are soon aware that we are not without guard. He is a strange guard, a German soldier bristling with arms. We do not see him because of the thick darkness, but we feel the hard contact every time that a lurch of the lorry throws us all in a heap. At a certain point he switches on a pocket torch and instead of shouting threats of damnation at us, he asks us courteously, one by one, in German and in pidgin language, if we have any money or watches to give him, seeing that they will not be useful to us any more. This is no order, no regulation: it is obvious that it is a small private initiative, of our Charon. The matter stirs us to anger and laughter and brings relief.

2

On the Bottom

The journey did not last more than twenty minutes. Then the lorry stopped, and we saw a large door, and above it a sign, brightly illuminated (its memory still strikes me in my dreams): *Arbeit Macht Frei*, 'Work Gives Freedom'.

We climb down, they make us enter an enormous empty room that is poorly heated. We have a terrible thirst. The weak gurgle of the water in the radiators makes us ferocious; we have had nothing to drink for four days. But there is also a tap – and above it a card which says that it is forbidden to drink as the water is dirty. Nonsense. It seems obvious that the card is a joke, 'they' know that we are dying of thirst and they put us in a room, and there is, a tap, and *Wassertrinken Verboten*. I drink and I incite my companions to do likewise, but I have to spit it out, the water is tepid and sweetish, with the smell of a swamp.

This is hell. Today, in our times, hell must be like this. A huge, empty room: we are tired, standing on our feet, with a tap which drips while we cannot drink the water, and we wait for something which will certainly be terrible, and nothing happens and nothing continues to happen. What can one think about? One cannot think any more, it is like being already dead. Someone sits down on the ground. The time passes drop by drop.

We are not dead. The door is opened and an SS man enters, smoking. He looks at us slowly and asks, '*Wer kann Deutsch?*'

One of us whom I have never seen, named Flesch, moves forward; he will be our interpreter. The SS man makes a long calm speech; the interpreter translates. We have to form rows of five, with intervals of two yards between man and man; then we have to undress and make a bundle of the clothes in a special manner, the woollen garments on one side, all the rest on the other; we must take off our shoes but pay great attention that they are not stolen.

Stolen by whom? Why should our shoes be stolen? And what about our documents, the few things we have in our pockets, our watches? We all look at the interpreter, and the interpreter asks the German, and the German smokes and looks him through and through as if he were transparent, as if no one had spoken.

I had never seen old men naked. Mr Bergmann wore a truss and asked the interpreter if he should take it off, and the interpreter hesitated. But the German understood and spoke seriously to the interpreter pointing to someone. We saw the interpreter swallow and then he said: 'The officer says, take off the truss, and you will be given that of Mr Coen.' One could see the words coming bitterly out of Flesch's mouth; this was the German manner of laughing.

Now another German comes and tells us to put the shoes in a certain corner, and we put them there, because now it is all over and we feel outside this world and the only thing is to obey. Someone comes with a broom and sweeps away all the shoes, outside the door in a heap. He is crazy, he is mixing them all together, ninety-six pairs, they will be all unmatched. The outside door opens, a freezing wind enters and we are naked and cover ourselves up with our arms. The wind blows and slams the door; the German reopens it and stands watching with interest how we writhe to hide from the wind, one behind the other. Then he leaves and closes it.

Now the second act begins. Four men with razors, soap-brushes and clippers burst in; they have trousers and jackets with stripes, with a number sewn on the front; perhaps they are the same sort as those others of this evening (this evening or yesterday evening?); but these are robust and flourishing. We ask many questions but they catch hold of us and in a moment we find ourselves shaved and sheared. What comic faces we have without hair! The four speak a language which does not seem of this world. It is certainly not German, for I understand a little German.

Finally another door is opened: here we are, locked in, naked, sheared and standing, with our feet in water – it is a shower-room. We are alone. Slowly the astonishment dissolves, and we speak, and everyone asks questions and no one answers. If we are naked in a shower-room, it means that we will have a shower. If we have a shower it is because they arc not going to kill us yet. But why then do they keep us standing, and give us nothing to drink, while nobody explains anything, and we have no shoes or clothes, but we are all naked with our feet in the water, and we have been travelling five days and cannot even sit down?

And our women?

Mr Levi asks me if I think that our women are like us at this moment, and where they are, and if we will be able to see them again. I say yes, because he is married and has a daughter; certainly we will see them again. But by now my belief is that all this is a game to mock and sneer at us. Clearly they will kill us, whoever thinks he is going to live is mad, it means that he has swallowed the bait, but I have not; I have understood that it will soon all be over, perhaps in this same room, when they get bored of seeing us naked, dancing from foot to foot and trying every now and again to sit down on the floor. But there are two inches of cold water and we cannot sit down.

We walk up and down without sense, and we talk, everybody talks to everybody else, we make a great noise. The door opens, and a German enters; it is the officer of before. He speaks briefly, the interpreter translates. 'The officer says you must be quiet, because this is not a rabbinical school.' One sees the words which are not his, the bad words, twist his mouth as they come out, as if he was spitting out a foul taste. We beg him to ask what we are waiting for, how long we will stay here, about our women, everything; but he says no, that he does not want to ask. This Flesch, who is most unwilling to translate into Italian the hard cold German phrases and refuses to turn into German our questions because he knows that it is useless, is a German Jew of about fifty, who has a large scar on his face from a wound received fighting the Italians on the Piave. He is a closed, taciturn man, for whom I feel an instinctive respect as I feel that he has begun to suffer before us.

The German goes and we remain silent, although we are a little ashamed of our silence. It is still night and we wonder if the day will ever come. The door opens again, and someone else dressed in stripes comes in. He is different from the others, older, with glasses, a more civilized face, and much less robust He speaks to us in Italian.

By now we are tired of being amazed. We seem to be watching some mad play, one of those plays in which the witches, the Holy Spirit and the devil appear. He speaks Italian badly, with a strong foreign accent. He makes a long speech, is very polite, and tries to reply to all our questions.

We are at Monowitz, near Auschwitz, in Upper Silesia, a region inhabited by both Poles and Germans. This camp is a work-camp, in German one says *Arbeitslager*; all the prisoners (there are about ten thousand) work in a factory which produces a type of rubber called Buna, so that the camp itself is called Buna.

We will be given shoes and clothes – no, not our own – other shoes, other clothes, like his. We are naked now because we are waiting for the shower and the disinfection, which will take place immediately after the reveille, because one cannot enter the camp without being disinfected.

Certainly there will be work to do, everyone must work here. But there is work and work: he, for example, acts as doctor. He is a Hungarian doctor who studied in Italy and he is the dentist of the Lager. He has been in the Lager for four and a half years (not in this one: Buna has only been open for a year and a half), but we can see that he is still quite well, not very thin. Why is he in the Lager? Is he Jewish like us? 'No,' he says simply, 'I am a criminal.'

We ask him many questions. He laughs, replies to some and not to others, and it is clear that he avoids certain subjects. He does not speak of the women: he says they are well, that we will see them again soon, but he does not say how or where. Instead he tells us other things, strange and crazy things, perhaps he too is playing with us. Perhaps he is mad – one goes mad in the Lager. He says that every Sunday there are concerts and football matches. He says that whoever boxes well can become cook. He says that whoever works well receives prize-coupons with which to buy tobacco and soap. He says that the water is really not drinkable, and that instead a coffee substitute is distributed every day, but generally nobody drinks it as the soup itself is sufficiently watery to quench thirst. We beg him to find us something to drink, but he says he cannot, that he has come to see us secretly, against SS orders, as we still have to be disinfected, and that he must leave at once; he has come because he has a liking for Italians, and because, he says, he 'has a little heart'. We ask him if there are other Italians in the camp and he says there are some, a few, he does not know how many; and he at once changes the subject. Meanwhile a bell rang and he immediately hurried off and left us stunned and disconcerted. Some feel refreshed but I do not. I still think that even this dentist, this incomprehensible person, wanted to amuse himself at our expense, and I do not want to believe a word of what he said.

At the sound of the bell, we can hear the still dark camp waking up. Unexpectedly the water gushes out boiling from the showers – five minutes of bliss; but immediately after, four men (perhaps they are the barbers) burst in yelling and shoving and drive us out, wet and steaming, into the adjoining room which is freezing; here other shouting people throw at us unrecognizable rags and thrust into our hands a pair of broken-down boots with wooden soles; we have no time to understand and we already find ourselves in the open, in the blue and icy snow of dawn, barefoot and naked, with all our clothing in our hands, with a hundred yards to run to the next hut. There we are finally allowed to get dressed.

When we finish, everyone remains in his own corner and we do not dare lift our eyes to look at one another. There is nowhere to look in a mirror, but our appearance stands in front of us, reflected in a hundred livid faces, in a hundred miserable and sordid puppets. We are transformed into the phantoms glimpsed yesterday evening.

Then for the first time we became aware that our language lacks words to express this offence, the demolition of a man. In a moment, with almost prophetic intuition, the reality was revealed to us: we had reached the bottom. It is not possible to sink lower than this; no human condition is more miserable than this, nor could it conceivably be so. Nothing belongs to us any more; they have taken away our clothes, our shoes, even our hair; if we speak, they will not listen to us, and if they listen, they will not understand. They will even take away our name: and if we want to keep it, we will have to find ourselves the strength to do so, to manage somehow so that behind the name something of us, of us as we were, still remains.

We know that we will have difficulty in being understood, and this is as it should be. But consider what value, what meaning is enclosed even in the smallest of our daily habits, in the hundred possessions which even the poorest beggar owns: a handkerchief, an old letter, the photo of a cherished person. These things are part of us, almost like limbs of our body; nor is it conceivable that we can be deprived of them in our world, for we immediately find others to substitute the old ones, other objects which are ours in their personification and evocation of our memories.

Imagine now a man who is deprived of everyone he loves, and at the same time of his house, his habits, his clothes, in short, of everything he possesses: he will be a hollow man, reduced to suffering and needs, forgetful of dignity and restraint, for he who loses all often easily loses himself. He will be a man whose life or death can be lightly decided with no sense of human affinity, in the most fortunate of cases, on the basis of a pure judgement of utility. It is in this way that one can understand the double sense of the term 'extermination camp', and it is now clear what we seek to express with the phrase: 'to lie on the bottom'.

*Häftling**: I have learnt that I am Häftling. My number is 174517; we have been baptized, we will carry the tattoo on our left arm until we die.

The operation was slightly painful and extraordinarily rapid: they placed us all in a row, and one by one, according to the alphabetical order of our names, we filed past a skilful official, armed with a sort of pointed tool with a very short needle. It

* Prisoner.

seems that this is the real, true initiation: only by 'showing one's number' can one get bread and soup. Several days passed, and not a few cuffs and punches, before we became used to showing our number promptly enough not to disorder the daily operation of food-distribution; weeks and months were needed to learn its sound in the German language. And for many days, while the habits of freedom still led me to look for the time on my wristwatch, my new name ironically appeared instead, a number tattooed in bluish characters under the skin.

Only much later, and slowly, a few of us learnt something of the funereal science of the numbers of Auschwitz, which epitomize the stages of destruction of European Judaism. To the old hands of the camp, the numbers told everything: the period of entry into the camp, the convoy of which one formed a part, and consequently the nationality. Everyone will treat with respect the numbers from 30,000 to 80,000: there are only a few hundred left and they represented the few survivals from the Polish ghettos. It is as well to watch out in commercial dealings with a 116,000 or a 117,000: they now number only about forty, but they represent the Greeks of Salonica, so take care they do not pull the wool over your eyes. As for the high numbers they carry an essentially comic air about them, like the words 'freshman' or 'conscript' in ordinary life. The typical high number is a corpulent, docile and stupid fellow: he can be convinced that leather shoes are distributed at the infirmary to all those with delicate feet, and can be persuaded to run there and leave his bowl of soup 'in your custody'; you can sell him a spoon for three rations of bread; you can send him to the most ferocious of the Kapos to ask him (as happened to me!) if it is true that his is the *Kartoffelschalenkommando*, the 'Potato Peeling Command', and if one can be enrolled in it

*

In fact, the whole process of introduction to what was for us a new order took place in a grotesque and sarcastic manner. When the tattooing operation was finished, they shut us in a vacant hut. The bunks are made, but we are severely forbidden to touch or sit on them: so we wander around aimlessly for half the day in the limited space available, still tormented by the parching thirst of the journey. Then the door opens and a boy in a striped suit comes in, with a fairly civilized air, small, thin and blond. He speaks French and we throng around him with a flood of questions which till now we had asked each other in vain.

But he does not speak willingly; no one here speaks willingly. We are new, we have nothing and we know nothing; why waste time on us? He reluctantly explains to us that all the others are out at work and will come back in the evening. He has come out of the infirmary this morning and is exempt from work for today. I asked him (with an ingenuousness that only a few days later already seemed incredible to me) if at least they would give us back our toothbrushes. He did not laugh, but with his face animated by fierce contempt, he threw at me '*Vous n'êtes pas à la maison.*' And it is this refrain that we hear repeated by everyone. You are not at home, this is not a sanatorium, the only exit is by way of the Chimney. (What did it mean? Soon we were all to learn what it meant.)

And it was in fact so. Driven by thirst, I eyed a fine icicle outside the window, within hand's reach. I opened the window and broke off the icicle but at once a large, heavy guard prowling outside brutally snatched it away from me. '*Warum?*' I asked him in my poor German. '*Hier ist kein warum*' (there is no why here), he replied, pushing me inside with a shove.

The explanation is repugnant but simple: in this place everything is forbidden, not for hidden reasons, but because the camp has been created for that purpose. If one wants to live one must learn this quickly and well:

'No Sacred Face will help thee here! it's not
A Serchio bathing-party ...'

Hour after hour, this first long day of limbo draws to its end.
While the sun sets in a tumult of fierce, blood-red clouds, they
finally make us come out of the hut. Will they give us something
to drink? No, they place us in line again, they lead us to a huge
square which takes up the centre of the camp and they arrange
us meticulously in squads. Then nothing happens for another
hour: it seems that we are waiting for someone.

A band begins to play, next to the entrance of the camp: it
plays *Rosamunda*, the well-known sentimental song, and this
seems so strange to us that we look sniggering at each other; we
feel a shadow of relief, perhaps all these ceremonies are nothing
but a colossal farce in Teutonic taste. But the band, on finishing
Rosamunda, continues to play other marches, one after the
other, and suddenly the squads of our comrades appear, returning from work. They walk in columns of five with a strange,
unnatural hard gait, like stiff puppets made of jointless bones;
but they walk scrupulously in time to the band.

They also arrange themselves like us in the huge square,
according to a precise order; when the last squad has returned,
they count and recount us for over an hour. Long checks are
made which all seem to go to a man dressed in stripes, who
accounts for them to a group of SS men in full battle dress.

Finally (it is dark by now, but the camp is brightly lit by head-
lamps and reflectors) one hears the shout '*Absperre!*' at which
all the squads break up in a confused and turbulent movement.
They no longer walk stiffly and erectly as before: each one drags
himself along with obvious effort. I see that all of them carry in
their hand or attached to their belt a steel bowl as large as a
basin.

We new arrivals also wander among the crowd, searching for

a voice, a friendly face or a guide. Against the wooden wall of a hut two boys are seated on the ground: they seem very young, sixteen years old at the outside, both with their face and hands dirty with soot. One of the two, as we are passing by, calls me and asks me in German some questions which I do not understand; then he asks where we come from. '*Italien*,' I reply; I want to ask him many things, but my German vocabulary is very limited.

'Are you a Jew?' I ask him.

'Yes, a Polish Jew.'

'How long have you been in the Lager?'

'Three years,' and he lifts up three fingers. He must have been a child when he entered, I think with horror; on the other hand this means that at least some manage to live here.

'What is your work?'

'*Schlosser*,' he replies. I do not understand. '*Eisen, Feuer*' (iron, fire), he insists, and makes a play with his hands of someone beating with a hammer on an anvil. So he is an ironsmith.

'*Ich Chemiker*,' I state; and he nods earnestly with his head, '*Chemiker gut*.' But all this has to do with the distant future: what torments me at the moment is my thirst.

'Drink, water. We no water,' I tell him.

He looks at me with a serious face, almost severe, and states clearly: 'Do not drink water, comrade,' and then other words that I do not understand.

'*Warum?*'

'*Geschwollen*,' he replies cryptically. I shake my head, I have not understood. '*Swollen*,' he makes me understand, blowing out his cheeks and sketching with his hands a monstrous tumefaction of the face and belly. '*Warten bis heute Abend*.' 'Wait until this evening,' I translate word by word.

Then he says: '*Ich Schlome. Du?*' I tell him my name, and he asks me: 'Where your mother?'

'In Italy.' Schlome is amazed: a Jew in Italy? 'Yes,' I explain as best I can, 'hidden, no one knows, run away, does not speak, no one sees her.' He has understood; he now gets up, approaches me and timidly embraces me. The adventure is over, and I feel filled with a serene sadness that is almost joy. I have never seen Schlome since, but I have not forgotten his serious and gentle face of a child, which welcomed me on the threshold of the house of the dead.

We have a great number of things to learn, but we have learnt many already. We already have a certain idea of the topography of the Lager; our Lager is a square of about six hundred yards in length, surrounded by two fences of barbed wire, the inner one carrying a high tension current. It consists of sixty wooden huts, which are called Blocks, ten of which are in construction. In addition, there is the body of the kitchens, which are in brick; an experimental farm, run by a detachment of privileged Häftlinge; the huts with the showers and the latrines, one for each group of six or eight Blocks. Besides these, certain Blocks are reserved for specific purposes. First of all, a group of eight, at the extreme eastern end of the camp, forms the infirmary and clinic; then there is Block 24 which is the *Krätze-block*, reserved for infectious skin-diseases; Block 7 which no ordinary Häftling has ever entered, reserved for the '*Prominenz*', that is, the aristocracy, the internees holding the highest posts; Block 47, reserved for the *Reichsdeutsche* (the Aryan Germans, 'politicals' or criminals); Block 49, for the Kapos alone; Block 12, half of which, for use of the *Reichsdeutsche* and the Kapos, serves as canteen, that is, a distribution centre for tobacco, insect powder and occasionally other articles; Block 37, which formed the Quartermaster's office and the Office for Work; and finally, Block 29, which always has its windows closed as it is the *Frauenblock*, the camp brothel, served by Polish Häftling girls, and reserved for the *Reichs-deutsche*.

The ordinary living Blocks are divided into two parts. In one *Tagesraum* lives the head of the hut with his friends. There is a long table, seats, benches, and on all sides a heap of strange objects in bright colours, photographs, cuttings from magazines, sketches, imitation flowers, ornaments; on the walls, great sayings, proverbs and rhymes in praise of order, discipline and hygiene; in one corner, a shelf with the tools of the *Blockfrisör* (official barber), the ladles to distribute the soup, and two rubber truncheons, one solid and one hollow, to enforce discipline should the proverbs prove insufficient. The other part is the dormitory: there are only one hundred and forty-eight bunks on three levels, fitted close to each other like the cells of a beehive, and divided by three corridors so as to utilize without wastage all the space in the room up to the roof. Here all the ordinary Häftlinge live, about two hundred to two hundred and fifty per hut. Consequently there are two men in most of the bunks, which are portable planks of wood, each covered by a thin straw sack and two blankets.

The corridors are so narrow that two people can barely pass together; the total area of the floor is so small that the inhabitants of the same Block cannot all stay there at the same time unless at least half are lying on their bunks. Hence the prohibition to enter a Block to which one does not belong.

In the middle of the Lager is the roll-call square, enormous, where we collect in the morning to form the work-squads and in the evening to be counted. Facing the roll-call square there is a bed of grass, carefully mown, where the gallows are erected when necessary.

We had soon learned that the guests of the Lager are divided into three categories: the criminals, the politicals and the Jews. All are clothed in stripes, all are Häftlinge, but the criminals wear a green triangle next to the number sewn on the jacket; the politicals wear a red triangle; and the Jews, who form the large majority, wear the Jewish star, red and yellow. SS men exist but are few and outside the camp, and are seen relatively infrequently. Our effective masters in practice are the green triangles, who have a free hand over us, as well as those of the other two categories who are ready to help them – and they are not few.

And we have learnt other things, more or less quickly, according to our intelligence: to reply '*Jawohl*', never to ask questions, always to pretend to understand. We have learnt the value of food; now we also diligently scrape the bottom of the bowl after the ration and we hold it under our chins when we eat bread so as not to lose the crumbs. We, too, know that it is not the same thing to be given a ladleful of soup from the top or from the bottom of the vat, and we are already able to judge, according to the capacity of the various vats, what is the most suitable place to try and reach in the queue when we line up.

We have learnt that everything is useful: the wire to tie up our shoes, the rags to wrap around our feet, waste paper to (illegally) pad out our jacket against the cold. We have learnt, on the other hand, that everything can be stolen, in fact is automatically stolen as soon as attention is relaxed; and to avoid this, we had to learn the art of sleeping with our head on a bundle made up of our jacket and containing all our belongings, from the bowl to the shoes.

We already know in good part the rules of the camp, which are incredibly complicated. The prohibitions are innumerable: to approach nearer to the barbed wire than two yards; to sleep with one's jacket, or without one's pants, or with one's cap on one's head; to use certain washrooms or latrines which are '*nur für Kapos*' or '*nur für Reichsdeutsche*'; not to go for the shower on the prescribed day, or to go there on a day not prescribed; to leave the hut with one's jacket unbuttoned, or with the collar raised; to carry paper or straw under one's clothes against the cold; to wash except stripped to the waist.

The rites to be carried out were infinite and senseless: every morning one had to make the 'bed' perfectly flat and smooth; smear one's muddy and repellent wooden shoes with the appropriate machine grease; scrape the mudstains off one's clothes (paint, grease and rust-stains were, however, permitted); in the evening one had to undergo the control for lice and the control of washing one's feet; on Saturday, have one's beard and hair shaved, mend or have mended one's rags; on Sunday, undergo the general control for skin diseases and the control of buttons on one's jacket, which had to be five.

In addition, there are innumerable circumstances, normally irrelevant, which here become problems. When one's nails grow long, they have to be shortened, which can only be done with one's teeth (for the toenails, the friction of the shoes is sufficient); if a button comes off, one has to tie it on with a piece of wire; if one goes to the latrine or the washroom, everything has to be carried along, always and everywhere, and while one washes one's face, the bundle of clothes has to be held tightly between one's knees: in any other manner it will be stolen in that second. If a shoe hurts, one has to go in the evening to the ceremony of the changing of the shoes: this tests the skill of the individual who, in the middle of the incredible crowd, has to be able to choose at an eye's glance one (not a pair, one) shoe which fits. Because once the choice is made, there can be no second chance.

And do not think that shoes form a factor of secondary importance in the life of the Lager. Death begins with the shoes; for most of us, they show themselves to be instruments of torture, which after a few hours of marching cause painful sores which become fatally infected. Whoever has them is forced to walk as if he was dragging a convict's chain (this explains the strange gait of the army which returns every evening on parade); he arrives last everywhere, and everywhere he receives blows. He cannot escape if they run after him; his feet swell and the more they swell, the more the friction with the wood and the cloth of the shoes becomes insupportable. Then only the hospital is left: but to enter the hospital with a diagnosis of '*dicke Füsse*' (swollen feet) is extremely dangerous, because it is well known to all, and especially to the SS, that here there is no cure for that complaint.

And in all this we have not yet mentioned the work, which in its turn is a Gordian knot of laws, taboos and problems.

We all work, except those who are ill (to be recognized as ill implies in itself an important equipment of knowledge and experience). Every morning we leave the camp in squads for Buna; every evening, in squads, we return. As regards the work, we are divided into about two hundred *Kommandos*, each of which consists of between fifteen and one hundred and fifty men and is commanded by a Kapo. There are good and bad Kommandos; for the most part they are used as transport and the work is quite hard, especially in the winter, if for no other reason merely because it always takes place in the open. There are also skilled Kommandos (electricians, smiths, bricklayers, welders, mechanics, concrete-layers, etc.), each attached to a certain workshop or department of Buna, and depending more directly on civilian foremen, mostly German and Polish. This naturally only applies to the hours of work; for the rest of the day the skilled workers (there are no more than three or four hundred in all) receive no different treatment from the ordinary workers. The detailing of individuals to the various Kommandos is organized by a special office of the Lager, the *Arbeitsdienst*, which is in continual touch with the civilian direction of Buna. The *Arbeitsdienst* decides on the basis of unknown criteria, often openly on the basis of protection or corruption, so that if anyone manages to find enough to eat, he is practically certain to get a good post at Buna.

The hours of work vary with the season. All hours of light are working hours: so that from a minimum winter working day (8–12 a.m. and 12.30–4 p.m.) one rises to a maximum summer one (6.30–12 a.m. and 1–6 p.m.). Under no excuse are the Häftlinge allowed to be at work during the hours of darkness or when there is a thick fog, but they work regularly even if it rains or snows or (as occurs quite frequently) if the fierce wind of the Carpathians blows; the reason being that the darkness or fog might provide opportunities to escape.

One Sunday in every two is a regular working day; on the so-called holiday Sundays, instead of working at Buna, one works normally on the upkeep of the Lager, so that days of real rest are extremely rare.

Such will be our life. Every day, according to the established rhythm, *Ausrücken* and *Einrücken*, go out and come in; work, sleep and eat; fall ill, get better or die.

... And for how long? But the old ones laugh at this question: they recognize the new arrivals by this question. They laugh and they do not reply. For months and years, the problem of the remote future has grown pale to them and has lost all intensity in face of the far more urgent and concrete problems of the near future: how much one will eat today, if it will snow, if there will be coal to unload.

If we were logical, we would resign ourselves to the evidence that our fate is beyond knowledge, that every conjecture is arbitrary and demonstrably devoid of foundation. But men are rarely logical when their own fate is at stake; on every occasion, they prefer the extreme positions. According to our character, some of us are immediately convinced that all is lost, that one cannot live here, that the end is near and sure; others are convinced that however hard the present life may be, salvation is probable and not far off, and if we have faith and strength, we will see our houses and our dear ones again. The two classes of pessimists and optimists are not so clearly defined, however, not because there are many agnostics, but because the majority, without memory or coherence, drift between the two extremes, according to the moment and the mood of the person they happen to meet.

Here I am, then, on the bottom. One learns quickly enough to wipe out the past and the future when one is forced to. A fortnight after my arrival I already had the prescribed hunger, that chronic hunger unknown to free men, which makes one dream at night, and settles in all the limbs of one's body. I have already learnt not to let myself be robbed, and in fact if I find a spoon lying around, a piece of string, a button which I can acquire without danger of punishment, I pocket them and consider them mine by full right. On the back of my feet I already have those numb sores that will not heal. I push wagons, I work with a shovel, I turn rotten in the rain, I shiver in the wind; already my own body is no longer mine: my belly is swollen, my limbs emaciated, my face is thick in the morning, hollow in the evening; some of us have yellow skin, others grey. When we do not meet for a few days we hardly recognize each other.

We Italians had decided to meet every Sunday evening in a corner of the Lager, but we stopped it at once, because it was too sad to count our numbers and find fewer each time, and to see each other ever more deformed and more squalid. And it was so tiring to walk those few steps and then, meeting each other, to remember and to think. It was better not to think.

3

Initiation

After the first day of capricious transfer from hut to hut and from Kommando to Kommando, I am assigned to Block 30 late one evening, and shown a bunk in which Diena is already sleeping. Diena wakes up, and although exhausted, makes room for me and receives me hospitably.

I am not sleepy, or more accurately, my sleepiness is masked by a state of tension and anxiety of which I have not yet managed to rid myself, and so I talk and talk.

I have too many things to ask. I am hungry and when will they distribute the soup tomorrow? And will I be able to eat it without a spoon? And where will I be able to find one? And where will they send me to work? Diena knows no more than I, and replies with other questions. But from above and below, from near by and from far away, from all corners of the now dark hut, sleepy and angry voices shout at me: '*Ruhe, Ruhe!*'

I understand that they are ordering me to be quiet, but the word is new to me, and since I do not know its meaning and implications, my inquietude increases. The confusion of languages is a fundamental component of the manner of living here: one is surrounded by a perpetual Babel, in which everyone shouts orders and threats in languages never heard before, and woe betide whoever fails to grasp the meaning. No one has time here, no one has patience, no one listens to you; we latest arrivals instinctively collect in the corners, against the walls, afraid of being beaten.

So I give up asking questions and soon slip into a bitter and tense sleep. But it is not rest: I feel myself threatened, besieged, at every moment I am ready to draw myself into a spasm of defence. I dream and I seem to sleep on a road, on a bridge, across a door through which many people are passing. And now, oh, so early, the reveille sounds. The entire hut shakes to its foundations, the lights are put on, everyone near me bustles around in a sudden frantic activity. They shake the blankets raising clouds of fetid dust, they dress with feverish hurry, they run outside into the freezing air half-dressed, they rush headlong towards the latrines and washrooms. Some, bestially, urinate while they run to save time, because within five minutes begins the distribution of bread, of bread-Brot-Broid-chleb-pain-lechem-keynér, of the holy grey slab which seems gigantic in your neighbour's hand, and in your own hand so small as to make you cry. It is a daily hallucination to which in the end one becomes accustomed: but at the beginning it is so irresistible that many of us, after long discussions on our own open and constant misfortune and the shameless luck of others, finally exchange our ration, at which the illusion is renewed inverted, leaving everyone discontented and frustrated.

Bread is also our only money: in the few minutes which elapse between its distribution and consumption, the Block resounds with claims, quarrels and scuffles. It is the creditors of yesterday who are claiming payment in the brief moment in which the debtor is solvent. After which a relative quiet begins and many take advantage to go to the latrines again to smoke half a cigarette, or to the washrooms to wash themselves properly.

The washroom is far from attractive. It is badly lighted, full of draughts, with the brick floor covered by a layer of mud. The water is not drinkable; it has a revolting smell and often fails for many hours. The walls are covered by curious didactic frescoes: for example, there is the good Häftling, portrayed stripped to the waist, about to diligently soap his sheared and rosy cranium, and the bad Häftling, with a strong Semitic nose and a greenish colour, bundled up in his ostentatiously stained clothes with a beret on his head, who cautiously dips a finger into the water of the washbasin. Under the first is written: '*So bist du rein*' (like this you are clean), and under the second: '*So gehst du ein*' (like this you come to a bad end); and lower down, in doubtful French but in Gothic script: '*La propreté, c'est la santé.*'

On the opposite wall an enormous white, red and black louse encamps, with the writing: '*Ein Laus, dein Tod*' (a louse is your death), and the inspired distich:

Nach dem Abort, vor dem Essen
Hände waschen, nicht vergessen.

(After the latrine, before eating, wash your hands, do not forget.)

For many weeks I considered these warnings about hygiene as pure examples of the Teutonic sense of humour, in the style of the dialogue about the truss which we had heard on our entry into the Lager. But later I understood that their unknown authors, perhaps without realizing it, were not far from some very important truths. In this place it is practically pointless to wash every day in the turbid water of the filthy washbasins for purposes of cleanliness and health; but it is most important as a symptom of remaining vitality, and necessary as an instrument of moral survival.

I must confess it: after only one week of prison, the instinct for cleanliness disappeared in me. I wander aimlessly around the washroom when I suddenly see Steinlauf, my friend aged almost fifty, with nude torso, scrub his neck and shoulders with little success (he has no soap) but great energy. Steinlauf sees me and greets me, and without preamble asks me severely why I do not wash. Why should I wash? Would I be better off than I am? Would I please someone more? Would I live a day, an hour longer? I would probably live a shorter time, because to wash is an effort, a waste of energy and warmth. Does not Steinlauf know that after half an hour with the coal sacks every difference between him and me will have disappeared? The more I think about it, the more washing one's face in our condition seems a stupid feat, even frivolous: a mechanical habit, or worse, a dismal repetition of an extinct rite. We will all die, we are all about to die: if they give me ten minutes between the reveille and work, I want to dedicate them to something else, to draw into myself, to weigh up things, or merely to look at the sky and think that I am looking at it perhaps for the last time; or even to let myself live, to indulge myself in the luxury of an idle moment.

But Steinlauf interrupts me. He has finished washing and is now drying himself with his cloth jacket which he was holding before wrapped up between his knees and which he will soon put on. And without interrupting the operation he administers me a complete lesson.

It grieves me now that I have forgotten his plain, outspoken words, the words of ex-sergeant Steinlauf of the Austro-Hungarian army, Iron Cross of the '14–'18 war. It grieves me because it means that I have to translate his uncertain Italian and his quiet manner of speaking of a good soldier into my language of an incredulous man. But this was the sense, not forgotten either then or later: that precisely because the Lager was a great machine to reduce us to beasts, we must not become beasts; that even in this place one can survive, and therefore one must want to survive, to tell the story, to bear witness; and that to survive we must force ourselves to save at least the skeleton, the scaffolding, the form of civilization. We are slaves, deprived of every right, exposed to every insult, condemned to certain death, but we still possess one power, and we must defend it with all our strength for it is the last – the power to refuse our consent. So we must certainly wash our faces without soap in dirty water and dry ourselves on our jackets. We must polish our shoes, not because the regulation states it, but for dignity and propriety. We must walk erect, without dragging our feet, not in homage to Prussian discipline but to remain alive, not to begin to die.

These things Steinlauf, a man of good will, told me; strange things to my unaccustomed ear, understood and accepted only in part, and softened by an easier, more flexible and blander doctrine, which for centuries has found its dwelling place on the other side of the Alps; according to which, among other things, nothing is of greater vanity than to force oneself to swallow whole a moral system elaborated by others, under another sky. No, the wisdom and virtue of Steinlauf, certainly good for him, is not enough for me. In the face of this complicated world my ideas of damnation are confused; is it really necessary to elaborate a system and put it into practice? Or would it not be better to acknowledge one's lack of a system?

4

Ka-Be

The days all seem alike and it is not easy to count them. For days now we have formed teams of two, from the railway to the store – a hundred yards over thawing ground. To the store, bending underneath the load, back again, arms hanging down one's sides, not speaking.

Around us, everything is hostile. Above us the malevolent clouds chase each other to separate us from the sun; on all sides the squalor of the toiling steel closes in on us. We have never seen its boundaries, but we feel all around us the evil presence of the barbed wire that separates us from the world. And on the scaffolding, on the trains being switched about, on the roads, in the pits, in the offices, men and more men, slaves and masters, the masters slaves themselves. Fear motivates the former, hatred the latter, all other forces are silent. All are enemies or rivals.

No, I honestly do not feel my companion of today, harnessed with me under the same load, to be either enemy or rival.

He is Null Achtzehn. He is not called anything except that, Zero Eighteen, the last three figures of his entry number; as if everyone was aware that only a man is worthy of a name, and that Null Achtzehn is no longer a man. I think that even he has forgotten his name, certainly he acts as if this was so. When he speaks, when he looks around, he gives the impression of being empty inside, nothing more than an involucre, like the slough of certain insects which one finds on the banks of swamps, held by a thread to the stones and shaken by the wind.

Null Achtzehn is very young, which is a grave danger. Not only because boys support exhaustion and fasting worse than adults, but even more because a long training is needed to survive here in the struggle of each one against all, a training which young people rarely have. Null Achtzehn is not even particularly weak, but all avoid working with him. He is indifferent to the point of not even troubling to avoid tiredness and blows or to search for food. He carries out all the orders that he is given, and it is foreseeable that when they send him to his death he will go with the same total indifference.

He has not even the rudimentary astuteness of a draught-horse, which stops pulling a little before it reaches exhaustion: he pulls or carries or pushes as long as his strength allows him, then he gives way at once, without a word of warning, without lifting his sad, opaque eyes from the ground. He made me think of the sledge-dogs in London's books, who slave until the last breath and die on the track.

But as all the rest of us try by every possible means to avoid work, Null Achtzehn is the one who works more than all. It is because of this, and because he is a dangerous companion, that no one wants to work with him; and as, on the other hand, no one wants to work with me, because I am weak and clumsy, it often happens that we find ourselves paired together.

As we come back once again from the store, with hands empty, dragging our feet, an engine whistles briefly and cuts off our path. Happy at the enforced delay, Null Achtzehn and I stop; bent and in rags, we wait for the wagons to pass slowly by.

. . . *Deutsche Reichsbahn. Deutsche Reichsbahn. SNCF.* Two

huge Russian goods wagons with the hammer and sickle badly rubbed off. Then, *Cavalli 8, Uomini 40, Tara, Portata*: an Italian wagon ... Oh, to climb into a corner, well-hidden under the coal, and to stay there quiet and still in the dark, to listen endlessly to the rhythm of the wheels, stronger than hunger or tiredness; until, at a certain moment, the train would stop and I would feel the warm air and the smell of hay and I would get out into the sun; then I would lie down on the ground to kiss the earth, as you read in books, with my face in the grass. And a woman would pass, and she would ask me 'Who are you?' in Italian, and I would tell her my story in Italian, and she would understand, and she would give me food and shelter. And she would not believe the things I tell her, and I would show her the number on my arm, and then she would believe ...

... It is over. The last wagon has passed, and as if the curtain had been raised, the pile of cast-iron supports lies before our eyes. The Kapo on his feet at the pile with a switch in his hand, the wan companions who come and go in pairs.

Alas for the dreamer: the moment of consciousness that accompanies the awakening is the acutest of sufferings. But it does not often happen to us, and they are not long dreams. We are only tired beasts.

We are once again at the foot of the pile. Mischa and the Galician lift a support and put it roughly on our shoulders. Their job is the least tiring, so that they show excess zeal to keep it: they shout at companions who dawdle, they incite them, they admonish them, they drive on the work at an unbearable pace. This fills me with anger, although I already know that it is in the normal order of things that the privileged oppress the unprivileged: the social structure of the camp is based on this human law.

This time it is my turn to walk in front. The support is heavy but very short, so that at every step I feel behind me Null Achtzehn's feet which tread on mine, as he is unable or cannot be bothered to keep in step.

Twenty steps, we have arrived at the railway, there is a cable to climb over. The load is badly placed, something is not right, it seems to be slipping from my shoulder. Fifty steps, sixty. The door of the store: still the same distance to walk and we can put it down. It is enough, I cannot go any further, the load is now weighing entirely on my arm. I cannot stand the pain and exhaustion any longer: I shout, I try to turn around, just in time to see Null Achtzehn trip and throw everything down.

If I had still had my agility of earlier days I could have jumped back: instead, here I am on the ground, with all my muscles contracted, the wounded foot tight between my hands, blind with pain. The corner of the piece of iron had cut across the back of my foot.

For a moment all is blank in the giddiness of pain. When I manage to look around, Null Achtzehn is still there on his feet, he has not moved, with his hands in his sleeves, his face expressionless, he does not say a word. Mischa and the Galician arrive, speaking Yiddish to each other, they give me incomprehensible advice. Templer and David and the others arrive: they profit from the distraction to stop work. The Kapo arrives, he distributes kicks, punches and abuse, and the comrades disperse like chaff in the wind. Null Achtzehn puts his hand to his nose and blankly looks at it, dirty with blood. I only receive two blows on the head, of the sort that do no harm but simply stun.

The incident is closed. It is proven, for good or bad, that I can stand up, so that the bone cannot be broken. I do not dare to cut the boot open for fear of wakening the pain again, and also because I know that the foot will swell and I will be unable to put the boot on again.

The Kapo sends me to take the place of the Galician at the pile, and the latter, glaring at me, takes his place alongside Null Achtzehn; but by now the English prisoners have passed, it will soon be time to return to the camp.

During the march I do my best to walk quickly, but I cannot keep up the pace. The Kapo picks out Null Achtzehn and Finder to help me as far as the procession in front of the SS, and finally (fortunately there is no roll-call this evening) I am in the hut and I can throw myself on the bunk and breathe.

Perhaps it is the heat, perhaps the fatigue of the march, but the pain has begun again, together with a strange feeling of humidity in the wounded foot. I take off my shoe: it is full of blood, by now congealed and kneaded into the mud and rags of the cloth I found a month ago, and which I use as a foot-pad, one day on the right, one day on the left foot.

This evening, after soup, I will go to Ka-Be.

Ka-Be is the abbreviation of Krankenbau, the infirmary. There are eight huts, exactly like the others in the camp, but separated by a wire-fence. They permanently hold a tenth of the population of the camp, but there are few who stay there longer than two weeks and none more than two months: within these limits they are held to die or be cured. Those who show signs of improvement are cured in Ka-Be, those who seem to get worse are sent from Ka-Be to the gas chambers. All this because we, fortunately, belong to the category of 'economically useful Jews'.

I have never been to Ka-Be nor to the clinic, and it is all new to me. There are two clinics, medical and surgical. In front of the door, exposed to the night and the wind, there are two long shadows. Some only have need of a bandage or a pill, others ask to be examined; some show death in their faces. Those at the front of both rows are already barefoot and ready to enter. Others, as their turn to enter approaches, contrive in the middle of the crush to loosen the haphazard laces and wire threads of their shoes and to unfold the precious foot-pads without tearing them; not too early, so as not to stand pointlessly in the mud in bare feet; not too late, so as not to lose their turn to enter, because it is rigorously forbidden to enter Ka-Be with shoes. A gigantic French Häftling, sitting in the porch between the doors of the two clinics, enforces respect for the prohibition. He is one of the few French officials of the camp. And do not think that to spend one's day among the muddy and broken shoes is a small privilege: it is enough to think of how many enter Ka-Be with shoes, and leave with no further need of them ...

When my turn comes I manage miraculously to take off my shoes and rags without losing any of them, without letting my bowl and gloves be stolen, without losing my balance and keeping my beret in my hand all the time, as for no reason can one wear it on entering a hut.

I leave the shoes at the deposit and am given the appropriate check, after which, barefoot and limping, my hands full of all my poor possessions that I dare not leave anywhere, I am admitted inside and join a new queue which ends in the examination rooms.

In this queue one progressively undresses so as to be naked when one arrives at the head, where a male nurse puts a thermometer under one's arm-pit. If anyone is dressed he loses his turn and goes back to join the queue. Everybody has to be given the thermometer, even if he only has a skin disease or toothache. In this way they make sure that whoever is not seriously ill will not submit himself to this complicated ritual for the sake of caprice.

My turn finally arrives and I am brought in front of the doctor. The nurse takes out the thermometer and presents me: '*Nummer 174517, kein Fieber.*' I do not need a long examination: I am immediately declared *Arztvormelder*. What it means I do not know, but this is certainly not the place to ask questions. I find myself thrown out, I get back my shoes and go back to the hut.

Chajim rejoices with me: I have a good wound, it does not seem dangerous, but it should be enough to guarantee me a discreet period of rest. I will spend the night in the hut with the others, but tomorrow morning, instead of going to work, I will have to show myself to the doctors for the definitive examination: this is what *Arztvormelder* means. Chajim is experienced in these matters and he thinks that I will probably be admitted tomorrow to Ka-Be. Chajim is my bed-companion and I trust him blindly. He is Polish, a religious Jew, learned in rabbinical law. He is about as old as I, a watchmaker by profession, and here in Buna works as a precision mechanic; so he is among the few who are able to preserve their dignity and self-assurance through the practice of a profession in which they are skilled.

And so it happened. After the reveille and the bread they called me out with three others from my hut. They took us to a corner of the roll-call square where there was a long queue, all the *Arztvormelder* of today; someone came and took away my bowl, spoon, beret and gloves. The others laughed. Did I not know that I had to hide them or leave them with someone, or best of all sell them, as they cannot be taken in Ka-Be? Then they look at my number and shake their heads: any stupidity is to be expected from one with so high a number.

Then they counted us, they made us undress outside in the cold, they took our shoes, they counted us again, and they made us take a shower. Then an SS man came, he looked at us without interest, stopping in front of one with a large hydrocele, whom he placed apart. After which they counted us again and made us take another shower, although we were still wet from the first one and some were trembling from a chill.

We are now ready for the definitive examination. Outside the window one can see the white sky and sometimes the sun; in this country one can look at it fixedly, through the clouds, as through a misty window. To judge by its position it must be past 2 p.m. Good-bye soup by now, and we have been on our feet for ten hours and naked for six.

This second medical examination is also extraordinarily rapid: the doctor (he has a striped suit like us, but with a white coat over it, with the number sewn on the coat, and he is much fatter than us) looks at and touches my swollen and bloody foot, at which I cry out from pain. Then he says: '*Aufgenommen, Block 23.*' I stand there with my mouth open, waiting for some other indication, but someone pulls me backwards brutally, throws a gown on my bare shoulders, gives me a pair of sandals and drives me out into the open.

A hundred yards away is Block 23; written on it is '*Schonungsblock*'. Who knows what it means? Inside they take off my gown and sandals and I find myself naked and last again in a queue of human skeletons – the inmates of today.

I have stopped trying to understand for a long time now. As far as I am concerned, I am by now so tired of standing on my wounded foot, still untended, so hungry and frozen, that nothing can interest me any more. This might easily be my last day and this room the gas chamber of which all speak, but what can I do about it? I might just as well lean against the wall, close my eyes and wait.

My neighbour cannot be Jewish. He is not circumcised and besides (this is one of the few things that I have so far learnt), so blond a skin, a face and a body so huge, are characteristics of non-Jewish Poles. He is a whole head taller than me but he has quite cordial features, as have only those who do not suffer from hunger.

I tried to ask him if he knew when they would let us enter. He turned to the nurse who resembled him like a twin and was smoking in the corner; they talked and laughed together without replying, as if I was not there. Then one of them took my arm and looked at my number and then both laughed still more strongly. Everyone knows that the 174000s are the Italian Jews, the well-known Italian Jews who arrived two months ago, all lawyers, all with degrees, who were more than a hundred and are now only forty; the ones who do not know how to work, and let their bread be stolen, and are slapped from the morning to the evening. The Germans call them '*zwei linke Hände*' (two left hands), and even the Polish Jews despise them as they do not speak Yiddish.

The nurse points to my ribs to show the other, as if I was a corpse in an anatomy class: he alludes to my eyelids and my swollen cheeks and my thin neck, he stoops to press on my tibia with his thumb, and shows the other the deep impression that his finger leaves in the pale flesh, as if it was wax.

I wish I had never spoken to the Pole: I feel as if I had never in all my life undergone an affront worse than this. The nurse, meanwhile, seems to have finished his demonstration in his language which I do not understand and which sounds terrible. He turns to me, and in near-German, charitably, tells me the conclusion: '*Du Jude, kaputt. Du schnell Krematorium fertig.*' (You Jew, finished. You soon ready for crematorium.)

Some more hours pass before all the inmates are seen, are given a shirt and their details taken. I, as usual, am the last. Someone in a brand-new striped suit asks me where I was born, what profession I practised 'as a civilian', if I had children, what diseases I had had, a whole series of questions. What use could they be? Is this a complicated rehearsal to make fools of us? Could this be the hospital? They make us stand naked and ask us questions.

Finally the door is opened, even for me, and I can enter the dormitory.

Here as everywhere there are bunks on three levels, in three rows throughout the hut, separated by two narrow corridors. The bunks are 150, the patients 250; so there are two in almost all the bunks. The patients in the upper bunks, squashed against the ceiling, can hardly sit up; they lean out, curious to see the new arrivals of today. It is the most interesting moment of the day, for one always finds some acquaintances. I am assigned bunk number 10 – a miracle! It is empty! I stretch myself out with delight; it is the first time since I entered the camp that I have a bunk all to myself. Despite my hunger, within ten minutes I am asleep.

The life of Ka-Be is a life of limbo. The material discomforts are relatively few, apart from hunger and the inherent pains of illness. It is not cold, there is no work to do, and unless you commit some grave fault, you are not beaten.

The reveille is at 4 a.m., even for the patients. One has to make one's bed and wash, but there is not much hurry and little severity. The bread is distributed at half past five, and one can cut it comfortably into thin slices and eat it lying down in complete peace; then one can fall asleep again until the soup is distributed at midday. Until about 4 p.m. it is *Mittagsruhe*, afternoon resttime; then there is often the medical visit and dispensing of medicines, and one has to climb down from the bunks, take off one's shirt and file past the doctor. The evening ration is also served in bed, after which, at 9 p.m., all the lights are turned off except for the shaded lamp of the night-guard, and there is silence.

... And for the first time since I entered the camp the reveille catches me in a deep sleep and its ringing is a return from nothingness. As the bread is distributed one can hear, far from the windows, in the dark air, the band beginning to play: the healthy comrades are leaving in squads for work.

One cannot hear the music well from Ka-Be. The beating of the big drums and the cymbals reach us continuously and monotonously, but on this weft the musical phrases weave a pattern only intermittently, according to the caprices of the wind. We all look at each other from our beds, because we all feel that this music is infernal.

The tunes are few, a dozen, the same ones every day, morning and evening: marches and popular songs dear to every German. They lie engraven on our minds and will be the last thing in Lager that we shall forget: they are the voice of the Lager, the perceptible expression of its geometrical madness, of the resolution of others to annihilate us first as men in order to kill us more slowly afterwards.

When this music plays we know that our comrades, out in the fog, are marching like automatons; their souls are dead and the music drives them, like the wind drives dead leaves, and takes the place of their wills. There is no longer any will: every beat of the drum becomes a step, a reflected contraction of exhausted muscles. The Germans have succeeded in this. They are ten thousand and they are a single grey machine; they are exactly determined; they do not think and they do not desire, they walk.

At the departure and the return march the SS are never lacking. Who could deny them their right to watch this choreography of their creation, the dance of dead men, squad after squad, leaving the fog to enter the fog? What more concrete proof of their victory?

Even those in Ka-Be recognize this departure and return from work, the hypnosis of the interminable rhythm, which kills thought and deadens pain; they have experienced it themselves and they will experience it again. But one had to escape from the enchantment, to hear the music from outside, as happened in Ka-Be, and as we think back now after the liberation and the rebirth, without obeying it, without enduring it, to understand what it was, for what meditated reason the Germans created this monstrous rite, and why even today, when we happen to remember some of those innocent songs, our blood freezes in our veins and we become aware that to escape from Auschwitz was no small fortune.

I have two neighbours in the adjoining bunk. They lie down all day and all night, side by side, skin against skin, crossed like the Pisces of the zodiac, so that each has the feet of the other beside his head.

One is Walter Bonn, a Dutchman, civilized and quite well mannered. He sees that I have nothing with which to cut my bread and loans me his knife, and then offers to sell it to me for half a ration of bread. I discuss the price and then turn it down, as I think that I will always find someone to lend me one here in Ka-Be, while outside it only costs a third of a ration. Walter is by no means less courteous because of this, and at midday, after eating his soup, he cleans his spoon with his mouth (which is a good rule before loaning it, so as to clean it and not to leave any traces of soup which may still be there) and spontaneously offers me it.

'What are you suffering from, Walter?'

'*Körperschwäche*', organic decay. The worst disease: it cannot be cured, and it is very dangerous to enter Ka-Be with such a diagnosis. If it had not been for the oedema of his ankles (and he shows me it) which hinders him from marching to work, he would have been very cautious about reporting ill.

I still have quite confused ideas about this kind of danger. Everybody speaks about it indirectly, by allusions, and when I ask some question they look at me and fall silent.

Is it true what one hears of selections, of gas, of crematoriums?

Crematoriums. The other one, Walter's neighbour, wakes up startled and sits up: who is talking about the crematorium? what is happening? cannot a sleeping person be left in peace? He is a Polish Jew, albino, with an emaciated and good-natured face, no longer young. His name is Schmulek, he is a smith. Walter tells him briefly.

So, '*der Italeyner*' does not believe in selections. Schmulek wants to speak German but speaks Yiddish; I understand him with difficulty, only because he wants to be understood. He silences Walter with a sign, he will see about persuading me:

'Show me your number: you are 174517. This numbering began eighteen months ago and applies to Auschwitz and the dependent camps. There are now ten thousand of us here at Buna-Monowitz; perhaps thirty thousand between Auschwitz and Birkenau. *Wo sind die Andere?* Where are the others?'

'Perhaps transferred to other camps?' I suggest.

Schmulek shakes his head, he turns to Walter.

'*Er will nix verstayen*,' he does not want to understand.

But destiny ordained that I was soon to understand, and at the expense of Schmulek himself. That evening the door of the hut opened, a voice shouted '*Achtung!*' and every sound died out to give way to a leaden silence.

Two SS men enter (one of them has many chevrons, perhaps he is an officer?). One can hear their steps in the hut as if it was empty; they speak to the chief doctor, and he shows them a register, pointing here and there. The officer notes down in a book. Schmulek touches my knee:

'*Pass' auf, pass' auf*,' keep your eyes open.

The officer, followed by the doctor, walks around in silence, nonchalantly, between the bunks; he has a switch in his hand,

and flicks at the edge of a blanket hanging down from a top bunk, the patient hurries to adjust it.

One has a yellow face; the officer pulls away his blankets, he starts back, the officer touches his belly, says, '*Gut, gut,*' and moves on.

Now he is looking at Schmulek; he brings out the book, checks the number of the bed and the number of the tattoo. I see it all clearly from above: he has drawn a cross beside Schmulek's number. Then he moves on.

I now look at Schmulek and behind him I see Walter's eyes, so I ask no questions.

The day after, in place of the usual group of patients who have recovered, two distinct groups are led out. The first have been shaved and sheared and have had a shower. The second left as they are, with long hair and without being treated, without a shower. Nobody said good-bye to the latter, nobody gave them messages for healthy comrades.

Schmulek formed part of this group.

In this discreet and composed manner, without display or anger, massacre moves through the huts of Ka-Be every day, touching here and there. When Schmulek left, he gave me his spoon and knife; Walter and I avoided looking at each other and remained silent for a long time. Then Walter asked me how I manage to keep my ration of bread so long, and explained to me that he usually cuts his bread lengthwise to have longer slices in order to smear on the margarine more easily.

Walter explains many things to me: *Schonungsblock* means the rest hut, where there are only the less serious patients or convalescents, or those not requiring attention. Among them, at least fifty more or less serious dysentery patients.

These are checked every third day. They are placed in a line along the corridor. At the end there are two tin-plate pots, and the nurse with a register, watch and pencil. Two at a time, the patients present themselves and have to show, on the spot and at once, that they still have diarrhoea; to prove it, they are given exactly one minute. After which, they show the result to the nurse who looks at it and judges. They wash the pots quickly in a wash-tub near by and the next two take over.

Of those waiting, some are contorted in the pain of keeping in their precious evidence another ten, another twenty minutes; others, without resources at the moment, strain veins and muscles in a contrary effort. The nurse watches, impassive, chewing his pencil, one eye on the watch, one eye on the specimens gradually presented him. In doubtful cases, he leaves with the pot to show it to the doctor.

I receive an unexpected visit: it is Piero Sonnino, my friend from Rome. 'Have you seen how I have fixed it?' Piero has mild enteritis, has been here for twenty days, and is quite happy, rested and growing fatter; he could not care less about the selections and has decided to stay in Ka-Be until the end of the winter, at all costs. His method consists of placing himself in line behind some authentic dysentery patient who offers a guarantee of success; when it is his turn he asks for his collaboration (to be rewarded with soup or bread), and if the latter agrees, and the nurse has a moment of inattention, he switches over the pots in the middle of the crowd, and the deed is done. Piero knows what he is risking, but it has gone well so far.

But life in Ka-Be is not this. It is not the crucial moments of the selections, it is not the grotesque episodes of the diarrhoea and lice controls, it is not even the illnesses.

Ka-Be is the Lager without its physical discomforts. So that, whoever still has some seeds of conscience, feels his conscience re-awaken; and in the long empty days, one speaks of other things than hunger and work and one begins to consider what they have made us become, how much they have taken away from us, what this life is. In this Ka-Be, an enclosure of relative peace, we have learnt that our personality is fragile, that it is much more in danger than our life; and the old wise ones, instead of warning us 'remember that you must die', would have done much better to remind us of this great danger that threatens us. If from inside the Lager, a message could have seeped out to free men, it would have been this: take care not to suffer in your own homes what is inflicted on us here.

When one works, one suffers and there is no time to think: our homes are less than a memory. But here the time is ours: from bunk to bunk, despite the prohibition, we exchange visits and we talk and we talk. The wooden hut, crammed with suffering humanity, is full of words, memories and of another pain. '*Heimweh*' the Germans call this pain; it is a beautiful word, it means 'longing for one's home'.

We know where we come from; the memories of the world outside crowd our sleeping and our waking hours, we become aware, with amazement, that we have forgotten nothing, every memory evoked rises in front of us painfully clear.

But where we are going we do not know. Will we perhaps be able to survive the illnesses and escape the selections, perhaps even resist the work and hunger which wear us out – but then, afterwards? Here, momentarily far away from the curses and the blows, we can re-enter into ourselves and meditate, and then it becomes clear that we will not return. We travelled here in the sealed wagons; we saw our women and our children leave towards nothingness; we, transformed into slaves, have marched a hundred times backwards and forwards to our silent labours, killed in our spirit long before our anonymous death. No one must leave here and so carry to the world, together with the sign impressed on his skin, the evil tidings of what man's presumption made of man in Auschwitz.

5

Our Nights

After twenty days of Ka-Be, when my wound was practically healed, I was discharged to my great displeasure.

The ceremony is simple, but implies a painful and dangerous period of readjustment. All who have no special contacts are not returned to their former Block and Kommando on leaving Ka-Be, but are enrolled, on the basis of criteria wholly unknown to me, in any other hut and given any kind of work. Moreover, they leave Ka-Be naked; they are given 'new' clothes and shoes (I mean not those left behind at their entry) which need to be adapted with speed and diligence to their own persons, which implies effort and expense. They have to worry about acquiring a new spoon and knife as at the beginning. And finally – and this is the gravest aspect – they find themselves inserted in an unknown environment, among hostile companions never seen before, with leaders whose characters they do not know and against whom it is consequently difficult to guard themselves.

Man's capacity to dig himself in, to secrete a shell, to build around himself a tenuous barrier of defence, even in apparently desperate circumstances, is astonishing and merits a serious study. It is based on an invaluable activity of adaptation, partly passive and unconscious, partly active: of hammering in a nail above his bunk from which to hang up his shoes; of concluding tacit pacts of non-aggression with neighbours; of understanding and accepting the customs and laws of a single Kommando, a single Block. By virtue of this work, one manages to gain a certain equilibrium after a few weeks, a certain degree of security in face of the unforeseen; one has made oneself a nest, the trauma of the transplantation is over.

But the man who leaves Ka-Be, naked and almost always insufficiently cured, feels himself ejected into the dark and cold of sidereal space. His trousers fall down, his shoes hurt him, his shirt has no buttons. He searches for a human contact and only finds backs turned on him. He is as helpless and vulnerable as a new-born baby, but the following morning he will still have to march to work.

It is in these conditions that I find myself when the nurse entrusts me, after various administrative rites, to the care of the *Blockältester* of Block 45. But at once a thought fills me with joy: I am in luck, this is Alberto's Block.

Alberto is my best friend. He is only twenty-two, two years younger than me, but none of us Italians have shown an equal capacity for adaptation. Alberto entered the Lager with his head high, and lives in here unscathed and uncorrupted. He understood before any of us that this life is war; he permitted himself no indulgences, he lost no time complaining and commiserating with himself and with others, but entered the battle from the beginning. He has the advantage of intelligence and intuition: he reasons correctly, often he does not even reason but is equally right. He understands everything at once: he knows a little French but understands whatever the Germans and Poles tell him. He replies in Italian and with gestures, he makes himself understood and at once wins sympathy. He fights for his life but still remains everybody's friend. He 'knows' whom to corrupt, whom to avoid, whose compassion to arouse, whom to resist.

Yet (and it is for this virtue of his that his memory is still dear and close to me) he himself did not become corrupt. I always saw, and still see in him, the rare figure of the strong yet peace-loving man against whom the weapons of night are blunted.

But I did not manage to gain permission to sleep in a bunk with him, and not even Alberto succeeded, although by now he enjoyed a certain popularity in Block 45. It is a pity, because to have a bed-companion whom one can trust, or at least with whom one can reach an understanding, is an inestimable advantage; and besides, it is winter now and the nights are long, and since we are forced to exchange sweats, smells and warmth with someone under the same blanket, and in a width little more than two feet, it is quite desirable that he be a friend.

In the winter the nights are long and we are allowed a considerable interval of time to sleep.

The tumult of the Block dies down; the distribution of the evening ration ended over an hour ago, and only a few stubborn people continue to scrape the by-now shining bottom of the bowl, turning it around with care under the lamp, frowning with attention. Engineer Kardos moves around the bunks, tending wounded feet and suppurating corns. This is his trade: there is no one who will not willingly renounce a slice of bread to soothe the torment of those numbed sores which bleed at every step all day. And so, in this manner, honestly, engineer Kardos solves the problem of living.

From the outside door, secretly and looking around cautiously, the story-teller comes in. He is seated on Wachsmann's bunk and at once gathers around him a small, attentive, silent crowd. He chants an interminable Yiddish rhapsody, always the same one, in rhymed quatrains, of a resigned and penetrating melancholy (but perhaps I only remember it so because of the time and the place that I heard it?); from the few words that I understand, it must be a song that he composed himself, in which he has enclosed all the life of the Lager in minute detail.

Some are generous and give the story-teller a pinch of tobacco or a needleful of thread; others listen intently but give nothing.

The bell rings suddenly for the last ceremony of the day: '*Wer hat kaputt die Schuhe?*' (who has broken shoes?), and at once the noise of forty or fifty claimants to the exchange breaks out as they rush towards the *Tagesraum* in desperate haste, well knowing that only the first ten, on the best of hypotheses, will be satisfied.

Then there is quiet. The light goes out a first time for a few seconds to warn the tailors to put away the precious needle and thread; then the bell sounds in the distance, the night-guard installs himself and all the lights are turned out definitively. There is nothing to do but to undress and go to bed.

I do not know who my neighbour is; I am not even sure that it is always the same person because I have never seen his face except for a few seconds amidst the uproar of the reveille, so that I know his back and his feet much better than his face. He does not work in my Kommando and only comes into the bunk at curfew time; he wraps himself in the blanket, pushes me aside with a blow from his bony hips, turns his back on me and at once begins to snore. Back against back, I struggle to regain a reasonable area of the straw mattress: with the base of my back I exercise a progressive pressure against his back; then I turn around and try to push with my knees; I take hold of his ankles and try to place them a little further over so as not to have his feet next to my face. But it is all in vain: he is much heavier than me and seems turned to stone in his sleep.

So I adapt myself to lie like this, forced into immobility, half-lying on the wooden edge. Nevertheless I am so tired and stunned that I, too, soon fall asleep, and I seem to be sleeping on the tracks of a railroad.

The train is about to arrive: one can hear the engine panting, it is my neighbour. I am not yet so asleep as not to be aware of the double nature of the engine. It is, in fact, the very engine which towed the wagons we had to unload in Buna today. I recognize it by the fact that even now, as when it passed close by us, I feel the heat it radiates from its black side. It is puffing, it is ever nearer, it is on the point of running over me, but instead it never arrives. My sleep is very light, it is a veil, if I want I can tear it. I will do it, I want to tear it, so that I can get off the railway track. Now I have done it and now I am awake: but not really awake, only a little more, one step higher on the ladder between the unconscious and the conscious. I have my eyes closed and I do not want to open them lest my sleep escape me, but I can register noises: I am sure this distant whistle is real, it does not come from an engine in a dream, it can be heard objectively. It is the whistle of the small-gauge track, it comes from the yard where they work at night as well. A long, firm note, then another one a semitone lower, then again the first, but short and cut off. This whistle is an important thing and in some ways essential: we have heard it so often associated with the suffering of the work and the camp that it has become a symbol and immediately evokes its image like certain music or smells.

This is my sister here, with some unidentifiable friend and many other people. They are all listening to me and it is this very story that I am telling: the whistle of three notes, the hard bed, my neighbour whom I would like to move, but whom I am afraid to wake as he is stronger than me. I also speak diffusely of our hunger and of the lice-control, and of the Kapo who hit me on the nose and then sent me to wash myself as I was bleeding. It is an intense pleasure, physical, inexpressible, to be at home, among friendly people and to have so many things to recount: but I cannot help noticing that my listeners do not follow me. In fact, they are completely indifferent: they speak confusedly of other things among themselves, as if I was not there. My sister looks at me, gets up and goes away without a word.

A desolating grief is now born in me, like certain barely remembered pains of one's early infancy. It is pain in its pure state, not tempered by a sense of reality and by the intrusion of extraneous circumstances, a pain like that which makes children cry; and it is better for me to swim once again up to the surface, but this time I deliberately open my eyes to have a guarantee in front of me of being effectively awake.

My dream stands in front of me, still warm, and although awake I am still full of its anguish: and then I remember that it is not a haphazard dream, but that I have dreamed it not once but many times since I arrived here, with hardly any variations of environment or details. I am now quite awake and I remember that I have recounted it to Alberto and that he confided to me, to my amazement, that it is also his dream and the dream of many others, perhaps of everyone. Why does it happen? Why is the pain of every day translated so constantly into our dreams, in the ever-repeated scene of the unlistened-to story?

While I meditate on this, I try to profit from the interval of wakefulness to shake off the painful remnants of the preceding sleep, so as not to compromise the quality of the next dream. I crouch in the dark, I look around and I listen.

One can hear the sleepers breathing and snoring; some groan and speak. Many lick their lips and move their jaws. They are dreaming of eating; this is also a collective dream. It is a pitiless dream which the creator of the Tantalus myth must have known. You not only see the food, you feel it in your hands, distinct and concrete, you are aware of its rich and striking smell; someone in the dream even holds it up to your lips, but every time a different circumstance intervenes to prevent the consummation of the act. Then the dream dissolves and breaks up into its elements, but it re-forms itself immediately after and begins again, similar, yet changed; and this without pause, for all of us, every night and for the whole of our sleep.

It must be later than 11 p.m. because the movement to and from the bucket next to the night-guard is already intense. It is an obscene torment and an indelible shame: every two or three hours we have to get up to discharge ourselves of the great dose of water which during the day we are forced to absorb in the form of soup in order to satisfy our hunger: that same water which in the evenings swells our ankles and the hollows of our eyes, conferring on all physiognomies a likeness of deformation, and whose elimination imposes an enervating toil on our kidneys.

It is not merely a question of a procession to a bucket; it is the rule that the last user of the bucket goes and empties it in the latrines; it is also the rule that at night one must not leave the hut except in night uniform (shirt and pants), giving one's number to the guard. It is easily foreseeable that the night-guard will try to exempt his friends, his co-nationals and the Prominents from this duty. Add to this that the old members of the camp have refined their senses to such a degree that, while still in their bunks, they are miraculously able to distinguish if the level is at a dangerous point, purely on the basis of the sound that the sides of the bucket make – with the result that they almost always manage to avoid emptying it. So the candidates for the bucket service are a fairly limited number in each hut, while the total volume to eliminate is at least forty gallons, which means that the bucket has to be emptied about twenty times.

In short, the risk which hangs over us, the inexperienced and non-privileged, when we are driven by necessity to the bucket every night is quite serious. The night-guard unexpectedly jumps from his corner and seizes us, scribbles down our number, hands us a pair of wooden shoes and the bucket and drives us out into the middle of the snow, shivering and sleepy. It is our task to shuffle to the latrine with the bucket which knocks against our bare calves, disgustingly warm; it is full beyond all reasonable limit, and inevitably with the shaking some of the content overflows on our feet, so that however repugnant this duty may be, it is always preferable that we, and not our neighbour, be ordered to do it.

So our nights drag on. The dream of Tantalus and the dream of the story are woven into a texture of more indistinct images: the suffering of the day, composed of hunger, blows, cold, exhaustion, fear and promiscuity, turns at night-time into shapeless nightmares of unheard-of violence, which in free life would only occur during a fever. One wakes up at every moment, frozen with terror, shaking in every limb, under the impression of an order shouted out by a voice full of anger in a language not understood. The procession to the bucket and the thud of bare heels on the wooden floor turns into another symbolic procession: it is us again, grey and identical, small as ants, yet so huge as to reach up to the stars, bound one against the other, countless, covering the plain as far as the horizon; sometimes melting into a single substance, a sorrowful turmoil in which we all feel ourselves trapped and suffocated; sometimes marching in a circle, without beginning or end, with a blinding giddiness and a sea of nausea rising from the praecordia to the gullet; until hunger or cold or the fullness of our bladders turn our dreams into their customary forms. We try in vain, when the nightmare itself or the discomforts wake us, to extricate the various elements and drive them back, separately, out of the field of our present attention, so as to defend our sleep from their intrusion: but as soon as we close our eyes, once again we feel our brain start up, beyond our control; it knocks and hums, incapable of rest, it fabricates phantasms and terrible symbols, and without rest projects and shapes their images, as a grey fog, on to the screen of our dreams.

But for the whole duration of the night, cutting across the alternating sleep, waking and nightmares, the expectancy and terror of the moment of the reveille keeps watch. By means of that mysterious faculty of which many are aware, even without watches we are able to calculate the moment with close accuracy. At the hour of the reveille, which varies from season to season but always falls a fair time before dawn, the camp bell rings for a long time, and the night-guard in every hut goes off duty; he switches on the light, gets up, stretches himself and pronounces the daily condemnation: '*Aufstehen*,' or more often in Polish: '*Wstavac*.'

Very few sleep on till the *Wstavac*: it is a moment of too acute pain for even the deepest sleep not to dissolve as it approaches. The night guard knows it and for this reason does not utter it in a tone of command, but with the quiet and subdued voice of one who knows that the announcement will find all ears waiting, and will be heard and obeyed.

Like a stone the foreign word falls to the bottom of every soul. 'Get up': the illusory barrier of the warm blankets, the thin armour of sleep, the nightly evasion with its very torments drops to pieces around us, and we find ourselves mercilessly awake, exposed to insult, atrociously naked and vulnerable. A day begins like every day, so long as not to allow us reasonably to conceive its end, so much cold, so much hunger, so much exhaustion separate us from it: so that it is better to concentrate one's attention and desires on the block of grey bread, which is small but which will certainly be ours in an hour, and which for five minutes, until we have devoured it, will form everything that the law of the place allows us to possess.

*

At the *Wstavac* the hurricane starts up again. The entire hut enters without transition into frantic activity: everybody climbs up and down, remakes his bed and tries at the same time to dress himself in a manner so as to leave none of his objects unguarded; the air is filled with so much dust as to become opaque; the quickest ones elbow their way through the crowd to go to the washroom and latrine before the queue begins. The hut-sweepers at once come on to the scene and drive everyone out, hitting and shouting at them.

When I have remade my bed and am dressed, I climb down on to the floor and put on my shoes. The sores on my feet reopen at once, and a new day begins.

6

The Work

Before Resnyk came, I slept with a Pole whose name no one knew; he was gentle and silent, with two old sores on his shin-bones, and during the night gave out a squalid smell of illness; he also had a weak bladder, and so woke up and woke me up eight or ten times a night.

One night he left his gloves in my care and entered the hospital. For half an hour I hoped that the quartermaster would forget that I was the sole occupant of my bunk, but when the curfew bell had already sounded, the bed trembled and a long, red-haired fellow, with the number of the French of Drancy, climbed up beside me.

To have a bed companion of tall stature is a misfortune and means losing hours of sleep; I always have tall companions as I am small and two tall ones cannot sleep together. But it could at once be seen that Resnyk, despite everything, was not a bad companion. He spoke little and courteously, he was clean, he did not snore, did not get up more than two or three times a night and always with great delicacy. In the morning he offered to make the bed (this is a complicated and difficult operation, and also carries a notable responsibility, as those who remake the bed badly, the '*schlechte Bettenbauer*', are diligently punished) and did it quickly and well; so that I experienced a certain fleeting pleasure later in the roll-call square on seeing that he had been assigned to my Kommando.

On the march to work, limping in our large wooden shoes on the icy snow, we exchanged a few words, and I found out that Resnyk is Polish; he lived twenty years at Paris but speaks an incredible French. He is thirty, but like all of us, could be taken for seventeen or fifty. He told me his story, and today I have forgotten it, but it was certainly a sorrowful, cruel and moving story; because so are all our stories, hundreds of thousands of stories, all different and all full of a tragic, disturbing necessity. We tell them to each other in the evening, and they take place in Norway, Italy, Algeria, the Ukraine, and are simple and incomprehensible like the stories in the Bible. But are they not themselves stories of a new Bible?

When we arrived at the yard they took us to the *Eisenröhreplatz*, which is the levelling where they unload the iron pipes, and then the normal things of every day began. The Kapo made a second roll-call, briefly made note of the new acquisition and arranged with the civilian *Meister* about the day's work. He then entrusted us to the *Vorarbeiter* and went to sleep in the tool cabin, next to the stove; he is not a Kapo who makes trouble, for he is not a Jew and so has no fear of losing his post. The *Vorarbeiter* distributed the iron levers among us and the jacks among his friends. The usual little struggle took place to get the lightest levers, and today it went badly for me: mine is the twisted one which weighs perhaps thirty-five pounds; I know that even if I had to use it without any weight on it, I would be dead of exhaustion in half an hour.

Then we left, each with his own lever, limping in the melting snow. At every step a little snow and mud stuck to the wooden soles of our shoes, until one walked unsteadily on two heavy, formless masses of which it was impossible to free oneself; then, when one suddenly came unstuck, it felt as if one leg was a hand shorter than the other.

Today we have to unload an enormous, cast-iron cylinder from the wagon: I think it is a synthesis tube and will weigh several tons. This is better for us, as it is notoriously less exhausting to work with big loads than with small ones; in fact, the work is better subdivided, and we are given adequate tools. However, it is dangerous, one dare not let one's attention wander, a moment's oversight is sufficient to find oneself crushed.

Meister Nogalla, the Polish superintendent, rigid, serious and taciturn, supervised in person the unloading operation. Now the cylinder lies on the ground and Meister Nogalla says: '*Bohlen holen.*'

Our hearts sink. It means 'carry the sleepers' in order to build the path in the soft mud on which the cylinder will be pushed by lever into the factory. But the wooden sleepers are mortized in the ground and weigh about 175 pounds; they are more or less at the limits of our strength. The more robust of us, working in pairs, are able to carry sleepers for a few hours; for me it is a torture, the load maims my shoulder-bone. After the first journey I am deaf and almost blind from the effort, and I would stoop to any baseness to avoid the second journey.

I will try and place myself with Resnyk; he seems a good worker and being taller will support the greater part of the weight. I know that it is in the natural order of events that Resnyk refuse me with disdain and form a pair with another more robust individual; then I will ask to go to the latrine and I will remain there as long as possible, and afterwards I will try to hide, with the certainty of being immediately traced, mocked at and hit; but anything is better than this work.

Instead Resnyk accepts, and even more, lifts up the sleeper by himself and rests it on my right shoulder with care; then he lifts up the other end, stoops to place it on his left shoulder and we leave.

The sleeper is coated with snow and mud; at every step it knocks against my ear and the snow slides down my neck. After fifty steps I am at the limit of what a person is theoretically able to support: my knees bend, my shoulder aches as if pressed in a vice, my equilibrium is in danger. At every step I feel my shoes sucked away by the greedy mud, by this omnipresent Polish mud whose monotonous horror fills our days.

I bite deeply into my lips; we know well that to gain a small, extraneous pain serves as a stimulant to mobilize our last reserves of energy. The Kapos also know it: some of them beat us from pure bestiality and violence, but others beat us when we are under a load almost lovingly, accompanying the blows with exhortations, as cart-drivers do with willing horses.

When we reach the cylinder we unload the sleeper on the ground and I remain stiff, with empty eyes, open mouth and hanging arms, sunk in the ephemeral and negative ecstasy of the cessation of pain. In a twilight of exhaustion I wait for the push which will force me to begin work again, and I try to take advantage of every second of waiting to recuperate some energy.

But the push never comes: Resnyk touches my elbow, we return as slowly as possible to the sleepers. There the others are wandering around in pairs, all trying to delay as long as possible before submitting to the load.

'*Allons, petit, attrape.*' This sleeper is dry and a little lighter, but at the end of the second journey I go to the *Vorarbeiter* and ask to go the latrine.

We have the advantage that our latrine is rather far; this permits us, once a day, a slightly longer absence than normal. Moreover, as it is also forbidden to go there alone, Wachsmann, the weakest and most clumsy of the Kommando, has been invested with the duty of *Scheissbegleiter*, 'toilet companion'; by the virtue of this appointment, Wachsmann is responsible for any hypothetical (laughable hypothesis!) attempt to escape, and more realistically, for every delay.

As my request was accepted, I leave in the mud and the grey snow among the scraps of metal, escorted by the small Wachsmann. I never manage to reach an understanding with him, as we have no language in common; but his comrades tell me that he is a rabbi, in fact a Melamed, a person learned in the Torah, and even more, in his own village in Galicia, was famed as a healer and a thaumaturge. Nor am I far from believing it when I think that this thin, fragile and soft figure has managed to work for two years without falling ill and without dying, but on the contrary is lit up by an amazing vitality in actions and words and spends long evenings discussing Talmudic questions incomprehensibly in Yiddish and Hebrew with Mendi, who is a modernist rabbi.

The latrine is an oasis of peace. It is a provisional latrine which the Germans have not yet provided with the customary wooden partitions to separate the various divisions: '*Nur für Engländer*', '*Nur für Polen*', '*Nur für Ukrainische Frauen*', and so on, with, a little apart '*Nur für Häftlinge*'. Inside, shoulder by shoulder, sit four hollow-faced Häftlinge; a bearded old Russian worker with the blue stripe OST on his left arm; a Polish boy, with a large white P on his back and chest; an English POW, with his face splendidly shaven and rosy and his khaki uniform neat, ironed and clean, except for a large KG (*Kriegsgefangener*) on his back. A fifth Häftling stands at the door patiently and monotonously asking every civilian who enters loosening his belt: '*Êtes-vous français?*'

When I return to work the lorries with the rations can be seen passing, which means it is ten o'clock. It is already a respectable hour, as the midday pause can be almost glimpsed in the fog of the remote future, allowing us to derive a little more strength from the expectation.

I do another two or three trips with Resnyk, searching attentively, even going to distant piles, to find lighter sleepers, but by now all the best ones have already been carried and only the other ones remain, repellent, with sharp corners, heavy with mud and ice, with metal plates nailed in to fix the rails.

When Franz comes to call Wachsmann to go and claim the ration, it means that it is already eleven o'clock and the morning has almost finished – no one thinks about the afternoon. Then the corvée returns at 11.30, and the standard interrogation begins: how much soup today, what quality, if we were given it from the top or the bottom of the vat; I force myself not to ask these questions, but I cannot help listening eagerly to the replies, sniffing at the smoke carried by the wind from the kitchen.

And at last, like a celestial meteor, superhuman and impersonal like a sign from heaven, the midday siren explodes, granting a brief respite to our anonymous and concord tiredness and hunger. And the usual things happen again: we all run to the hut, and we queue up with our bowls ready and we all have an animal hurry to swell our bellies with the warm stew, but no one wants to be first, as the first person receives the most liquid ration. As usual, the Kapo mocks and insults us for our voracity and takes care not to stir the pot, as the bottom belongs notoriously to him. Then comes the bliss (positive, from the belly) of the distension and warmth of the stomach and of the cabin around the noisy stove. The smokers, with miserly and reverent gestures, roll a thin cigarette, while everybody's clothes, humid with mud and snow, give out a dense smoke at the heat of the stove, with the smell of a kennel or of a sheepfold.

A tacit convention ordains that no one speak: within a minute everyone is sleeping, jammed elbow against elbow, falling suddenly forwards and recovering with a stiffening of the back. Behind the barely-closed eyelids, dreams break out violently, the usual dreams. To be at home, in a wonderfully hot bath. To be at home, seated at a table. To be at home, and tell the story of this hopeless work of ours, of this never-ending hunger, of the slave's way of sleeping.

Then, in the bosom of the vapours of our torpid digestions, a painful nucleus condenses, and jars us and grows until it crosses the threshold of the consciousness and takes away the joy of sleep. '*Es wird bald ein Uhr sein*': it is almost one o'clock. Like a rapid, voracious cancer, it kills our sleep and oppresses us with a foreboding anguish: we listen to the wind blowing outside, and to the light rustle of the snow against the window, '*es wird schnell ein Uhr sein*'. While everyone clings on to his sleep, so as not to allow it to abandon him, all senses are taut with the horror of the signal which is about to come, which is outside the door, which is here ...

Here it is. A thud at the window: Meister Nogalla has thrown a snowball against the window pane, and now stands stiffly outside, holding his watch with its face turned towards us. The Kapo gets up, stretches himself, and says quietly as one who does not doubt that he will be obeyed: '*Alles heraus*', all out.

Oh, if one could only cry! Oh, if one could only affront the wind as we once used to, on equal terms, and not as we do here, like cringing dogs.

We are outside and everyone picks up his lever. Resnyk drops his head between his shoulders, pulls his beret over his ears and lifts his face up to the low grey sky where the inexorable snow whirls around: '*Si j'avey une chien, je ne le chasse pas dehors.*'

7

A Good Day

The conviction that life has a purpose is rooted in every fibre of man, it is a property of the human substance. Free men give many names to this purpose, and think and talk a lot about its nature. But for us the question is simpler.

Today, in this place, our only purpose is to reach the spring. At the moment we care about nothing else. Behind this aim there is not at the moment any other aim. In the morning while we wait endlessly lined up in the roll-call square for the time to leave for work, while every breath of wind penetrates our clothes and runs in violent shivers over our defenceless bodies, and everything is grey around us, and we are grey; in the morning, when it is still dark, we all look at the sky in the east to spot the first signs of a milder season, and the rising of the sun is commented on every day: today a little earlier than yesterday, today a little warmer than yesterday, in two months, in a month, the cold will call a truce and we will have one enemy less.

Today the sun rose bright and clear for the first time from the horizon of mud. It is a Polish sun, cold, white and distant, and only warms the skin, but when it dissolved the last mists a murmur ran through our colourless numbers, and when even I felt its lukewarmth through my clothes I understood how men can worship the sun.

'*Das Schlimmste ist vorüber*,' said Ziegler, turning his pointed shoulders to the sun: the worst is over. Next to us there is a group of Greeks, those admirable and terrible Jews of Salonica, tenacious, thieving, wise, ferocious and united, so determined to live, such pitiless opponents in the struggle for life; those Greeks who have conquered in the kitchens and in the yards, and whom even the Germans respect and the Poles fear. They are in their third year of camp, and nobody knows better than them what the camp means. They now stand closely in a circle, shoulder to shoulder, and sing one of their interminable chants.

Felicio the Greek knows me. '*L'année prochaine à la maison!*' he shouts at me, and adds: '*à la maison par la Cheminée!*' Felicio has been at Birkenau. And they continue to sing and beat their feet in time and grow drunk on songs.

When we finally left by the main entrance of the camp, the sun was quite high and the sky serene. At midday one could see the mountains; to the west, the steeple of Auschwitz (a steeple here!), and all around the barrage balloons. The smoke from the Buna lay still in the cold air, and a row of low hills could be seen, green with forests: and our hearts tighten because we all know that Birkenau is there, that our women finished there, and that soon we too will finish there; but we are not used to seeing it.

For the first time we are aware that on both sides of the road, even here, the meadows are green; because, without a sun, a meadow is as if it were not green.

Buna is not: Buna is desperately and essentially opaque and grey. This huge entanglement of iron, concrete, mud and smoke is the negation of beauty. Its roads and buildings are named like us, by numbers or letters, not by weird and sinister names. Within its bounds not a blade of grass grows, and the soil is impregnated with the poisonous saps of coal and petroleum, and the only things alive are machines and slaves – and the former are more alive than the latter.

*

Buna is as large as a city; besides the managers and German technicians, forty thousand foreigners work there, and fifteen to twenty languages are spoken. All the foreigners live in different Lagers which surround Buna: the Lager of the English prisoners-of-war, the Lager of the Ukrainian women, the Lager of the French volunteers and others we do not know. Our Lager (*Judenlager, Vernichtungslager, Kazett*) by itself provides ten thousand workers who come from all the nations of Europe. We are the slaves of the slaves, whom all can give orders to, and our name is the number which we carry tattooed on our arm and sewn on our jacket.

The Carbide Tower, which rises in the middle of Buna and whose top is rarely visible in the fog, was built by us. Its bricks were called *Ziegel, briques, tegula, cegli, kamenny, mattoni, téglak*, and they were cemented by hate; hate and discord, like the Tower of Babel, and it is this that we call it: – *Babelturm, Bobelturm*; and in it we hate the insane dream of grandeur of our masters, their contempt for God and men, for us men.

And today just as in the old fable, we all feel, and the Germans themselves feel, that a curse – not transcendent and divine, but inherent and historical – hangs over the insolent building based on the confusion of languages and erected in defiance of heaven like a stone oath.

As will be told, the Buna factory, on which the Germans were busy for four years and for which countless of us suffered and died, never produced a pound of synthetic rubber.

But today the eternal puddles, on which a rainbow veil of petroleum trembles, reflect the serene sun. Pipes, rails, boilers, still cold from the freezing of the night, are dripping with dew. The earth dug up from the pits, the piles of coal, the blocks of concrete, exhale in light vapours the humidity of the winter.

Today is a good day. We look around like blind people who have recovered their sight, and we look at each other. We have never seen each other in sunlight: someone smiles. If it was not for the hunger!

For human nature is such that grief and pain – even simultaneously suffered – do not add up as a whole in our consciousness, but hide, the lesser behind the greater, according to a definite law of perspective. It is providential and is our means of surviving in the camp. And this is the reason why so often in free life one hears it said that man is never content. In fact it is not a question of a human incapacity for a state of absolute happiness, but of an ever-insufficient knowledge of the complex nature of the state of unhappiness; so that the single name of the major cause is given to all its causes, which are composite and set out in an order of urgency. And if the most immediate cause of stress comes to an end, you are grievously amazed to see that another one lies behind; and in reality a whole series of others.

So that as soon as the cold, which throughout the winter had seemed our only enemy, had ceased, we became aware of our hunger; and repeating the same error, we now say: 'If it was not for the hunger! ...'

But how could one imagine not being hungry? The Lager *is* hunger: we ourselves are hunger, living hunger.

On the other side of the road a steam-shovel is working. Its mouth, hanging from its cables, opens wide its steel jaws, balances a moment as if uncertain in its choice, then rushes upon the soft, clayey soil and snaps it up voraciously, while a satisfied snort of thick white smoke rises from the control cabin. Then it rises, turns half around, vomits backwards its mouthful and begins again.

Leaning on our shovels, we stop to watch, fascinated. At every bite of its mouth our mouths also open, our Adam's apples dance up and down, wretchedly visible under the flaccid skin. We are unable to tear ourselves away from the sight of the steam-shovel's meal.

Sigi is seventeen years old and is hungrier than everybody, although he is given a little soup every evening by his probably not disinterested protector. He had begun to speak of his home in Vienna and of his mother, but then he slipped on to the subject of food and now he talks endlessly about some marriage luncheon and remembers with genuine regret that he failed to finish his third plate of bean soup. And everyone tells him to keep quiet, but within ten minutes Bela is describing his Hungarian countryside and the fields of maize and a recipe to make meat-pies with corncobs and lard and spices and ... and he is cursed, sworn at and a third one begins to describe ...

How weak our flesh is! I am perfectly well aware how vain these fantasies of hunger are, but dancing before my eyes I see the spaghetti which we had just cooked, Vanda, Luciana, Franco and I, at the sorting-camp when we suddenly heard the news that we would leave for here the following day; and we were eating it (it was so good, yellow, filling), and we stopped, fools, stupid as we were – if we had only known! And if it happened again ... Absurd. If there is one thing sure in this world it is certainly this: that it will not happen to us a second time.

Fischer, the newest arrival, pulls out of his pocket a bundle, tied together with the painstaking exactitude of the Hungarians, and inside there is a half-ration of bread: half the bread of this morning. It is notorious that only the High Numbers keep their bread in their pockets; none of us old ones are able to preserve our bread for an hour. Various theories circulate to justify this incapacity of ours: bread eaten a little at a time is not wholly assimilated; the nervous tension needed to preserve the bread without touching it when one is hungry is in the highest degree harmful and debilitating; bread which is turning stale soon loses its alimentary value, so that the sooner it is eaten, the more nutritious it is; Alberto says that hunger and bread in one's pocket are terms of opposite sign which automatically cancel each other out and cannot exist in the same individual; and the majority affirm justly that, in the end, one's stomach is the securest safe against thefts and extortions. '*Moi, on m'a jamais volé mon pain!*' David snarls, hitting his concave stomach: but he is unable to take his eyes off Fischer who chews slowly and methodically, 'lucky' enough to still have half a ration at ten in the morning: '*Sacré veinard, va!*'

But it is not only because of the sun that today is a happy day: at midday a surprise awaits us. Besides the normal morning ration, we discover in the hut a wonderful pot of over eleven gallons, one of those from the factory kitchen, almost full. Templer looks at us, triumphant; this 'organization' is his work.

Templer is the official organizer of the Kommando: he has an astonishing nose for the soup of civilians, like bees for flowers. Our Kapo, who is not a bad Kapo, leaves him a free hand, and with reason: Templer slinks off, following imperceptible tracks like a bloodhound, and returns with the priceless news that the Methanol Polish workers, one mile from here, have abandoned ten gallons of soup that tasted rancid, or that a wagonload of turnips is to be found unguarded on the siding next to the factory kitchen.

Today there are ninety pints and we are fifteen, Kapo and *Vorarbeiter* included. This means six pints each: we will have two at midday as well as the normal ration, and will come back to the hut in turns for the other four during the afternoon, besides being granted an extra five minutes' suspension of work to fill ourselves up.

What more could one want? Even our work seems light, with the prospect of four hot, dense pints waiting for us in the hut. The Kapo comes to us periodically and calls: '*Wer hat noch zu fressen?*' He does not say it from derision or to sneer, but because this way of eating on our feet, furiously, burning our mouths and throats, without time to breathe, really is *'fressen'*, the way of eating of animals, and certainly not *'essen'*, the human way of eating, seated in front of a table, religiously. *'Fressen'* is exactly the word, and is used currently among us.

Meister Nogalla watches and closes an eye at our absences from work. Meister Nogalla also has a hungry look about him, and if it was not for the social conventions, perhaps he would not despise a couple of pints of our warm broth.

Templer's turn comes. By plebiscitary consensus, he has been allowed ten pints, taken from the bottom of the pot. For Templer is not only a good organizer, but an exceptional soup-eater, and is uniquely able to empty his bowels at his own desire and in anticipation of a large meal, which contributes to his amazing gastric capacity.

Of this gift of his, he is justly proud, and everybody, even Meister Nogalla, knows about it. Accompanied by the gratitude of all, Templer the benefactor enters the latrine for a few moments and comes out beaming and ready, and amidst the general benevolence prepares to enjoy the fruits of his work:

'Nu, Templer, hast du Platz genug für die Suppe gemacht?'

At sunset, the siren of the *Feierabend* sounds, the end of work; and as we are all satiated, at least for a few hours, no quarrels arise, we feel good, the Kapo feels no urge to hit us, and we are able to think of our mothers and wives, which usually does not happen. For a few hours we can be unhappy in the manner of free men.

8

This Side of Good and Evil

We had an incorrigible tendency to see a symbol and a sign in every event. For seventy days we had been waiting for the *Wäschetauschen*, the ceremony of the change of underclothes, and a rumour circulated persistently that the change of washing had not taken place because, as the front had moved forward, the Germans were unable to gather together new transport at Auschwitz, and 'therefore' the liberation was near. And equally, the opposite interpretation circulated: that the delay in the change was a sure sign of an approaching integral liquidation of the camp. Instead the change took place, and as usual, the directors of the Lager took every care to make it occur unexpectedly and at the same time in all the huts.

It has to be realized that cloth is lacking in the Lager and is precious; and that our only way of acquiring a rag to blow our noses, or a pad for our shoes, is precisely that of cutting off the tail of a shirt at the time of the exchange. If the shirt has long sleeves, one cuts the sleeves; if not, one has to make do with a square from the bottom, or by unstitching one of the many patches. But in all cases a certain time is needed to get hold of needle and thread and to carry out the operation with some skill, so as not to leave the damage too obvious at the time of handing it in. The dirty, tattered washing is passed on, thrown together, to the tailor's workshop in the camp, where it is summarily pieced up, sent to the steam disinfection (not washed!) and is then re-distributed; hence the need to make the exchanges as unexpected as possible, so as to save the soiled washing from the above mutilations.

But, as always happens, it was not possible to prevent a cunning glance piercing through the canvas of the cart which was leaving after the disinfection, so that within a few minutes the camp knew of the imminence of a *Wäschetauschen*, and in addition, that this time there were new shirts from a convoy of Hungarians which had arrived three days ago.

The news had immediate repercussions. All who illegally possessed second shirts, stolen or organized, or even honestly bought with bread as a protection against the cold or to invest capital in a moment of prosperity, immediately rushed to the Exchange Market, hoping to arrive in time to barter their reserve shirts for food products before the flood of new shirts, or the certainty of their arrival, irreparably devalued the price of the article.

The Market is always very active. Although every exchange (in fact, every form of possession) is explicitly forbidden, and although frequent swoops of Kapos or *Blockältester* sent merchants, customers and the curious periodically flying, nevertheless, the north-east corner of the Lager (significantly the corner furthest from the SS huts) is permanently occupied by a tumultuous throng, in the open during the summer, in a washroom during the winter, as soon as the squads return from work.

Here scores of prisoners driven desperate by hunger prowl around, with lips half-open and eyes gleaming, lured by a deceptive instinct to where the merchandise shown makes the gnawing of their stomachs more acute and their salvation more assiduous. In the best cases they possess a miserable half-ration of bread which, with painful effort, they have saved since the morning, in the senseless hope of a chance to make an advantageous bargain with some ingenuous person, unaware of the prices of the moment. Some of these, with savage patience, acquire with their half-ration two pints of soup which, once in their possession, they subject to a methodical examination with a view to extracting the few pieces of potato lying at the bottom; this done, they exchange it for bread, and the bread for another two pints to denaturalize, and so on until their nerves are exhausted, or until some victim, catching them in the act, inflicts on them a severe lesson, exposing them to public derision. Of the same kind are those who come to the market to sell their only shirt; they well know what will happen on the next occasion that the Kapo finds out that they are bare underneath their jackets. The Kapo will ask them what they have done with their shirt; it is a purely rhetorical question, a formality useful only to begin the game. They will reply that their shirt was stolen in the washroom; this reply is equally customary, and is not expected to be believed; in fact, even the stones of the Lager know that ninety-nine times out of a hundred whoever has no shirt has sold it because of hunger, and that in any case one is responsible for one's shirt because it belongs to the Lager. Then the Kapo will beat them, they will be issued another shirt, and sooner or later they will begin again.

The professional merchants stand in the market, each one in his normal corner; first among them come the Greeks, as immobile and silent as sphinxes, squatting on the ground behind their bowls of thick soup, the fruits of their labour, of their cooperation and of their national solidarity. The Greeks have been reduced to very few by now, but they have made a contribution of the first importance to the physiognomy of the camp and to the international slang in circulation. Everyone knows that '*caravana*' is the bowl, and that '*la comedera es buena*' means that the soup is good; the word that expresses the generic idea of

theft is 'klepsiklepsi', of obvious Greek origin. These few survivors from the Jewish colony of Salonica, with their two
languages, Spanish and Greek, and their numerous activities, are
the repositories of a concrete, mundane, conscious wisdom, in
which the traditions of all the Mediterranean civilizations blend
together. That this wisdom was transformed in the camp into
the systematic and scientific practice of theft and seizure of positions and the monopoly of the bargaining Market, should not
let one forget that their aversion to gratuitous brutality, their
amazing consciousness of the survival of at least a potential
human dignity, made of the Greeks the most coherent national
nucleus in Lager, and in this respect, the most civilized.

At the Market you can find specialists in kitchen thefts, their
jackets swollen with strange bulges. While there is a virtually
stable price for soup (half a ration of bread for two pints), the
quotations for turnips, carrots, potatoes are extremely variable
and depend greatly, among other factors, on the diligence and
the corruptibility of the guards at the stores.

Mahorca is sold. Mahorca is a third-rate tobacco, crude and
wooden, which is officially on sale at the canteen in one and a
half ounce packets, in exchange for the prize-coupons that the
Buna ought to distribute to the best workers. Such a distribution
occurs irregularly, with great parsimony and open injustice, so
that the greatest number of the coupons end up, either legitimately or through abuse of authority, in the hands of the Kapos
and of the Prominents; nevertheless the prize-coupons still
circulate on the market in the form of money, and their value
changes in strict obedience to the laws of classical economics.

There have been periods in which the prize-coupon was
worth one ration of bread, then one and a quarter, even one
and a third; one day it was quoted at one and a half rations,
but then the supply of Mahorca to the canteen failed, so that,
lacking a coverage, the money collapsed at once to a quarter

of a ration. Another boom period occurred for a singular reason: the arrival of a fresh contingent of robust Polish girls in place of the old inmates of the Frauenblock. In fact, as the prize-coupon is valid for entry to the Frauenblock (for the criminals and the politicals; not for the Jews, who on the other hand, do not feel affected by this restriction), those interested actively and rapidly cornered the market: hence the revaluation, which, in any case, did not last long.

Among the ordinary Häftlinge there are not many who search for Mahorca to smoke it personally; for the most part it leaves the camp and ends in the hands of the civilian workers of Buna. The traffic is an instance of a kind of '*kombinacja*' frequently practised: the Häftling, somehow saving a ration of bread, invests it in Mahorca; he cautiously gets in touch with a civilian addict who acquires the Mahorca, paying in cash with a portion of bread greater than that initially invested. The Häftling eats the surplus, and puts back on the market the remaining ration. Speculations of this kind establish a tie between the internal economy of the Lager and the economic life of the outside world: the accidental failure of the distribution of tobacco among the civilian population of Cracow, overcoming the barrier of barbed wire which segregates us from human society, had an immediate repercussion in camp, provoking a notable rise in the quotation of Mahorca, and consequently of the prize-coupon.

The process outlined above is no more than the most simple of examples: another more complex one is the following. The Häftling acquires in exchange for Mahorca or bread, or even obtains as a gift from a civilian, some abominable, ragged, dirty shred of a shirt, which must however have three holes suitable to fit more or less over the head and arms. So long as it only carries signs of wear, and not of artificially created mutilations, such an object, at the time of the *Wäschetauschen*, is valid as a shirt and carries the right of an exchange; at the most, the person who presents it will receive an adequate measure of blows for having taken so little care of camp clothing.

Consequently, within the Lager, there is no great difference in value between a shirt worthy of the name and a tattered thing full of patches; the Häftling described above will have no difficulty in finding a comrade in possession of a shirt of commercial value who is unable to capitalize on it as he is not in touch with civilian workers, either because of his place of work, or through difficulties of language or intrinsic incapacity. This latter will be satisfied with a modest amount of bread for the exchange, and in fact the next *Wäschetauschen* will to a certain extent re-establish equilibrium, distributing good and bad washing in a perfectly casual manner. But the first Häftling will be able to smuggle the good shirt into Buna and sell it to the original civilian (or to any other) for four, six, even ten rations of bread. This high margin of profit is correlative to the gravity of the risk of leaving camp wearing more than one shirt or re-entering with none.

There are many variations on this theme. There are some who do not hesitate to have the gold fillings of their teeth extracted to sell them in Buna for bread or tobacco. But the most common of cases is that such traffic takes place through an intermediary. A 'high number', that is, a new arrival, only recently but sufficiently besotted by hunger and by the extreme tension of life in the camp, is noticed by a 'low number' for the number of his gold teeth; the 'low' offers the 'high' three or four rations of bread to be paid in return for extraction. If the high number accepts, the low one pays, carries the gold to Buna, and if in contact with a civilian of trust, from whom he fears neither denunciation nor fraudulent dealing, he can make a gain of ten or even as much as twenty or more rations, which are paid to him gradually, one or two a day. It is worth noting in this respect that contrary to what takes place in the Buna, the maximum total of any transaction negotiated *within* the camp is four rations of bread, because it would be practically impossible either to make contracts on credit, or to preserve a larger quantity of bread from the greed of others or one's own hunger.

Traffic with civilians is a characteristic element of the *Arbeitslager*, and as we have seen, determines its economic life. On the other hand, it is a crime, explicitly foreseen by the camp regulations, and considered equivalent to 'political' crimes; so that it is punished with particular severity. The Häftling convicted of '*Handel mit Zivilisten*', unless he can rely on powerful influences, ends up at Gleiwitz III, at Janina or at Heidebreck in the coal-mines; which means death from exhaustion in the course of a few weeks. Moreover, his accomplice, the civilian worker, may also be denounced to the competent German authority and condemned to pass a period in *Vernichtungslager*, under the same conditions as us; a period varying, as far as I can see, from a fortnight to eight months. The workmen who experience this retaliation have their possessions taken away like us on their entry, but their personal effects are kept in a special store room. They are not tattooed and they keep their hair, which makes them easily recognizable, but for the whole duration of the punishment they are subjected to the same work and the same discipline as us – except, of course, the selections.

They work in separate Kommandos and they have no contact of any sort with the common Häftlinge. In fact, the Lager is for them a punishment, and if they do not die of exhaustion or illness they can expect to return among men; if they could communicate with us, it would create a breach in the wall which keeps us dead to the world, and a ray of light into the mystery which prevails among free men about our condition. For us, on the contrary, the Lager is not a punishment; for us, no end is foreseen and the Lager is nothing but a manner of living assigned to us, without limits of time, in the bosom of the Germanic social organism.

One section of the camp itself is in fact set aside for civilian workers of all nationalities who are compelled to stay there for a longer or shorter period in expiation of their illicit relations with Häftlinge. This section is separated from the rest of the camp by barbed wire, and is called E-Lager, and its guests E-Häftlinge. 'E' is the initial for '*Erziehung*' which means education.

All the bargaining-transactions outlined above are based on the smuggling of materials belonging to the Lager. This is why the SS are so eager to suppress them: the very gold of our teeth is their property, as sooner or later, torn from the mouths of the living or the dead, it ends up in their hands. So it is natural that they should take care that the gold does not leave the camp.

But against theft in itself, the direction of the camp has no prejudice. The attitude of open connivance by the SS as regards smuggling in the opposite direction shows this clearly.

Here things are generally more simple. It is a question of stealing or receiving any of the various tools, utensils, materials, products, etc. with which we come in daily contact in Buna in the course of our work, of introducing them into the camp in the evening, of finding a customer and of effecting the exchange for bread or soup. This traffic is intense: for certain articles, although they are necessary for the normal life of the Lager, this method of theft in Buna is the only and regular way of provisioning. Typical are the instances of brooms, paint, electric wire, grease for shoes. The traffic in this last item will serve as an example.

As we have stated elsewhere, the camp regulations prescribe the greasing and polishing of shoes every morning, and every *Blockältester* is responsible to the SS for obedience to this order by all the men in his hut. One would think that each hut would enjoy a periodic assignment of grease for shoes, but this is not so; the mechanism is completely different. It needs to be stated first that each hut receives an assignment of soup somewhat higher than that prescribed for regulation rations; the extra is divided according to the discretion of the *Blockältester*, who first of all distributes the gifts to his friends and protégés, then the recompense to the hut-sweepers, to the night-guards, to the lice-controllers and to all other Prominents and functionaries in the hut. What is still left over (and every smart *Blockältester* makes sure that there is always some over) is used precisely for these acquisitions.

The rest is obvious. Those Häftlinge at Buna who have the chance to fill their bowl with grease or machine-oil (or anything else: any blackish and greasy substance is considered suitable for the purpose), on their return to the camp in the evening, make a systematic tour of the huts until they find a *Blockältester* who has run out of the article and wants a fresh supply. In addition, every hut usually has its habitual supplier, who has been allotted a fixed daily recompense on condition that he provides the grease every time that the reserve is about to run out.

Every evening, beside the doors of the *Tagesräume*, the groups of suppliers stand patiently around; on their feet for hours and hours in the rain or snow, they discuss excitedly matters relating to the fluctuation of prices and value of the prize-coupon. Every now and again one of them leaves the group, makes a quick visit to the Market and returns with the latest news.

Besides the articles already described, there are innumerable others to be found in Buna which might be useful to the Block or welcomed by the *Blockältester*, or might excite the interest or curiosity of the prominents: light-bulbs, ordinary or shaving-soap, files, pliers, sacks, nails; methylic alcohol is sold to make drinks; while petrol is useful for the rudimentary lighters, prodigies of the secret industry of the Lager craftsmen.

In this complex network of thefts and counter-thefts, nourished by the silent hostility between the SS command and the civilian authorities of Buna, Ka-Be plays a part of prime importance. Ka-Be is the place of least resistance, where the regulations can most easily be avoided and the surveillance of the Kapos eluded. Everyone knows that it is the nurses themselves who send back on the market, at low prices, the clothes and shoes of the dead and of the selected who leave naked for Birkenau; it is the nurses and doctors who export the restricted sulphonamides to Buna, selling them to civilians for articles of food.

The nurses also make huge profits from the trade in spoons. The Lager does not provide the new arrivals with spoons, although the semi-liquid soup cannot be consumed without them. The spoons are manufactured in Buna, secretly and in their spare moments, by Häftlinge who work as specialists in the iron- and tin-smith Kommandos: they are rough and clumsy tools, shaped from iron-plate worked by hammer, often with a sharp handle-edge to serve at the same time as a knife to cut the bread. The manufacturers themselves sell them directly to the new arrivals: an ordinary spoon is worth half a ration, a knife-spoon three quarters of a ration of bread. Now it is a law that although one can enter Ka-Be with one's spoon, one cannot leave with it. At the moment of release, before the clothes are given, the healthy patient's spoon is confiscated by the nurses and placed on sale in the Market. Adding the spoons of the patients about to leave to those of the dead and selected, the nurses receive the gains of the sale of about fifty spoons every day. On the other hand, the dismissed patients are forced to begin work again with the initial disadvantage of half a ration of bread, set aside to acquire a new spoon.

Finally, Ka-Be is the main customer and receiver of thefts occurring in Buna: of the soup assigned to Ka-Be, a good forty pints are set aside every day as the theft-fund to acquire the most varied of goods from the specialists. There are those who steal thin rubber tubing which is used in Ka-Be for enemas and for stomach-tubes; others offer coloured pencils and inks, necessary for Ka-Be's complicated book-keeping system; and thermometers and glass instruments and chemicals, which come from the Buna stores in the Häftlinge's pockets and are used in the infirmary as sanitary equipment

And I would not like to be accused of immodesty if I add that it was our idea, mine and Alberto's, to steal the rolls of graph-paper from the thermographs of the Desiccation Department, and offer them to the Medical Chief of Ka-Be with the suggestion that they be used as paper for pulse-temperature charts.

In conclusion: theft in Buna, punished by the civil direction, is authorized and encouraged by the SS; theft in camp, severely repressed by the SS, is considered by the civilians as a normal exchange operation; theft among Häftlinge is generally punished, but the punishment strikes the thief and the victim with equal gravity. We now invite the reader to contemplate the possible meaning in the Lager of the words 'good' and 'evil', 'just' and 'unjust'; let everybody judge, on the basis of the picture we have outlined and of the examples given above, how much of our ordinary moral world could survive on this side of the barbed wire.

9

The Drowned and the Saved

What we have so far said and will say concerns the ambiguous life of the Lager. In our days many men have lived in this cruel manner, crushed against the bottom, but each for a relatively short period; so that we can perhaps ask ourselves if it is necessary or good to retain any memory of this exceptional human state.

To this question we feel that we have to reply in the affirmative. We are in fact convinced that no human experience is without meaning or unworthy of analysis, and that fundamental values, even if they are not positive, can be deduced from this particular world which we are describing. We would also like to consider that the Lager was pre-eminently a gigantic biological and social experiment.

Thousands of individuals, differing in age, condition, origin, language, culture and customs, are enclosed within barbed wire: there they live a regular, controlled life which is identical for all and inadequate to all needs, and which is more rigorous than any experimenter could have set up to establish what is essential and what adventitious to the conduct of the human animal in the struggle for life.

We do not believe in the most obvious and facile deduction: that man is fundamentally brutal, egoistic and stupid in his conduct once every civilized institution is taken away, and that the Häftling is consequently nothing but a man without inhibitions.

We believe, rather, that the only conclusion to be drawn is that in the face of driving necessity and physical disabilities many social habits and instincts are reduced to silence.

But another fact seems to us worthy of attention: there comes to light the existence of two particularly well differentiated categories among men – the saved and the drowned. Other pairs of opposites (the good and the bad, the wise and the foolish, the cowards and the courageous, the unlucky and the fortunate) are considerably less distinct, they seem less essential, and above all they allow for more numerous and complex intermediary gradations.

This division is much less evident in ordinary life; for there it rarely happens that a man loses himself. A man is normally not alone, and in his rise or fall is tied to the destinies of his neighbours; so that it is exceptional for anyone to acquire unlimited power, or to fall by a succession of defeats into utter ruin. Moreover, everyone is normally in possession of such spiritual, physical and even financial resources that the probabilities of a shipwreck, of total inadequacy in the face of life, are relatively small. And one must take into account a definite cushioning effect exercised both by the law, and by the moral sense which constitutes a self-imposed law; for a country is considered the more civilized the more the wisdom and efficiency of its laws hinder a weak man from becoming too weak or a powerful one too powerful.

But in the Lager things are different: here the struggle to survive is without respite, because everyone is desperately and ferociously alone. If some Null Achtzehn vacillates, he will find no one to extend a helping hand; on the contrary, someone will knock him aside, because it is in no one's interest that there will be one more 'musselman'* dragging himself to work every

---

* This word '*Muselmann*', I do not know why, was used by the old ones of the camp to describe the weak, the inept, those doomed to selection.

day; and if someone, by a miracle of savage patience and cunning, finds a new method of avoiding the hardest work, a new art which yields him an ounce of bread, he will try to keep his method secret, and he will be esteemed and respected for this, and will derive from it an exclusive, personal benefit; he will become stronger and so will be feared, and who is feared is, ipso facto, a candidate for survival.

In history and in life one sometimes seems to glimpse a ferocious law which states: 'to he that has, will be given; from he that has not, will be taken away'. In the Lager, where man is alone and where the struggle for life is reduced to its primordial mechanism, this unjust law is openly in force, is recognized by all. With the adaptable, the strong and astute individuals, even the leaders willingly keep contact, sometimes even friendly contact, because they hope later to perhaps derive some benefit. But with the musselmans, the men in decay, it is not even worth speaking, because one knows already that they will complain and will speak about what they used to eat at home. Even less worthwhile is it to make friends with them, because they have no distinguished acquaintances in camp, they do not gain any extra rations, they do not work in profitable Kommandos and they know no secret method of organizing. And in any case, one knows that they are only here on a visit, that in a few weeks nothing will remain of them but a handful of ashes in some near-by field and a crossed-out number on a register. Although engulfed and swept along without rest by the innumerable crowd of those similar to them, they suffer and drag themselves along in an opaque intimate solitude, and in solitude they die or disappear, without leaving a trace in anyone's memory.

The result of this pitiless process of natural selection could be read in the statistics of Lager population movements. At Auschwitz, in 1944, of the old Jewish prisoners (we will not speak of the others here, as their condition was different), '*kleine Nummer*', low numbers less than 150,000, only a few hundred had survived; not one was an ordinary Häftling, vegetating in the ordinary Kommandos, and subsisting on the normal ration. There remained only the doctors, tailors, shoemakers, musicians, cooks, young attractive homosexuals, friends or compatriots of some authority in the camp; or they were particularly pitiless, vigorous and inhuman individuals, installed (following an investiture by the SS command, which showed itself in such choices to possess satanic knowledge of human beings) in the posts of Kapos, *Blockältester*, etc.; or finally, those who, without fulfilling particular functions, had always succeeded through their astuteness and energy in successfully organizing, gaining in this way, besides material advantages and reputation, the indulgence and esteem of the powerful people in the camp. Whosoever does not know how to become an 'Organisator', 'Kombinator', 'Prominent' (the savage eloquence of these words!) soon becomes a 'musselman'. In life, a third way exists, and is in fact the rule; it does not exist in the concentration camp.

To sink is the easiest of matters; it is enough to carry out all the orders one receives, to eat only the ration, to observe the discipline of the work and the camp. Experience showed that only exceptionally could one survive more than three months in this way. All the musselmans who finished in the gas chambers have the same story, or more exactly, have no story; they followed the slope down to the bottom, like streams that run down to the sea. On their entry into the camp, through basic incapacity, or by misfortune, or through some banal incident, they are overcome before they can adapt themselves; they are beaten by time, they do not begin to learn German, to disentangle the infernal knot of laws and prohibitions until their body is already in decay, and nothing can save them from selections or from death by exhaustion. Their life is short, but their number is endless; they, the *Muselmänner,* the drowned, form the backbone of the camp, an anonymous mass, continually renewed and always identical, of non-men who march and labour in silence, the divine spark dead within them, already too empty to really suffer. One hesitates to call them living: one hesitates to call their death death, in the face of which they have no fear, as they are too tired to understand.

They crowd my memory with their faceless presences, and if I could enclose all the evil of our time in one image, I would choose this image which is familiar to me: an emaciated man, with head dropped and shoulders curved, on whose face and in whose eyes not a trace of a thought is to be seen.

If the drowned have no story, and single and broad is the path to perdition, the paths to salvation are many, difficult and improbable.

The most travelled road, as we have stated, is the '*Prominenz*'. '*Prominenten*' is the name for the camp officials, from the Häftling-director (*Lagerältester*) to the Kapos, the cooks, the nurses, the night-guards, even to the hut-sweepers and to the *Scheissminister* and *Bademeister* (superintendents of the latrines and showers). We are more particularly interested in the Jewish Prominents, because while the others are automatically invested with offices as they enter the camp in virtue of their natural supremacy, the Jews have to plot and struggle hard to gain them.

The Jewish Prominents form a sad and notable human phenomenon. In them converge present, past and atavistic sufferings, and the tradition of hostility towards the stranger makes of them monsters of asociality and insensitivity.

They are the typical product of the structure of the German Lager: if one offers a position of privilege to a few individuals in a state of slavery, exacting in exchange the betrayal of a natural solidarity with their comrades, there will certainly be someone who will accept. He will be withdrawn from the common law and will become untouchable; the more power that he is given, the more he will be consequently hateful and hated. When he is given the command of a group of unfortunates, with the right of life or death over them, he will be cruel and tyrannical, because he will understand that if he is not sufficiently so, someone else, judged more suitable, will take over his post. Moreover, his capacity for hatred, unfulfilled in the direction of the oppressors, will double back, beyond all reason, on the oppressed; and he will only be satisfied when he has unloaded on to his underlings the injury received from above.

We are aware that this is very distant from the picture that is usually given of the oppressed who unite, if not in resistance, at least in suffering. We do not deny that this may be possible when oppression does not pass a certain limit, or perhaps when the oppressor, through inexperience or magnanimity, tolerates or favours it. But we state that in our days, in all countries in which a foreign people have set foot as invaders, an analogous position of rivalry and hatred among the subjected has been brought about; and this, like many other human characteristics, could be experienced in the Lager in the light of particularly cruel evidence.

About the non-Jewish Prominents there is less to say, although they were far and away the most numerous (no 'Aryan' Häftling was without a post, however modest). That they were stolid and bestial is natural when one thinks that the majority were ordinary criminals, chosen from the German prisons for the very purpose of their employment as superintendents of the camps for Jews; and we maintain that it was a very apt choice, because we refuse to believe that the squalid human specimens whom we saw at work were an average example, not of Germans in general, but even of German prisoners in particular. It is difficult to explain how in Auschwitz the political

German, Polish and Russian Prominents rivalled the ordinary convicts in brutality. But it is known that in Germany the qualification of political crime also applied to such acts as clandestine trade, illicit relations with Jewish women, theft from Party officials. The 'real' politicals lived and died in other camps, with names now sadly famous, in notoriously hard conditions, which, however, in many aspects differed from those described here.

But besides the officials in the strict sense of the word, there is a vast category of prisoners, not initially favoured by fate, who fight merely with their own strength to survive. One has to fight against the current; to battle every day and every hour against exhaustion, hunger, cold and the resulting inertia; to resist enemies and have no pity for rivals; to sharpen one's wits, build up one's patience, strengthen one's willpower. Or else, to throttle all dignity and kill all conscience, to climb down into the arena as a beast against other beasts, to let oneself be guided by those unsuspected subterranean forces which sustain families and individuals in cruel times. Many were the ways devised and put into effect by us in order not to die: as many as there are different human characters. All implied a weakening struggle of one against all, and a by no means small sum of aberrations and compromises. Survival without renunciation of any part of one's own moral world – apart from powerful and direct interventions by fortune – was conceded only to very few superior individuals, made of the stuff of martyrs and saints.

We will try to show in how many ways it was possible to reach salvation with the stories of Schepschel, Alfred L., Elias and Henri.

Schepschel has been living in the Lager for four years. He has seen the death of tens of thousands of those like him, beginning with the pogrom which had driven him from his village in

Galicia. He had a wife and five children and a prosperous business as a saddler, but for a long time now he has grown accustomed to thinking of himself only as a sack which needs periodic refilling. Schepschel is not very robust, nor very courageous, nor very wicked; he is not even particularly astute, nor has he ever found a method which allows him a little respite, but he is reduced to small and occasional expedients, '*kombinacje*' as they are called here.

Every now and again he steals a broom in the Buna and sells it to the *Blockältester*; when he manages to set aside a little bread-capital, he hires the tools of the cobbler in the Block, his compatriot, and works on his own account for a few hours; he knows how to make braces with interlaced electric wires. Sigi told me that he has seen him during the midday interval singing and dancing in front of the hut of the Slovak workers, who sometimes reward him with the remainders of their soup.

This said, one would be inclined to think of Schepschel with indulgent sympathy, as of a poor wretch who retains only a humble and elementary desire to live, and who bravely carries on his small struggle not to give way. But Schepschel was no exception, and when the opportunity showed itself, he did not hesitate to have Moischl, his accomplice in a theft from the kitchen, condemned to a flogging, in the mistaken hope of gaining favour in the eyes of the *Blockältester* and furthering his candidature for the position of *Kesselwäscher*, 'vat-washer'.

The story of engineer Alfred L. shows among other things how vain is the myth of original equality among men.

In his own country L. was the director of an extremely important factory of chemical products, and his name was (and is) well known in industrial circles throughout Europe. He was a robust man of about fifty; I do not know how he had been arrested, but he entered the camp like all others: naked, alone and unknown. When I knew him he was very wasted away, but still showed on his face the signs of a disciplined and methodical energy; at that time, his privileges were limited to the daily cleaning of the Polish workers' pots; this work, which he had gained in some manner as his exclusive monopoly, yielded him half a ladleful of soup per day. Certainly it was not enough to satisfy his hunger; nevertheless, no one had ever heard him complain. In fact, the few words that he let slip implied imposing secret resources, a solid and fruitful 'organization'.

This was confirmed by his appearance. L. had a 'line': with his hands and face always perfectly clean, he had the rare self-denial to wash his shirt every fortnight, without waiting for the bi-monthly change (we would like to point out here that to wash a shirt meant finding soap, time and space in the over-crowded washroom; adapting oneself to carefully keep watch on the wet shirt without losing attention for a moment, and to put it on, naturally still wet, in the silence-hour when the lights are turned out); he owned a pair of wooden shoes to go to the shower, and even his striped suit was singularly adapted to his appearance, clean and new. L. had acquired in practice the whole appearance of a Prominent considerably before becoming one; only a long time after did I find out that L. was able to earn all this show of prosperity with incredible tenacity, paying for his individual acquisitions and services with bread from his own ration, so imposing upon himself a regime of supplementary privations.

His plan was a long-term one, which is all the more notable as conceived in an environment dominated by a mentality of the provisional; and L. carried it out with rigid inner discipline, without pity for himself or – with greater reason – for comrades who crossed his path. L. knew that the step was short from being judged powerful to effectively becoming so, and that everywhere, and especially in the midst of the general levelling of the Lager, a respectable appearance is the best guarantee of being respected. He took every care not to be confused with the mass; he worked with stubborn duty, even occasionally admonishing his lazy comrades in a persuasive and deprecatory tone of voice; he avoided the daily struggle for the best place in the queue for the ration, and prepared to take the first ration, notoriously the most liquid, every day, so as to be noticed by his *Blockältester* for his discipline. To complete the separation, he always behaved in his relations with his comrades with the maximum courtesy compatible with his egotism, which was absolute.

When the Chemical Kommando was formed, as will be described, L. knew that his hour had struck: he needed no more than his spruce suit and his emaciated and shaved face in the midst of the flock of his sordid and slovenly colleagues to at once convince both Kapo and *Arbeitsdienst* that he was one of the genuinely saved, a potential Prominent; so that (to he who has, shall be given) he was without hesitation appointed 'specialist', nominated technical head of the Kommando, and taken on by the Direction of Buna as analyst in the laboratory of the styrene department. He was subsequently appointed to examine all the new intake to the Chemical Kommando, to judge their professional ability; which he always did with extreme severity, especially when faced with those in whom he smelled possible future rivals.

I do not know how his story continued; but I feel it is quite probable that he managed to escape death, and today is still living his cold life of the determined and joyless dominator.

Elias Lindzin, 141565, one day rained into the Chemical Kommando. He was a dwarf, not more than five feet high, but I have never seen muscles like his. When he is naked you can see every muscle taut under his skin, like a poised animal; his body, enlarged without alteration of proportions, would serve as a good model for a Hercules: but you must not look at his head.

Under his scalp, the skull sutures stand out immoderately. The cranium is massive and gives the impression of being made of metal or stone; the limit of his shaven hair shows up barely a finger's width above his eyebrows. The nose, the chin, the forehead, the cheekbones are hard and compact, the whole face looks like a battering ram, an instrument made for butting. A sense of bestial vigour emanates from his body.

To see Elias work is a disconcerting spectacle; the Polish *Meister*, even the Germans sometimes stop to admire Elias at work. Nothing seems impossible to him. While we barely carry one sack of cement, Elias carries two, then three, then four, keeping them balanced no one knows how, and while he hurries along on his short, squat legs, he makes faces under the load, he laughs, curses, shouts and sings without pause, as if he had lungs made of bronze. Despite his wooden shoes Elias climbs like a monkey on to the scaffolding and runs safely on crossbeams poised over nothing; he carries six bricks at a time balanced on his head; he knows how to make a spoon from a piece of tin, and a knife from a scrap of steel; he finds dry paper, wood and coal everywhere and knows how to start a fire in a few moments even in the rain. He is a tailor, a carpenter, a cobbler, a barber; he can spit incredible distances; he sings, in a not unpleasant bass voice, Polish and Yiddish songs never heard before; he can ingest ten, fifteen, twenty pints of soup without vomiting and without having diarrhoea, and begin work again immediately after. He knows how to make a big hump come out between his shoulders, and goes around the hut, bow-legged and mimicking, shouting and declaiming incomprehensibly, to the joy of the Prominents of the camp. I saw him fight a Pole a whole head taller than him and knock him down with a blow of his cranium into the stomach, as powerful and accurate as a catapult. I never saw him rest, I never saw him quiet or still, I never saw him injured or ill.

Of his life as a free man, no one knows anything; and in any case, to imagine Elias as a free man requires a great effort of fantasy and induction; he only speaks Polish, and the surly and deformed Yiddish of Warsaw; besides it is impossible to keep him to a coherent conversation. He might be twenty or forty years old; he usually says that he is thirty-three, and that he has begot seventeen children – which is not unlikely. He talks continuously on the most varied of subjects; always in a resounding voice, in an oratorical manner, with the violent mimicry of the deranged; as if he was always talking to a dense crowd – and as is natural, he never lacks a public. Those who understand his language drink up his declamations, shaking with laughter; they pat him enthusiastically on the back – a back as hard as iron – inciting him to continue; while he, fierce and frowning, whirls around like a wild animal in the circle of his audience, apostrophizing now one, now another of them; he suddenly grabs hold of one by the chest with his small hooked paw, irresistibly drags him to himself, vomits into his face an incomprehensible invective, then throws him back like a piece of wood, and amidst the applause and laughter, with his arms reaching up to the heavens like some little prophetic monster, continues his raging and crazy speech.

His fame as an exceptional worker spread quite soon, and by the absurd law of the Lager, from then on he practically ceased to work. His help was requested directly by the *Meister* only for such work as required skill and special vigour. Apart from these services he insolently and violently supervised our daily, flat exhaustion, frequently disappearing on mysterious visits and adventures in who knows what recesses of the yard, from which he returned with large bulges in his pockets and often with his stomach visibly full.

Elias is naturally and innocently a thief: in this he shows the instinctive astuteness of wild animals. He is never caught in the act because he only steals when there is a good chance; but when this chance comes Elias steals as fatally and foreseeably as a stone drops. Apart from the fact that it is difficult to surprise him, it is obvious that it would be of no use punishing him for his thefts: to him they imply a vital act like breathing or sleeping.

We can now ask who is this man Elias. If he is a madman, incomprehensible and para-human, who ended in the Lager by chance. If he is an atavism, different from our modern world, and better adapted to the primordial conditions of camp life. Or if he is perhaps a product of the camp itself, what we will all become if we do not die in the camp, and if the camp itself does not end first

There is some truth in all three suppositions. Elias has survived the destruction from outside, because he is physically indestructible; he has resisted the annihilation from within because he is insane. So, in the first place, he is a survivor: he is the most adaptable, the human type most suited to this way of living.

If Elias regains his liberty he will be confined to the fringes of human society, in a prison or a lunatic asylum. But here in the Lager there are no criminals nor madmen; no criminals because there is no moral law to contravene, no madmen because we are wholly devoid of free will, as our every action is, in time and place, the only conceivable one.

In the Lager Elias prospers and is triumphant. He is a good worker and a good organizer, and for this double reason, he is safe from selections and respected by both leaders and comrades. For those who have no sound inner resources, for those who do not know how to draw from their own consciences sufficient force to cling to life, the only road to salvation leads to

Elias: to insanity and to deceitful bestiality. All the other roads are dead-ends.

This said, one might perhaps be tempted to draw conclusions, and perhaps even rules for our daily life. Are there not all around us some Eliases, more or less in embryo? Do we not see individuals living without purpose, lacking all forms of self-control and conscience, who live not *in spite of* these defects, but like Elias precisely because of them?

The question is serious, but will not be further discussed as we want these to be stories of the Lager, while much has already been written on man outside the Lager. But one thing we would like to add: Elias, as far as we could judge from outside, and as far as the phrase can have meaning, was probably a happy person.

Henri, on the other hand, is eminently civilized and sane, and possesses a complete and organic theory on the ways to survive in Lager. He is only twenty-two, he is extremely intelligent, speaks French, German, English and Russian, has an excellent scientific and classical culture.

His brother died in Buna last winter, and since then Henri has cut off every tie of affection; he has closed himself up, as if in armour, and fights to live without distraction with all the resources that he can derive from his quick intellect and his refined education. According to Henri's theory, there are three methods open to man to escape extermination which still allow him to retain the name of man: organization, pity and theft.

He himself practises all three. There is no better strategist than Henri in seducing ('cultivating' he says) the English POWs. In his hands they become real geese with golden eggs – if you remember that in exchange for a single English cigarette you can make enough in the Lager not to starve for a day. Henri was once seen in the act of eating a real hard-boiled egg.

The traffic in products of English origin is Henri's monopoly, and this is all a matter of organization; but his instrument of penetration, with the English and with others, is pity. Henri has the delicate and subtly perverse body and face of Sodoma's San Sebastian: his eyes are deep and profound, he has no beard yet, he moves with a natural languid elegance (although when necessary he knows how to run and jump like a cat, while the capacity of his stomach is little inferior to that of Elias). Henri is perfectly aware of his natural gifts and exploits them with the cold competence of a physicist using a scientific instrument: the results are surprising. Basically it is a question of a discovery: Henri has discovered that pity, being a primary and instinctive sentiment, grows quite well if ably cultivated, particularly in the primitive minds of the brutes who command us, those very brutes who have no scruples about beating us up without a reason, or treading our faces into the ground; nor has the great practical importance of the discovery escaped him, and upon it he has built up his personal trade.

As the ichneumon paralyses the great hairy caterpillar, wounding it in its only vulnerable ganglion, so Henri at a glance sizes up the subject, '*son type*'; he speaks to him briefly, to each with the appropriate language, and the '*type*' is conquered: he listens with increasing sympathy, he is moved by the fate of this unfortunate young man, and not much time is needed before he begins to yield returns.

There is no heart so hardened that Henri cannot breach it if he sets himself to it seriously. In the Lager, and in Buna as well, his protectors are very numerous: English soldiers, French, Ukrainian, Polish civilian workers: German 'politicals'; at least four *Blockältester*, a cook, even an SS man. But his favourite field is Ka-Be: Henri has free entry into Ka-Be; Doctor Citron and Doctor Weiss are more than his protectors, they are his friends and take him in whenever he wants and with the diagnosis he wants. This takes place especially immediately before selections, and in the periods of the most laborious work: 'hibernation', as he says.

Possessing such conspicuous friendships, it is natural that Henri is rarely reduced to the third method, theft; on the other hand, he naturally does not talk much about this subject.

It is very pleasant to talk to Henri in moments of rest. It is also useful: there is nothing in the camp that he does not know and about which he has not reasoned in his close and coherent manner. Of his conquests, he speaks with educated modesty, as of prey of little worth, but he digresses willingly into an explanation of the calculation which led him to approach Hans asking him about his son at the front, and Otto instead showing him the scars on his shins.

To speak with Henri is useful and pleasant: one sometimes also feels him warm and near; communication, even affection seems possible. One seems to glimpse, behind his uncommon personality, a human soul, sorrowful and aware of itself. But the next moment his sad smile freezes into a cold grimace which seems studied at the mirror; Henri politely excuses himself ('... *j'ai quelque chose à faire*,' '... *j'ai quelqu'un à voir*') and here he is again, intent on his hunt and his struggle; hard and distant enclosed in armour, the enemy of all, inhumanly cunning and incomprehensible like the Serpent in Genesis.

From all my talks with Henri, even the most cordial, I have always left with a slight taste of defeat; of also having been, somehow inadvertently, not a man to him, but an instrument in his hands.

I know that Henri is living today. I would give much to know his life as a free man, but I do not want to see him again.

10

Chemical Examination

Kommando 98, called the Chemical Kommando, should have been a squad of skilled workers.

The day on which its formation was officially announced a meagre group of fifteen Häftlinge gathered in the grey of dawn around the new Kapo in the roll-call square.

This was the first disillusion: he was a 'green triangle', a professional delinquent; the *Arbeitsdienst* had not thought it necessary for the Kapo of the Chemical Kommando to be a chemist. It was pointless wasting one's breath asking him questions; he would not have replied, or else he would have replied with kicks and shouts. On the other hand, his not very robust appearance and his smaller than average stature were reassuring.

He made a short speech in the foul German of the barracks, and the disillusion was confirmed. So these were the chemists: well, he was Alex, and if they thought they were entering paradise, they were mistaken. In the first place, until the day production began, Kommando 98 would be no more than an ordinary transport-Kommando attached to the magnesium chloride warehouse. Secondly, if they imagined, being *Intelligenten*, intellectuals, that they could make a fool of him, Alex, a *Reichsdeutscher*, well, *Herrgottsacrament*, he would show them, he would ... (and with his fist clenched and index finger extended he cut across the air with the menacing gesture of the Germans);

and finally, they should not imagine that they would fool anyone, if they had applied for the position without any qualifications – an examination, yes, gentlemen, in the very near future; a chemistry examination, before the triumvirate of the Polymerization Department: Doktor Hagen, Doktor Probst and Doktor Ingenieur Pannwitz.

And with this, *meine Herren*, enough time had been lost, Kommandos 96 and 97 had already started, forward march, and to begin with, whosoever failed to walk in line and step would have to deal with him.

He was a Kapo like all the other Kapos.

Leaving the camp, in front of the musical band and the SS counting-post we march in rows of five, beret in hand, arms hanging down our sides and neck rigid; speaking is forbidden. Then we change to threes and it is possible to exchange a few words amidst the clatter of ten thousand pairs of wooden shoes.

Who are my new comrades? Next to me walks Alberto; he is in his third year at university, and once again we have managed to stay together. The third person on my left I have never seen; he seems very young, is as pale as wax and has the number of the Dutch. The three backs in front of me are also new. It is dangerous to turn around, I might lose step or stumble; but I try for a moment, and see the face of Iss Clausner.

So long as one walks there is no time to think, one has to take care not to step on the shoes of the fellow hobbling in front, and not let them be stepped on by the fellow behind; every now and again there is a hole to be walked over, an oily puddle to be avoided. I know where we are, I have already come here with my preceding Kommando, it is the H-Strasse, the road of the stores, I tell Alberto, we are really going to the magnesium chloride warehouse, at least that was not a lie.

We have arrived, we climb down into a large damp cellar, full of draughts; this is the headquarters of the Kommando, the Bude as it is called here. The Kapo divides us into three squads: four to unload the sacks from the wagon, seven to carry them down, four to pile them up in the deposit. We form the last squad, I, Alberto, Iss and the Dutchman.

At last we can speak, and to each one of us what Alex said seems a madman's dream.

With these empty faces of ours, with these sheared craniums, with these shameful clothes, to take a chemical examination. And obviously it will be in German; and we will have to go in front of some blond Aryan doctor hoping that we do not have to blow our noses, because perhaps he will not know that we do not have handkerchiefs, and it will certainly not be possible to explain it to him. And we will have our old comrade hunger with us, and we will hardly be able to stand still on our feet, and he will certainly smell our odour, to which we are by now accustomed, but which persecuted us during the first days, the odour of turnips and cabbages, raw, cooked and digested.

Exactly so, Clausner confirms. But have the Germans such great need of chemists? Or is it a new trick, a new machine '*pour faire chier les Juifs*'? Are they aware of the grotesque and absurd test asked of us, of us who are no longer alive, of us who have already gone half-crazy in the dreary expectation of nothing?

Clausner shows me the bottom of his bowl. Where others have carved their numbers, and Alberto and I our names, Clausner has written: '*Ne pas chercher à comprendre.*'

Although we do not think for more than a few minutes a day, and then in a strangely detached and external manner, we well know that we will end in selections. I know that I am not made of the stuff of those who resist, I am too civilized, I still think too much, I use myself up at work. And now I also know that I can save myself if I become a Specialist, and that I will become a Specialist if I pass a chemistry examination.

Today, at this very moment as I sit writing at a table, I myself am not convinced that these things really happened.

Three days passed, three of those usual immemorable days, so long while they are passing, and so short afterwards, and we were already all tired of believing in the chemistry examination.

The Kommando was reduced to twelve men: three had disappeared in the customary manner of down there, perhaps into the hut next door, perhaps cancelled from this world. Of the twelve, five were not chemists; all five had immediately requested permission from Alex to return to their former Kommandos. They were given a few kicks, but unexpectedly, and by who knows whose authority, it was decided that they should remain as auxiliaries to the Chemical Kommando.

Down came Alex into the magnesium chloride yard and called us seven out to go and face the examination. We go like seven awkward chicks behind the hen, following Alex up the steps of the *Polimerisations-Büro*. We are in the lobby, there is a brass-plate on the door with the three famous names. Alex knocks respectfully, takes off his beret and enters. We can hear a quiet voice; Alex comes out again. '*Ruhe, jetzt. Warten*,' wait in silence.

We are satisfied with this. When one waits time moves smoothly without need to intervene and drive it forward, while when one works, every minute moves painfully and has to be laboriously driven away. We are always happy to wait; we are capable of waiting for hours with the complete obtuse inertia of spiders in old webs.

Alex is nervous, he walks up and down and we move out of his way each time. We too, each in our own way, are uneasy; only Mendi is not. Mendi is a rabbi; he comes from sub-Carpathian Russia, from that confusion of peoples where everyone speaks at least three languages, and Mendi speaks seven. He knows a great number of things; besides being a rabbi, he is a militant Zionist, a comparative philologist, he has been a partisan and a lawyer; he is not a chemist, but he wants to try all the same, he is a stubborn, courageous, keen little man.

Balla has a pencil and we all crowd around him. We are not sure if we still know how to write, we want to try.

Kohlenwasserstoffe, Massenwirkungsgesetz. The German names of compounds and laws float back into my memory. I feel grateful towards my brain: I have not paid much attention to it, but it still serves me so well.

Here is Alex. I am a chemist. What have I to do with this man Alex? He plants his feet in front of me, he roughly adjusts the collar of my jacket, he takes out my beret and slaps it on my head, then he steps backwards, eyes the result with a disgusted air, and turns his back, muttering: '*Was für ein Muselmann Zugang.*' What a messy recruit!

The door opens. The three doctors have decided that six candidates will be examined in the morning. The seventh will not. I am the seventh, I have the highest entry number, I have to return to work. Alex will only come to fetch me in the afternoon. What ill-luck, I cannot even talk to the others to hear what questions they are asking.

This time it really is my turn. Alex looks at me blackly on the doorstep; he feels himself in some way responsible for my miserable appearance. He dislikes me because I am Italian, because I am Jewish and because of all of us, I am the one furthest from his sergeants' mess ideal of virility. By analogy, without understanding anything, and proud of this very ignorance, he shows a profound disbelief in my chances for the examination.

We have entered. There is only Doktor Pannwitz; Alex, beret in hand, speaks to him in an undertone: ' ... an Italian, has been here only three months, already half kaputt ... *Er sagt er ist Chemiker* ... ' But he, Alex, apparently has his reservations on the subject.

Alex is briefly dismissed and put aside, and I feel like Oedipus in front of the Sphinx. My ideas are clear, and I am aware even at this moment that the position at stake is important; yet I feel a mad desire to disappear, not to take the test.

Pannwitz is tall, thin, blond; he has eyes, hair and nose as all Germans ought to have them, and sits formidably behind a complicated writing-table. I, Häftling 174517, stand in his office, which is a real office, shining, clean and ordered, and I feel that I would leave a dirty stain whatever I touched.

When he finished writing, he raised his eyes and looked at me.

From that day I have thought about Doktor Pannwitz many times and in many ways. I have asked myself how he really functioned as a man; how he filled his time, outside of the Polymerization and the Indo-Germanic conscience; above all when I was once more a free man, I wanted to meet him again, not from a spirit of revenge, but merely from a personal curiosity about the human soul.

Because that look was not one between two men; and if I had known how completely to explain the nature of that look, which came as if across the glass window of an aquarium between two beings who live in different worlds, I would also have explained the essence of the great insanity of the third Germany.

One felt in that moment, in an immediate manner, what we all thought and said of the Germans. The brain which governed those blue eyes and those manicured hands said: 'This something in front of me belongs to a species which it is obviously opportune to suppress. In this particular case, one has to first make sure that it does not contain some utilizable element.' And in my head, like seeds in an empty pumpkin: 'Blue eyes and fair hair are essentially wicked. No communication possible. I am a specialist in mine chemistry. I am a specialist in organic syntheses. I am a specialist ...'

And the interrogation began, while in the corner that third zoological specimen, Alex, yawned and chewed noisily.

'*Wo sind Sie geboren?*' He addresses me as *Sie*, the polite form of address: Doktor Ingenieur Pannwitz has no sense of humour. Curse him, he is not making the slightest effort to speak a slightly more comprehensible German.

I took my degree at Turin in 1941, *summa cum laude* – and while I say it I have the definite sensation of not being believed, of not even believing it myself; it is enough to look at my dirty hands covered with sores, my convict's trousers encrusted with mud. Yet I am he, the B. Sc. of Turin, in fact, at this particular moment it is impossible to doubt my identity with him, as my reservoir of knowledge of organic chemistry, even after so long an inertia, responds at request with unexpected docility. And even more, this sense of lucid elation, this excitement which I feel warm in my veins, I recognize it, it is the fever of examinations, *my* fever of *my* examinations, that spontaneous mobilization of all my logical faculties and all my knowledge, which my friends at university so envied me.

The examination is going well. As I gradually realize it, I seem to grow in stature. He is asking me now on what subject I wrote my degree thesis. I have to make a violent effort to recall that sequence of memories, so deeply buried away: it is as if I was trying to remember the events of a previous incarnation.

Something protects me. My poor old 'Measurements of dielectrical constants' are of particular interest to this blond Aryan who lives so safely: he asks me if I know English, he shows me Gatterman's book, and even this is absurd and impossible, that down here, on the other side of the barbed wire, a Gatterman should exist, exactly similar to the one I studied in Italy in my fourth year, at home.

Now it is over: the excitement which sustained me for the whole of the test suddenly gives way and, dull and flat, I stare at the fair skin of his hand writing down my fate on the white page in incomprehensible symbols.

'*Los, ab!*' Alex enters the scene again, I am once more under his jurisdiction. He salutes Pannwitz, clicking his heels, and in return receives a faint nod of the eyelids. For a moment I grope around for a suitable formula of leave-taking: but in vain. I know how to say to eat, to work, to steal, to die in German; I also know how to say sulphuric acid, atmospheric pressure, and short-wave generator, but I do not know how to address a person of importance.

Here we are again on the steps. Alex flies down the stairs: he has leather shoes because he is not a Jew, he is as light on his feet as the devils of Malabolge. At the bottom he turns and looks at me sourly as I walk down hesitantly and noisily in my two enormous unpaired wooden shoes, clinging on to the rail like an old man.

It seems to have gone well, but I would be crazy to rely on it. I already know the Lager well enough to realize that one should never anticipate, especially optimistically. What is certain is that I have spent a day without working, so that tonight I will have a little less hunger, and this is a concrete advantage, not to be taken away.

To re-enter Bude, one has to cross a space cluttered up with piles of cross-beams and metal frames. The steel cable of a crane cuts across the road, and Alex catches hold of it to climb over: *Donnerwetter*, he looks at his hand black with thick grease. In the meanwhile I have joined him. Without hatred and without sneering, Alex wipes his hand on my shoulder, both the palm and the back of the hand, to clean it; he would be amazed, the poor brute Alex, if someone told him that today, on the basis of this action, I judge him and Pannwitz and the innumerable others like him, big and small, in Auschwitz and everywhere.

11

The Canto of Ulysses

There were six of us, scraping and cleaning the inside of an underground petrol tank; the daylight only reached us through a small manhole. It was a luxury job because no one supervised us; but it was cold and damp. The powder of the rust burnt under our eyelids and coated our throats and mouths with a taste almost like blood.

The rope-ladder hanging from the manhole began to sway: someone was coming. Deutsch extinguished his cigarette, Goldner woke Sivadjan; we all began to vigorously scrape the resonant steelplate wall.

It was not the *Vorarbeiter*, it was only Jean, the Pikolo of our Kommando. Jean was an Alsatian student; although he was already twenty-four, he was the youngest Häftling of the Chemical Kommando. So that he was given the post of Pikolo, which meant the messenger-clerk, responsible for the cleaning of the hut, for the distribution of tools, for the washing of bowls and for keeping record of the working hours of the Kommando.

Jean spoke French and German fluently: as soon as we recognized his shoes on the top step of the ladder we all stopped scraping.

'*Also, Pikolo, was gibt es Neues?*'

'*Qu'est ce qu'il y a comme soupe aujourd'hui?*'

... in what mood was the Kapo? And the affair of the

twenty-five lashes given to Stern? What was the weather like outside? Had he read the newspaper? What smell was coming from the civilian kitchen? What was the time?

Jean was liked a great deal by the Kommando. One must realize that the post of Pikolo represented a quite high rank in the hierarchy of the Prominents: the Pikolo (who is usually no more than seventeen years old) does no manual work, has an absolute right to the remainder of the daily ration to be found on the bottom of the vat and can stay all day near the stove. He 'therefore' has the right to a supplementary half-ration and has a good chance of becoming the friend and confidant of the Kapo, from whom he officially receives discarded clothes and shoes. Now Jean was an exceptional Pikolo. He was shrewd and physically robust, and at the same time gentle and friendly: although he continued his secret individual struggle against death, he did not neglect his human relationships with less privileged comrades; at the same time he had been so able and persevering that he had managed to establish himself in the confidence of Alex, the Kapo.

Alex had kept all his promises. He had shown himself a violent and unreliable rogue, with an armour of solid and compact ignorance and stupidity, always excepting his intuition and consummate technique as convict-keeper. He never let slip an opportunity of proclaiming his pride in his pure blood and his green triangle, and displayed a lofty contempt for his ragged and starving chemists: '*Ihr Doktoren! Ihr Intelligenten!*' he sneered every day, watching them crowd around with their bowls held out for the distribution of the ration. He was extremely compliant and servile before the civilian *Meister* and with the SS he kept up ties of cordial friendship.

He was clearly intimidated by the register of the Kommando and by the daily report of work, and this had been the path that Pikolo had chosen to make himself indispensable. It had been a long, cautious and subtle task which the entire Kommando had followed for a month with bated breath; but at the end the porcupine's defence was penetrated, and Pikolo confirmed in his office to the satisfaction of all concerned.

Although Jean had never abused his position, we had already been able to verify that a single word of his, said in the right tone of voice and at the right moment, had great power; many times already it had saved one of us from a whipping or from being denounced to the SS. We had been friends for a week: we discovered each other during the unusual occasion of an air-raid alarm, but then, swept by the fierce rhythm of the Lager, we had only been able to greet each other fleetingly, at the latrines, in the washroom.

Hanging with one hand on the swaying ladder, he pointed to me: '*Aujourd'hui c'est Primo qui viendra avec moi chercher la soupe.*'

Until yesterday it had been Stern, the squinting Transylvanian; now he had fallen into disgrace for some story of brooms stolen from the store, and Pikolo had managed to support my candidature as assistant to the '*Essenholen*', the daily corvée of the ration.

He climbed out and I followed him, blinking in the brightness of the day. It was warmish outside, the sun drew a faint smell of paint and tar from the greasy earth, which made me think of a holiday beach of my infancy. Pikolo gave me one of the two wooden poles, and we walked along under a clear June sky.

I began to thank him, but he stopped me: it was not necessary. One could see the Carpathians covered in snow. I breathed in the fresh air, I felt unusually light-hearted.

'*Tu es fou de marcher si vite. On a le temps, tu sais.*' The ration was collected half a mile away; one had to return with the pot weighing over a hundred pounds supported on the two poles. It was quite a tiring task, but it meant a pleasant walk there without a load, and the ever-welcome chance of going near the kitchens.

We slowed down. Pikolo was expert. He had chosen the path cleverly so that we would have to make a long detour, walking at least for an hour, without arousing suspicion. We spoke of our houses, of Strasbourg and Turin, of the books we had read, of what we had studied, of our mothers: how all mothers resemble each other! His mother too had scolded him for never knowing how much money he had in his pocket; his mother too would have been amazed if she had known that he had found his feet, that day by day he was finding his feet.

An SS man passed on a bicycle. It is Rudi, the *Blockführer*. Halt! Attention! Take off your beret! '*Sale brute, celui-là. Ein ganz gemeiner Hund.*' Can he speak French and German with equal facility? Yes, he thinks indifferently in both languages. He spent a month in Liguria, he likes Italy, he would like to learn Italian. I would be pleased to teach him Italian: why not try? We can do it. Why not immediately, one thing is as good as another, the important thing is not to lose time, not to waste this hour.

Limentani from Rome walks by, dragging his feet, with a bowl hidden under his jacket. Pikolo listens carefully, picks up a few words of our conversation and repeats them smiling: '*Zup-pa, cam-po, acqua.*'

Frenkl the spy passes. Quicken our pace, one never knows, he does evil for evil's sake.

... The canto of Ulysses. Who knows how or why it comes into my mind. But we have no time to change, this hour is already less than an hour. If Jean is intelligent he will understand. He *will* understand – today I feel capable of so much.

... Who is Dante? What is the Comedy? That curious sensation of novelty which one feels if one tries to explain briefly what is the Divine Comedy. How the Inferno is divided up, what are its punishments. Virgil is Reason, Beatrice is Theology.

Jean pays great attention, and I begin slowly and accurately:

'Then of that age-old fire the loftier horn
Began to mutter and move, as a wavering flame
Wrestles against the wind and is over-worn;
And, like a speaking tongue vibrant to frame
Language, the tip of it nickering to and fro
Threw out a voice and answered: "When I came ... "'

Here I stop and try to translate. Disastrous – poor Dante and poor French! All the same, the experience seems to promise well: Jean admires the bizarre simile of the tongue and suggests the appropriate word to translate 'age-old'.

And after 'When I came?' Nothing. A hole in my memory. 'Before Aeneas ever named it so.' Another hole. A fragment floats into my mind, not relevant: ' ... nor piety To my old father, not the wedded love That should have comforted Penelope ... ', is it correct?

' ... So on the open sea I set forth.'

Of this I am certain, I am sure, I can explain it to Pikolo, I can point out why 'I set forth'* is not 'je me mis', it is much stronger and more audacious, it is a chain which has been broken, it is throwing oneself on the other side of a barrier, we know the impulse well. The open sea: Pikolo has travelled by sea, and knows what it means: it is when the horizon closes in on itself, free, straight ahead and simple, and there is nothing but the smell of the sea; sweet things, ferociously far away.

* 'misi me' [translator's note].

We have arrived at Kraftwerk, where the cable-laying Kommando works. Engineer Levi must be here. Here he is, one can only see his head above the trench. He waves to me, he is a brave man, I have never seen his morale low, he never speaks of eating.

'Open sea', 'open sea', I know it rhymes with 'left me': '... and that small band of comrades that had never left me', but I cannot remember if it comes before or after. And the journey as well, the foolhardy journey beyond the Pillars of Hercules, how sad, I have to tell it in prose – a sacrilege. I have only rescued two lines, but they are worth stopping for:

'... that none should prove so hardy
To venture the uncharted distances ...'

'To venture':* I had to come to the Lager to realize that it is the same expression as before: 'I set forth'. But I say nothing to Jean, I am not sure that it is an important observation. How many things there are to say, and the sun is already high, midday is near. I am in a hurry, a terrible hurry.

Here, listen, Pikolo, open your ears and your mind, you have to understand, for my sake:

'Think of your breed; for brutish ignorance
Your mettle was not made; you were made men,
To follow after knowledge and excellence.'

As if I also was hearing it for the first time: like the blast of a trumpet, like the voice of God. For a moment I forget who I am and where I am.

Pikolo begs me to repeat it. How good Pikolo is, he is aware

* 'si metta' [translator's note].

that it is doing me good. Or perhaps it is something more: perhaps, despite the wan translation and the pedestrian, rushed commentary, he has received the message, he has felt that it has to do with him, that it has to do with all men who toil, and with us in particular; and that it has to do with us two, who dare to reason of these things with the poles for the soup on our shoulders.

'My little speech made every one so keen ...'

... and I try, but in vain, to explain how many things this 'keen' means. There is another lacuna here, this time irreparable. '... the light kindles and grows Beneath the moon' or something like it; but before it? ... Not an idea, '*keine Ahnung*' as they say here. Forgive me, Pikolo, I have forgotten at least four triplets.

'*Ça ne fait rien, vas-y tout de même.*'
'... When at last hove up a mountain, grey
With distance, and so lofty and so steep,
I never had seen the like on any day.'

Yes, yes, 'so lofty and so steep', not 'very steep',* a consecutive proposition. And the mountains when one sees them in the distance ... the mountains ... oh, Pikolo, Pikolo, say something, speak, do not let me think of my mountains which used to show up against the dusk of evening as I returned by train from Milan to Turin!

Enough, one must go on, these are things that one thinks but does not say. Pikolo waits and looks at me.

I would give today's soup to know how to connect 'the like on any day' to the last lines. I try to reconstruct it through the

* 'alta tanto', not 'molto alta' [translator's note].

rhymes, I close my eyes, I bite my fingers – but it is no use, the rest is silence. Other verses dance in my head: '... The sodden ground belched wind ...', no, it is something else. It is late, it is late, we have reached the kitchen, I must finish:

> 'And three times round she went in roaring smother
> With all the waters; at the fourth the poop
> Rose, and the prow went down, as pleased Another.'

I keep Pikolo back, it is vitally necessary and urgent that he listen, that he understand this 'as pleased Another' before it is too late; tomorrow he or I might be dead, or we might never see each other again, I must tell him, I must explain to him about the Middle Ages, about the so human and so necessary and yet unexpected anachronism, but still more, something gigantic that I myself have only just seen, in a flash of intuition, perhaps the reason for our fate, for our being here today ...

We are now in the soup queue, among the sordid, ragged crowd of soup-carriers from other Kommandos. Those just arrived press against our backs. '*Kraut und Rüben? Kraut und Rüben.*' The official announcement is made that the soup today is of cabbages and turnips: '*Choux et navets. Kaposzta és répak.*'

> 'And over our heads the hollow seas closed up.'

12

The Events of the Summer

Throughout the spring, convoys arrived from Hungary; one prisoner in two was Hungarian, and Hungarian had become the second language in the camp after Yiddish.

In the month of August 1944, we who had entered the camp five months before now counted among the old ones. As such, we of Kommando 98 were not amazed that the promises made to us and the examination we had passed had brought no result; neither amazed nor exceptionally saddened. At bottom, we all had a certain dread of changes: 'When things change, they change for the worse' was one of the proverbs of the camp. More generally, experience had shown us many times the vanity of every conjecture: why worry oneself trying to read into the future when no action, no word of ours could have the minimum influence? We were old Häftlinge: our wisdom lay in 'not trying to understand', not imagining the future, not tormenting ourselves as to how and when it would all be over; not asking others or ourselves any questions.

We preserved the memories of our previous life, but blurred and remote, profoundly sweet and sad, like the memories of early infancy. While for everybody, the moment of entry into the camp was the starting point of a different sequence of thoughts, those near and sharp, continually confirmed by present experience, like wounds re-opened every day.

The news heard in the Buna yards of the Allied landing in Normandy, of the Russian offensive and of the failed attempt against Hitler, had given rise to waves of violent but ephemeral hope. Day by day everyone felt his strength vanish, his desire to live melt away, his mind grow dim; and Normandy and Russia were so far away, and the winter so near; hunger and desolation so concrete, and all the rest so unreal, that it did not seem possible that there could really exist any other world or time other than our world of mud and our sterile and stagnant time, whose end we were by now incapable of imagining.

For living men, the units of time always have a value, which increases in ratio to the strength of the internal resources of the person living through them; but for us, hours, days, months spilled out sluggishly from the future into the past, always too slowly, a valueless and superfluous material, of which we sought to rid ourselves as soon as possible. With the end of the season when the days chased each other, vivacious, precious and irrecoverable, the future stood in front of us, grey and inarticulate, like an invincible barrier. For us, history had stopped.

But in August '44 the bombardments of Upper Silesia began, and they continued with irregular pauses and renewals throughout the summer and the autumn until the definite crisis.

The monstrously unanimous labour of gestation of Buna stopped brusquely, and at once degenerated into a disconnected, frantic and paroxysmal confusion. The day on which the production of synthetic rubber should have begun, which seemed imminent in August, was gradually postponed until the Germans no longer spoke about it.

Constructive work stopped; the power of the countless multitudes of slaves was directed elsewhere, and day by day showed itself more riotous and passively hostile. At every raid there was new damage to be repaired; the delicate machinery assembled with care just before had to be dismantled again and evacuated; air-raid shelters and walls had to be hurriedly erected to show themselves at the next test as ironically ineffective as sand castles.

We had thought that anything would be preferable to the monotony of the identical and inexorably long days, to the systematic and ordered squalor of Buna at work; but we were forced to change our minds when Buna began to fall in pieces around us, as if struck by a curse in which we ourselves felt involved. We had to sweat amidst the dust and smoking ruins, and tremble like beasts, flattened against the earth by the anger of aeroplanes; broken by exhaustion and parched with thirst, we returned in the long, windy evenings of the Polish summer to find the camp upside down, no water to drink or wash in, no soup for our empty bellies, no light by which to defend our piece of bread against someone else's hunger, or find our shoes and clothes in the morning in the dark, shrieking hole of the Block.

At Buna the German civilians raged with the fury of the secure man who wakes up from a long dream of domination and sees his own ruin and is unable to understand it. The *Reichsdeutsche* of the Lager as well, politicals included, felt the ties of blood and soil in the hour of danger. This new fact reduced the complications of hatreds and incomprehensions to their elementary terms and redivided the camp: the politicals, together with the green triangles and the SS, saw, or thought they saw, in all our faces the mockery of revenge and the vicious joy of the vendetta. They found themselves in unanimous agreement on this, and their ferocity redoubled. No German could now forget that we were on the other side: on the side of the terrible sowers who furrowed the German sky as masters, high above every defence, and twisted the living metal of their constructions, carrying slaughter every day into their very homes, into the hitherto unviolated homes of the German people.

As for us, we were too destroyed to be really afraid. The few who could still judge and feel rightly, drew new strength and hope from the bombardments; those whom hunger had not yet reduced to a definitive inertia often profited from the moments of general panic to undertake doubly rash expeditions (since, besides the direct risk of the raid, theft carried out in conditions of emergency was punished by hanging) to the factory kitchen or the stores. But the greater number bore the new danger and the new discomforts with unchanged indifference: it was not a conscious resignation, but the opaque torpor of beasts broken in by blows, whom the blows no longer hurt.

Entry to the reinforced shelters was forbidden us. When the earth began to tremble, we dragged ourselves, stunned and limping, through the corrosive fumes of the smoke bombs to the vast waste areas, sordid and sterile, closed within the boundary of Buna; there we lay inert, piled up on top of each other like dead men, but still aware of the momentary pleasure of our bodies resting. We looked with indifferent eyes at the smoke and flames breaking out around us: in moments of quiet, full of the distant menacing roar that every European knows, we picked from the ground the stunted chicory leaves and dandelions, trampled on a hundred times, and chewed them slowly in silence.

When the alarm was over, we returned from all parts to our posts, a silent innumerable flock, accustomed to the anger of men and things; and continued that work of ours, as hated as ever, now even more obviously useless and senseless.

In this world shaken every day more deeply by the omens of its nearing end, amidst new terrors and hopes, with intervals of exasperated slavery, I happened to meet Lorenzo.

The story of my relationship with Lorenzo is both long and short, plain and enigmatic: it is the story of a time and condition now effaced from every present reality, and so I do not think it can be understood except in the manner in which we nowadays understand events of legends or the remotest history.

In concrete terms it amounts to little: an Italian civilian worker brought me a piece of bread and the remainder of his ration every day for six months; he gave me a vest of his, full of patches; he wrote a postcard on my behalf to Italy and brought me the reply. For all this he neither asked nor accepted any reward, because he was good and simple and did not think that one did good for a reward.

All this should not sound little. My case was not the only one; as has already been said, there were others of us who had contacts of various kinds with civilians, and derived from them the means to survive; but they were relationships of a different nature. Our comrades spoke of them in the same ambiguous manner, full of overtones, in which men of the world speak of their feminine relationships: that is, of adventures of which one can justly be proud and for which one wants to be envied, but which, even for the most pagan consciences, always remain on the margins of the permissible and the honest; so that it is incorrect and improper to boast about them. It is in this way that the Häftlinge speak of their civilian 'protectors' and 'friends'; with an ostentatious discretion, without stating names, so as not to compromise them, and especially and above all so as not to create undesirable rivals. The most consummate, the professional seducers like Henri, do not in fact speak of them; they surround their successes with an aura of equivocal mystery, and they limit themselves to hints and allusions, calculated to arouse in their audience a confused and disquieting legend that they enjoy the good graces of boundlessly powerful and generous civilians. This in view of a deliberate aim: the reputation of good luck, as we have said elsewhere, shows itself of fundamental utility to whosoever knows how to surround himself by it.

The reputation of being a seducer, of being 'organized', excites at once envy, scorn, contempt and admiration. Whoever allows himself to be seen eating 'organized' food is judged quite severely; he shows a serious lack of modesty and tact, besides an open stupidity. It would be equally stupid and impertinent to ask 'who gave it to you? where did you find it? how did you manage it?' Only the High Numbers, foolish, useless and help-less, who know nothing of the rules of the Lager, ask such questions; one does not reply to these questions, or one replies *'Verschwinde, Mensch!'*, *'Hau' ab'*, *'Uciekaj'*, *'Schiess in den Wind'*, *'Va chier'*; in short, with one of those countless equiva-lents of 'Go to hell' in which camp jargon is so rich.

There are also those who specialize in complex and patient campaigns of spying to identify who is the civilian or group of civilians to whom so-and-so turns, and then try in various ways to supplant him. Interminable controversies of priority break out, made all the more bitter for the loser by the knowledge that a 'tried' civilian is almost more profitable, and above all safer than a civilian making his first contact with us. He is a civilian who is worth much more for obvious sentimental and technical reasons: he already knows the principles of the 'organization', its regulations and dangers, and even more he has shown him-self capable of overcoming the caste barrier.

In fact, we are the untouchables to the civilians. They think, more or less explicitly – with all the nuances lying between contempt and commiseration – that as we have been con-demned to this life of ours, reduced to our condition, we must be tainted by some mysterious, grave sin. They hear us speak in many different languages, which they do not understand and which sound to them as grotesque as animal noises; they see us reduced to ignoble slavery, without hair, without honour and without names, beaten every day, more abject every day, and they never see in our eyes a light of rebellion, or of peace, or of faith. They know us as thieves and untrustworthy, muddy, ragged and starving, and mistaking the effect for the cause, they judge us worthy of our abasement. Who could tell one of our faces from the other? For them we are 'Kazett', a singular neuter word.

This naturally does not stop many of them throwing us a piece of bread or a potato now and again, or giving us their bowls, after the distribution of the '*Zivilsuppe*' in the work-yards, to scrape and give back washed. They do it to get rid of some importunate starved look, or through a momentary impulse of humanity, or through simple curiosity to see us running from all sides to fight each other for the scrap, bestially and without restraint, until the strongest one gobbles it up, where-upon all the others limp away, frustrated.

Now nothing of this sort occurred between me and Lorenzo. However little sense there may be in trying to specify why I, rather than thousands of others, managed to survive the test, I believe that it was really due to Lorenzo that I am alive today; and not so much for his material aid, as for his having con-stantly reminded me by his presence, by his natural and plain manner of being good, that there still existed a just world out-side our own, something and someone still pure and whole, not corrupt, not savage, extraneous to hatred and terror; something difficult to define, a remote possibility of good, but for which it was worth surviving.

The personages in these pages are not men. Their humanity is buried, or they themselves have buried it, under an offence received or inflicted on someone else. The evil and insane SS men, the Kapos, the politicals, the criminals, the Prominents, great and small, down to the indifferent slave Häftlinge, all the

grades of the mad hierarchy created by the Germans paradoxically fraternized in a uniform internal desolation.

But Lorenzo was a man; his humanity was pure and uncontaminated, he was outside this world of negation. Thanks to
Lorenzo, I managed not to forget that I myself was a man.

13

October 1944

We fought with all our strength to prevent the arrival of winter. We clung to all the warm hours, at every dusk we tried to keep the sun in the sky for a little longer, but it was all in vain. Yesterday evening the sun went down irrevocably behind a confusion of dirty clouds, chimney stacks and wires, and today it is winter.

We know what it means because we were here last winter; and the others will soon learn. It means that in the course of these months, from October till April, seven out of ten of us will die. Whoever does not die will suffer minute by minute, all day, every day: from the morning before dawn until the distribution of the evening soup we will have to keep our muscles continually tensed, dance from foot to foot, beat our arms under our shoulders against the cold. We will have to spend bread to acquire gloves, and lose hours of sleep to repair them when they become unstitched. As it will no longer be possible to eat in the open, we will have to eat our meals in the hut, on our feet, everyone will be assigned an area of floor as large as a hand, as it is forbidden to rest against the bunks. Wounds will open on everyone's hands, and to be given a bandage will mean waiting every evening for hours on one's feet in the snow and wind.

Just as our hunger is not that feeling of missing a meal, so our way of being cold has need of a new word. We say 'hunger', we say 'tiredness', 'fear', 'pain', we say 'winter' and they are different things. They are free words, created and used by free men who lived in comfort and suffering in their homes. If the Lagers had lasted longer a new, harsh language would have been born; and only this language could express what it means to toil the whole day in the wind, with the temperature below freezing, wearing only a shirt, underpants, cloth jacket and trousers, and in one's body nothing but weakness, hunger and knowledge of the end drawing nearer.

In the same way in which one sees a hope end, winter arrived this morning. We realized it when we left the hut to go and wash: there were no stars, the dark cold air had the smell of snow. In roll-call square, in the grey of dawn, when we assembled for work, no one spoke. When we saw the first flakes of snow, we thought that if at the same time last year they had told us that we would have seen another winter in Lager, we would have gone and touched the electric wire-fence; and that even now we would go if we were logical, were it not for this last senseless crazy residue of unavoidable hope.

Because 'winter' means yet another thing.

Last spring the Germans had constructed huge tents in an open space in the Lager. For the whole of the good season each of them had catered for over a thousand men: now the tents had been taken down, and an excess two thousand guests crowded our huts. We old prisoners knew that the Germans did not like these irregularities and that something would soon happen to reduce our number.

One feels the selections arriving. 'Selekcja': the hybrid Latin and Polish word is heard once, twice, many times, interpolated in foreign conversations; at first we cannot distinguish it, then it forces itself on our attention, and in the end it persecutes us.

This morning the Poles had said 'Selekcja'. The Poles are the first to find out the news, and they generally try not to let it spread around, because to know something which the others still do not know can always be useful. By the time that everyone realizes that a selection is imminent, the few possibilities of evading it (corrupting some doctor or some prominent with bread or tobacco; leaving the hut for Ka-Be or vice-versa at the right moment so as to cross with the commission) are already their monopoly.

In the days which follow, the atmosphere of the Lager and the yard is filled with '*Selekcja*': nobody knows anything definite, but all speak about it, even the Polish, Italian, French civilian workers whom we secretly see in the yard. Yet the result is hardly a wave of despondency: our collective morale is too inarticulate and flat to be unstable. The fight against hunger, cold and work leaves little margin for thought, even for this thought. Everybody reacts in his own way, but hardly anyone with those attitudes which would seem the most plausible as the most realistic, that is with resignation or despair.

All those able to find a way out, try to take it; but they are the minority because it is very difficult to escape from a selection. The Germans apply themselves to these things with great skill and diligence.

Whoever is unable to prepare for it materially, seeks defence elsewhere. In the latrines, in the washroom, we show each other our chests, our buttocks, our thighs, and our comrades reassure us: 'You are all right, it will certainly not be your turn this time, ... *du bist kein Muselmann* ... more probably mine ...' and they undo their braces in turn and pull up their shirts.

Nobody refuses this charity to another: nobody is so sure of his own lot to be able to condemn others. I brazenly lied to old Wertheimer; I told him that if they questioned him, he should reply that he was forty-five, and he should not forget to have a shave the evening before, even if it cost him a quarter-ration of bread; apart from that he need have no fears, and in any case it was by no means certain that it was a selection for the gas chamber; had he not heard the *Blockältester* say that those chosen would go to Jaworszno to a convalescent camp?

It is absurd of Wertheimer to hope: he looks sixty, he has enormous varicose veins, he hardly even notices the hunger any more. But he lies down on his bed, serene and quiet, and replies to someone who asks him with my own words; they are the command-words in the camp these days: I myself repeated them just as – apart from details – Chajim told them to me, Chajim, who has been in Lager for three years, and being strong and robust is wonderfully sure of himself; and I believed them.

On this slender basis I also lived through the great selection of October 1944 with inconceivable tranquillity. I was tranquil because I managed to lie to myself sufficiently. The fact that I was not selected depended above all on chance and does not prove that my faith was well-founded.

Monsieur Pinkert is also, a priori, condemned: it is enough to look at his eyes. He calls me over with a sign, and with a confidential air tells me that he has been informed – he cannot tell me the source of information – that this time there is really something new: the Holy See, by means of the International Red Cross … in short, he personally guarantees both for himself and for me, in the most absolute manner, that every danger is ruled out; as a civilian he was, as is well known, attaché to the Belgian embassy at Warsaw.

Thus in various ways, even those days of vigil, which in the telling seem as if they ought to have passed every limit of human torment, went by not very differently from other days.

The discipline in both the Lager and Buna is in no way relaxed: the work, cold and hunger are sufficient to fill up every thinking moment.

*

Today is working Sunday, *Arbeitssonntag*: we work until 1 p.m., then we return to camp for the shower, shave and general control for skin diseases and lice. And in the yards, everyone knew mysteriously that the selection would be today.

The news arrived, as always, surrounded by a halo of contradictory or suspect details: the selection in the infirmary took place this morning; the percentage was seven per cent of the whole camp, thirty, fifty per cent of the patients. At Birkenau, the crematorium chimney has been smoking for ten days. Room has to be made for an enormous convoy arriving from the Poznan ghetto. The young tell the young that all the old ones will be chosen. The healthy tell the healthy that only the ill will be chosen. Specialists will be excluded. German Jews will be excluded. Low Numbers will be excluded. You will be chosen. I will be excluded.

At 1 p.m. exactly the yard empties in orderly fashion, and for two hours the grey unending army files past the two control stations where, as on every day, we are counted and recounted, and past the military band which for two hours without interruption plays, as on every day, those marches to which we must synchronize our steps at our entrance and our exit.

It seems like every day, the kitchen chimney smokes as usual, the distribution of the soup is already beginning. But then the bell is heard, and at that moment we realize that we have arrived.

Because this bell always sounds at dawn, when it means the reveille; but if it sounds during the day, it means '*Blocksperre*', enclosure in huts, and this happens when there is a selection to prevent anyone avoiding it, or when those selected leave for the gas, to prevent anyone seeing them leave.

Our *Blockältester* knows his business. He has made sure that we have all entered, he has the door locked, he has given everyone his card with his number, name, profession, age and nationality and he has ordered everyone to undress completely, except for shoes. We wait like this, naked, with the card in our hands, for the commission to reach our hut. We are hut 48, but one can never tell if they are going to begin at hut 1 or hut 60. At any rate, we can rest quietly at least for an hour, and there is no reason why we should not get under the blankets on the bunk and keep warm.

Many are already drowsing when a barrage of orders, oaths and blows proclaims the imminent arrival of the commission. The *Blockältester* and his helpers, starting at the end of the dormitory, drive the crowd of frightened, naked people in front of them and cram them in the *Tagesraum* which is the Quartermaster's office. The *Tagesraum* is a room seven yards by four: when the drive is over, a warm and compact human mass is jammed into the *Tagesraum*, perfectly filling all the corners, exercising such a pressure on the wooden walls as to make them creak.

Now we are all in the *Tagesraum*, and besides there being no time, there is not even any room in which to be afraid. The feeling of the warm flesh pressing all around is unusual and not unpleasant. One has to take care to hold up one's nose so as to breathe, and not to crumple or lose the card in one's hand.

The *Blockältester* has closed the connecting-door and has opened the other two which lead from the dormitory and the *Tagesraum* outside. Here, in front of the two doors, stands the arbiter of our fate, an SS subaltern. On his right is the *Blockältester,* on his left, the quartermaster of the hut. Each one of us, as he comes naked out of the *Tagesraum* into the cold October air, has to run the few steps between the two doors, give the card to the SS man and enter the dormitory door. The SS man, in the fraction of a second between two successive crossings, with a glance at one's back and front, judges everyone's fate, and in turn gives the card to the man on his right or his left, and this is the life or death of each of us. In three or four minutes a hut of two hundred men is 'done', as is the whole camp of twelve thousand men in the course of the afternoon.

Jammed in the charnel-house of the *Tagesraum*, I gradually felt the human pressure around me slacken, and in a short time it was my turn. Like everyone, I passed by with a brisk and elastic step, trying to hold my head high, my chest forward and my muscles contracted and conspicuous. With the corner of my eye I tried to look behind my shoulders, and my card seemed to end on the right.

As we gradually come back into the dormitory we are allowed to dress ourselves. Nobody yet knows with certainty his own fate, it has first of all to be established whether the condemned cards were those on the right or the left. By now there is no longer any point in sparing each other's feelings with superstitious scruples. Everybody crowds around the oldest, the most wasted away, and most 'muselman'; if their cards went to the left, the left is certainly the side of the condemned.

Even before the selection is over, everybody knows that the left was effectively the '*schlechte Seite*', the bad side. There have naturally been some irregularities: René, for example, so young and robust, ended on the left; perhaps it was because he has glasses, perhaps because he walks a little stooped like a myope, but more probably because of a simple mistake: Rendé passed the commission immediately in front of me and there could have been a mistake with our cards. I think about it, discuss it with Alberto, and we agree that the hypothesis is probable; I do not know what I will think tomorrow and later; today I feel no distinct emotion.

It must equally have been a mistake about Sattler, a huge Transylvanian peasant who was still at home only twenty days ago; Sattler does not understand German, he has understood nothing of what has taken place, and stands in a corner mending his shirt. Must I go and tell him that his shirt will be of no more use?

There is nothing surprising about these mistakes: the examination is too quick and summary, and in any case, the important thing for the Lager is not that the most useless prisoners be eliminated, but that free posts be quickly created, according to a certain percentage previously fixed.

The selection is now over in our hut, but it continues in the others, so that we are still locked in. But as the soup-pots have arrived in the meantime, the *Blockältester* decides to proceed with the distribution at once. A double ration will be given to those selected. I have never discovered if this was a ridiculously charitable initiative of the *Blockältester*, or an explicit disposition of the SS, but in fact, in the interval of two or three days (sometimes even much longer) between the selection and the departure, the victims at Monowitz-Auschwitz enjoyed this privilege.

Ziegler holds out his bowl, collects his normal ration and then waits there expectantly. 'What do you want?' asks the *Blockältester*: according to him, Ziegler is entitled to no supplement, and he drives him away, but Ziegler returns and humbly persists. He was on the left, everybody saw it, let the *Blockältester* check the cards; he has the right to a double ration. When he is given it, he goes quietly to his bunk to eat.

Now everyone is busy scraping the bottom of his bowl with his spoon so as not to waste the last drops of the soup; a confused, metallic clatter, signifying the end of the day. Silence slowly prevails and then, from my bunk on the top row, I see and hear old Kuhn praying aloud, with his beret on his head, swaying backwards and forwards violently. Kuhn is thanking God because he has not been chosen.

Kuhn is out of his senses. Does he not see Beppo the Greek in the bunk next to him, Beppo who is twenty years old and is going to the gas chamber the day after tomorrow and knows it and lies there looking fixedly at the light without saying anything and without even thinking any more? Can Kuhn fail to realize that next time it will be his turn? Does Kuhn not understand that what has happened today is an abomination, which no propitiatory prayer, no pardon, no expiation by the guilty, which nothing at all in the power of man can ever clean again? If I was God, I would spit at Kuhn's prayer.

14

Kraus

When it rains we would like to cry. It is November, it has been raining for ten days now and the ground is like the bottom of a swamp. Everything made of wood gives out a smell of mushrooms.

If I could walk ten steps to the left I would be under shelter in the shed; a sack to cover my shoulders would be sufficient, or even the prospect of a fire where I could dry myself; or even a dry rag to put between my shirt and my back. Between one movement of the shovel and another I think about it, and I really believe that to have a dry rag would be positive happiness.

By now it would be impossible to be wetter; I will just have to pay attention to move as little as possible, and above all not to make new movements, to prevent some other part of my skin coming into unnecessary contact with my soaking, icy clothes.

It is lucky that it is not windy today. Strange, how in some way one always has the impression of being fortunate, how some chance happening, perhaps infinitesimal, stops us crossing the threshold of despair and allows us to live. It is raining, but it is not windy. Or else, it is raining and is also windy: but you know that this evening it is your turn for the supplement of soup, so that even today you find the strength to reach the evening. Or it is raining, windy and you have the usual hunger, and then you think that if you really had to, if you really felt nothing in your heart but suffering and tedium – as sometimes happens, when you really seem to lie on the bottom – well, even in that case, at any moment you want you could always go and touch the electric wire-fence, or throw yourself under the shunting trains, and then it would stop raining.

We have been stuck in the mud since the morning, legs akimbo, with our feet sinking ever deeper in the selfsame holes in the glutinous soil. We sway on our haunches at every swing of the shovel. I am half-way down the pit, Kraus and Clausner are at the bottom, Gounan is above me at surface level. Only Gounan can look around, and every now and again he warns Kraus curtly of the need to quicken the pace or even to rest, according to who is passing by in the road. Clausner uses the pickaxe, Kraus lifts the earth up to me on his shovel, and I gradually pass it up to Gounan who piles it up on one side. Others form a shuttle service with wheelbarrows and carry the earth somewhere, of no interest to us. Our world today is this hole of mud.

Kraus misses his stroke, a lump of mud flies up and splatters over my knees. It is not the first time it has happened, I warn him to be careful, but without much hope: he is Hungarian, he understands German badly and does not know a word of French. He is tall and thin, wears glasses and has a curious, small, twisted face; when he laughs he looks like a child, and he often laughs. He works too much and too vigorously: he has not yet learnt our underground art of economizing on everything, on breath, movements, even thoughts. He does not yet know that it is better to be beaten, because one does not normally die of blows, but one does of exhaustion, and badly, and when one grows aware of it, it is already too late. He still thinks ... oh no, poor Kraus, his is not reasoning, it is only the stupid honesty of a small employee, he brought it along with him, and he seems to think that his present situation is like outside, where it is honest and logical to work, as well as being of advantage, because according to what everyone says, the more one works the more one earns and eats.

'*Regardez-moi ça! ... Pas si vite, idiot!*' Gounan swears at him from above; then he remembers to translate it in German: '*Langsam, du blöder Einer, langsam, verstanden?*' Kraus can kill himself through exhaustion if he wants to, but not today, because we are working in a chain and the rhythm of the work is set by him.

There goes the siren of the Carbide factory, now the English prisoners are leaving; it is half past four. Then the Ukrainian girls will leave and it will be five o'clock and we will be able to straighten our backs, and only the return march, the roll-call and the lice-control will separate us from our rest.

It is assembly time, '*Antreten*' from all sides; from all sides the mud puppets creep out, stretch their cramped limbs, carry the tools back to the huts. We extract our feet from the ditch cautiously so as not to let our shoes be sucked off, and leave, dripping and swaying, to line up for the return march. '*Zu dreine*', in threes. I tried to place myself near to Alberto as we had worked separately today and we both wanted to ask each other how it had gone; but someone hit me in the stomach and I finished behind him, right next to Kraus.

Now we leave. The Kapo marks time in a hard voice: '*Links, links, links*'; at first, our feet hurt, then we slowly grow warm and our nerves relax. We have bored our way through all the minutes of the day, this very day which seemed invincible and eternal this morning; now it lies dead and is immediately forgotten; already it is no longer a day, it has left no trace in anybody's memory. We know that tomorrow will be like today: perhaps it will rain a little more or a little less, or perhaps instead of digging soil we will go and unload bricks at the Carbide factory. Or the war might even finish tomorrow, or we might all be killed or transferred to another camp, or one of those great changes might take place which, ever since the Lager has been the Lager, have been infatigably foretold as imminent and certain. But who can seriously think about tomorrow?

Memory is a curious instrument: ever since I have been in the camp, two lines written by a friend of mine a long time ago have been running through my mind:

'... Until one day
there will be no more sense in saying: tomorrow.'

It is like that here. Do you know how one says 'never' in camp slang? '*Morgen früh*', tomorrow morning. It is now the hour of '*links, links, links und links*', the hour in which one must not lose step. Kraus is clumsy, he has already been kicked by the Kapo because he is incapable of walking in line: and now he is beginning to gesticulate and chew a miserable German, listen, listen, he wants to apologise for the spadeful of mud, he has not yet understood where we are, I must say Hungarians are really a most singular people.

To keep step and carry on a complicated conversation in German is too much. This time it is I who warn him that he has lost step; I look at him and I see his eyes behind the drops of water on his glasses, and they are the eyes of the man Kraus.

Then an important thing happened, and it is worth telling now, perhaps for the same reason that it happened then. I began to make a long speech to Kraus: in bad German, but slowly, separating the words, making sure after each sentence that he had understood.

I told him that I had dreamt that I was at home, the home where I was born, with my family, sitting with my legs under the table, and on the table a great deal, a very great deal to eat. And it was summer and it was in Italy – at Naples? ... yes, at Naples, this is hardly the time to quibble. Then all of a sudden the bell rang, and I got up hurriedly and went to open the door, and who did I see? I saw him, this very Kraus Páli, with hair grown, clean and well nourished and dressed as a free man, with a loaf of bread in his hand. Yes, a loaf of four pounds, still warm. Then 'Servus, Páli, wie geht's?' and I felt filled with joy and made him come in, and I explained to my parents who he was, and that he had come from Budapest, and why he was so wet; because he was soaking, just like now. And I gave him food and drink and a good bed to sleep in, and it was night-time, but there was a wonderful warmth so that we were all dry in a moment (yes, I was also very wet).

What a good boy Kraus must have been as a civilian: he will not survive very long here, one can see it at the first glance, it is as logical as a theorem. I am sorry I do not know Hungarian, for his emotion has broken the dykes, and he is breaking out in a flood of outlandish Magyar words. I cannot understand anything except my name, but by the solemn gestures one would say that he is making promises and prophecies.

Poor silly Kraus. If he only knew that it is not true, that I have really dreamt nothing about him, that he is nothing to me except for a brief moment, nothing like everything is nothing down here, except the hunger inside and the cold and the rain around.

15

Die drei Leute vom Labor

How many months have gone by since we entered the camp? How many since the day I was dismissed from Ka-Be? And since the day of the chemistry examination? And since the October selection?

Alberto and I often ask ourselves these questions, and many others as well. We were ninety-six when we arrived, we, the Italians of convoy 174,000; only twenty-nine of us survived until October, and of these, eight went in the selection. We are now twenty-one and the winter has hardly begun. How many of us will be alive at the new year? How many when spring begins?

There have been no air raids now for several weeks; the November rain has turned to snow, and the snow has covered the ruins. The Germans and Poles go to work in rubber jackboots, woollen ear-pads and padded overalls; the English prisoners have their wonderful fur-lined jackets. They have distributed no overcoats in our Lager except to a few of the privileged; we are a specialized Kommando, which – in theory – only works under shelter; so we are left in our summer outfits.

We are the chemists, 'therefore' we work at the phenylbeta sacks. We cleared out the warehouse after the first air raids in the height of the summer. The phenylbeta seeped under our clothes and stuck to our sweating limbs and chafed us like leprosy; the skin came off our faces in large burnt patches. Then the air raids temporarily stopped and we carried the sacks back into the warehouse. Then the warehouse was hit and we took the sacks into the cellar of the styrene department. Now the warehouse has been repaired and once again we have to pile up the sacks there. The caustic smell of the phenylbeta impregnates our only suit, and follows us day and night like our shadows. So far, the advantages of being in the Chemical Kommando have been limited to the following: the others have received overcoats while we have not; the others carry 100 pound cement sacks, while we carry 125 pound phenylbeta sacks. How can we still think about the chemistry examination and our illusions of that time? At least four times during the summer we have heard speak of Doktor Pannwitz's laboratory in Bau 939, and the rumour spread that the analysts for the Polymerization Department would be chosen among us.

But now it is time to stop, it is all over now. This is the last act: the winter has begun, and with it our last battle. There is no longer any reason to doubt that it will be the last. Any time during the day when we happen to listen to the voice of our bodies, or ask our limbs, the answer is always the same: our strength will not last out. Everything around us speaks of a final decay and ruin. Half of Bau 939 is a heap of twisted metal and smashed concrete; large deformed blue icicles hang like pillars from the enormous tubings where the overheated steam used to roar. Buna is silent now, and when the wind is propitious, if one listens hard, one can hear the continuous dull underground rumbling of the front which is getting nearer. Three hundred prisoners have arrived in the Lager from the Lodz ghetto, transferred by the Germans before the Russian advance: they told us rumours about the legendary battle of the Warsaw ghetto, and they described how the Germans had liquidated the Lublin camp over a year ago: four machine-guns in the corners and the huts set on fire; the civilized world will never know about it. When will it be our turn?

This morning the Kapo divided up the squads as usual. The Magnesium Chloride ten to the Magnesium Chloride: and they leave, dragging their feet, as slowly as possible, because the Magnesium Chloride is an extremely unpleasant job; you stand all day up to your ankles in cold, briny water, which soaks into your shoes, your clothes and your skin. The Kapo grabs hold of a brick and throws it among the group; they get clumsily out of the way, but do not quicken their pace. This is almost a custom, it happens every morning, and does not always mean that the Kapo has a definite intent to hurt.

The four of the *Scheisshaus*, to their work: and the four attached to the building of the new latrine leave. For when we exceeded the force of fifty Häftlinge with the arrival of the convoys from Lodz and Transylvania, the mysterious German bureaucrat who supervises these matters authorized us to build a '*Zweiplatziges Kommandoscheisshaus*', i.e. a two-seated closet reserved for our Kommando. We are not unaware of this mark of distinction, which makes ours one of the few Kommandos of which one can with reason boast of one's membership: but it is evident that we will lose one of the simplest of pretexts to absent ourselves from work and arrange combinations with civilians. '*Noblesse oblige*,' says Henri, who has other strings to his bow.

The twelve for the bricks. Meister Dahm's five. The two for the tanks. How many absent? Three absent. Homolka gone into Ka-Be this morning, the ironsmith dead yesterday, François transferred who knows where or why. The roll-call is correct; the Kapo notes it down and is satisfied. There are only us eighteen of the phenylbeta left, beside the Prominents of the Kommando. And now the unexpected happens.

The Kapo says: Doktor Pannwitz has communicated to the *Arbeitsdienst* that three Häftlinge have been chosen for the Laboratory: 169509, Brackier; 175633, Kandel; 174517, Levi. For a moment my ears ring and Buna whirls around me. There are three Levis in Kommando 98, but *Hundert Vierundsiebzig Fünf Hundert Siebzehn* is me, there is no possible doubt. I am one of the three chosen.

The Kapo looks us up and down with a twisted smile. A Belgian, a Russian and an Italian: three '*Franzosen*' in short. Is it possible that three *Franzosen* have really been chosen to enter the paradise of the Laboratory?

Many comrades congratulate us; Alberto first of all, with genuine joy, without a shadow of envy. Alberto holds nothing against my fortune, he is really very pleased, both because of our friendship and because he will also gain from it. In fact, by now we two are bound by a tight bond of alliance, by which every 'organized' scrap is divided into two strictly equal parts. He has no reason to envy me, as he neither hoped nor desired to enter the Laboratory. The blood in his veins is too free for this untamed friend of mine to think of relaxing in a system; his instinct leads him elsewhere, to other solutions, towards the unforeseen, the impromptu, the new. Without hesitating, Alberto prefers the uncertainties and battles of the 'free profession' to a good employment.

I have a ticket from the *Arbeitsdienst* in my pocket, on which it is written that Häftling 174517, as a specialized worker, has the right to a new shirt and underpants and must be shaved every Wednesday.

The ravaged Buna lies under the first snows, silent and stiff like an enormous corpse; every day the sirens of the *Fliegeralarm* wail; the Russians are fifty miles away. The electric power station has stopped, the methanol rectification columns no longer exist, three of the four acetylene gasometers have been blown up. Prisoners 'reclaimed' from all the camps in east Poland pour into our Lager haphazardly; the minority are set to work, the majority leave immediately for Birkenau and the Chimney. The ration has been still further reduced. Ka-Be is overflowing, the E-Häftlinge have brought scarlet fever, diphtheria and petechial typhus into the camp.

But Häftling 174517 has been promoted as a specialist and has the right to a new shirt and underpants and has to be shaved every Wednesday. No one can boast of understanding the Germans.

We entered the Laboratory timid, suspicious and bewildered like three wild beasts slinking into a large city. How clean and polished the floor is! It is a laboratory surprisingly like any other laboratory. Three long work-benches covered with hundreds of familiar objects. The glass instruments in a corner to drip, the precision balance, a Heraeus oven, a Höppler thermostat. The smell makes me start back as if from the blow of a whip: the weak aromatic smell of organic chemistry laboratories. For a moment the large semi-dark room at the university, my fourth year, the mild air of May in Italy comes back to me with brutal violence and immediately vanishes.

Herr Stawinoga gives us our work-places. Stawinoga is a German Pole, still young, with an energetic, but sad and tired face. He is also Doktor: not of chemistry, but (*ne pas chercher à comprendre*) of comparative philology; all the same, he is head of the Laboratory. He does not speak to us willingly, but does not seem ill-disposed. He calls us 'Monsieur' which is ridiculous and disconcerting.

The temperature in the Laboratory is wonderful; the thermometer reads 65° F. We agree that they can make us wash the glass instruments, sweep the floor, carry the hydrogen flasks, anything so as to remain here, and so solve the problem of the winter for us. And then, on a second examination, even the problem of hunger should not be difficult to solve. Will they really want to search us at the exit every day? And even if they want to, will they do it every time that we ask to go to the latrine? Obviously not. And there is soap, petrol, alcohol here. I will stitch a secret pocket inside my jacket, and combine with the Englishman who works in the repairs-yard and trades in petrol. We will see how strict the supervision is: but by now I have spent a year in the Lager and I know that if one wants to steal and seriously sets one's mind to it, no supervision and no searchings can prevent it.

So it would seem that fate, by a new unsuspected path, has arranged that we three, the object of envy of all the ten thousand condemned, suffer neither hunger nor cold this winter. This means a strong probability of not falling seriously ill, of not being frozen, of overcoming the selections. In these conditions, those less expert than us about things in the Lager might even be tempted by the hope of survival and by the thought of liberty. But we are not, we know how these matters go; all this is the gift of fortune, to be enjoyed as intensely as possible and at once; for there is no certainty about tomorrow. At the first glass I break, the first error in measurement, the first time my attention is distracted, I will go back to waste away in the snow and the winds until I am ready for the Chimney. And besides, who knows what will happen when the Russians come?

Because the Russians will come. The ground trembles day and night under our feet; the muffled dull rumbling of their artillery now bursts uninterrupted into the novel silence of Buna. One breathes a tense air, an air of resolution. The Poles no longer work, the French again walk with their head high. The English wink at us and greet us on the aside with a 'V' sign; and not always on the aside.

But the Germans are deaf and blind, enclosed in an armour of obstinacy and of wilful ignorance. Once again they have named the date for the beginning of the production of synthetic rubber: it will be the first of February 1945. They construct shelters and trenches, they repair the damage, they build, they fight, they command, they organize and they kill. What else could they do? They are Germans. This way of behaviour is not meditated and deliberate, but follows from their nature and from the destiny they have chosen. They could not act differently: if you wound the body of a dying man, the wound will begin to heal, even if the whole body dies within a day.

Every morning now, when the squads are divided, the Kapo calls us three of the Laboratory before all the others, '*die drei Leute vom Labor*'. In camp, in the evenings and the mornings, nothing distinguishes me from the flock, but during the day, at work, I am under shelter and warm, and nobody beats me; I steal and sell soap and petrol without risk, and perhaps I will be given a coupon for a pair of leather shoes. Even more, can this be called work? To work is to push wagons, carry sleepers, break stones, dig earth, press one's bare hands against the iciness of the freezing iron. But I sit all day, I have a notebook and a pencil and they have even given me a book to refresh my memory about analytical methods. I have a drawer where I can put my beret and gloves, and when I want to go out I only have to tell Herr Stawinoga, who never says no and asks no questions if I delay; he has the air of suffering in his flesh for the ruin which surrounds him.

My comrades in the Kommando envy me, and they are right; should I not be contented? But in the morning, I hardly escape the raging wind and cross the doorstep of the Laboratory when I find at my side the comrade of all my peaceful moments, of Ka-Be, of the rest-Sundays – the pain of remembering, the old ferocious suffering of feeling myself a man again, which attacks me like a dog the moment my conscience comes out of the gloom. Then I take my pencil and notebook and write what I would never dare tell anyone.

Then there are the women. How long is it since I have seen a woman? In Buna we quite often met the Polish and Ukrainian women workers, in trousers and leather jackets, huge and violent like their men. They were sweaty and dishevelled in the summer, padded out with thick clothes in the winter and worked with spades and pickaxes. We did not feel ourselves next to women.

It is different here. Faced with the girls of the Laboratory, we three feel ourselves sink into the ground from shame and embarrassment. We know what we look like: we see each other and sometimes we happen to see our reflection in a clean window. We are ridiculous and repugnant. Our cranium is bald on Monday, and covered by a short brownish mould by Saturday. We have a swollen and yellow face, marked permanently by the cuts made by the hasty barber, and often by bruises and numbed sores; our neck is long and knobbly, like that of plucked chickens. Our clothes are incredibly dirty, stained by mud, grease and blood; Kandel's breeches only arrive half-way down his calves, showing his bony, hairy ankles; my jacket runs off my shoulders as if off a wooden clothes-hanger. We are full of fleas, and we often scratch ourselves shamelessly; we have to ask permission to go to the latrines with humiliating frequency. Our wooden shoes are insupportably noisy and are plastered with alternate layers of mud and regulation grease.

Besides which, we are accustomed to our smell, but the girls are not and never miss a chance of showing it. It is not the generic smell of the badly washed, but the smell of the Häftling, faint and sweetish, which greeted us at our arrival in the Lager and which tenaciously pervades the dormitories, kitchens, washrooms and closets of the Lager. One acquires it at once and one never loses it: 'so young and already stinking!' is our way of greeting new arrivals.

To us the girls seem outside this world. There are three young German girls, Fräulein Liczba, the Polish store-keeper, and Frau Meyer, the secretary. They have smooth, rosy skin, beautiful attractive clothes, clean and warm, blond hair, long and well-set; they speak with grace and self-possession, and instead of keeping the Laboratory clean and in order, as they ought to, they smoke in the corners, scandalously eat bread and jam, file their nails, break a lot of glass vessels and then try to put the blame on us; when they sweep, they sweep our feet. They never speak to us and turn up their noses when they see us shuffling across the Laboratory, squalid and filthy, awkward and insecure in our shoes. I once asked Fräulein Liczba for some information, and she did not reply but turned with an annoyed face to Stawinoga and spoke to him quickly. I did not understand the sentence, but I clearly grasped '*Stinkjude*' and my blood froze. Stawinoga told me that for anything to do with the work we should turn directly to him.

These girls sing, like girls sing in laboratories all over the world, and it makes us deeply unhappy. They talk among themselves: they talk about the rationing, about their fiancés, about their homes, about the approaching holidays ...

'Are you going home on Sunday? I am not, travelling is so uncomfortable!'

'I am going home for Christmas. Only two weeks and then it will be Christmas again; it hardly seems real, this year has gone by so quickly!'

... This year has gone by so quickly. This time last year I was a free man: an outlaw but free, I had a name and a family, I had an eager and restless mind, an agile and healthy body. I used to think of many, far-away things: of my work, of the end of the war, of good and evil, of the nature of things and of the laws which govern human actions; and also of the mountains, of singing and loving, of music, of poetry. I had an enormous, deep-rooted, foolish faith in the benevolence of fate; to kill and to die seemed extraneous literary things to me. My days were both cheerful and sad, but I regretted them equally, they were all full and positive; the future stood before me as a great treasure. Today the only thing left of the life of those days is what one needs to suffer hunger and cold; I am not even alive enough to know how to kill myself.

If I spoke German better I could try to explain all this to Frau Meyer; but she would certainly not understand, or if she was so good and intelligent as to understand, she would be unable to bear my proximity, and would flee from me, as one flees from contact with an incurable invalid, or from a man condemned to death. Or perhaps she would give me a coupon for a pint of civilian soup.

This year has gone by so quickly.

16

The Last One

By now Christmas is approaching. Alberto and I are walking side by side in the long grey file, bending forwards to resist the wind better. It is night and it is snowing; it is not easy to keep on one's feet, and even more difficult to keep up the pace in line; every now and again someone in front of us stumbles and falls in the black mud, and one has to be careful to avoid him and keep one's place in the column.

Since I started work in the Laboratory, Alberto and I work separately and we always have many things to tell each other on the return march. They are not usually things on a high level: about work, or our comrades, or the bread or the cold. But for a week now there had been something new: every evening Lorenzo brings us six or eight pints of soup from the Italian civilian workers. To solve the problem of transport, we had to procure what is called a '*menaschka*' here, that is, a zincpot, made to order, more like a bucket than a pot. Silberlust, the tin-smith, made it for us from two scraps of a gutter in exchange for three rations of bread; it was a splendid, sturdy, capacious pitcher, with the characteristic shape of a neolithic tool.

In the whole camp there are only a few Greeks who have a *menaschka* larger than ours. Besides the material advantages, it carries with it a perceptible improvement in our social standing. A *menaschka* like ours is a diploma of nobility, a heraldic emblem: Henri is becoming our friend and speaks to us on equal terms; L. has assumed a paternal and condescending air; as for Elias, he is perpetually at our side, and although he spies on us with tenacity to discover the secret of our '*organisacja*', he overwhelms us at the same time with incomprehensible declarations of solidarity and affection, and deafens us with a litany of portentous obscenities and oaths in Italian and French which he learnt somewhere and by which he obviously means to honour us.

As for the moral aspect of the new state of affairs, Alberto and I are forced to agree that there is nothing to be very proud of; but it is so easy to find justifications! Besides, the very fact that we have new things to talk about is no negligible gain.

We talk about our plan to buy a second *menaschka* to rotate with the first, so that to make only one expedition a day to the remote corner of the yard where Lorenzo is now working will be sufficient. We speak about Lorenzo and how to reward him; later, if we return, we will of course do everything we can for him; but of what use is it to talk about that? He knows as well as us that we can hardly hope to return. We ought to do something at once; we could try to have his shoes repaired at the cobbler's shop in our Lager where repairs are free (it seems a paradox, but officially everything was free in the extermination camps). Alberto will try: he is a friend of the head-cobbler, perhaps a few pints of soup will be enough.

We talk about three new exploits of ours, and we agree that for obvious reasons of professional secrecy it is inadvisable to talk about them at large: it is a pity, our personal prestige would be greatly increased.

As for the first, it is my brain-child. I knew that the *Blockältester* of Block 44 was short of brooms and I stole one in the yard; as far as this goes there is nothing extraordinary. The difficulty was to smuggle the broom into Lager on the return

march, and I solved it in what I believe to be a completely original way: I took apart the handle and the head of the broom,
sawing the former into two pieces and carrying the various parts
separately into camp (the two pieces of the handle tied to my
thighs inside my trousers) and then reconstructed the whole article. This required a piece of tin-plate, a hammer and nails to join
together the two pieces of wood. The whole business only took
four days.

Contrary to what I feared, the customer not only did not
devalue my broom but showed it as a curiosity to several of his
friends, who gave me a regular order for two other brooms 'of
the same model'.

But Alberto had other irons in the fire. In the first place he
had put the finishing touches to 'Operation File' and had
already carried it out successfully twice. Alberto goes to the
tool-store, asks for a file and chooses a largish one. The store-
keeper writes 'one file' next to his number and Alberto leaves.
He goes straight to a safe civilian (a gem of a rascal from Trieste,
as shrewd as they make them, who helps Alberto more for love
of the art than for interest or philanthropy), who has no difficulty in exchanging the large file on the open market for two
small ones of equal or lesser value. Alberto gives back 'one file'
to the store and sells the other.

And he has just crowned his achievements with his master-
piece, an audacious new combination of singular elegance. It
must first be stated that for some weeks now Alberto had been
entrusted with a special duty: at the yard in the morning he is
given a bucket with pliers, screwdrivers and several hundred cel-
luloid labels in different colours, which he has to fit on to
suitable clips in order to tag the numerous and lengthy pipes of
hot and cold water, steam, compressed air, gas, naphtha,
vacuum, etc. which run in all directions throughout the
Polymerization Department. It must also be stated (and here

there seems to be no connection: but does not ingenuity consist in the finding or creating of connections between apparently extraneous orders of ideas?) that for all us Häftlinge the shower constitutes a quite unpleasant occurrence for various reasons (the water is lacking and is cold or otherwise boiling, there is no changing-room, we have no towels nor soap, and during our enforced absence it is easy to be robbed). As the shower is obligatory, the *Blockältester* need a system of control enabling them to apply sanctions against whoever tries to evade it: usually a trusted member of the Block is placed at the door, and like Polyphemus touches everyone who comes out to feel if he is wet; if he is, he is given a ticket, if he is dry, he is given five blows from a truncheon. One can only claim one's bread the following morning by presenting the ticket.

Alberto's attention concentrated on the tickets. In general they are only wretched pieces of paper which are given back damp, crumpled and unrecognizable. Alberto knows his Germans and the *Blockältester* are all German, or German-trained: they love order, systems, bureaucracy; even more, although rough and irascible blockheads, they cherish an infantile delight in glittering, many-coloured objects.

Having played the theme, there follows the brilliant development. Alberto systematically withdrew a series of labels of the same colour; from each one he made three small disks (I organized the necessary instrument, a cork-borer, in the Laboratory): when two hundred disks were ready, enough for a Block, he went to the *Blockältester* and offered him his '*Spezialität*' at the mad price of ten rations of bread, payment by instalments. The customer accepted with enthusiasm, and Alberto now has at his disposal a formidable article in fashion which is guaranteed to be accepted in every hut, one colour per hut: for no *Blockältester* wants to be regarded as niggardly or reactionary. Even more important, he has no need to be afraid of rivals, as he alone has access to the primary material. Is it not well thought out?

We talk about these things, stumbling from one puddle to the other, between the black of the sky and the mud of the road. We talk and we talk. I carry the two empty bowls, Alberto the happy weight of the full *menaschka*. Once again the music from the band, the ceremony of *'Mützen ab'*, hats smartly off in front of the SS; once more *Arbeit Macht Frei*, and the announcement of the Kapo: *'Kommando 98, zwei and sechzig Häftlinge, Stärke stimmt'*, sixty-two prisoners, number correct. But the column has not broken up, they have made a march as far as the roll-call square. Is there to be a roll-call? It is not a roll-call. We have seen the crude glare of the searchlight and the well-known profile of the gallows.

For more than an hour the squads continued to return, with the hard clatter of their wooden shoes on the frozen snow. When all the Kommandos had returned, the band suddenly stopped and a raucous German voice ordered silence. Another German voice rose up in the sudden quiet, and spoke for a long time angrily into the dark and hostile air. Finally the condemned man was brought out into the blaze of the searchlight.

All this pomp and ruthless ceremony are not new to us. I have already watched thirteen hangings since I entered the camp; but on the other occasions they were for ordinary crimes, thefts from the kitchen, sabotage, attempts to escape. Today it is different.

Last month one of the crematoriums at Birkenau had been blown up. None of us knows (and perhaps no one will ever know) exactly how the exploit was carried out: there was talk of the *Sonderkommando*, the Special Kommando attached to the gas chambers and the ovens, which is itself periodically exterminated, and which is kept scrupulously segregated from the rest of the camp. The fact remains that a few hundred men at Birkenau, helpless and exhausted slaves like ourselves, had found in themselves the strength to act, to mature the fruits of their hatred.

The man who is to die in front of us today in some way took part in the revolt. They said he had contacts with the rebels of Birkenau, that he carried arms into our camp, that he was plotting a simultaneous mutiny among us. He is to die today before our very eyes: and perhaps the Germans do not understand that this solitary death, this man's death which has been reserved for him, will bring him glory, not infamy.

At the end of the German's speech, which nobody understood, the raucous voice of before again rose up: '*Habt ihr verstanden?*' Have you understood?

Who answered '*Jawohl*'? Everybody and nobody: it was as if our cursed resignation took body by itself, as if it turned into a collective voice above our heads. But everybody heard the cry of the doomed man, it pierced through the old thick barriers of inertia and submissiveness, it struck the living core of man in each of us:

'*Kameraden, ich bin der Letz!*' (Comrades, I am the last one!)

I wish I could say that from the midst of us, an abject flock, a voice rose, a murmur, a sign of assent. But nothing happened. We remained standing, bent and grey, our heads dropped, and we did not uncover our heads until the German ordered us to do so. The trapdoor opened, the body wriggled horribly; the band began playing again and we were once more lined up and filed past the quivering body of the dying man.

At the foot of the gallows, the SS watch us pass with indifferent eyes: their work is finished, and well finished. The Russians can come now: there are no longer any strong men among us, the last one is now hanging above our heads, and as for the others, a few halters had been enough. The Russians can come now: they will only find us, the slaves, the worn-out, worthy of the unarmed death which awaits us.

To destroy a man is difficult, almost as difficult as to create one: it has not been easy, nor quick, but you Germans have succeeded. Here we are, docile under your gaze; from our side you have nothing more to fear; no acts of violence, no words of defiance, not even a look of judgement.

Alberto and I went back to the hut, and we could not look each other in the face. That man must have been tough, he must have been made of another mettle than us if this condition of ours, which has broken us, could not bend him.

Because we also are broken, conquered: even if we know how to adapt ourselves, even if we have finally learnt how to find our food and to resist the fatigue and cold, even if we return home.

We lifted the *menaschka* on to the bunk and divided it, we satisfied the daily ragings of hunger, and now we are oppressed by shame.

17

The Story of Ten Days

Already for some months now the distant booming of the Russian guns had been heard at intervals when, on 11 January 1945, I fell ill of scarlet fever and was once more sent into Ka-Be. '*Infektionsabteilung*': it meant a small room, really quite clean, with ten bunks on two levels, a wardrobe, three stools and a closet seat with the pail for corporal needs. All in a space of three yards by five.

It was difficult to climb to the upper bunks as there was no ladder; so, when a patient got worse he was transferred to the lower bunks.

When I was admitted I was the thirteenth in the room. Four of the others – two French political prisoners and two young Hungarian Jews – had scarlet fever; there were three with diphtheria, two with typhus, while one suffered from a repellent facial erysipelas. The other two had more than one illness and were incredibly wasted away.

I had a high fever. I was lucky enough to have a bunk entirely to myself: I lay down with relief knowing that I had the right to forty days' isolation and therefore of rest, while I felt myself still sufficiently strong to fear neither the consequences of scarlet fever nor the selections.

Thanks to my by-now long experience of camp life I managed to bring with me all my personal belongings: a belt of interlaced electric wire, the knife-spoon, a needle with three needlefuls, five buttons and last of all eighteen flints which I had stolen from the laboratory. From each of these, shaping them patiently with a knife, it was possible to make three smaller flints, just the right gauge for a normal cigarette lighter. They were valued at six or seven rations of bread.

I enjoyed four peaceful days. Outside it was snowing and very cold, but the room was heated. I was given strong doses of sulpha drugs, I suffered from an intense feeling of sickness and was hardly able to eat; I did not want to talk.

The two Frenchmen with scarlet fever were quite pleasant. They were provincials from the Vosges who had entered the camp only a few days before with a large convoy of civilians swept up by the Germans in their retreat from Lorraine. The elder one was named Arthur, a peasant, small and thin. The other, his bed-companion, was Charles, a school teacher, thirty-two years old; instead of a shirt he had been given a summer vest, ridiculously short.

On the fifth day the barber came. He was a Greek from Salonica: he spoke only the beautiful Spanish of his people, but understood some words of all the languages spoken in the camp. He was called Askenazi and had been in the camp for almost three years. I do not know how he managed to get the post of *Frisör* of Ka-Be: he spoke neither German nor Polish, nor was he in fact excessively brutal. Before he entered, I heard him speaking excitedly for a long time in the corridor with one of the doctors, a compatriot of his. He seemed to have an unusual look on his face, but as the expressions of the Levantines are different from ours, I could not tell whether he was afraid or happy or merely upset. He knew me, or at least knew that I was Italian.

When it was my turn I climbed down laboriously from the bunk. I asked him in Italian if there was anything new: he stopped shaving me, winked in a serious and allusive manner, pointed to the window with his chin, and then made a sweeping gesture with his hand towards the west.

'*Morgen, alle Kamerad weg.*'

He looked at me for a moment with his eyes wide-open, as if waiting for a reaction, and then he added: '*todos, todos*' and returned to his work. He knew about my flints and shaved me with a certain gentleness.

The news excited no direct emotion in me. Already for many months I had no longer felt any pain, joy or fear, except in that detached and distant manner characteristic of the Lager, which might be described as conditional: if I still had my former sensitivity, I thought, this would be an extremely moving moment.

My ideas were perfectly clear; for a long time now Alberto and I had foreseen the dangers which would accompany the evacuation of the camp and the liberation. As for the rest, Askenazi's news was merely a confirmation of rumours which had been circulating for some days: that the Russians were at Częstochowa, sixty miles to the north; that they were at Zakopane, sixty miles to the south; that at Buna the Germans were already preparing the sabotage mines.

I looked at the faces of my comrades one by one: it was clearly useless to discuss it with any of them. They would have replied: 'Well?' and it would all have finished there. The French were different, they were still fresh.

'Did you hear?' I said to them. 'Tomorrow they are going to evacuate the camp.'

They overwhelmed me with questions. 'Where to? On foot? ... The ill ones as well? Those who cannot walk?' They knew that I was an old prisoner and that I understood German, and deduced that I knew much more about the matter than I wanted to admit.

I did not know anything more: I told them so but they continued to ask questions. How stupid of them! But of course, they had only been in the Lager for a week and had not yet learnt that one did not ask questions.

In the afternoon the Greek doctor came. He said that all patients able to walk would be given shoes and clothes and would leave the following day with the healthy ones on a twelve mile march. The others would remain in Ka-Be with assistants to be chosen from the patients least ill.

The doctor was unusually cheerful, he seemed drunk. I knew him: he was a cultured, intelligent man, egoistic and calculating. He added that everyone, without distinction, would receive a triple ration of bread, at which the patients visibly cheered up. We asked him what would happen to us. He replied that probably the Germans would leave us to our fate: no, he did not think that they would kill us. He made no effort to hide the fact that he thought otherwise. His very cheerfulness boded ill.

He was already equipped for the march. He had hardly gone out when the two Hungarian boys began to speak excitedly to each other. They were in an advanced state of convalescence but extremely wasted away. It was obvious that they were afraid to stay with the patients and were deciding to go with the healthy ones. It was not a question of reasoning: I would probably also have followed the instinct of the flock if I had not felt so weak; fear is supremely contagious, and its immediate reaction is to make one try to run away.

Outside the hut the camp sounded unusually excited. One of the two Hungarians got up, went out and returned half an hour later laden with filthy rags. He must have taken them from the store-house of clothes still to be disinfected. He and his comrade dressed feverishly, putting on rag after rag. One could see that they were in a hurry to have the matter over with before the fear itself made them hesitate. It was crazy of them to think of walking even for one hour, weak as they were, especially in the snow with those broken-down shoes found at the last moment. I tried to explain, but they looked at me without replying. Their eyes were like those of terrified cattle.

Just for a moment it flashed through my mind that they might even be right. They climbed awkwardly out of the window; I saw them, shapeless bundles, lurching into the night. They did not return; I learnt much later that, unable to continue, they had been killed by the SS a few hours after the beginning of the march.

It was obvious that I, too, needed a pair of shoes. But it took me an hour to overcome the feeling of sickness, fever and inertia. I found a pair in the corridor. (The healthy prisoners had ransacked the deposit of patients' shoes and had taken the best ones; those remaining, with split soles and unpaired, lay all over the place.) Just then I met Kosman, the Alsatian. As a civilian he had been a Reuters correspondent at Clermont-Ferrand; he also was excited and euphoric. He said: 'If you return before me, write to the mayor of Metz that I am about to come back.'

Kosman was notorious for his acquaintances among the Prominents, so his optimism seemed a good sign and I used it to justify my inertia to myself; I hid the shoes and returned to bed.

Late that night the Greek doctor returned with a rucksack on his shoulders and a woollen hood. He threw a French novel on my bed. 'Keep it, read it, Italian. You can give it back to me when we meet again.' Even today I hate him for those words. He knew that we were doomed.

And then finally Alberto came, defying the prohibition, to say good-bye to me from the window. We were inseparable: we were 'the two Italians' and foreigners even mistook our names. For six months we had shared a bunk and every scrap of food 'organized' in excess of the ration; but he had had scarlet fever as a child and I was unable to infect him. So he left and I remained. We said good-bye, not many words were needed, we had already discussed our affairs countless times. We did not think we would be separated for very long. He had found a sturdy pair of leather shoes in a reasonable condition: he was one of those fellows who immediately find everything they need.

He also was cheerful and confident, as were all those who were leaving. It was understandable: something great and new was about to happen; we could finally feel a force around us which was not of Germany; we could concretely feel the impending collapse of that hated world of ours. At any rate, the healthy ones who, despite all their tiredness and hunger, were still able to move, could feel this. But it is obvious that whoever is too weak, or naked or barefoot, thinks and feels in a different way, and what dominated our thoughts was the paralysing sensation of being totally helpless in the hands of fate.

All the healthy prisoners (except a few prudent ones who at the last moment undressed and hid themselves in the hospital beds) left during the night of 18 January 1945. They must have been about twenty thousand, coming from different camps. Almost in their entirety they vanished during the evacuation march: Alberto was among them. Perhaps someone will write their story one day.

So we remained in our bunks, alone with our illnesses, and with our inertia stronger than fear.

In the whole Ka-Be we numbered perhaps eight hundred. In our room there were eleven of us, each in his own bunk, except for Charles and Arthur who slept together. The rhythm of the great machine of the Lager was extinguished. For us began the ten days outside both world and time.

18 January. During the night of the evacuation the camp-kitchens continued to function, and on the following morning the last distribution of soup took place in the hospital. The central-heating plant had been abandoned; in the huts a little heat still lingered on, but hour by hour the temperature dropped and it was evident that we would soon suffer from the cold. Outside it must have been at least 5°F. below zero; most of the patients had only a shirt and some of them not even that.

Nobody knew what our fate would be. Some SS men had remained, some of the guard-towers were still occupied.

About midday an SS officer made a tour of the huts. He appointed a chief in each of them, selecting from among the remaining non-Jews, and ordered a list of the patients to be made at once, divided into Jews and non-Jews. The matter seemed clear. No one was surprised that the Germans preserved their national love of classification until the very end, nor did any Jew seriously expect to live until the following day.

The two Frenchmen had not understood and were frightened. I translated the speech of the SS man. I was annoyed that they should be afraid: they had not even experienced a month of the Lager, they hardly suffered from hunger yet, they were not even Jews, but they were afraid.

There was one more distribution of bread. I spent the afternoon reading the book left by the doctor: it was interesting and I can remember it with curious accuracy. I also made a visit to the neighbouring ward in search of blankets; many patients had been sent out from there and their blankets were free. I brought back some quite heavy ones.

When Arthur heard that they came from the dysentery ward, he looked disgusted: '*Y avait point besoin de la dire*'; in fact, they were polluted. But I thought that in any case, knowing what awaited us, we might as well sleep comfortably.

It was soon night but the electric light remained on. We saw with tranquil fear that an armed SS man stood at the corner of the hut. I had no desire to talk and was not afraid except in that external and conditional manner I have described. I continued reading until late.

There were no clocks, but it must have been about 11 p.m.

when all the lights went out, even those of the reflectors on the guard-towers. One could see the searchlight beams in the distance. A cluster of intense lights burst out in the sky, remaining immobile, crudely illuminating the earth. One could hear the roar of the aeroplanes.

Then the bombardment began. It was nothing new: I climbed down to the ground, put my bare feet into my shoes and waited.

It seemed far away, perhaps over Auschwitz.

But then there was a near explosion, and before one could think, a second and a third one, loud enough to burst one's eardrums. Windows were breaking, the hut shook, the spoon I had fixed in the wall fell down.

Then it seemed all over. Cagnolati, a young peasant also from the Vosges, had apparently never experienced a raid. He had jumped out naked from his bed and was concealed in a corner, screaming. After a few minutes it was obvious that the camp had been struck. Two huts were burning fiercely, another two had been pulverized, but they were all empty. Dozens of patients arrived, naked and wretched, from a hut threatened by fire: they asked for shelter. It was impossible to take them in. They insisted, begging and threatening in many languages. We had to barricade the door. They dragged themselves elsewhere, lit up by the flames, barefoot in the melting snow. Many trailed behind them streaming bandages. There seemed no danger to our hut, so long as the wind did not change.

The Germans were no longer there. The towers were empty.

Today I think that if for no other reason than that an Auschwitz existed, no one in our age should speak of Providence. But without doubt in that hour the memory of biblical salvations in times of extreme adversity passed like a wind through all our minds.

It was impossible to sleep; a window was broken and it was very cold. I was thinking that we would have to find a stove to set up and get some coal, wood and food. I knew that it was all essential, but without some help I would never have had the energy to carry it out. I spoke about it to the two Frenchmen.

19 January. The Frenchmen agreed. We got up at dawn, we three. I felt ill and helpless, I was cold and afraid.

The other patients looked at us with respectful curiosity: did we not know that patients were not allowed to leave Ka-Be? And if the Germans had not all left? But they said nothing, they were glad that someone was prepared to make the test.

The Frenchmen had no idea of the topography of the Lager, but Charles was courageous and robust, while Arthur was shrewd, with the practical commonsense of the peasant. We went out into the wind of a freezing day of fog, poorly wrapped up in blankets.

What we saw resembled nothing that I had ever seen or heard described.

The Lager, hardly dead, had already begun to decompose. No more water, or electricity, broken windows and doors slamming to in the wind, loose iron-sheets from the roofs screeching, ashes from the fire drifting high, afar. The work of the bombs had been completed by the work of man: ragged, decrepit, skeleton-like patients at all able to move dragged themselves everywhere on the frozen soil, like an invasion of worms. They had ransacked all the empty huts in search of food and wood; they had violated with senseless fury the grotesquely adorned rooms of the hated *Blockältester*, forbidden to the ordinary Häftlinge until the previous day; no longer in control of their own bowels, they had fouled everywhere, polluting the precious snow, the only source of water remaining in the whole camp.

Around the smoking ruins of the burnt huts, groups of patients lay stretched out on the ground, soaking up its last warmth. Others had found potatoes somewhere and were roasting them on the embers of the fire, glaring around with fierce eyes. A few had had the strength to light a real fire, and were melting snow in it in any handy receptacle.

We hurried to the kitchens as fast as we could; but the potatoes were almost finished. We filled two sacks and left them in Arthur's keeping. Among the ruins of the *Prominenzblock* Charles and I finally found what we were searching for: a heavy cast-iron stove, with the flue still usable. Charles hurried over with a wheelbarrow and we loaded it on; he then left me with the task of carrying it to the hut and ran back to the sacks. There he found Arthur unconscious from the cold. Charles picked up both sacks and carried them to safety, then he took care of his friend.

Meanwhile, staggering with difficulty, I was trying to manoeuvre the heavy wheelbarrow as best as possible. There was the roar of an engine and an SS man entered the camp on a motor-cycle. As always when I saw their hard faces I froze from terror and hatred. It was too late to disappear and I did not want to abandon the stove. The rules of the Lager stated that one must stand at attention with head uncovered. I had no hat and was encumbered by the blanket. I moved a few steps away from the wheelbarrow and made a sort of awkward bow. The German moved on without seeing me, turned behind a hut and left. Only later did I realize the danger I had run.

I finally reached the entrance of the hut and unloaded the stove into Charles's hands. I was completely breathless from the effort, large black spots danced before my eyes.

It was essential to get it working. We all three had our hands paralysed while the icy metal stuck to the skin of our fingers, but it was vitally urgent to set it up to warm ourselves and to boil the potatoes. We had found wood and coal as well as embers from the burnt huts.

When the broken window was repaired and the stove began to spread its heat, something seemed to relax in everyone, and at that moment Towarowski (a Franco-Pole of twenty-three, typhus) proposed to the others that each of them offer a slice of bread to us three who had been working. And so it was agreed.

Only a day before a similar event would have been inconceivable. The law of the Lager said: 'eat your own bread, and if you can, that of your neighbour', and left no room for gratitude. It really meant that the Lager was dead.

It was the first human gesture that occurred among us. I believe that that moment can be dated as the beginning of the change by which we who had not died slowly changed from Häftlinge to men again.

Arthur recovered quite well, but from then on always avoided exposing himself to the cold; he undertook the upkeep of the stove, the cooking of the potatoes, the cleaning of the room and the helping of the patients. Charles and I shared the various tasks outside. There was still an hour of light: an expedition yielded us a pint of spirits and a tin of yeast, thrown in the snow by someone; we made a distribution of potatoes and one spoonful of yeast per person. I thought vaguely that it might help against lack of vitamins.

Darkness fell; in the whole camp ours was the only room with a stove, of which we were very proud. Many invalids from other wards crowded around the door, but Charles's imposing stature held them back. Nobody, neither us nor them, thought that the inevitable promiscuity with our patients made it extremely dangerous to stay in our room, and to fall ill of diphtheria in those conditions was more surely fatal than jumping off a fourth floor.

I myself was aware of it, but I did not dwell long on the idea:

for too long I had been accustomed to think of death by illness as a possible event, and in that case unavoidable, and anyhow beyond any possible intervention on our part. And it did not even pass through my mind that I could have gone to another room in another hut with less danger of infection. The stove, our creation, was here, and spread a wonderful warmth; I had my bed here; and by now a tie united us, the eleven patients of the *lnfektionsabteilung*.

Very occasionally we heard the thundering of artillery, both near and far, and at intervals the crackling of automatic rifles. In the darkness, lighted only by the glow of the embers, Arthur and I sat smoking cigarettes made of herbs found in the kitchen, and spoke of many things, both past and future. In the middle of this endless plain, frozen and full of war, in the small dark room swarming with germs, we felt at peace with ourselves and with the world. We were broken by tiredness, but we seemed to have finally accomplished something useful – perhaps like God after the first day of creation.

20 January. The dawn came and it was my turn to light the stove. Besides a general feeling of weakness, the aching of my joints reminded me all the time that my scarlet fever was far from over. The thought of having to plunge into the freezing air to find a light in the other huts made me shudder with disgust. I remembered my flints: I sprinkled a piece of paper with spirits, and patiently scraped a small pile of black dust on top of it and then scraped the flint more vigorously with my knife. And finally, after a few sparks, the small pile caught fire and the small bluish flame of alcohol rose from the paper.

Arthur climbed down enthusiastically from his bed and heated three potatoes per person from those boiled the day before; after which, Charles and I, starved and shivering violently, left again to explore the decaying camp.

We had enough food (that is, potatoes) for two days only; as for water, we were forced to melt the snow, an awkward operation in the absence of large pots, which yielded a blackish, muddy liquid which had to be filtered.

The camp was silent. Other starving spectres like ourselves wandered around searching, unshaven, with hollow eyes, greyish skeleton bones in rags. Shaky on their legs, they entered and left the empty huts carrying the most varied of objects: axes, buckets, ladles, nails; anything might be of use, and those looking furthest ahead were already thinking of profitable commerce with the Poles of the surrounding countryside.

In the kitchen we found two of them squabbling over the last handfuls of putrid potatoes. They had seized each other by their rags, and were fighting with curiously slow and uncertain movements, cursing in Yiddish between their frozen lips.

In the courtyard of the storehouse there were two large piles of cabbages and turnips (those large, insipid turnips, the basis of our diet). They were so frozen that they could only be separated with a pickaxe. Charles and I took turns, using all our energy at each stroke, and we carried out about 100 pounds. There was still more: Charles discovered a packet of salt and ('*Une fameuse trouvaille!*') a can of water of perhaps twelve gallons, frozen in a block.

We loaded everything on to a small cart (formerly used to distribute the rations for the huts; there were a great number of them abandoned everywhere), and we turned back, toiling over the snow.

We contented ourselves that day with boiled potatoes again and slices of turnips roasted on the stove, but Arthur promised important innovations for the following day.

In the afternoon I went to the ex-surgery, searching for anything that might prove of use. I had been preceded: everything had been upset by inexpert looters. Not a bottle intact, the floor covered by a layer of rags, excrement and soiled bandages. A naked, contorted corpse. But there was something that had escaped my predecessors: a battery from a lorry. I touched the poles with a knife – a small spark. It was charged.

That evening we had light in our room.

Sitting in bed, I could see a large stretch of the road through the window. For the past three days the Wehrmacht in flight passed by in waves. Armoured cars, Tiger tanks camouflaged in white, Germans on horseback, Germans on bicycles, Germans on foot, armed and unarmed. During the night, long before the tanks came into sight, one could hear the grinding of their tracks.

Charles asked: '*Ça route encore?*'

'*Ça route toujours.*'

It seemed as if it would never end.

21 January. Instead it ended. On the dawn of the 21st we saw the plain deserted and lifeless, white as far as the eye could see, lying under the flight of the crows, deathly sad. I would almost have preferred to see something moving again. The Polish civilians had also disappeared, hiding who knows where. Even the wind seemed to have stopped. I wanted only one thing: to stay in bed under my blankets and abandon myself to a complete exhaustion of muscles, nerve and willpower; waiting as indifferently as a dead man for it to end or not to end.

But Charles had already lighted the stove, Charles, our active, trusting, alive friend, and he called me to work:

'*Vas-y, Primo, descends-toi de là-haut; it y a Jules à attraper par les oreilles . . .*'

'Jules' was the lavatory bucket, which every morning had to be taken by its handles, carried outside and emptied into the cesspool; this was the first task of the day, and if one remembers that it was impossible to wash one's hands and that three of us were ill with typhus, it can be understood that it was not a pleasant job.

We had to inaugurate the cabbages and turnips. While I went to search for wood and Charles collected the snow for water, Arthur mobilized the patients who could sit up to help with the peeling. Towarowski, Sertelet, Alcalai and Schenck answered the call.

Sertelet was also a peasant from the Vosges, twenty years old; he seemed in good shape, but day by day his voice assumed an ever more sinister nasal timbre, reminding us that diphtheria seldom relaxes its hold.

Alcalai was a Jewish glazier from Toulouse; he was quiet and discreet, and suffered from erysipelas on the face.

Schenck was a Slovak businessman, Jewish; a typhus patient, he had a formidable appetite. Likewise Towarowski, a Franco-Polish Jew, stupid and talkative, but useful to our community through his communicative optimism.

So while the patients scraped with their knives, each one seated on his bunk, Charles and I devoted ourselves to finding a suitable site for the kitchen operations. An indescribable filth had invaded every part of the camp. All the latrines were over-flowing, as naturally nobody cared any more about their upkeep, and those suffering from dysentery (more than a hun-dred) had fouled every corner of Ka-Be, filling all the buckets, all the bowls formerly used for the rations, all the pots. One could not move an inch without watching one's step; in the dark it was impossible to move around. Although suffering from the cold, which remained acute, we thought with horror of what would happen if it thawed: the diseases would spread irreparably, the stench would be suffocating, and even more, with the snow melted we would remain definitively without water.

After a long search we finally found a small area of floor not excessively soiled in a spot formerly used for the laundry. We lit a live fire to save time and complications and disinfected our hands, rubbing them with chloramine mixed with snow.

The news that a soup was being cooked spread rapidly through the crowd of the semi-living; a throng of starved faces gathered at the door. Charles, with ladle uplifted, made a short, vigorous speech, which although in French needed no translation.

The majority dispersed but one came forward. He was a Parisian, a high-class tailor (he said), suffering from tuberculosis. In exchange for two pints of soup he offered to make us clothes from the many blankets still to be found in the camp.

Maxime showed himself really able. The following day Charles and I were in possession of a jacket, trousers and gloves of a rough fabric of striking colours.

In the evening, after the first soup, distributed with enthusiasm and devoured with greed, the great silence of the plain was broken. From our bunks, too tired to be really worried, we listened to the bangs of mysterious artillery groups apparently hidden on all the points of the horizon, and to the whistle of the shells over our heads.

I was thinking life outside was beautiful and would be beautiful again, and that it would really be a pity to let ourselves be overcome now. I woke up the patients who were dozing and when I was sure that they were all listening I told them, first in French and then in my best German, that they must all begin to think of returning home now, and that as far as depended on us, certain things were to be done and others to be avoided. Each person should carefully look after his own bowl and spoon; no one should offer his own soup to others; no one should climb down from his bed except to go to the latrine; if anyone was in need of anything, he should only turn to us three. Arthur in particular was given the task of supervising the discipline and hygiene, and was to remember that it was better to leave bowls and spoons dirty rather than wash them with the danger of changing those of a diphtheria patient with those of someone suffering from typhus.

I had the impression that the patients by now were too indifferent to everything to pay attention to what I had said; but I had great faith in Arthur's diligence.

22 January. If it is courageous to face a grave danger with a light heart, Charles and I were courageous that morning. We extended our explorations to the SS camp, immediately outside the electric wire-fence.

The camp guards must have left in a great hurry. On the tables we found plates half-full of a by-now frozen soup which we devoured with an intense pleasure, mugs full of beer, transformed into a yellowish ice, a chess board with an unfinished game. In the dormitories, piles of valuable things.

We loaded ourselves with a bottle of vodka, various medicines, newspapers and magazines and four first-rate eiderdowns, one of which is today in my house in Turin. Cheerful and irresponsible, we carried the fruits of our expedition back to the dormitory, leaving them in Arthur's care. Only that evening did we learn what happened perhaps only half an hour later.

Some SS men, perhaps dispersed, but still armed, penetrated into the abandoned camp. They found that eighteen Frenchmen had settled in the dining-hall of the SS-Waffe. They killed them all methodically, with a shot in the nape of the neck, lining up their twisted bodies in the snow on the road; then they left. The eighteen corpses remained exposed until the arrival of the Russians; nobody had the strength to bury them.

But by now there were beds in all the huts occupied by corpses as rigid as wood, whom nobody troubled to remove.

The ground was too frozen to dig graves; many bodies were piled up in a trench, but already early on the heap showed out of the hole and was shamefully visible from our window.

Only a wooden wall separated us from the ward of the dysentery patients, where many were dying and many dead. The floor was covered by a layer of frozen excrement. None of the patients had strength enough to climb out of their blankets to search for food, and those who had done it at the beginning had not returned to help their comrades. In one bed, clasping each other to resist the cold better, there were two Italians. I often heard them talking, but as I spoke only French, for a long time they were not aware of my presence. That day they heard my name by chance, pronounced with an Italian accent by Charles, and from then on they never ceased groaning and imploring.

Naturally I would have liked to have helped them, given the means and the strength, if for no other reason than to stop their crying. In the evening when all the work was finished, conquering my tiredness and disgust, I dragged myself gropingly along the dark, filthy corridor to their ward with a bowl of water and the remainder of our day's soup. The result was that from then on, through the thin wall, the whole diarrhoea ward shouted my name day and night with the accents of all the languages of Europe, accompanied by incomprehensible prayers, without my being able to do anything about it. I felt like crying, I could have cursed them.

The night held ugly surprises.

Lakmaker, in the bunk under mine, was a poor wreck of a man. He was (or had been) a Dutch Jew, seventeen years old, tall, thin and gentle. He had been in bed for three months; I have no idea how he had managed to survive the selections. He had had typhus and scarlet fever successively; at the same time a serious cardiac illness had shown itself, while he was smothered with bedsores, so much so that by now he could only lie on his stomach. Despite all this, he had a ferocious appetite. He only spoke Dutch, and none of us could understand him.

Perhaps the cause of it all was the cabbage and turnip soup, of which Lakmaker had wanted two helpings. In the middle of the night he groaned and then threw himself from his bed. He tried to reach the latrine, but was too weak and fell to the ground, crying and shouting loudly.

Charles lit the lamp (the battery showed itself providential) and we were able to ascertain the gravity of the incident. The boy's bed and the floor were filthy. The smell in the small area was rapidly becoming insupportable. We had but a minimum supply of water and neither blankets nor straw mattresses to spare. And the poor wretch, suffering from typhus, formed a terrible source of infection, while he could certainly not be left all night to groan and shiver in the cold in the middle of the filth.

Charles climbed down from his bed and dressed in silence. While I held the lamp, he cut all the dirty patches from the straw mattress and the blankets with a knife. He lifted Lakmaker from the ground with the tenderness of a mother, cleaned him as best as possible with straw taken from the mattress and lifted him into the remade bed in the only position in which the unfortunate fellow could lie. He scraped the floor with a scrap of tinplate, diluted a little chloramine and finally spread disinfectant over everything, including himself.

I judged his self-sacrifice by the tiredness which I would have had to overcome in myself to do what he had done.

23 January. Our potatoes were finished. For days past the rumour had circulated through all the huts that an enormous trench of potatoes lay somewhere outside the barbed wire, not far from the camp.

Some unknown pioneer must have carried out patient explorations, or else someone knew the spot with precision. In fact, by the morning of the 23rd a section of the barbed wire had been beaten down and a double file of wretches went in and out through the opening.

Charles and I left, into the wind of the leaden plain. We were beyond the broken barrier.

'*Dis donc, Primo, on est dehors!*'

It was exactly like that; for the first time since the day of my arrest I found myself free, without armed guards, without wire-fences between myself and home.

Perhaps 400 yards from the camp lay the potatoes – a treasure. Two extremely long ditches, full of potatoes and covered by alternate layers of soil and straw to protect them from the cold. Nobody would die of hunger any more.

But to extract them was by no means easy work. The cold had made the surface of the earth as hard as iron. By strenuous work with a pickaxe it was possible to break the crust and lay bare the deposit; but the majority preferred to work the holes abandoned by others and continue to deepen them, passing the potatoes to their companions standing outside.

An old Hungarian had been surprised there by death. He lay there like hunger personified: head and shoulders under a pile of earth, belly in the snow, hands stretched out towards the potatoes. Someone came later and moved the body about a yard, so freeing the hole.

From then on our food improved. Besides boiled potatoes and potato soup, we offered our patients potato pancakes, on Arthur's recipe: rub together raw potatoes with boiled, soft ones, and roast the mixture on a red-hot iron-plate. They tasted of soot.

But Sertelet, steadily getting worse, was unable to enjoy them. Besides speaking with an ever more nasal tone, that day he was unable to force down any food; something had closed up in his throat, every mouthful threatened to suffocate him.

I went to look for a Hungarian doctor left as a patient in the hut in front. When he heard the word diphtheria he started back and ordered me to leave.

For pure propaganda purposes I gave everyone nasal drops of camphorated oil. I assured Sertelet that they would help him; I even tried to convince myself.

24 January. Liberty. The breach in the barbed wire gave us a concrete image of it. To anyone who stopped to think, it signified no more Germans, no more selections, no work, no blows, no roll-calls, and perhaps, later, the return.

But we had to make an effort to convince ourselves of it, and no one had time to enjoy the thought. All around lay destruction and death.

The pile of corpses in front of our window had by now overflowed out of the ditch. Despite the potatoes everyone was extremely weak: not a patient in the camp improved, while many fell ill with pneumonia and diarrhoea; those who were unable to move themselves, or lacked the energy to do so, lay lethargic in their bunks, benumbed by the cold, and nobody realized when they died.

The others were all incredibly tired: after months and years of the Lager it needs more than potatoes to give back strength to a man. Charles and I, as soon as we had dragged the fifty pints of daily soup from the laundry to our room, threw ourselves panting on the bunks, while Arthur, with that domesticated air of his, diligently divided the food, taking care to save the three rations of '*rabiot pour les travailleurs*' and a little of the sediment '*pour les italiens d'à côté*'.

In the second room of the contagious ward, likewise adjoining ours and occupied mainly by tuberculosis patients, the situation was quite different. All those who were able to had gone to other huts. Their weakest comrades and those who were most seriously ill died one by one in solitude.

I went in there one morning to try and borrow a needle. A patient was wheezing in one of the upper bunks. He heard me, struggled to sit up, then fell dangling, head downwards over the edge towards me, with his chest and arms stiff and his eyes white. The man in the bunk below automatically stretched up his arms to support the body and then realized that he was dead. He slowly withdrew from under the weight and the body slid to the ground where it remained. Nobody knew his name.

But in hut 14 something new had happened. It was occupied by patients recovering from operations, some of them quite healthy. They organized an expedition to the English prisoner-of-war camp, which it was assumed had been evacuated. It proved a fruitful expedition. They returned dressed in khaki with a cart full of wonders never seen before: margarine, custard powders, lard, soya-bean flour, whisky.

That evening there was singing in hut 14.

None of us felt strong enough to walk the one mile to the English camp and return with a load. But indirectly the fortunate expedition proved of advantage to many. The unequal division of goods caused a reflourishing of industry and commerce. Our room, with its lethal atmosphere, transformed itself into a factory of candles poured into cardboard moulds, with wicks soaked in boracic acid. The riches of hut 14 absorbed our entire production, paying us in lard and flour.

I myself had found the block of beeswax in the *Elektromagazin*; I remember the expression of disappointment of those who saw me carry it away and the dialogue that followed:

'What do you want to do with that?'

It was inadvisable to reveal a shop secret; I heard myself

replying with the words I had often heard spoken by the old ones of the camp, expressing their favourite boast – of being hard-boiled, 'old hands', who always knew how to find their feet: '*Ich verstehe verschiedene Sachen*.' I know how to do many things ...

25 January. It was Sómogyi's turn. He was a Hungarian chemist, about fifty years old, thin, tall and taciturn. Like the Dutchman he suffered from typhus and scarlet fever. He had not spoken for perhaps five days; that day he opened his mouth and said in a firm voice:

'I have a ration of bread under the sack. Divide it among you three. I shall not be eating any more.'

We could not find anything to say, but for the time being we did not touch the bread. Half his face had swollen. As long as he retained consciousness he remained closed in a harsh silence.

But in the evening and for the whole of the night and for two days without interruption the silence was broken by his delirium. Following a last interminable dream of acceptance and slavery he began to murmur: '*Jawohl*' with every breath, regularly and continuously like a machine, '*Jawohl*', at every collapsing of his wretched frame, thousands of times, enough to make one want to shake him, to suffocate him, at least to make him change the word.

I never understood so clearly as at that moment how laborious is the death of a man.

Outside the great silence continued. The number of ravens had increased considerably and everybody knew why. Only at distant intervals did the dialogue of the artillery wake up.

We all said to each other that the Russians would arrive soon, at once; we all proclaimed it, we were all sure of it, but at bottom nobody believed it. Because one loses the habit of hoping in the Lager, and even of believing in one's own reason.

In the Lager it is useless to think, because events happen for the most part in an unforeseeable manner; and it is harmful, because it keeps alive a sensitivity which is a source of pain, and which some providential natural law dulls when suffering passes a certain limit.

Like joy, fear and pain itself, even expectancy can be tiring. Having reached 25 January, with all relations broken already for eight days with that ferocious world that still remained a world, most of us were too exhausted even to wait.

In the evening, around the stove, Charles, Arthur and I felt ourselves become men once again. We could speak of everything. I grew enthusiastic at Arthur's account of how one passed the Sunday at Provenchères in the Vosges, and Charles almost cried when I told him the story of the armistice in Italy, of the turbid and desperate beginning of the Partisan resistance, of the man who betrayed us and of our capture in the mountains.

In the darkness, behind and above us, the eight invalids did not lose a syllable, even those who did not understand French. Only Sómogyi implacably confirmed his dedication to death.

26 January. We lay in a world of death and phantoms. The last trace of civilization had vanished around and inside us. The work of bestial degradation, begun by the victorious Germans, had been carried to its conclusion by the Germans in defeat.

It is man who kills, man who creates or suffers injustice; it is no longer man who, having lost all restraint, shares his bed with a corpse. Whoever waits for his neighbour to die in order to take his piece of bread is, albeit guiltless, further from the model of thinking man than the most primitive pigmy or the most vicious sadist.

Part of our existence lies in the feelings of those near to us. This is why the experience of someone who has lived for days during which man was merely a thing in the eyes of man is non-human. We three were for the most part immune from it, and we owe each other mutual gratitude. This is why my friendship with Charles will prove lasting.

But thousands of feet above us, in the gaps in the grey clouds, the complicated miracles of aerial duels began. Above us, bare, helpless and unarmed, men of our time sought reciprocal death with the most refined of instruments. A movement of a finger could cause the destruction of the entire camp, could annihilate thousands of men; while the sum total of all our efforts and exertions would not be sufficient to prolong by one minute the life of even one of us.

The saraband stopped at night and the room was once again filled with Sómogyi's monologue.

In full darkness I found myself suddenly awake. '*L'pauv'-vieux*' was silent; he had finished. With the last gasp of life, he had thrown himself to the ground: I heard the thud of his knees, of his hips, of his shoulders, of his head.

'*La mort l'a chasse de son lit*,' Arthur defined it.

We certainly could not carry him out during the night. There was nothing for it but to go back to sleep again.

27 January. Dawn. On the floor, the shameful wreck of skin and bones, the Sómogyi thing.

There are more urgent tasks: we cannot wash ourselves, so that we dare not touch him until we have cooked and eaten. And besides: '... *rien de si dégoûtant que les débordements*,' said Charles justly; the latrine had to be emptied. The living are more demanding; the dead can wait. We began to work as on every day.

The Russians arrived while Charles and I were carrying Sómogyi a little distance outside. He was very light. We over-turned the stretcher on the grey snow.

Charles took off his beret. I regretted not having a beret.

Of the eleven of the *Infektionsabteilung* Sómogyi was the only one to die in the ten days. Sertelet, Cagnolati, Towarowski, Lakmaker and Dorget (I have not spoken of him so far; he was a French industrialist who, after an operation for peritonitis, fell ill of nasal diphtheria) died some weeks later in the temporary Russian hospital of Auschwitz. In April, at Katowice, I met Schenck and Alcalai in good health. Arthur has reached his family happily and Charles has taken up his teacher's profession again; we have exchanged long letters and I hope to see him again one day.

THE TRUCE

A SURVIVOR'S JOURNEY HOME
FROM AUSCHWITZ

Dreams used to come in the brutal nights,
Dreams crowding and violent
Dreamt with body and soul,
Of going home, of eating, of telling our story.
Until, quickly and quietly, came
The dawn reveille:

> *Wstawàch*.
> And the heart cracked in the breast.

Now we have found our home again,
Our hunger is quenched,
All the stories have been told.
It is time. Soon we shall hear again
The alien command:

> *Wstawàch*.
> 11 January 1946

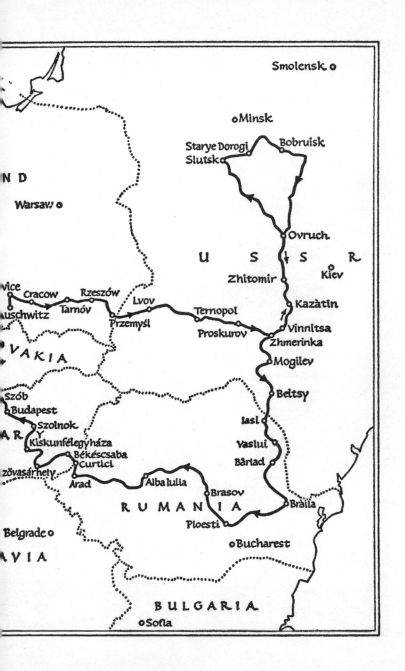

Smolensk o

oMinsk

Starye Dorogi   Bobruisk
Slutsk o

N D

Warsaw o

Ovruch

U   S   S   R

Zhitomir o   Kiev

vice Cracow   Rzeszów
           Tarnóv   Lvov   Kazàtin
uschwitz   Ternopol
         Przemyśl   Proskurov   Vinnitsa

Zhmerinka

VAKIA   Mogilev

Szób   Beltsy
Budapest
  Szolnok
R   Y   Iasi o
Kiskunfélegyháza
    Békéscsaba   Vaslui o
zövasárhely Curtici   Bârlad
   Arad   Alba Iulia
              Brasov
R U M A N I A   Brăila
          Ploesti o
Belgrade o
        o Bucharest
VIA

BULGARIA
    o Sofia

1

The Thaw

In the first days of January 1945, hard pressed by the Red Army, the Germans hastily evacuated the Silesian mining region. But whereas elsewhere, in analogous conditions, they had not hesitated to destroy the Lagers and their inhabitants by fire or arms, they acted differently in the district of Auschwitz: superior orders had been received (given personally, it would seem, by Hitler) to recover at all costs every man fit for work. Thus all healthy prisoners were evacuated, in frightful conditions, in the direction of Buchenwald and Mauthausen, while the sick were abandoned to their fate. One can legitimately deduce from the evidence that originally the Germans did not intend to leave one man alive in the concentration camps; but a fierce night air raid and the rapidity of the Russian advance induced them to change their minds and flee, leaving their task unfinished.

In the sick bay of the Lager at Buna-Monowitz eight hundred of us remained. Of these about five hundred died from illness, cold and hunger before the Russians arrived, and another two hundred succumbed in the following days, despite the Russians' aid.

The first Russian patrol came in sight of the camp about midday on 27 January 1945. Charles and I were the first to see them: we were carrying Sómogyi's body to the common grave, the first of our room mates to die. We tipped the stretcher on to the defiled snow, as the pit was now full, and no other grave was at hand: Charles took off his beret as a salute to both the living and the dead.

They were four young soldiers on horseback, who advanced along the road that marked the limits of the camp, cautiously holding their sten-guns. When they reached the barbed wire, they stopped to look, exchanging a few timid words, and throwing strangely embarrassed glances at the sprawling bodies, at the battered huts and at us few still alive.

To us they seemed wonderfully concrete and real, perched on their enormous horses, between the grey of the snow and the grey of the sky, immobile beneath the gusts of damp wind which threatened a thaw.

It seemed to us, and so it was, that the nothing full of death in which we had wandered like spent stars for ten days had found its own solid centre, a nucleus of condensation; four men, armed, but not against us: four messengers of peace, with rough and boyish faces beneath their heavy fur hats.

They did not greet us, nor did they smile; they seemed oppressed not only by compassion but by a confused restraint, which sealed their lips and bound their eyes to the funereal scene. It was that shame we knew so well, the shame that drowned us after the selections, and every time we had to watch, or submit to, some outrage: the shame the Germans did not know, that the just man experiences at another man's crime; the feeling of guilt that such a crime should exist, that it should have been introduced irrevocably into the world of things that exist, and that his will for good should have proved too weak or null, and should not have availed in defence.

So for us even the hour of liberty rang out grave and muffled, and filled our souls with joy and yet with a painful sense of pudency, so that we should have liked to wash our consciences and our memories clean from the foulness that lay upon them;

and also with anguish, because we felt that this should never happen, that now nothing could ever happen good and pure enough to rub out our past, and that the scars of the outrage would remain within us for ever, and in the memories of those who saw it, and in the places where it occurred and in the stories that we should tell of it. Because, and this is the awful privilege of our generation and of my people, no one better than us has ever been able to grasp the incurable nature of the offence, that spreads like a contagion. It is foolish to think that human justice can eradicate it. It is an inexhaustible fount of evil; it breaks the body and the spirit of the submerged, it stifles them and renders them abject; it returns as ignominy upon the oppressors, it perpetuates itself as hatred among the survivors, and swarms around in a thousand ways, against the very will of all, as a thirst for revenge, as a moral capitulation, as denial, as weariness, as renunciation.

These things, at that time blurred, and felt by most as no more than an unexpected attack of mortal fatigue, accompanied the joy of liberation for us. This is why few among us ran to greet our saviours, few fell in prayer. Charles and I remained standing beside the pit overflowing with discoloured limbs, while others knocked down the barbed wire; then we returned with the empty stretcher to break the news to our companions.

For the rest of the day nothing happened; this did not surprise us, and we had long been accustomed to it. In our room the dead Sómogyi's bunk was immediately occupied by old Thylle, to the visible disgust of my two French companions.

Thylle, so far as I then knew, was a 'red triangle', a German political prisoner, and one of the old inhabitants of the Lager; as such, he had belonged by right to the aristocracy of the camp, he had not worked manually (at least in the last years), and he had received food and clothes from home. For these reasons the

German 'politicals' were rarely inmates of the sick bay, where however they enjoyed various privileges: the first of them that of escaping from the selections. As Thylle was the only political prisoner at the moment of liberation, the SS in flight had appointed him head of Block 20, where, besides our room of highly infectious patients, there were also the TB and dysentery wards.

Being a German, he had taken this precarious appointment very seriously. In the ten days between the departure of the SS and the arrival of the Russians, while everyone was fighting his last battle against hunger, cold and disease, Thylle had carried out diligent inspections of his new fief, checking the state of the floors and the bowls and the number of blankets (one for each inmate, alive or dead). On one of his visits to our room he had even praised Arthur for the order and cleanliness he kept; Arthur, who did not understand German, and even less the Saxon dialect of Thylle, had replied *'vieux dégoûtant'* and *'putain de boche'*; nevertheless, Thylle, from that day on, in open abuse of his authority, had acquired the habit of coming into our room every evening to use the comfortable latrine-bucket installed there, the only one regularly cleaned in the whole camp, and the only one near a stove.

Thus, up to that day old Thylle had been a foreigner to me, and therefore an enemy – a powerful person, moreover, and therefore a dangerous enemy. For people like myself, that is to say for the majority of the Lager, there were no other distinctions: during the whole interminable year spent in the Lager, I had never had either the curiosity or the occasion to investigate the complex structure of the hierarchy of the camp. The gloomy edifice of vicious powers lay wholly above us, and our looks were turned to the ground. Yet this Thylle, an old combatant hardened by a hundred struggles both for and within his party, and petrified by ten years of ferocious and ambiguous life within

the Lager, was the companion and confidant of my first night of
liberty.

For the whole day we had been too busy to remark upon the
event, which we still felt marked the crucial point of our entire
existence; and perhaps, unconsciously, we had sought something
to do precisely to avoid spare time, because face to face with
liberty we felt ourselves lost, emptied, atrophied, unfit for our
part.

But night came, and our sick companions fell asleep. Charles
and Arthur also dropped into the sleep of innocence, because
they had been in the Lager for one month only, and had not yet
absorbed its poison. I alone, although exhausted, could not fall
asleep because of my very tiredness and illness. All my limbs
ached, my blood throbbed violently in my head and I felt myself
overwhelmed by fever. But it was not this alone; in the very hour
in which every threat seemed to vanish, in which a hope of a
return to life ceased to be crazy, I was overcome – as if a dyke
had crumbled – by a new and greater pain, previously buried
and relegated to the margins of my consciousness by other more
immediate pains: the pain of exile, of my distant home, of lone-
liness, of friends lost, of youth lost and of the host of corpses all
around.

In my year at Buna I had seen four-fifths of my companions
disappear, but I had never faced the concrete presence, the
blockade, of death, its sordid breath a step away, outside the
window, in the bunk next to me, in my own veins. Thus I lay in
a sickly state of semi-consciousness, full of gloomy thoughts.

But very soon I realized that someone else was awake. The
heavy breathing of the sleepers was drowned at intervals by a
hoarse and irregular panting, interrupted by coughs and groans
and stifled sighs. Thylle was weeping, with the difficult and
shameless tears of an old man, as intolerable as senile nudity.
Perhaps he saw me move in the dark; and the solitude, which up

to that day we had both sought for different reasons, must have weighed upon him as much as upon me, because in the middle of the night he asked me 'are you awake?' and, not waiting for a reply, toiled up to my bunk, and, without asking permission, sat beside me.

It was not easy to understand each other; not only because of linguistic difficulties, but also because the thoughts that weighed upon us in that long night were immense, marvellous and terrible, but above all confused. I told him that I was suffering from nostalgia; and he exclaimed, after he had stopped crying, 'ten years, ten years'; and after ten years of silence, in a low stridulous voice, grotesque and solemn at the same time, he began to sing the *Internationale*, leaving me perturbed, diffident and moved.

The morning brought us the first signs of liberty. Some twenty Polish men and women, clearly summoned by the Russians, arrived and with little enthusiasm began to fumble around, attempting to bring some order and cleanliness into the huts and to clear away the bodies. About midday a frightened child appeared, dragging a cow by the halter; he made us understand that it was for us, that the Russians had sent it, then he abandoned the beast and fled like a bolt. I don't know how, but within minutes the poor animal was slaughtered, gutted and quartered and its remains distributed to all the corners of the camp where survivors nestled.

During the following days, we saw more Polish girls wander around the camp, pale with disgust and pity: they cleaned the patients and tended to their sores as best they could. They also lit an enormous fire in the middle of the camp, which they fed with planks from broken-down huts, and on which they cooked soup in whatever pots came to hand. Finally, on the third day, we saw a cart enter the camp led joyfully by Yankel, a Häftling*: he was a young Russian Jew, perhaps the only Russian among the survivors, and as such he naturally found himself acting as interpreter and liaison officer with the Soviet HQ. Between resounding cracks of his whip, he announced that he had the task of carrying all the survivors, in small groups of thirty or forty a day, beginning with the most seriously ill, to the central Lager of Auschwitz, now transformed into a gigantic lazaret.

In the meantime, the thaw we had been fearing for so many days had started, and as the snow slowly disappeared, the camp began to change into a squalid bog. The bodies and the filth made the misty, muggy air impossible to breathe. Nor had death ceased to take its toll: the sick died in their cold bunks by the dozen, and here and there along the muddy roads, as if suddenly struck down, died the greediest of the survivors, those who had followed blindly the imperious command of our age-old hunger and had stuffed themselves with the rations of meat that the Russians, still engaged in fighting, sent irregularly to the camp: sometimes little, sometimes nothing, sometimes in crazy abundance.

But I was aware of what was going on around me in only a disconnected and hazy manner. It seemed as if the weariness and the illness, like ferocious and cowardly beasts, had waited in ambush for the moment when I dismantled my defences, in order to attack me from behind. I lay in a feverish torpor, semi-conscious, tended fraternally by Charles, and tormented by thirst and acute pains in my joints. There were no doctors or drugs. I also had a sore throat, and half my face had swollen; my skin had become red and rough and hurt me like a burn; perhaps I was suffering from more than one illness at the same time. When it was my turn to climb on to Yankel's cart, I was no longer able to stand on my feet.

* Prisoner.

I was hoisted on to the cart by Charles and Arthur, together with a load of dying men, from whom I did not feel very different. It was drizzling, and the sky was low and gloomy. While the slow steps of Yankel's horses drew me towards remote liberty, for the last time there filed before my eyes the huts where I had suffered and matured, the roll-call square where the gallows and the gigantic Christmas tree still towered side by side, and the gate to slavery, on which one could still read the three, now hollow, words of derision: '*Arbeit Macht Frei*', 'Work Gives Freedom'.

2

The Main Camp

At Buna we did not know much of 'the main camp', of Ausch-witz proper: the Häftlinge transferred from one camp to another were few, hardly talkative (no Häftling ever was), and not easily believed.

When Yankel's cart crossed the famous threshold, we were amazed. Buna-Monowitz, with its twelve thousand inhabitants, was a village in comparison: what we were entering now was a boundless metropolis. There were no one-storey 'Blocks', but innumerable gloomy, square, grey stone edifices, three floors high, all identical; between them ran paved roads, straight and at right angles, as far as the eye could see. Everything was deserted, silent, flattened by the heavy sky, full of mud and rain and abandonment.

Here too, as at every turn of our long itinerary, we were sur-prised to be greeted with a bath, when we had need of so many other things. But this was no bath of humiliation, no grotesque-devilish-sacral bath, no black-mass bath like the first one which had marked our descent into the concentration-camp universe, nor was it a functional, antiseptic, highly automatized bath, like that of our passage into American hands many months later: it was a bath in the Russian manner, to human measure, extem-poraneous and crude.

I am not questioning that a bath was opportune for us in our condition: in fact it was necessary, and not unwelcome. But in that bath, and at each of those three memorable christenings, it was easy to perceive behind the concrete and literal aspect a great symbolic shadow, the unconscious desire of the new authorities, who absorbed us in turn within their own sphere, to strip us of the vestiges of our former life, to make of us new men consistent with their own models, to impose their brand upon us.

The robust arms of two Soviet nurses lifted us down from the cart: '*Po malu!*' ('gently, gently!'); these were the first Russian words I heard. They were two energetic and experienced girls. They led us to one of the installations of the Lager, which had been summarily restored, undressed us, made us lie down on the wooden laths that covered the floor, and with tender hands, but without too much regard, soaped, rubbed, massaged and dried us from head to foot

The operation went smoothly and quickly for all of us, except for some moralistic-jacobin protests from Arthur, who proclaimed himself *libre citoyen*, and in whose subconscious the contact of those feminine hands upon his bare skin conflicted with ancestral taboos. But a serious obstacle intervened when it came to the turn of the last of our group.

None of us knew who he was, because he was in no condition to speak. He was a shadow, a bald little figure, twisted like a root, skeleton-like, knotted up by a horrible contraction of all his muscles; they had lifted him out of the cart bodily, like an inanimate block, and now he lay on the ground on his side, curled up and stiff, in a desperate position of defence, with his knees pressed up against his forehead, his elbows squeezed against his sides, and his hands like wedges, with the fingers pressing against his shoulders. The Russian sisters, perplexed, sought in vain to stretch him on his back, at which he let out shrill mouse-like squeaks: it was in any case a useless effort; his limbs yielded elastically under pressure, but as soon as they were released, they shot back to their initial position. Then the nurses came to a decision and carried him under the shower as he was; and because they had definite orders, they washed him as best they could, forcing the sponge and soap into the entangled knots of his body; finally, they rinsed him conscientiously, throwing a couple of buckets of tepid water over him.

Charles and I, naked and steaming, watched the scene with compassion and horror. When one of the arms was stretched out, we saw the tattooed number for a moment: he was a 200,000, one from the Vosges: *'Bon dieu, c'est un français!'* exclaimed Charles, and turned in silence towards the wall.

We were given a shirt and pants, and led to the Russian barber, so that our heads might be shaved for the last time in our careers. The barber was a dark-skinned giant, with wild and delirious eyes: he practised his art with uncouth violence, and for reasons unknown to me carried a sten-gun slung on his shoulder. *'Italiano Mussolini,'* he said to me grimly; and to the Frenchmen *'Fransé Laval'*; from which one sees how little general ideas help the understanding of individual cases.

Here we split up: Charles and Arthur, cured and relatively healthy, rejoined the French group and disappeared from my horizon. I, being ill, was taken to the infirmary, given a summary medical check and urgently relegated to a new 'Infectious Ward'.

The infirmary was such both by design, and also because it was indeed overflowing with invalids (in fact the Germans in flight had left only the most seriously ill at Monowitz, Auschwitz, and Birkenau, and these had all been collected together by the Russians in the Main Camp); it was not, nor could it be, a place for treatment, because the doctors (mostly ill themselves) numbered only a few dozen, drugs and sanitary equipment were wholly lacking, while at least three-quarters of the five thousand camp-inmates were in need of treatment.

The place to which I was consigned was a huge and gloomy dormitory, filled to the ceiling with suffering and moaning. For perhaps eight hundred patients there was only one doctor on duty and no nurse: the patients had themselves to provide for their most urgent needs, and for those of their sicker companions. I spent only one night there, which I still remember as a nightmare; in the morning the corpses in the bunks or sprawling on the floor could be counted by the dozen.

The following day I was transferred to a smaller ward with only twenty bunks; I lay in one of these for three or four days, prostrated by a high fever, conscious only intermittently, incapable of eating, and tormented by thirst.

On the fifth day the fever had disappeared. I felt as light as a cloud, famished and frozen, but my head was clear, my eyes and ears felt as if purified by the enforced vacation, and I was able to re-establish contact with the world.

In the course of those few days a striking change had occurred around me. It was the last great sweep of the scythe, the closing of accounts; the dying were dead, in all the others life was beginning to flow again tumultuously. Outside the windows, despite the steady snowfall, the mournful roads of the camp were no longer deserted, but teemed with a brisk, confused and noisy ferment, which seemed to be an end in itself. Cheerful or wrathful calls, shouts and songs rang out till late at night. All the same, my attention, and that of my neighbours in the near-by beds, rarely managed to escape from the obsessive presence, the mortal power of affirmation of the smallest and most harmless among us, of the most innocent, of a child, of Hurbinek.

Hurbinek was a nobody, a child of death, a child of Auschwitz. He looked about three years old, no one knew anything of him, he could not speak and he had no name; that curious name, Hurbinek, had been given to him by us, perhaps by one of the women who had interpreted with those syllables one of the inarticulate sounds that the baby let out now and again. He was paralysed from the waist down, with atrophied legs, as thin as sticks; but his eyes, lost in his triangular and wasted face, flashed terribly alive, full of demand, assertion, of the will to break loose, to shatter the tomb of his dumbness. The speech he lacked, which no one had bothered to teach him, the need of speech charged his stare with explosive urgency: it was a stare both savage and human, even mature, a judgement, which none of us could support, so heavy was it with force and anguish.

None of us, that is, except Henek; he was in the bunk next to me, a robust and hearty Hungarian boy of fifteen. Henek spent half his day beside Hurbinek's pallet. He was maternal rather than paternal; had our precarious coexistence lasted more than a month, it is extremely probable that Hurbinek would have learnt to speak from Henek; certainly better than from the Polish girls who, too tender and too vain, inebriated him with caresses and kisses, but shunned intimacy with him.

Henek, on the other hand, calm and stubborn, sat beside the little sphinx, immune to the distressing power he emanated; he brought him food to eat, adjusted his blankets, cleaned him with skilful hands, without repugnance; and he spoke to him, in Hungarian naturally, in a slow and patient voice. After a week, Henek announced seriously, but without a shadow of self-consciousness, that Hurbinek 'could say a word'. What word? He did not know, a difficult word, not Hungarian: something like '*mass-klo*', '*matisklo*'. During the night we listened carefully: it was true, from Hurbinek's corner there occasionally came a sound, a word. It was not, admittedly, always exactly the same word, but it was certainly an articulated word; or better, several slightly different articulated words, experimental variations on a theme, on a root, perhaps on a name.

Hurbinek continued in his stubborn experiments for as long as he lived. In the following days everybody listened to him in silence, anxious to understand, and among us there were speakers of all the languages of Europe; but Hurbinek's word remained secret. No, it was certainly not a message, it was not a revelation; perhaps it was his name, if it had ever fallen to his lot to be given a name; perhaps (according to one of our hypotheses) it meant 'to eat', or 'bread'; or perhaps 'meat' in Bohemian, as one of us who knew that language maintained.

Hurbinek, who was three years old and perhaps had been born in Auschwitz and had never seen a tree; Hurbinek, who had fought like a man, to the last breath, to gain his entry into the world of men, from which a bestial power had excluded him; Hurbinek, the nameless, whose tiny forearm – even his – bore the tattoo of Auschwitz; Hurbinek died in the first days of March 1945, free but not redeemed. Nothing remains of him: he bears witness through these words of mine.

Henek was a good companion, and a perpetual source of surprise. His name too, like that of Hurbinek, was artificial: his real name, which was König, had been changed into Henek, a Polish diminutive for Henry, by the two Polish girls who, although at least ten years older than him, felt for Henek an ambiguous sympathy which soon turned into open desire.

Henek-König, alone of our microcosm of affliction, was neither ill nor convalescent; in fact he enjoyed splendid physical and spiritual health. He was of small stature and mild aspect, but he had the muscles of an athlete; he was affectionate and obliging towards Hurbinek and us, yet harboured sedate, sanguinary instincts. The Lager, a mortal trap, a 'bone-crusher' for the others, had been a good school for him; in a few months it had made of him a young carnivore, alert, shrewd, ferocious and prudent.

In the long hours we passed together he told me the chief events of his short life. He was born and lived on a farm in the middle of a wood in Transylvania, near the Rumanian border. On Sundays, he and his father often went to the woods, both with guns. Why with guns? To hunt? Yes, to hunt; but also to shoot at Rumanians. And why shoot at Rumanians? Because they are Rumanians, Henek explained to me with disarming simplicity. Every now and again they also shot at us.

He had been captured and deported to Auschwitz with his whole family. The others had been killed at once; he had told the SS that he was eighteen years old and a bricklayer, when he was really only fourteen and a schoolboy. So he entered Birkenau; but at Birkenau he had insisted on his real age, had been assigned to the children's Block, and, as he was the oldest and most robust, had become their Kapo. The children at Birkenau were like birds of passage: after a few days they were transferred to the Experiments Block, or directly to the gas chambers. Henek had understood the situation immediately, and like a good Kapo he had 'organized' himself, he had established solid relations with an influential Hungarian Häftling, and had remained until the liberation. When there were selections at the children's Block he was the one who chose. Did he feel no remorse? No: why should he? Was there any other way to survive?

At the evacuation of the Lager, he had wisely decided to hide; from his hiding-place, through the small window of a cellar, he had seen the Germans empty the fabulous storehouses of Auschwitz in great haste, and he had noted that in the hurry of their departure, they had scattered a fair number of tins of food on the road. They had not stopped to recover them, but had sought to destroy them by driving their half-tracks over them. Many tins had been driven into the mud and snow without splitting open; at night Henek had come out with a sack and had collected a fantastic hoard of tins, deformed, flattened, but still full: meat, lard, fish, fruit, vitamins. Naturally he had not said anything to anybody: he told me about it, because I was in the neighbouring bunk, and because I could be of use to him in guarding them. In fact, as Henek spent many hours wandering around the Lager on mysterious errands, while I was incapable of moving, my work as custodian was quite useful to him. He had faith in me; he settled the sack under my bed, and during the following days recompensed me with a fair wage in kind, authorizing me to take such extra rations as he judged proportionate to my services and suitable, in quality and quantity, to my condition as an invalid.

Hurbinek was not the only child. There were others, in relatively good health; they had formed a little 'club', very closed and reserved, in which the intrusion of adults was visibly unwelcome. They were wild and judicious little animals, who conversed in languages I could not understand. The most authoritative member of the clan was no more than five years old, and his name was Peter Pavel.

Peter Pavel spoke to nobody and had need of nobody. He was a beautiful blond and robust child, with an intelligent and impassive face. In the morning he climbed down from his bunk, which was on the third tier, with slow but sure movements, went to the showers to fill his bowl with water, and washed himself meticulously. Then he disappeared for the whole day, making a brief appearance only at noon to collect his soup in the same bowl. In the evening he came back for dinner, ate, went out again, re-entered soon afterwards with a chamber pot, placed it in the corner behind the stove, sat there for a few moments, left again with the pot, came back without it, climbed up quietly to his own place, punctiliously adjusted the blankets and pillow, and slept until the morning without changing position.

A few days after my arrival, I saw with discomfort a well-known face appear: the pathetic and disagreeable shape of Kleine Kiepura, the mascot of Buna-Monowitz. They all knew him at Buna; he was the youngest of the prisoners, no more than twelve years old. Everything was irregular about him, beginning with his presence in Lager, which normally children did not enter alive. No one knew how or why he had been admitted, yet at the same time everybody knew only too well. His position there was irregular, because he did not march to work, but lived in semi-isolation in the officials' Block; moreover, his whole appearance was strikingly irregular. He had grown too much and badly; enormously long arms, and legs stuck out from his squat, short body, like those of a spider; below his pale face, whose features were not lacking in infantile grace, a huge jaw jutted out, more prominent than his nose. Kleine Kiepura was the attendant and protégé of the Lager-Kapo, the Kapo of all the Kapos.

Nobody loved him, except his protector. In the shadow of authority, well fed and dressed, exempt from work, he had led until the very end the ambiguous and frivolous existence of a favourite, amid a web of denunciations and twisted affections; his name, wrongly I hope, was always whispered in the most notorious anonymous denunciations to the Political Bureau and to the SS. Hence all feared him and shrank from him.

But now the Lager-Kapo, deprived of all power, was marching towards the west, and Kleine Kiepura, recovering from a slight illness, shared our lot. He was given a bunk and a bowl, and he inserted himself into our limbo. Henek and I addressed only a few cautious words to him, hindered as we were by diffidence and hostile compassion; but he barely replied. He stayed silent for two days; he sat huddled in his bunk, staring into space with his fists tight against his chest. Then all of a sudden he began to speak – and we longed for his silence. Kleine Kiepura spoke as if in a dream: and his dream was of a success

story, of becoming a Kapo. It was difficult to tell if it was madness or a puerile sinister game; endlessly, from the height of his
bunk immediately below the ceiling, the boy sang and whistled
the marches of Buna, the brutal rhythms that ruled our tired
steps every morning and evening; he shouted imperious commands in German at a troop of non-existent slaves.

'Get up, swine, understand? Make your beds, quickly; clean
your shoes. All in line, lice inspection, feet inspection! Show
your feet, scum! Dirty again, you shit-heap! Watch out, I'm not
joking. If I catch you once more, it's the crematorium for you!'
Then, yelling in the manner of German soldiers: 'Fall in!
Dressed! Covered! Collar down; in step, keep time! Hands in
line with the seams of your trousers!' And then again, after a
pause, in an arrogant and stridulous voice: 'This isn't a sanatorium! This is a German Lager, its name is Auschwitz, and no one
leaves except through the Chimney. If you like it, all right; if you
don't, all you have to do is touch the electric wire!'

Kleine Kiepura disappeared after a few days, to everybody's
relief. His presence among us, weak and ill, but full of the timid
and flickering joy of our new-found liberty, offended like that of
a corpse, and the compassion he aroused in us was mixed with
horror. We tried in vain to tear him from his delirium: the infection of the Lager had gained too much ground.

The two Polish girls, who carried out the duties of nurse (pretty
badly), were named Hanka and Jadzia. Hanka was an ex-Kapo,
as one could tell from her unshaven hair, and even more surely
from her insolent manner. She could hardly have been more
than twenty-four; she was of average height, with a dark complexion and hard vulgar features. In that purgatory, full of past
and present sufferings, of hopes and pity, she spent her days in
front of the mirror, filing her nails or strutting in front of the
indifferent and ironical Henek.

She was, or considered herself, of a higher social standing than Jadzia: but it needed very little indeed to surpass in authority so humble a creature. Jadzia was a small and timid girl, of a sickly-rosy colour; but her sheath of anaemic flesh was tormented, torn apart from inside, convulsed by a continual secret tempest. She had a desire, an urge, an impelling need of a man, of any man, at once, of all men. Every male who crossed her path attracted her; attracted her materially, heavily, as a magnet attracts iron. Jadzia stared at him with bewitched and stupefied eyes, she rose from her corner, advanced towards him with the uncertain step of a somnambulist, sought contact with him; if the man then drew away, she followed him at a distance, in silence, for a few yards, then, with her eyes lowered, returned to her inertia; if the man waited for her, Jadzia wrapped herself around him, incorporated him, took possession of him, with the blind, mute, tremulous, slow, but sure movements which amoebae show under the microscope.

Her first and principal objective was naturally Henek; but Henek did not want her, he derided and insulted her. But being the practical boy he was, he had not lost interest in the case, and had mentioned it to Noah, his great friend.

Noah did not live in our dormitory; in fact he lived nowhere and everywhere. He was a nomad, a free man, rejoicing in the air he breathed and the ground he trod upon. He was Scheissminister of free Auschwitz, Minister of latrines and cesspits; but notwithstanding this monatto-like post of his (which in any case he had assumed voluntarily) there was nothing sordid about him, or if there were anything, it was cancelled out by the impetus of his vital energy. Noah was a young Pantagruel, as strong as a horse, voracious and lecherous. As Jadzia wanted all men, so Noah wanted all women; but while the feeble Jadzia limited herself to throwing out her tenuous threads, like a rock-mollusc, Noah, a high-flying bird, cruised along all the roads of the camp from dawn to dusk, on the seat of his repugnant cart, cracking his whip and singing at the top of his voice; the cart stopped before the entrance of each Block, and while his troop, filthy and stinking, hurried, cursing, through their repulsive task, Noah wandered around the feminine dormitories like an oriental prince, dressed in an arabesque many-coloured coat, full of patches and braid. His encounters were like so many hurricanes. He was the friend of all men and the lover of all women. The deluge was over; in the black sky of Auschwitz, Noah saw the rainbow shine out, and the world was his, to repopulate.

Frau Vitta (or rather Frau Vita, as every Italian called her,)* on the other hand, loved all human beings with a love both simple and fraternal. Frau Vita, with her ruined figure and clear gentle face, was a young widow from Trieste, half Jewish, a survivor of Birkenau. She spent many hours beside my bed, speaking to me of a thousand things at the same time with Triestine volubility, laughing and crying. She was in good health, but deeply wounded, ulcerated, by what she had undergone and seen in a year of Lager, and during those last gruesome days. In fact, she had been 'commandeered' for the transport of corpses, of lumps of corpses, of wretched anonymous remains, and these final images weighed upon her like a mountain; she sought to exorcise them, to wash herself clean of them, throwing herself headlong into a tumultuous activity. She was the only person to bother about the invalids and the children; she did it with frantic compassion, and when she still had free time she washed the floors and windows with wild fury, rinsed the bowls and glasses noisily, ran around the dormitories to carry real or fictitious messages; then she came back exhausted, and sat panting on my bunk, with tearful eyes, starved of words, of intimacy, of human warmth. In the evening, when all the jobs of the day were over,

* 'Vita' in Italian means 'life'.

incapable of enduring solitude, she suddenly jumped up from her bunk, and danced by herself between the bunks, to the sound of her own songs, affectionately clasping an imaginary man to her breast.

It was Frau Vita who closed André's and Antoine's eyes. They were two young peasants from the Vosges, both my companions for the ten days of the interregnum, both ill with diphtheria. I seemed to have known them for centuries. With strange parallelism, they were simultaneously struck by a form of dysentery, which soon showed itself to be extremely serious, of tubercular origin; in a few days the scales of their fate tipped down. They were in two neighbouring bunks, they did not complain, they endured the atrocious colic with clenched teeth, without understanding its mortal nature; they spoke only to each other, timidly, and they never asked anyone for help. André was the first to go, while he was speaking, in mid-sentence, as a candle goes out. For two days no one arrived to take him away; the children came to look at him with bewildered curiosity, then continued to play in their corner.

Antoine remained silent and alone, wholly shut in a suspense that transformed him. His state of nutrition was reasonable, but in two days he underwent a metamorphosis of dissolution, as if sucked up by his companion. Together with Frau Vita we managed to get a doctor, after many vain attempts; I asked him, in German, if there was anything to be done, if there was any hope, and I counselled him not to speak in French. He replied in Yiddish, with a brief phrase I did not understand; then he translated into German: '*Sein Kamerad ruft ihn*', 'His companion is calling him'. Antoine obeyed the call that same evening. They were not yet twenty, and they had been in the Lager only one month.

Finally Olga came, in a night full of silence, to bring me the dismal news of the Birkenau camp, and of the fate of the women deported with me. I had been waiting for her for many days; I did not know her personally, but Frau Vita, who, despite sanitary injunctions, also frequented patients in other wards in search of troubles to alleviate and of impassioned conversations, had informed us of our respective presences, and had organized the illegal meeting in the depth of the night while everyone was sleeping.

Olga was a Jewish Croat partisan, who in 1942 had fled to Piedmont with her family and had been interned there; she belonged to that flood of thousands of foreign Jews who had found hospitality, and a brief peace, in the paradoxical Italy of those years, officially anti-Semitic. She was a woman of great intelligence and culture, strong, beautiful and with insight: deported to Birkenau, she had survived there, alone of her family.

She spoke Italian perfectly; from reasons of gratitude and temperament, she had soon become a friend of the Italian women in the camp, and in particular of those who had been deported in the same train as I. She told me their story by candlelight, with her eyes fixed on the ground. The furtive light illumined only her face in the darkness, accentuating its precocious lines, and transforming it into a tragic mask. A handkerchief covered her head; she untied it at one point and the mask became as macabre as a skull. Olga's cranium was bare, covered only with a short grey down.

They had all died. All the children and all the old people had died immediately. Of the 550 people of whom I had lost trace when I entered the Lager, only twenty-nine women had been admitted to the Birkenau camp: of these, five alone had survived. Vanda had died by gas, fully conscious, in the month of October; Olga herself had procured two sleeping tablets for her, but they had not proved sufficient.

3

The Greek

Towards the end of February, after a month in bed, I was not yet cured, and indeed began to feel but little improvement. I had a clear impression that I would not regain my health and my strength until I stood upright again (albeit with difficulty), and put shoes on my feet. So, on one of the rare days when the doctor called, I asked him to let me out. The doctor examined me, or pretended to do so; he noted that the desquamation of the scarlet fever had finished; he told me that as far as he was concerned I could go; he warned me, absurdly, not to expose myself to fatigue or cold, and he wished me good luck.

I cut myself a pair of socks from a blanket, grabbed as many jackets and pairs of trousers as I could find (for no other clothing was to hand), said good-bye to Frau Vita and Henek and went out.

I stood on my feet somewhat shakily. Immediately outside the door, there was a Soviet officer; he photographed me and gave me five cigarettes. A little farther on, I was unable to avoid a fellow in civilian dress, who was hunting for men to clear away the snow; he captured me, deaf to my protests, gave me a spade and attached me to a squad of shovellers.

I offered him the five cigarettes but he refused them with contempt. He was an ex-Kapo, and had naturally remained in office; who else in fact could have managed to make people like us clear the snow? I tried to shovel, but it was physically impossible. If I could get round the corner, no one would see me any more, but first I had to free myself of the spade; it would have been interesting to sell it, but I did not know to whom; and to carry it with me even for a few steps was dangerous. There was not enough snow to bury it. In the end I dropped it through a cellar window, and I found myself free again.

I walked into a Block; there was a guardian, an old Hungarian, who did not want to let me enter, but the cigarettes convinced him. Inside it was warm, full of smoke and noise and unknown faces; but in the evening they gave soup to me as well. I was hoping for a few days of rest and of gradual training for an active life, but I did not know that I had tripped up badly. No later than the following morning, I got caught up in a Russian transport convoy towards a mysterious transit camp.

I cannot say that I remember exactly how and when my Greek sprang up from nowhere. In those days and in those parts, soon after the front had passed by, a high wind was blowing over the face of the earth; the world around us seemed to have returned to primeval Chaos, and was swarming with scalene, defective, abnormal human specimens; each of them bestirred himself, with blind or deliberate movements, in anxious search of his own place, of his own sphere, as the particles of the four elements are described as doing in the verse-cosmogonies of the Ancients.

I too, swept up by the whirlwind, found myself, one bitter night, after a heavy snowfall, loaded on to a horse-drawn military cart many hours before dawn, together with a dozen unknown companions. The cold was intense; the sky, thick with stars, slowly lightened in the east, promising one of those marvellous daybreaks of the plain, which, at the time of our slavery, we had watched interminably in the roll-call square of the Lager.

Our guide and escort was a Russian soldier. He sat in front singing full-throatedly to the stars, and every now and again spoke to the horses in that strangely affectionate way that Russians have, with gentle inflections and long modulated phrases. Naturally, we had asked him about our destination, but we got nothing comprehensible from him, except – as far as we could gather from certain rhythmic puffings of his and from the movement of his elbows bent like piston-rods – that his task was limited to taking us as far as a railway.

This was in fact what happened. As the sun rose, the cart stopped at the foot of an embankment which carried the railway lines, interrupted and destroyed for about fifty yards by a recent bombardment. The soldier pointed to one of the two sections, helped us climb down from the cart (it was necessary: the journey had lasted nearly two hours, the cart was small, and many of us, because of the uncomfortable position and the penetrating cold, were so numb as to be unable to move), took leave of us with jovial incomprehensible words, turned the horses round, and departed, singing sweetly.

The sun, which had barely risen, had disappeared behind a veil of mist; from the top of the railway embankment we could only see an interminable flat, deserted countryside, buried under the snow, without a roof, without a tree. More hours passed; not one of us had a watch.

As I have already said, we were about a dozen. There was a *Reichsdeutscher* who, like many other 'Aryan' Germans, had assumed relatively courteous and frankly ambiguous attitudes after the liberation (this was an amusing metamorphosis, which I had already seen happen in others, sometimes gradually, sometimes in a few minutes at the first appearance of the new lords of the Red Star, on whose large faces it was easy to read the tendency not to split hairs). There were two tall, thin brothers, Viennese Jews about fifty years old, silent and cautious like all

the old Häftlinge; an officer of the regular Yugoslav Army, who
seemed as if he had not yet succeeded in throwing off the com-
pliance and inertia of the Lager, and who looked at us with
empty eyes. There was a sort of human wreck, of indefinable
age, who spoke ceaselessly to himself in Yiddish; one of the
many whom the ferocious life of the camp had half destroyed,
and then left to their fate, sealed up (and perhaps protected) by
a thick armour of insensitivity or open madness. And finally
there was the Greek, with whom destiny was to unite me for an
unforgettable week of vagabondage.

His name was Mordo Nahum, and at first sight he seemed
nothing exceptional, except for his shoes (of leather, almost new,
of elegant design: a real portent, given the time and the place),
and the sack that he carried on his back, which was of conspicuous size and corresponding weight, as I myself was to
ascertain in the following days. Besides his own language, he
spoke Spanish (like all Jews from Salonica), French, a halting
Italian but with a good accent, and, as I found out later, Turkish,
Bulgarian and a little Albanian. He was about forty; of fairly tall
stature, he walked with curved shoulders, his head pushed forward like a myope. Red of hair and skin, he had large pale
watery eyes and a great curved nose, which gave his whole body
a rapacious yet halting appearance, like a night-bird surprised
by light, or a shark outside its natural environment.

He was recovering from some indeterminate illness, which
caused attacks of extremely high, enervating fever; in the first
nights of the journey he still sometimes fell into a state of pros-
tration, with attacks of shivering and delirium. Although we did
not feel particularly attracted to each other, we were drawn
together by having two languages in common, and by the fact,
quite noticeable in the circumstances, that we were the only two
Mediterraneans in the small group.

The waiting was interminable; we were hungry and cold, and

we were forced to stand or lie down in the snow, because there was no roof or shelter as far as the eye could see. It must have been nearly midday when, heralded from afar by the puffing and smoke, the hand of civilization was stretched out to us charitably in the form of an emaciated string of three or four goods trucks dragged by a small locomotive, such as is used in normal times for shunting wagons.

The train stopped in front of us, at the end of the interrupted line. We were unable to gain any sensible information from the few Polish peasants who got out; they looked at us with closed faces, and avoided us as if we were pestiferous. In fact, we were, probably in the strict sense of the word, and in any case our aspect could hardly have been pleasing: but we had misguidedly hoped for a more cordial welcome from the first 'civilians' we met after our liberation. We all climbed into one end of the trucks, and the small train left almost at once in the opposite direction, pushed and no longer pulled by the toy locomotive. At the next stopping place two peasant women climbed on; once the first diffidence and linguistic obstacles had been overcome, we learnt from them some important geographical facts, and some news which, if true, sounded little less than disastrous to our ears.

The break in the railway line was a little way from a locality named Neu Berun, which had formerly been the junction for a branch line, later destroyed, to Auschwitz. The two sections which started from the interruption led to Katowice (to the west), and to Cracow (to the east). Both of these localities lay about forty miles from Neu Berun, which, in the frightful conditions in which the war had left the line, meant at least two days' journey, with an unspecified number of stops and changes. The train on which we found ourselves was travelling towards Cracow; until a few days before, the Russians had gathered an enormous number of ex-prisoners at Cracow, and now all the barracks, schools, hospitals and convents were overflowing with people in a condition of desperate need. The very streets of Cracow, according to our informers, were swarming with men and women of all races, who in a moment had transformed themselves into smugglers, clandestine merchants, even into thieves and bandits.

For several days now, the ex-prisoners had been concentrated into other camps, around Katowice. The two women were amazed to find us travelling towards Cracow, where, they said, the Russian garrison itself was suffering from hunger. After they had heard our story they consulted briefly, then they declared themselves convinced that it must simply have been a mistake on the part of our escort, the Russian cart-driver, who, with little knowledge of the country, had directed us towards the eastern section instead of towards the western.

The news plunged us into a riddle of doubts and anxiety. We had hoped for a short and safe journey, towards a camp equipped to receive us, towards an acceptable substitute for our homes; and this hope formed part of a far greater hope, that of an upright and just world, miraculously re-established on its natural foundations after an eternity of upheavals, of errors and massacres, after our long patient wait. It was a naïve hope, like all those that rest on too sharp a division between good and evil, between past and future, but it was on this that we were living. That first crack, and the other inevitable ones, small and large, that followed it, were for us a cause of grief, the more hardly felt because they were unforeseen; for one does not dream for years, for decades, of a better world, without representing it as perfect.

It was not so; something had happened that only the few wise ones among us had foreseen. Liberty, the improbable, the impossible liberty, so far removed from Auschwitz that we had only dared to hope for it in our dreams, had come, but it had not taken us to the Promised Land. It was around us, but in the form of a pitiless deserted plain. More trials, more toil, more hunger, more cold, more fears awaited us.

I had been fasting now for twenty-four hours. We were sitting on the wooden floor of the truck, huddled together to protect ourselves from the cold; the railway lines were loose, and at every bump our heads, unsteady on our necks, knocked against the wooden planks of the walls. I felt exhausted, not only physically; like an athlete who has run for hours, using up all his own resources, those of nature first, and then those that he squeezes out, that he creates from nothing in moments of extreme need; like an athlete who arrives at his goal, and who, in the act of falling spent to the ground, is brutally hauled to his feet, and forced to start running again, in the dark, towards another goal of unknown distance.

The train travelled slowly. In the evening dark, apparently deserted villages emerged; then total night came down, atrociously cold, without light in heaven or on earth. Only the bumping of the truck prevented us from drifting into a sleep which the cold would have rendered mortal. After interminable hours of travel, perhaps about three o'clock at night, we finally stopped at a wrecked, dark little station. The Greek was delirious; of the others, none wanted to get down from the truck, some from fear, some from sheer inertia, some in the hope that the train would leave soon. I got down, and wandered into the dark with my ridiculous baggage until I saw a small lighted window. It was the telegraph hut, packed with people: there was a lighted stove. I entered cautiously, like a stray dog, ready to disappear at the first sign of a threat, but nobody bothered about me. I threw myself on the floor and fell asleep at once, as one learns to do in the Lager.

I woke up some hours later at dawn. The hut was empty. The telegraphist saw me raise my head, and placed an enormous slice of bread and cheese beside me on the ground. I was startled (apart from being half paralysed by the cold and sleep) and I fear I did not thank him. I pushed the food into my stomach and went outside; the train had not moved. In the truck, my companions were lying besotted; when they saw me they shook themselves, all except the Yugoslav, who strove to move in vain. The cold and immobility had paralysed his legs; when we touched him he shouted and groaned. We had to massage him for a long time, and then to move his limbs cautiously, as one inches a rusty mechanism.

It had been a terrible night for everyone, perhaps the worst of our whole exile. I spoke to the Greek about it; we agreed to join forces so as to avoid at all costs another freezing night, which we felt we should not survive.

I think that the Greek, thanks to my nocturnal outing, had somehow overestimated my qualities of 'débrouillard et démerdard', as they were elegantly described at the time. As for myself, I confess that I was impressed mainly by his big sack and his quality of a Salonikite, which, as everyone in Auschwitz knew, was equivalent to a guarantee of highly skilled mercantile ability, and of knowing how to get oneself out of any situation. Sympathy, bilateral, and esteem, unilateral, came later.

The train left again, and by a tortuous and vague route led us to a place called Szczakowa. Here the Polish Red Cross had established a marvellous field-kitchen; a quite substantial hot soup was distributed at all hours of the day and night, and to anyone, without distinction, who presented himself. A miracle that none of us would have dared to dream of in our most audacious dreams: in a certain sense, the Lager upside down. I do not remember the behaviour of my companions; as for myself, I was so voracious that the Polish sisters, used as they were to the famished clientele of the place, crossed themselves.

We left again in the afternoon. The sun was out. Our poor

train stopped at dusk, in trouble; far away the spires of Cracow glowed red. The Greek and I got down from the truck and went to interrogate the engine-driver, who stood in the middle of the snow, busy and dirty, fighting long jets of steam that shot out from some burst pipe. '*Masheena kaputt*,' he replied to us epigraphically. We were no longer slaves, we were no longer protected, we had left our tutelage. For us the hour of trial was sounding.

The Greek, revived by the hot soup of Szczakowa, felt quite strong. '*On y va?*' – '*On y va*.' So we left the train and our perplexed companions, whom we were never to see again, and we started out on foot in the problematical search for human kind.

At his peremptory request I shouldered the famous bundle. In vain I had tried to protest. 'But it's your stuff!' 'Exactly, because it is mine. I organized it and you carry it. That's the division of work. Later you too will profit from it.' So we started off, he first and I second, on the hard snow of a minor road; the sun had gone down.

I have spoken already of the Greek's shoes; as for myself, I was wearing a pair of curious foot-coverings which in Italy I had only seen worn by priests: of extremely delicate leather, reaching higher than the ankle, without laces, but with two large clasps, and two lateral patches of elastic fabric which should have ensured that they remained tight-fitting. I was also wearing four pairs of Häftling-style cloth trousers on top of each other, a cotton shirt, a jacket, also striped – and that was all. My baggage consisted of a blanket and a cardboard box in which I had formerly kept a few pieces of bread, but which was now empty. The Greek eyed the whole lot with unconcealed contempt and annoyance.

We had deceived ourselves grossly about the distance from Cracow: we should have to walk at least four miles. After about

twenty minutes, my shoes were finished; the sole of one of them
had come off, and the other began to unstitch itself. Until then
the Greek had maintained a pregnant silence; when he saw me
put down the sack and sit by the side of the road to contemplate
the disaster, he asked me:

'How old are you?'

Twenty-five,' I replied.

'What do you do?'

'I'm a chemist'

'Then you're a fool,' he said calmly. 'A man who has no shoes
is a fool.'

He was a great Greek. Few times in my life, before or after,
have I felt such concrete wisdom weigh upon me. There was
little to say in reply. The validity of the argument was manifest,
plain: the two shapeless pieces of trash on my feet, and the two
shining marvels on his. There was no justification. I was no
longer a slave; but after my first steps on the path of liberty, here
was I seated by the road, with my feet in my hands clumsy and
useless like the broken-down locomotive we had just left. Was
I really entitled to my liberty? The Greek seemed to doubt it

'... But I had scarlet fever, a high temperature, I was in the
sick bay; the shoe store was a long way off, it was forbidden to
go near it, and anyway they said that it had been sacked by the
Poles. And didn't I have the right to believe that the Russians
would have provided?'

'Words,' said the Greek. 'Anyone can talk. I had a temperature of 104, and I didn't know if it was day or night; but one
thing I did know, that I needed shoes and other things; so I got
up, and I went as far as the store to study the situation. There
was a Russian with a sten-gun in front of the door, but I wanted
the shoes, and so I walked to the back, I broke open a small
window and I entered. So I got my shoes, and also the sack, and
everything that is inside the sack, which will prove useful later

on. That is foresight; yours is stupidity. It's a failure to understand the reality of things.'

'Now it's you who are just talking,' said I. 'I may have made
a mistake, but now the problem is how to reach Cracow before
nightfall, with or without shoes'; and so saying I fumbled
around with numbed fingers, and with bits of wire I found on
the road, trying to tie the soles to the uppers, at least provi-
sionally.

'Hold it; that'll be no use at all.' He gave me two pieces of
robust cloth that he had dragged out of his bundle, and showed
me how to pack together shoes and feet, firmly enough at least
to hobble along. Then we proceeded in silence.

The suburbs of Cracow were anonymous and squalid. The
roads were wholly deserted: the shops were empty, all the doors
and windows were barred or smashed. We reached the terminus
of a tram line; I hesitated, because we had no money to pay the
fare, but the Greek said: 'Climb on, then we'll see.' The tram
was empty; after a quarter of an hour the driver arrived, but not
the conductor (from which we see that once more the Greek was
right; as we shall see, he was to prove right in all the succeed-
ing situations, except one); we left, and during the journey
discovered with joy that one of the passengers who had climbed
on in the meantime was a Frenchman. He explained to us that
he was staying in an old convent, which our tram would soon
pass; at the following stop, we should find a barracks requisi-
tioned by the Russians and full of Italian soldiers. My heart
rejoiced; I had found a home.

In reality, things did not all go so smoothly. At first, the Polish
guard on duty at the barracks told us abruptly to go away.
'Where?' 'What do I care? Away from here, anywhere.' After
much insistence and begging, he was finally induced to go and
call an Italian sergeant, on whom the decision to admit other
guests clearly depended. It was not easy, he explained to us; the

barracks were already bursting, rations were limited; he conceded that I was an Italian, but I was not a soldier; as for my companion, he was Greek, and it was impossible to put him in with veterans of the Greek and Albanian campaigns; disorders and fights would inevitably result. I countered with my best eloquence, and with genuine tears in my eyes; I guaranteed that we would only stay one night (and I thought to myself: once inside . . .) and that the Greek spoke Italian well and in any case would open his mouth as little as possible. My arguments were weak, and I was aware of it, but the Greek knew how to work all the skives in the world, and while I was speaking he was rooting about in the sack hanging on my back. At a certain point he pushed me aside, and in silence placed under the nose of the Cerberus a dazzling tin of pork, embellished with a many-coloured label, and with futile instructions in six languages on the correct way to handle the contents. So we won a roof and a bed at Cracow.

It was already night. Contrary to what the sergeant had led us to believe, the most sumptuous abundance reigned inside the barracks; there were lighted stoves, candles and acetylene lamps, food and drink and straw to sleep on. The Italians were distributed ten or twelve to a dormitory, but we at Monowitz had been two per cubic yard. They were wearing good military clothing, thick jackets, many of them had wrist watches, all of them had hair shining with brilliantine; they were noisy, cheerful and obliging and overwhelmed us with kindness. As for the Greek, they virtually carried him in triumph. A Greek! A Greek has come! The news rang from dormitory to dormitory, and in a short time a festive crowd gathered around my surly partner. They spoke Greek, some of them with ease, these veterans of the most compassionate military occupation that history records: they talked of places and events with colourful sympathy, in a chivalrous tacit recognition of the desperate valour of the invaded country. But there was something more, which opened the way for them; mine was no ordinary Greek, he was visibly a master, an authority, a super-Greek. In a few moments of conversation, he had accomplished a miracle, he had created an atmosphere.

He possessed the right equipment; he could speak Italian, and (what matters more, and what is missing in many Italians themselves) he knew of what to speak in Italian. He amazed me; he showed himself an expert about girls and spaghetti, Juventus* and lyrical music, the war and blennorrhoea, wine and the black market, motor-bikes and spivs. Mordo Nahum, so laconic with me, in a brief time became the pivot of the evening. I realized that his eloquence, his successful attempt at *captatio benevolentiae*, did not derive solely from opportunist considerations. He too had fought in the Greek campaign, with the rank of sergeant; on the other side of the front, naturally, but this detail at the moment seemed trifling to everybody. He had been at Tepeleni, many Italians had also been there; like them he had suffered cold, hunger, mud and bombardments, and in the end, like them, he had been captured by the Germans. He was a colleague, a fellow-soldier.

He told curious stories of the war; of how, after the Germans had broken through the front, he had found himself with six of his soldiers ransacking the first floor of a bombed and abandoned villa, searching for provisions; he had heard suspicious noises on the floor below, had cautiously climbed down the stairs with his sten-gun at the ready, and had met an Italian sergeant, who with six soldiers was doing exactly the same thing on the ground floor. The Italian in turn had levelled his gun, but the Greek had pointed out that in those conditions a gun fight

* A leading Italian football club.

would have been particularly stupid, that they all found themselves, Greeks and Italians, in the same boat, and that he did not see why they should not make a small separate local peace and continue their researches in their respective occupied territories – to which proposal the Italian had rapidly agreed.

For me too he was a revelation. I knew that he was nothing but a rogue, a merchant, expert in deceit and lacking in scruples, selfish and cold; yet I felt blossom out in him, encouraged by the sympathy of the audience, a warmth, an unsuspected humanity, singular but genuine, rich with promise.

Late at night, heaven knows how, a flask of wine suddenly appeared. It was the *coup de grâce*: for me everything sank celestially into a warm purple fog, and I barely managed to drag myself on all fours to the straw bed that the Italians, with maternal care, had prepared in a corner for the Greek and myself.

Dawn had barely risen when the Greek woke me. Alas! Where had last night's jovial guest disappeared to? The Greek who stood in front of me was hard, secretive, taciturn. 'Get up,' he said in a tone of voice that admitted no reply, 'put your shoes on, get the sack and let's go.'

'Go where?'

'To work, to the market. Do you think it's a nice thing to be supported?'

I felt wholly opposed to this argument It seemed to me, besides being convenient, extremely natural and also pleasant that someone should keep me; I had found the explosion of national solidarity, or rather of spontaneous humanity, the evening before both enjoyable and exhilarating. Even more, full as I was of self-pity, it seemed to me just, good, that the world should at last pity me. Moreover, I had no shoes, I was ill, I was cold, I was tired; and finally, in the name of all the gods, what the hell could I do at the market?

I disclosed all these considerations, obvious to me. But, '*c'est pas des raisons d'homme*,' he replied sharply; I was forced to realize that I had infringed an important moral principle of his, that he was seriously scandalized, that on this point he was not prepared for compromise or discussion. Moral codes, all of them, are rigid by definition; they do not admit blurrings, compromises, or reciprocal contaminations. They are to be accepted or rejected *en bloc*. This is one of the principal reasons why man is gregarious and searches more or less consciously for the company not of his generic neighbour, but only of someone who shares his profound beliefs (or lack of them). I was obliged to recognize, with disappointment and amazement, that Mordo Nahum was such a man, a man of deep-rooted beliefs, and, what is more, beliefs far removed from mine. Now everyone knows how awkward it is to do business, in fact to live together, with an ideological opponent.

The basis of his ethic was work, which to him was a sacred duty, but which he understood in a very wide sense. To him, work included everything, but with the condition that it should bring profit without limiting liberty. The concept of work thus included, as well as certain permissible activities, smuggling, theft and fraud (not robbery; he was not a violent man). On the other hand he considered reprehensible, because humiliating, all activities which did not involve initiative or risk, or which presupposed a discipline and a hierarchy; any relationship of employment, any services, even if they were well paid, he lumped together as 'servile work'. But it was not servile work to plough your own field, or to sell false antiques to tourists at a port.

As for the more elevated activities of the spirit, as for creative work, I soon understood that the Greek was divided. These were delicate judgements, to be made on the merits of each case; it was permissible for example to pursue success for its own sake, even by selling false paintings or literary trash, or, more generally, by harming one's neighbour; it was reprehensible obstinately to pursue an unprofitable ideal; it was sinful to withdraw from the world in contemplation; the path of the man who dedicated himself to meditation and the acquisition of wisdom, on the other hand, was permissible, in fact commendable – so long as he did not believe that he had the right to receive his bread free from mankind, for wisdom was also merchandise, which could and should be exchanged.

Since Mordo Nahum was no fool, he clearly realized that these principles might not be shared by individuals of a different origin and formation, and in particular by me; he was however firmly persuaded of them, and it was his ambition to put them into practice, to demonstrate their general validity.

In conclusion, my proposal to wait quietly for food from the Russians could only appear detestable to him; because it was 'unearned bread'; because it implied a relationship of subjection; and because every form of order, of structure, was suspect, whether it brought a loaf of bread a day, or a monthly pay-packet.

So I followed the Greek to the market, not really because I was convinced by his arguments, but mainly through inertia and curiosity. The evening before, when I was already navigating in a sea of vinous vapours, he had diligently enquired about the location, customs, tariffs, supply and demand of the free market of Cracow, and his duty now called him.

We left, he with the sack (which I carried), I in my disintegrating shoes, which turned each step into a problem. The market of Cracow had blossomed out spontaneously, as soon as the front had passed by, and in a few days it had invaded an entire suburb. Everything was bought and sold there, and the whole city centred on it; townsfolk were selling furniture, books, paintings, clothes and silver; peasant women, padded out like mattresses, offered meat, poultry, eggs, cheese; boys and girls, with noses and cheeks reddened by the icy wind, searched for tobacco-addicts to buy their ration, which the Soviet military administration distributed with extravagant munificence (ten ounces a month to everybody, including babies).

With joy I met a group of compatriots: quick-witted folk, three soldiers and a girl, jovial and spendthrift, who carried on an excellent business in those days of cold and hunger with a sort of hot fritter, cooked with unusual ingredients in a doorway nearby.

After a preliminary survey, the Greek decided on shirts. Were we partners? Well then, he would contribute the capital and business experience; I, my (feeble) knowledge of German and the physical work. 'Off you go,' he told me, 'wander around all the stalls where they are selling shirts, ask how much they cost, reply that it's too much, then report back to me. Don't let yourself be noticed too much.' Reluctantly I prepared to carry out this market research; I still harboured a fossil hunger, cold and inertia, and at the same time curiosity, lightheartedness and a new and sapid willingness to converse, to open up human contacts, to parade and squander my immeasurable liberty. But the Greek, behind the back of my would-be vendors, followed me with severe eye; hurry up, damn you, time is money, and business is business.

I came back from my investigation with some comparative prices, which the Greek noted mentally; and with a fair number of disordered philological oddments: that one says something like *koshoola* for a shirt; that Polish numbers resemble Greek ones; that for 'how much?' and 'what time is it?' one says something like *eela kostooya* and *ktoora gojeena*; a termination of the genitive in –*ago* that clarified the sense of some Polish oaths I had often heard in the Lager; and other scraps of information which filled me with a foolish and puerile joy.

The Greek was calculating to himself. A shirt could be sold for fifty to one hundred zloty; an egg cost five or six zloty; for ten zloty, according to the Italian fritter-mongers, one could eat soup and another course at the soup-kitchen behind the cathedral. The Greek decided to sell only one of the three shirts he owned, and to eat at the soup-kitchen; the surplus would be invested in eggs. Then we would see what to do.

So he gave me the shirt, and ordered me to hold it up and shout: 'A shirt, gentlemen, a shirt.' For 'shirt', I was already documented; as for 'gentlemen', I believed that the correct form was *Panovye*, which I had heard used a few minutes before by my rivals and which I interpreted as a plural vocative of *Pan*, gentleman. As for this last term, I had no doubts: it is to be found in an important dialogue in *The Brothers Karamazov*. It really must have been the correct word, as various clients addressed me in Polish, asking me incomprehensible questions about the shirt. I was in difficulties; the Greek intervened authoritatively, pushed me aside and personally conducted the negotiations, which were long and laborious, but which ended happily. At the purchaser's request, the consignment of the article took place, not in the public square, but in a doorway.

Seventy zloty, equivalent to seven meals or a dozen eggs. I don't know about the Greek; as for myself, I had not possessed so large a sum of foodstuffs all at one time for fourteen months. But did I really possess them? It seemed highly doubtful; the Greek had pocketed the sum silently, and his whole attitude led one to understand that he intended to keep the administration of the profits to himself.

We wandered round the egg-stalls, where we learnt that hard-boiled and raw eggs sold at the same price. We bought six for dinner: the Greek proceeded to their purchase with extreme care, choosing the largest after detailed comparisons and much perplexity and changes of mind, wholly insensitive to the dis-approving looks of the seller.

The soup-kitchen was behind the cathedral; it remained only to determine which, of the many and beautiful churches of Cracow, was the cathedral. Whom could one ask, and how? A priest walked by; I would ask the priest. Now the priest, young and of benign appearance, understood neither French nor German; as a result, for the first and only time in my post-scholastic career, I reaped the fruits of years of classical studies, carrying on the most extravagant and chaotic of conversations in Latin. After the initial request for information (*Pater optime, ubi est menas pauperorum?*), we began to speak confusedly of everything, of my being a Jew, of the Lager (*castra?* Better: Lager, only too likely to be understood by everybody), of Italy, of the danger of speaking German in public (which I was to understand soon after, by direct experience), and of innumerable other things, to which the unusual dress of the language gave a curious air of the remotest past.

I had completely forgotten the hunger and the cold, so true is it that the need for human contact is to be numbered among the primordial needs. I had also forgotten the Greek; but he had not forgotten me, and he emerged brutally after a few minutes, interrupting the conversation pitilessly. It was not that he was incapable of human contact, or that he did not understand its value (I had seen that the evening before in the barracks); but it was something for outside office hours, for holidays, something supplementary, not to be mixed up with the serious and stren-uous business that was daily work. To my feeble protests, he replied only with a morose look. We walked on; the Greek was silent for a long time, then, as a conclusive judgement on my collaboration, he said to me in a thoughtful tone: '*Je n'ai pas encore compris si tu es idiot ou fainéant.*'

By following the priest's valuable directions, we reached the soup-kitchen. It was a somewhat depressing place, but warm and full of voluptuous smells. The Greek ordered two soups and only one ration of beans with lard; this was the punishment for my indecorous and fatuous behaviour in the morning. He was angry; but after he had gulped down his soup he softened perceptibly, so much so as to leave me a good quarter of his beans. Outside it had begun to snow, and a vicious wind was blowing. Whether from pity at the sight of my striped clothes, or from indifference to the regulations, the kitchen staff left us in peace for a good part of the afternoon to meditate and make plans for the future. The Greek's mood seemed to have changed; perhaps his fever had returned, or perhaps, after the bargains of the morning, he felt that he was on holiday. In fact he was in a benevolently pedagogic mood; as the hours slowly passed, the tone of his discourse grew gradually warmer, and on a parallel plane the tie that united us changed: from owner–slave at midday, to employer–employee at one o'clock, from master–disciple at two o'clock, to elder brother–younger brother at three o'clock. The discourse came back to my shoes, which neither of us, for different reasons, could forget. He explained to me that to be without shoes is a very serious fault. When war is waging, one has to think of two things before all others: in the first place of one's shoes, in the second place of food to eat; and not vice versa, as the common herd believes, because he who has shoes can search for food, but the inverse is not true. 'But the war is over,' I objected: and I thought it was over, as did many in those months of truce, in a much more universal sense than one dares to think today. 'There is always war,' replied Mordo Nahum memorably.

It is common knowledge that nobody is born with a decalogue already formed, but that everyone builds his own either during his life or at the end, on the basis of his own experiences, or of those of others which can be assimilated to his own; so that everybody's moral universe, suitably interpreted, comes to be identified with the sum of his former experiences, and so represents an abridged form of his biography. The biography of my Greek was linear; it was that of a strong and cold man, solitary and logical, who had acted from his infancy within the rigid framework of a mercantile society. He was also (or had been) open to other claims; he was not indifferent to the sky and the sea of his own country, to the pleasures of the home and of the family, to dialectical encounters; but he had been conditioned to drive all this back to the margins of his day and life, so that it would not disturb what he called the '*travail d'homme*'. His life had been one of war, and he considered anyone who refused this iron universe of his to be despicable and blind. The Lager had happened to both of us; I had felt it as a monstrous upheaval, a loathsome anomaly in my history and in the history of the world; he, as a sad confirmation of things well known. 'There is always war', man is wolf to man: an old story. He never spoke to me of his two years of Auschwitz.

He spoke to me instead, with eloquence, of his multiple activities in Salonica, of goods bought, sold, smuggled by sea or across the Bulgarian frontier by night; of frauds shamefully endured and of others gloriously perpetrated; and finally, of the happy and serene hours spent after the day's work by the shores of his bay, with his merchant colleagues, in cafés built on piles which he described to me with unusual freedom, and of the long discussions that took place there. What discussions? Of money, customs, freight charges, naturally, but of other things as well. What is the meaning of 'knowledge', 'spirit', 'justice', 'truth'? What is the nature of the slender tie that binds the soul to the body, how is it established at birth and dissolved at death? What is liberty, and how can one reconcile the conflict between the liberty of the spirit and fate? What follows death?; and other great Greek matters. But naturally, all this in the evening, when business was over, with coffee or wine or olives, a lucid intellectual game between men active even in idleness; without passion.

Why the Greek recounted these matters to me, why he confessed to me, is not clear. Perhaps in front of me, so different, so foreign, he still felt alone, and his discourse was a monologue.

We left the kitchen in the evening, and returned to the Italians' barracks; after much insistence, we had gained permission from the Italian colonel, the head of the camp, to stay in the barracks one more night – but only one. No food, and we were not to show ourselves too much, he did not want trouble with the Russians. The morning after we should have to leave. We dined on two eggs apiece, from those purchased in the morning, keeping the last two for breakfast. After the events of the day, I felt myself very 'junior' compared to the Greek. When we came to the eggs, I asked him if he knew how to distinguish a raw egg from a hard-boiled one from the outside. (One spins the egg rapidly, for example on a table; if it is hard boiled it spins for a long time, if it is raw it stops almost at once); it was a little trick I was proud of, I hoped the Greek did not know it, and that I could thus rehabilitate myself in his eyes, at least in small measure.

But the Greek stared at me coldly, like a wise serpent: 'What do you take me for? Do you think I was born yesterday? Do you think I have never dealt in eggs? Come on, tell me an article I have never dealt in!'

I had to beat a retreat. The episode, negligible in itself, came back to me many months later, in the height of summer in the heart of White Russia, on the occasion of what was to be my third and last meeting with Mordo Nahum.

*

We left the following morning, at dawn (this is a story inter-woven with freezing dawns), aiming at Katowice: we had received confirmation that various assembly centres really existed there for dispersed Italians, French, Greeks, etc. Kato-wice was only about fifty miles from Cracow, little more than an hour by train in normal times. But in those days one could hardly travel a dozen miles without changing trains, many bridges had been blown up, and because of the bad state of the lines the trains travelled with extreme slowness by day, and not at all by night. It was a labyrinthine journey, which lasted three days, with nocturnal halts in places ridiculously far from the straight line between the two extremes; a journey of cold and hunger, which took us on the first day to a place called Trze-binia. Here the train stopped, and I climbed down on the platform to stretch my legs, rigid from the cold. Perhaps I was among the first dressed in 'zebra' clothes to appear in that place called Trzebinia; I immediately found myself the centre of a dense group of curious people, who interrogated me volubly in Polish. I replied as best I could in German; and in the middle of the group of workers and peasants a bourgeois appeared, with a felt hat, glasses and a leather briefcase in his hand – a lawyer.

He was Polish, he spoke French and German well, he was an extremely courteous and benevolent person; in short, he pos-sessed all the requisites enabling me finally, after the long year of slavery and silence, to recognize in him the messenger, the spokesman of the civilized world, the first that I had met.

I had a torrent of urgent things to tell the civilized world: my things, but everyone's, things of blood, things which (it seemed to me) ought to shake every conscience to its very foundations. In truth, the lawyer was courteous and benevolent: he questioned me, and I spoke at dizzy speed of those so recent experiences of mine, of Auschwitz nearby, yet, it seemed, unknown to all, of the hecatomb from which I alone had escaped, of everything. The lawyer translated into Polish for the public. Now I do not know Polish, but I know how one says 'Jew' and how one says 'political'; and I soon realized that the translation of my account, although sympathetic, was not faithful to it. The lawyer described me to the public not as an Italian Jew, but as an Italian political prisoner.

I asked him why, amazed and almost offended. He replied, embarrassed: '*C'est mieux pour vous. La guerre n'est pas finie.*' The words of the Greek.

I felt my sense of freedom, my sense of being a man among men, of being alive, like a warm tide ebb from me. I found myself suddenly old, lifeless, tired beyond human measure; the war was not over, there was always war. My listeners began to steal away; they must have understood. I had dreamed, we had always dreamed, of something like this, in the nights at Auschwitz: of speaking and not being listened to, of finding liberty and remaining alone. After a while I remained alone with the lawyer; a few minutes later he also left me, urbanely excusing himself. He warned me, as the priest had done, against speaking German; when I asked for an explanation, he replied vaguely: 'Poland is a sad country.' He wished me good luck, he offered me money which I refused; he seemed to me deeply moved.

The locomotive was whistling its imminent departure. I climbed on the goods truck again, where the Greek was waiting for me, but I did not tell him of the episode.

This was not the only halt; others followed, and in one of them, in the evening, we realized that Szczakowa, the place with hot soup for everybody, was not far away. It was in fact to the north, and we had to go west, but as there was hot soup for everybody at Szczakowa, and we had no other programme except to satisfy our hunger, why not aim at Szczakowa? So we got down, waited until a suitable train passed and presented ourselves again and again at the Red Cross counter; I think that the Polish sisters recognized me easily, and that they still remember me today.

When night came, we prepared to sleep on the floor in the middle of the waiting-room, as all the places by the walls were already taken. Some hours later a Polish policeman arrived, moustached, ruddy and corpulent. Perhaps out of pity or perhaps out of curiosity about my dress, he interrogated me in vain in Polish; I replied with the first phrase that one learns in every foreign language, and that is, '*nye rozumyen po polsku*', I do not understand Polish. I added, in German, that I was Italian and that I spoke a little German. At which, miracle! the policeman began to speak Italian.

He spoke a terrible Italian, guttural and aspirated, interwoven with portentous oaths unknown to me. He had learnt it, and this explained everything, in a valley of northern Italy, where he had worked for some years as a miner. He too, and he was the third, had warned me not to speak German. I asked him why; he replied with an eloquent gesture, passing his index and middle fingers, like a knife, between his chin and larynx, and adding very cheerfully: Tonight all Germans kaputt.'

It was undoubtedly an exaggeration, or at any rate wishful thinking; but in fact the next day we passed a long train of cattle-trucks, closed from the outside; they were going east, and from the slits one could see many human mouths gaping for air. This spectacle, strongly evocative, aroused in me a mixture of confused and contradictory feelings, which even today I have difficulty in disentangling.

The policeman, with great kindness, proposed that the Greek and myself spend the rest of the night in warmth, in the jail; we accepted willingly, and only woke up in the unusual surroundings late in the morning, after a refreshing sleep.

We left Szczakowa the day after, for the last lap of our

journey. We reached Katowice without trouble, where there really existed an assembly camp for Italians, and another for Greeks. We left each other without many words: but at the moment of farewell, in a fleeting but distinct manner, I felt a solitary wave of friendliness towards my Greek, streaked with tenuous gratitude, contempt, respect, animosity, curiosity and regret that I should not see him again.

I was in fact to see him again – twice. I saw him in May, in the glorious and turbulent days at the end of the war, when all the Greeks of Katowice, about a hundred men and women, passed singing in front of our camp, as they marched towards the station; they were going back to their country, to their homes. At the head of the column was he, Mordo Nahum, a lord among the Greeks, and it was he who bore the blue and white standard; but he put it down when he saw me, came out of the ranks to salute me (a little ironically, for he was leaving and I was staying; but it was just, he explained to me, because Greece belonged to the United Nations), and with an unaccustomed gesture took a gift out of his famous sack: a pair of trousers, of the type used in Auschwitz in the last months, that is with a large 'window' on the left hip, closed by a patch of striped cloth. Then he disappeared.

But he was to appear once more, many months later, against the most improbable of backgrounds and in the most unexpected of incarnations.

4

Katowice

The transit camp of Katowice, which welcomed me hungry and tired after the week of wanderings with the Greek, was situated on a low hill in a suburb of the city called Bogucice. Formerly it had been a small German Lager, and had housed the miner-slaves working in a near-by coal pit. It consisted of a dozen brick huts, of small dimensions, and a single storey; there still existed the double barbed-wire enclosure, now purely symbolic. The entrance was guarded by a solitary Soviet soldier, of a somnolent and idle mien; on the opposite side there was a large hole in the enclosure, through which one could leave without even bending down: the Russian Command did not seem to worry about it at all. The kitchens, canteen, infirmary and washrooms were outside the enclosure, so that the entrance was subject to a continual traffic.

The guard was a huge Mongolian, about fifty years old, armed with a sten-gun and bayonet, with enormous knobbly hands, grey drooping Stalin-type moustaches and fiery eyes; but his ferocious and barbaric appearance was wholly inconsistent with his innocent duties. He was never relieved, and so died of boredom. His behaviour towards those who used the entrance was unforeseeable; sometimes he demanded your *propusk*, that is, your permit; at other times he only asked your name; at other times again a little tobacco, or nothing at all. On certain other days, however, he ferociously repulsed everybody, but did not mind if he then saw them leaving by the hole at the back of the camp, even though it was plainly visible. When it was cold, he simply left his post, entered one of the dormitories where he saw a chimney smoking, threw his sten-gun on a bunk, lit his pipe, offered vodka if he had some, or asked for it if he had none, and swore despondently if no one gave him any. Sometimes he even gave his sten-gun to the first of us he came across, and by gestures and shouts made him understand that he was to act as substitute at the guard-post; then he dozed off near the stove.

When I arrived there with Mordo Nahum, the camp was occupied by an extremely promiscuous population of about four hundred. There were French, Italians, Dutch, Greeks, Czechs, Hungarians and others; some had been civilian workers of the Todt Organization, others military internees, still others ex-Häftlinge. There were also about a hundred women.

In practice, the organization of the camp was really left to individual or group initiative; but nominally the camp was under a Soviet Kommandantur which was the most picturesque example of a gypsy encampment that one could imagine. There was a captain, Ivan Antonovich Egorov, a little man, no longer young, with a rustic and repulsive air; three lieutenants; a sergeant, athletic and jovial; a dozen territorial-army soldiers (including the guard with moustaches described above); a quartermaster; a *doktorka*; a medical doctor, Pyotr Grigoryevich Danchenko, extremely young, a great drinker, smoker, lover, a negligent person; a nurse, Marya Fydorovna Prima, who soon became my friend; and an indefinite flock of girls as solid as oaks; nobody knew if they were military personnel or mobilized or auxiliaries or civilians or dilettanti. This last group had various and vague duties: washer-women, cooks, typists, secretaries, waitresses, lovers *pro tem,* of one or another man, intermittent fiancées, wives, daughters.

The whole troupe lived in harmony, without timetable or regulations, near the camp, lodged in the buildings of an abandoned primary school. The only person to take care of us was the quartermaster, who seemed to be the highest in authority, although not in rank, of the whole Command. In any case, their entire hierarchical relationships were indecipherable; for the most part, they lived together with friendly simplicity, like a large temporary family, without military formalism; sometimes furious quarrels and fights broke out, even between officers and soldiers, but they ended quickly without disciplinary consequences or bitterness, as if nothing had happened.

The war was about to finish, the long war that had devastated their country; for them it was already over. It was the great truce; for the other harsh season which was to follow had not yet begun, nor as yet had the ill-omened name of Cold War been pronounced. They were cheerful, sad and tired, and took pleasure in food and wine, like Ulysses' companions after the ships had been pulled ashore. And yet, under their slovenly and anarchical appearance, it was easy to see in them, in each of those rough and open faces, the good soldiers of the Red Army, the valiant men of the old and new Russia, gentle in peace and fierce in war, strong from an inner discipline born from concord, from reciprocal love and from love of their country; a stronger discipline, because it came from the spirit, than the mechanical and servile discipline of the Germans. It was easy to understand, living among them, why this former discipline, and not the latter, had finally triumphed.

One of the buildings in the camp was inhabited by Italians only, almost all civilian workers, who had gone to Germany more or less voluntarily. They were builders and miners, no longer young, quiet folk, sober, laborious, of gentle spirit.

But the camp leader of the Italians, to whom I was directed

to be 'enlisted', was very different. Accountant Rovi had become camp leader not by election from below, nor by Russian investiture, but by self-nomination; in fact, although he was an individual of somewhat meagre intellectual and moral qualities, he possessed to a notable degree that virtue which under any sky is the most necessary to win power – the love of power for its own sake.

To watch the behaviour of a man who acts not according to reason, but according to his own deep impulses, is a spectacle of extreme interest, similar to that which the naturalist enjoys when he studies the activities of an animal of complex instincts. Rovi had achieved his office by acting with the same atavistic spontaneity as a spider spinning its web; like the spider without its web, so Rovi did not know how to live without his office. He had begun to spin immediately; he was basically foolish, and did not know a word of German or Russian, but from the first day he had secured for himself the services of an interpreter, and had presented himself in a ceremonial manner to the Soviet Command as plenipotentiary for Italian interests. He had organized a desk, with official forms (in beautiful handwriting with flourishes), rubber stamps, variously coloured pencils and a ledger; although he was not a colonel, in fact not even a soldier, he had hung outside his door an ostentatious placard 'Italian Command – Colonel Rovi'; he had surrounded himself with a small court of scullions, scribes, acolytes, spies, messengers and bullies, whom he paid in kind, with food taken from the rations of the community, and with exemption from all jobs of common interest. His courtiers, who, as always happens, were far worse than he, ensured (even by force, which was rarely necessary) that his orders were carried out, served him, gathered information for him and flattered him intensely.

With surprising foresight, which is another way of saying by

a highly complex and mysterious mental process, he had understood the importance, in fact the necessity, of owning a uniform,
given that he had to deal with people in uniform. He had created
quite a theatrical one, not without fantasy, out of a pair of Soviet
boots, a Polish railwayman's cap and a jacket and pair of
trousers found heaven knows where, which seemed to have
belonged to a Fascist uniform and perhaps had; he had had
badges sewn on the collar, gold braid on the cap, stripes and
chevrons on the sleeves, and had covered his chest with medals.

However, he was not a tyrant, and not even a bad admin-
istrator. He had the good sense to keep molestations,
extortions and abuses of authority within modest limits, and
possessed an undeniable vocation for red tape. Now, since
these Russians were curiously sensitive to the fascination of
red tape (of which however they wholly missed the ultimate
rational significance), and since, it seemed, they loved bureaucracy with that platonic and spiritual love which does not
arrive at or desire possession, Rovi was benevolently tolerated,
albeit not really appreciated, in the environment of the
Kommandantur. Furthermore, he was bound to Captain
Egorov by a paradoxical impossible tie of sympathy between
misanthropes; for both were sad individuals, afflicted, disgusted and dyspeptic, and sought isolation in the general
euphoria.

In the camp of Bogucice I found Leonardo, already accredited
as a doctor, and besieged by a scarcely profitable but extremely
numerous clientele; like myself he had come from Buna, and had
arrived at Katowice a few weeks earlier, following less intricate
paths than mine. Among the Häftlinge of Buna there were far
too many doctors, and few (in practice, only those who spoke
German, or who were extremely skilled in the art of survival)
succeeded in gaining recognition as such by the head doctor of
the SS. So Leonardo had not enjoyed any privileges; he had been

subjected to the most wearing manual tasks, and had lived his year of Lager in an extremely precarious manner. He painfully endured the fatigue and the cold, and had been sent to the infirmary countless times, for oedema of the feet, infected wounds and general undernourishment. Three times, in three infirmary selections, he had been chosen to die in the gas chamber, and three times he had narrowly escaped his fate through the solidarity of his colleagues in office. However, besides good fortune, he also possessed another virtue essential for those places: an unlimited capacity for endurance, a silent courage, not innate, not religious, not transcendent, but deliberate and willed hour by hour, a virile patience, which sustained him miraculously to the very edge of collapse.

The infirmary of Bogucice was to be found in the same school which lodged the Russian Command, in two small, quite clean rooms. It had been created from nothing by Marya Fyodorovna: Marya was a military nurse of about forty, with oblique and wild eyes, short nose with flared nostrils, and the agile, silent movements of a forest cat. In fact, she came from the forests; she was born in the heart of Siberia.

Marya was an energetic, stormy, disorderly and brisk woman. She procured drugs, partly through the normal administrative channels, drawing on the Soviet military depots; partly through the multiple channels of the black market; and partly (and it was the major part) by co-operating actively in sacking the warehouses of the former German Lagers and the abandoned German infirmaries and pharmacies, whose reserves had previously been the fruit of sacks carried out by the Germans among all the nations of Europe. So every day supplies arrived at the infirmary of Bogucice without plan or method: hundreds of boxes of pharmaceutical specialities, with labels and instructions in every language, which needed to be ordered and catalogued for possible use.

One of the most important things I had learnt in Auschwitz was that one must always avoid being a nobody. All roads are closed to a person who appears useless, all are open to a person who has a function, even the most fatuous. So after I had taken counsel with Leonardo, I presented myself to Marya, and offered my services as a polyglot-pharmacist

Marya Fyodorovna examined me with an eye expert in weighing up males. Was I a '*doktor*'? Yes, I was, I maintained, assisted in my ambiguity by the strong linguistic discord; the Siberian woman, in fact, did not speak German, but (although she was not Jewish) she knew a little Yiddish, learnt heaven knows where. I did not have a very professional or a very attractive air, but perhaps I was passable for work in a back room: Marya took a crumpled piece of paper out of her pocket, and asked me what was my name.

When I added 'Primo' to 'Levi', her green eyes lit up, at first suspectingly, then inquiringly, finally benevolently. But then we were almost relations, she explained to me. I 'Primo' and she 'Prima'; 'Prima' was her surname, her '*familia*', Marya Fyodorovna Prima. Excellent, I could have the job. Shoes and clothes? Well, it was no easy matter, she would speak about it to Egorov and to some of her acquaintances, perhaps something could be found later. She scribbled my name on the piece of paper and the following day solemnly gave me the *propusk*, a permit of a somewhat homely appearance, which authorized me to enter and leave the camp at any hour of the day or night.

I lived in a room with eight Italian workers, and every morning I went to the infirmary to work. Marya Fyodorovna passed on to me many hundreds of coloured boxes to classify, and gave me small friendly presents: boxes of glucose (extremely welcome), liquorice and mint tablets; shoelaces; sometimes a packet of salt or custard powder. One evening she invited me for tea in her room, and I noticed that on the wall above her bed hung seven or eight photographs of men in uniform; they were almost all portraits of well-known faces, of the soldiers and officers of the Kommandantur. Marya called them all familiarly by name and spoke of them with affectionate simplicity; she had known them for so many years now, and they had fought the whole war together.

After a few days, as my work as pharmacist left me with a lot of free time, Leonardo called me to help him in the surgery. The Russian intention had been to restrict the surgery to the members of the Bogucice camp; in fact, as the treatment was free and without any formalities, Russian soldiers, civilians from Katowice, people passing through, beggars and doubtful figures who did not want to have anything to do with the authorities also came to ask for examination or medicines.

Neither Marya nor Dr Danchenko had anything to say about this state of affairs (not that Danchenko ever had anything to say about anything; nor did he concern himself about anything except courting the girls, which he did with the mannerisms of an operetta grand duke; early in the morning, when he came for a rapid inspection, he was already drunk and full of happiness). Nevertheless, a few weeks later, Marya summoned me, and with a very official air informed me that 'by order of Moscow' the activities of the surgery had to be subjected to a minute control. So I would have to keep a register, and each evening note down the name and age of the patients, their illness and the type and quantity of medicines provided or prescribed.

In itself, the matter did not seem without sense; but it was necessary to clarify certain practical details, which I discussed with Marya. For example, how could we be sure of the identity of the patients? But Marya thought the objection trifling; 'Moscow' would certainly be satisfied if I wrote down the general particulars as declared. But a more serious difficulty arose;

in what language was the register to be kept? Not in Italian or French or German, which neither Marya nor Danchenko knew. In Russian? No, I did not know Russian. Marya meditated, perplexed, then she brightened up, and exclaimed: 'Galina!' Galina would save the situation.

Galina was one of the girls attached to the Kommandantur; she knew German, so I could dictate the minutes to her in German, and she could translate them into Russian on the spot. Marya immediately sent for Galina (Marya's authority, although ill-defined, seemed great), and so began our collaboration.

Galina was eighteen, and came from Kazàtin in the Ukraine. She was dark, cheerful and graceful; she had an intelligent face with sensitive, petite features, and was the only one of her group to dress with a certain elegance, and the only one with shoulders, hands and feet of acceptable dimensions. She spoke German reasonably; with her help the famous minutes were laboriously manufactured evening by evening, with the stub of a pencil, on a block of greyish paper that Marya had handed to me like a holy relic. How does one say 'asthma' in German? And 'ankle'? And 'sprain'? And what are the corresponding Russian terms? At every linguistic obstacle we were forced to stop full of doubt and to fall back on complicated gestures, which ended in peals of laughter from Galina.

Far more rarely from me. Face to face with Galina I felt weak, ill and dirty; I was painfully conscious of my miserable appearance, of my badly shaved face, of my Auschwitz clothes; I was acutely conscious of Galina's glance, still almost infantile, in which vague compassion was mixed with definite repulsion.

Nevertheless, after a few weeks of working together, an atmosphere of tenuous reciprocal confidence had settled between us. Galina gave me to understand that the business of the minutes was not all that serious, that Marya Fyodorovna was 'old and mad' and would be satisfied so long as the sheets she received were covered with writing, and that Doctor Danchenko was busy in wholly other matters (known to Galina in amazing detail) with Anna, with Tanya, with Vassilissa, and that he was as interested in the minutes as in 'last year's snow'. So the time dedicated to the melancholic bureaucratic gods began to dwindle, and Galina profited from the intervals to tell me her story in bits and pieces, while smoking distractedly.

In the middle of the war, two years previously, she had been conscripted by this very Kommandantur in the Caucasus where she had taken refuge with her family; conscripted in the simplest of ways, that is stopped on the road, and taken to the Command HQ to type a few letters. She had gone there and she had stayed; she had been unable to detach herself (or more probably, I thought, she had not even tried). The Kommandantur had become her real family; she had followed it for thousands of miles, along the dislocated supply lines and interminable front, from the Crimea to Finland. She did not have a uniform, or even a specific post or rank, but she was useful to her fighting companions, she was their friend, and so she followed them, because there was the war, and everyone had to do his duty; moreover, the world was large and varied, and it was fun to wander around when one was young and without worries.

Galina had not even the shade of a worry. One met her in the morning going to the laundry with a bundle of washing balanced on her head, singing like a thrush; or in the offices of the Command HQ barefooted, hammering away at a typewriter; or on Sundays walking along the boulevard, arm in arm with a soldier, never the same one; or in the evening on the balcony, romantically entranced, while a smitten Belgian, in rags, serenaded her on the guitar. She was a country girl, alert, ingenious, a bit of a flirt, very vivacious, not particularly well educated, or particularly serious; yet one felt in her the same force, the same dignity as in her comrades and boyfriends, the dignity of a man who works and knows why, of a man who fights and knows that he is in the right, of a man who has his life ahead of him.

In the middle of May, a few days after the end of the war, she came to say good-bye to me. She was leaving: they had told her she could go home. Did she have her travel-warrant? Did she have her train fare? 'No,' she replied smiling, '*Nye nada*,' there was no need, in these matters one always found a way out; and she disappeared, sucked up into the emptiness of Russian space, along the paths of her endless country, leaving behind her a sharp scent of earth, of youth and of joy.

I also had other duties; to help Leonardo in the surgery, naturally; and to help Leonardo in the daily check for lice.

This last service was necessary in those countries and in those times, when petechial typhus crept about, endemic and mortal. The job was not very attractive; we had to go through all the huts, and ask everybody to strip to the waist and hand us his shirt, in whose creases and seams the lice normally nestled and laid eggs. This type of louse has a red spot on its back; according to a pleasantry which was repeated endlessly by our patients, if the spot was sufficiently enlarged a minute hammer and sickle would be seen. Lice are also called 'the infantry', with fleas as the artillery, mosquitoes as the air force, bugs as the parachutists and crab-lice as the sappers. In Russia they are called *vshi*; I learnt that from Marya, who had given me a second block of paper on which to note each day the number and name of those with lice, and to underline the backsliders in red.

The backsliders were rare, with the single notable exception of Ferrari. Ferrari was a prodigy of inertia. He belonged to a small group of ordinary criminals, formerly held at San Vittore, the main prison at Milan, to whom the Germans had given the option in 1944 of imprisonment in Italy or labour service in Germany, and who had opted for the latter. There were about forty, almost all thieves or receivers; they formed a closed, colourful and turbulent microcosm, a perpetual source of trouble for the Russian Command and for Mr Rovi.

But Ferrari was treated by his colleagues with open contempt, and so found himself relegated to an obligatory solitude. He was a small man, about forty, thin and sallow, almost bald, with an absent-minded expression. He spent his days stretched out on his bunk, and was an indefatigable reader. He read everything that came to hand: Italian, French, German, Polish newspapers and books. Every two or three days, at the moment of the check, he told me: 'I've finished that book. Have you another one to lend me? But not in Russian: you know that I have difficulty with Russian.' Not that he was a polyglot: in fact, he was practically illiterate. But he still 'read' every book, from the first line to the last, identifying the individual letters with satisfaction, pronouncing them with his lips and laboriously reconstructing the words without bothering about their meaning. That was enough for him as, on different levels, others take pleasure in solving crossword puzzles, or integrating differential equations or calculating the orbits of the asteroids.

He was a singular individual, as was confirmed by his story, which he willingly told me, and which I narrate here.

'For many years I attended the school for thieves at Loreto. There was this dummy fixed up with bells and a wallet in its pocket; one had to filch the wallet without the bells sounding, and I never succeeded. So they never authorized me to steal; they made me a guard. I was a guard for two years. The earnings are small and it's risky; it's not a good job.

'Chewing over this, one fine day I decided that, with or without authorization, if I wanted to earn my living I would have to set up on my own.

'There was the war, the evacuation, the black market, a crowd of people on the trams. I was on a Number Two tram, at Porta Ludovica, as no one knew me in that area. Near me there was a woman with a large bag; in her coat pocket I could feel a wallet. I took out my *saccagno* very slowly and began to cut the pocket.'

I must open a brief technical parenthesis. The *saccagno*, Ferrari explained to me, is a precision instrument which is made by breaking in two the blade of an open razor. Its purpose is to cut bags and pockets, so it must be extremely sharp. Occasionally it is also used to disfigure people, in questions of honour; and this is why disfigured people are also called *saccagnati*.

'I had almost finished, when a woman, not the one with the pocket, mark you, but another, began to cry "Thief, thief!" I was doing nothing to her, she did not know me, and she didn't even know the woman with the pocket. She was not even from the police, she was somebody who had nothing to do with the matter at all. At any rate, the tram stopped, they caught me, I ended in San Vittore, and from there in Germany, and from Germany here. You see? That's what can happen if you're too enterprising.'

Since then, Ferrari had not been at all enterprising. He was the most submissive and docile of my patients; he undressed immediately without protest, handed me his shirt with the inevitable lice and the morning after submitted to the disinfection without putting on airs like an offended lord. But the following day, the lice, heaven knows how, were there again. He was like that; he was no longer enterprising, he no longer put up resistance, not even to the lice.

My professional activity brought at least two advantages: the *propusk* and better food.

Food in Bogucice camp, in fact, was not short; we were given the Russian military ration, which consisted of two pounds of bread, two plates of soup a day, a *kasha* (that is, a dish with meat, lard, millet or other vegetables), and Russian-style tea, diluted, abundant and sweet. But Leonardo and I had to repair the damage caused by a year of Lager; we were still subject to an uncontrollable hunger, for the most part psychological, and the ration was not enough for us.

Marya had authorized us to eat our midday meal at the infirmary. The infirmary kitchen was run by two Parisian *maquisardes*, working-class women no longer young, also survivors from the Lager, where they had lost their husbands; they were taciturn and mournful women, whose past and recent sufferings appeared to be mastered and kept within limits on their precociously aged faces by the sharp moral consciousness of political fighters.

One of them, Simone, served at our table. She ladled out the soup once, and a second time. Then she looked at me, almost with mistrust: '*Vous répétez, jeune homme?*' Timidly I nodded assent, ashamed of my bestial greed. Under Simone's severe look, I rarely dared to '*répéter*' a fourth time.

As for the *propusk*, it formed a sign of social distinction rather than a specific advantage; in fact, anybody could easily leave through the hole in the fence, and go to the city as free as a bird in the sky. This is what many of the thieves did, to exercise their art at Katowice or even farther afield; they did not come back, or else they came back to the camp after a few days, often giving different names, not that anybody cared.

However, the *propusk* allowed one to make for Katowice without the long walk through the mud surrounding the camp. As my strength and the good season returned, I too felt an increasingly lively temptation to leave for a cruise through the unknown city; what use was it to have been liberated, if we still had to spend our days in a frame, of barbed wire? Moreover, the people of Katowice were friendly towards us, and we had free tickets for the trams and cinemas.

One evening I spoke of this to Cesare, and we decided on a general programme for the following days, which would combine utility with pleasure, that is to say business with vagabondage.

5

Cesare

I had got to know Cesare in the last days of the Lager, but he
was then a different Cesare. After the Germans had abandoned
the camp of Buna, the infectious patients' ward, where the two
French and I had succeeded in surviving and in installing an
appearance of civilization, represented an island of relative comfort; in the adjoining ward, that of the dysentery patients, death
ruled unopposed.

Through the wooden wall, a few inches from my head, I
heard Italian being spoken. One evening, mustering what little
energy I still possessed, I decided to go and see who was still
living on the other side. I walked through the dark and frozen
corridor, opened the door and found myself thrown headlong
into a kingdom of horror.

There were about a hundred bunks; at least half were filled
with corpses stiffened by the cold. Only two or three candles
broke the darkness; the walls and ceilings were lost in the shadows, so that it seemed like penetrating an enormous cavern.
There was no heating except for the infectious breath of the fifty
living patients. Despite the cold, the stink of faeces and death
was so intense as to choke my breath, and I had to do violence
to my lungs to force them to inhale the foul air.

Yet about fifty men were still living. They lay huddled under their blankets; some were groaning or shouting, others climbing painfully down from the bunks to relieve themselves on the floor. They were calling out names, praying, swearing, begging for help in all the languages of Europe.

I dragged myself gropingly along one of the passages between the three-storey bunks, stumbling and swaying in the dark on the layer of frozen excrement. On hearing my steps, the cries redoubled; bony hands came out from under the blankets, grabbed hold of my clothes, touched me icily on the face, tried to block my path. At last I reached the dividing wall at the end of the passage, and found whom I was looking for. There were two Italians in a single bunk, clinging to each other to keep out the cold: Cesare and Marcello.

I knew Marcello well; he came from Cannaregio, the old ghetto of Venice; he had been at Fossoli with me and had crossed the Brenner in the wagon next to mine. He was healthy and strong, and up to the last weeks of the Lager had held out valiantly, resisting the hunger and fatigue; but the cold of the winter had broken him. He no longer spoke, and in the light of my match I could barely recognize him: a yellow face, black with beard, all nose and teeth; his eyes bright and dilated with fever, staring into emptiness. For him there was little to be done.

Cesare, on the other hand, I barely knew, for he had arrived at Buna from Birkenau only a few months before. He asked for water before food: water, because he had not drunk for four days, and his fever was burning him, and his dysentery empty-ing him. I brought him some, together with the remains of our soup; I did not know that in this way I was laying the basis of a long and singular friendship.

His recuperative capacities must have been extraordinary, for I found him in the camp of Bogucice two months later, not only restored, but little less than flourishing, and as lively as a grasshopper; and this, despite an additional adventure which had severely tested the natural qualities of his astuteness, strengthened in the hard school of the Lager.

After the arrival of the Russians, he had been placed among the patients in Auschwitz, and as his illness was not serious, and his constitution robust, he recovered quickly – in fact, a little too quickly. About the middle of March, the German army in flight had concentrated around Breslau, and had tried one last desperate counter-offensive in the direction of the Silesian mining zone. The Russians had been taken by surprise; perhaps over-estimating the enemy's initiative, they hastened to prepare a defensive line. They needed a long anti-tank trench to close the valley of the Oder between Oppeln and Gleiwitz; manpower was short, the work colossal, the need urgent, and the Russians saw to it according to their custom in an extremely expeditious and summary manner.

One morning, about nine o'clock, armed Russians suddenly blocked some of the main streets of Katowice. In Katowice, and in all Poland, there was a shortage of men; the male population of working age had disappeared, prisoners in Germany and Russia, dispersed among the partisan bands, massacred in battle, in the bombardments, in the reprisals, in the Lagers, in the ghettos. Poland was a country in mourning, a country of old men and widows. At nine in the morning there were only women in the street; housewives with their bags or handcarts, searching for food and fuel in the shops and markets. The Russians lined them up in rows of four, bags and all, took them to the station and sent them to Gleiwitz.

Simultaneously, that is five or six days before I arrived there with the Greek, they had unexpectedly surrounded the camp of Bogucice; they shouted like cannibals and fired shots in the air to frighten anybody attempting to run away. Without much ado they silenced their peaceful colleagues of the Kommandantur, who had sought timidly to intervene, they entered the camp with their sten-guns at the ready, and made everybody come out of the huts.

Thus on the main square of the camp a sort of parodied version of the German selections took place. A considerably less bloody version, as it was a question of going to work and not to death; but to make up for this, a far more chaotic and impromptu one.

While some of the soldiers went through the dormitories to dislodge the shirkers and then chase after them in a mad race like a great game of hide and seek, others stood by the door and examined one by one the men and women who were gradually presented to them by their hunters, or who presented themselves spontaneously. The judgement whether '*bolnoy*' or '*zdorovy*' (ill or healthy) was pronounced collectively, by acclamation, not without noisy disputes in controversial cases. The '*bolnoy*' was sent back to his hut; the '*zdorovy*' was lined up in front of the barbed-wire fence.

Cesare was among the first to understand the situation ('to make out the movement', as he used to say in his colourful jargon); he had behaved with praiseworthy perspicacity, and only just failed to escape scot-free; he had hidden in the wood-deposit, a place nobody had thought about, and had remained there to the end of the hunt, very quiet and still under the pile of logs which he had pulled over himself. And then, some fool, in search of refuge, had come to hide there, bringing a Russian chasing after him. Cesare had been taken and declared healthy, purely as a reprisal, for when he came out of the woodpile he looked like a crucified Christ, or rather a defective cripple, and would have made a stone weep: he was trembling all over, he forced himself to slobber, and walked bandy-legged, limping, dragging a leg, with squinting, demented eyes. All the same, they had put him in the row of healthy people; after a few seconds, with a lightning change of tactics, he had taken to his heels and tried to re-enter the camp by the hole at the back. But he had been overtaken, had received a clout and a kick on the shins, and had accepted defeat.

The Russians had taken them beyond Gleiwitz on foot, more than twenty miles; there they had lodged them as best they could in stables and barns, and had given them a dog's life with precious little to eat, and sixteen hours a day with pickaxe and spade, in rain or sun, with a Russian always there, sten-gun at the ready; the men at the trench, and the women (those from the camp and the Polish women they had found in the streets) peeling potatoes, cooking and cleaning.

It was tough; but the insult needled Cesare more than the work and hunger. To be caught with his pants down – he: a man who had kept a stall at Porta Portese: all Trastevere would laugh at him. He had to redeem his reputation.

He worked for three days; on the fourth, he bartered his bread for two cigars. One of them he ate; the other, he soaked in water and held in his armpit all night. The next day he was ready to report sick; he had all the symptoms, a galloping fever, terrible colic, giddiness, vomiting. They put him to bed; he stayed there until the intoxication had worked itself out, then at night-time he slipped away like a wraith and returned to Bogucice by short stages, with his conscience clear. I managed to settle him in my room, and we remained inseparable until the return journey.

'Here we are again,' said Cesare, pulling on his trousers gloomily when, a few days after his return, the nocturnal quiet of the camp was dramatically broken. It was an explosion, it was the Last Trumpet; Russian soldiers were running up and down the corridors, knocking on the doors with their rifle butts, yelling excited and incomprehensible orders; shortly after, the general staff arrived, Marya in hair curlers, Egorov and Danchenko half dressed, followed by Mr Rovi, bewildered and sleepy but in full uniform. We had to get up and dress, immediately. Why? Had the Germans come back? Were they transferring us? Nobody knew anything.

We finally managed to capture Marya. No, the Germans had not broken the front, but the situation was still very serious. '*Inspektsiya*': that very morning a general was coming from Moscow to inspect the camp. The entire Kommandantur was filled with panic and despair, a *dies irae* state of mind.

Rovi's interpreter galloped from dormitory to dormitory, shouting orders and counter-orders. Brooms, dusters, buckets appeared; everyone was mobilized, the heaps of rubbish had to disappear, the windows had to be cleaned, the floors swept, the door handles polished, the cobwebs dusted away. We all began to work, yawning and swearing. Two o'clock went by, three o'clock, four o'clock.

About dawn, one began to hear people speaking of '*ubornaya*': the camp latrine really presented a problem.

It was a brick building, placed in the middle of the camp, large, striking, impossible to hide or camouflage. For months, nobody had bothered about its cleanliness or upkeep; inside, the floor was covered by a layer of stagnant filth, so deep that we had fixed large stones and bricks in it, which we could jump along in precarious equilibrium. From the doors and the cracks in the walls the filthy liquid overflowed outside, crossed the camp in the form of a stinking stream and vanished downhill in the midst of the fields.

Captain Egorov, who was sweating blood and had completely lost his head, chose a work squad of ten of us to go and clean up the latrine with brooms and buckets of chloride. But a child would have realized that ten men, even if given the right equipment, and not just brooms, would have taken at least a week; and as for the chloride, all the perfumes of Arabia would not have sweetened the place.

Not infrequently, senseless decisions emerge from the clash of two necessities where it would have been wiser to leave the dilemma to solve itself. An hour later (when the whole camp was buzzing like a disturbed beehive) the work squad was recalled, and we saw all twelve of the Command's territorial army men arrive, with planks, nails, hammers and rolls of barbed wire. In a twinkling all the doors and windows of the scandalous latrine were closed, barred, sealed with thick planks, and all the walls, up to the roof, were covered by an inextricable tangle of barbed wire. Decency had been saved; the most diligent of inspectors quite literally could not have placed a foot inside.

Midday came, then evening, and still no sign of the general. The following morning there was already less talk about him, on the third day none at all; the Russians of the Kommandantur had returned to their habitual and benign negligence and botchery, two planks had been taken down from the back door of the latrine and everything had returned to the old routine.

However, an inspector did come, a few weeks later; he came to check the running of the camp, and especially of the kitchens; he was not a general, but a captain wearing an armlet with the slightly ominous letters NKVD. He came, and he must have found particular pleasure in his duties – or in the girls of the Kommandantur, or in the air of Upper Silesia, or in the vicinity of the Italian cooks, because he did not go away, but stayed to inspect the kitchens every day until June (when we left) without apparently performing any other useful activity.

The kitchen, run by a barbaric cook from Bergamo, and an indeterminate number of fat, greasy voluntary helpers, was situated immediately outside the fence, and consisted of a large hut, almost wholly occupied by the two huge cauldrons resting on cement kilns. To enter one climbed two steps; there was no door.

The inspector carried out his first inspection with great dignity and seriousness, jotting down notes. He was a Jew, about thirty years old, extremely tall and bony, with a fine ascetic Don Quixote-like face. But by the second day he had dug out a motor-cycle, from heaven knows where, and he fell so passionately in love with it that henceforth the two were never seen apart.

The ceremony of the inspection became a public spectacle, watched by the citizens of Katowice in ever-growing numbers. The inspector arrived at about eleven o'clock, like a hurricane; he braked suddenly with a terrible squeal, and pivoting on the front wheel made the back of the motor-cycle skid through ninety degrees. Without stopping, he aimed at the kitchen with lowered head, like a charging bull; he mounted the two steps with fearful bumpings, performed two cramped figures of eight round the cauldrons, the throttle wide open, once more flew past the steps on his way down, gave the public a military salute with a radiant smile, bent over the handlebars and disappeared in a cloud of glaucous smoke and much backfiring.

The game went smoothly for some weeks; then one day neither motor-cycle nor captain were to be seen. The latter was in hospital, with a broken leg; the former was in the loving hands of a cenacle of Italian *aficionados*. But they soon reappeared; the captain had had a bracket fitted to the frame of the motor-cycle and held his plastered leg on it in a horizontal position. His face, noble in its pallor, was bright with ecstatic happiness; fitted up like this, he once more began his daily inspection with hardly less impetus.

*

Only when April came, when the last snows had melted and the mild sun had dried the Polish mud, did we begin to feel ourselves truly free. Cesare had already been to town on various occasions, and insisted that I accompany him on his expeditions; I finally decided to overcome my inertia, and we left together on a glorious spring day.

At Cesare's request, as the experiment interested him, we did not leave by the hole in the fence. I left first by the main gate; the sentry asked my name, then asked for my permit and I gave it him. He checked it; the name corresponded. I turned the corner, and passed the piece of cardboard to Cesare through the barbed wire. The sentry asked Cesare his name: Cesare replied 'Primo Levi'. He asked for the permit: the name corresponded again, and Cesare left in a wholly legal manner. Not that Cesare is much concerned about acting legally; but he likes a sense of style, gamesmanship, putting one over on the next man without making him suffer.

We had entered Katowice as cheerful as schoolboys on holiday, but our happy-go-lucky mood was continually jarred by the spectacle which confronted us. At every step we came across the traces of the fearful tragedy which had touched us but had miraculously spared us. Graves at every corner, mute and hasty graves, without a cross but with the Red Star, of Soviet soldiers killed in battle. In one of the city's parks there was an endless war cemetery with crosses and stars intermingled, almost all bearing the same date: the date of the street battle, or perhaps of the last German massacre. In the middle of the main street stood three or four German tanks, seemingly intact, transformed into trophies and monuments, the gun of one of the tanks still aiming at an enormous hole, half-way up the house in front: the monster had died in the throes of destruction. Ruins everywhere, concrete frames, scorched wooden joists, corrugated-iron huts, people in rags, with a wild and famished look. At the important crossings, there were road signs put up by the Russians, forming a curious contrast to the tidiness and pre-fabricated precision of the analogous German signs we had seen earlier, and of the American ones we were to see later; rough planks of unvarnished wood, with hand-written names painted on in tar, in uneven Cyrillic characters: Gleiwitz, Cracow, Częstochowa; or rather, since the name was too long, 'Czestoch' on one plank, and then 'owa' on another smaller plank nailed underneath.

And yet the town was still living, after the nightmare years of the Nazi occupation, and the hurricane of the passing of the front. Many shops and cafés were open; the free market actually proliferated; the trams, coal-mines, schools, cinemas were all functioning.

Since, on that first day, we did not have a penny between us, we satisfied ourselves with a reconnaissance. After a few hours of walking in the sharp air, our chronic hunger had once more become acute: 'Come with me,' said Cesare, 'we're going to have lunch.'

He took me to the market, to the part where the fruit stalls were. At the first stall, under the jaundiced eyes of the stall-holder, he took a strawberry, only one strawberry, but a large one; he chewed it very slowly, with the air of an expert, then shook his head: 'Nyedobre,' he said severely. ('It's Polish,' he explained to me; 'it means it's no good.') He passed to the next stall and repeated the scene; and so on with all the stalls until the last one. 'Well? What are you waiting for?' he then said to me with cynical pride; 'if you are hungry, you only have to act like me.'

All the same, the strawberry technique was not enough for our hunger; Cesare had understood the situation: it was high time to dedicate ourselves seriously to business.

He explained his intentions to me: he was a friend of mine,

and was not asking me for anything; if I wanted, I could come
to the market with him, perhaps even help him and learn the
business, but what he really needed was a professional partner,
with a small initial capital and some experience. In fact, he had
already found such a man, a certain Giacomantonio, a villain-
ous-looking old acquaintance of his from San Lorenzo prison.
The terms of the partnership were extremely simple: Giacomantonio would buy, he would sell and they would divide the profits
equally.

Buy what? Everything, he told me: anything that came along.
Although Cesare was little more than twenty years old, he
boasted of a remarkable trading experience, comparable to that
of the Greek. But, once the superficial analogies were over, I
soon realized that an abyss lay between him and the Greek.
Cesare was full of human warmth, always, at every moment of
his life, not just outside office hours like Mordo Nahum. For
Cesare, 'work' was sometimes an unpleasant necessity, at other
times an amusing opportunity to meet people, and not a frigid
obsession, or a luciferesque affirmation of himself. One of them
was free, the other was a slave to himself; one was miserly and
reasonable, the other prodigal and fantastic. The Greek was a
lone wolf, in an eternal war against all, old before his time,
closed in the circle of his own joyless pride; Cesare was a child
of the sun, everybody's friend; he knew no hatred or contempt,
was as changeable as the sky, joyous, cunning and ingenuous,
bold and cautious, very ignorant, very innocent and very civilized.

I did not want to enter the agreement with Giacomantonio,
but I willingly accepted Cesare's invitation to accompany him
sometimes to the market, as an apprentice, an interpreter and a
porter. I accepted it not only out of friendship, and a desire to
escape the boredom of the camp, but above all because to watch
Cesare's enterprises, even the most modest and trivial ones,

constituted a unique experience, a live and fortifying spectacle, which reconciled me to the world and once more lit in me that joy of living which Auschwitz had extinguished.

A virtue like Cesare's is good in itself, in an absolute sense; it is enough to confer nobility upon a man, to redeem his many other defects, to save his soul. But at the same time, and on a more practical level, it is of priceless value for someone intending to practise his trade on a public square: in fact, nobody was insensitive to Cesare's charm, neither the Russians of the Command, nor our motley comrades of the camp, nor the citizens of Katowice who frequented the market. Now it is equally clear from the hard laws of commerce that what is of advantage to the seller is of disadvantage to the purchaser and vice versa.

April was drawing to its close, and the sun was already warm and generous, when Cesare came to wait for me at the end of the surgery. His murderous-looking companion had carried out a series of brilliant coups: for a total of fifty zloty he had bought a fountain pen which did not write, a chronometer and a woollen shirt in quite good condition. Then this man Giacomantonio, with the expert nose of a receiver, had had the excellent idea of mounting guard at Katowice station in order to wait for the Russian trains returning from Germany: these soldiers, now demobilized and on their way home, were the easiest dupes imaginable. They were in carefree holiday spirits, had plenty of booty, did not know the local prices and needed ready money.

Apart from any utilitarian aim, it was in any case worthwhile passing a few hours at the station, merely to watch the extraordinary spectacle of the Red Army returning home: a spectacle as dramatic and solemn as a biblical migration, and at the same time as rambling and colourful as the passage of a circus. Endless strings of cattle-trucks, used as military transports, stopped at

Katowice: they were fitted out to travel for months, perhaps as far as the Pacific Ocean, and carried, all mixed together, thousands of soldiers and civilians, men and women, former Russian prisoners of the Germans, and fresh German prisoners of the Russians, as well as goods, furniture, cattle, dismantled industrial plant, food, war materials, scrap metal. They were travelling villages: some trucks contained what seemed to be a family nucleus, one or two double beds, a wardrobe with mirrors, a stove, a radio, chairs and tables. Electric wires ran haphazardly between one truck and another, originating in the first truck with a generator; they served for the lighting system and at the same time for hanging out the washing to dry (and to grow black with soot). When the sliding doors were opened in the morning half-dressed men and women appeared with large sleepy faces, who looked out puzzled from the background of these domestic settings, with little idea of which part of the world they found themselves in; then they got down to wash in the freezing water of the hydrants, and offered round tobacco and sheets of *Pravda* to roll cigarettes.

So I left for the market with Cesare, who intended to sell the three objects described above, perhaps to the Russians themselves. By now the market had lost its primitive character of a fair of human miseries. Rationing had been abolished, or rather had fallen into disuse; the peasants' carts arrived from the rich surrounding countryside with tons of lard and cheese, eggs, chickens, sugar, fruit, butter: a garden of temptations, a cruel challenge to our obsessive hunger, and to our lack of means, an imperious incitement to procure money.

Cesare sold the pen at the first attempt, for twenty zloty, without bargaining. He had absolutely no need of an interpreter: he spoke only Italian, or to be precise Roman dialect, or to be still more precise Roman ghetto slang, studded with corrupt Hebrew words. Clearly he had no choice, because he did

not know any other language; but, unknown to him, this ignorance played heavily in his favour. Cesare was playing on his
home ground, to use sporting terms; on the other hand,
his clients, intent on interpreting his incomprehensible speech
and novel gestures, were distracted from the necessary concentration; if they made counter-offers, Cesare did not understand
them, or stubbornly pretended not to understand them.

The art of the charlatan is not so widespread as I thought; the
Polish public seemed to be unaware of it, and was fascinated.
Moreover, Cesare was also a first-class mimic; he waved the
shirt in the sun, holding it tightly by the collar (under the collar
there was a hole, but Cesare held the shirt in his hand at the very
place with the hole), and he declaimed its praises with torrential
eloquence, with new and senseless additional digressions, suddenly addressing one or another member of the public with
obscene nicknames which he invented on the spot. He stopped
abruptly (he knew by instinct the oratorical value of pauses),
kissed the shirt with affection and then began again, with a resolute yet desolate voice, as if it tore his heart to part with it, and
he was only doing it for love of his neighbour: 'You, Big Belly,'
he said, 'how much will you give me for this little *koshoola* of
mine?'

The Big Belly was dumbfounded. He looked at 'the little koshoola' with desire, and glanced around out of the corner of his
eye, half hoping and half fearing that someone else would make
the first offer. Then he came forward hesitantly, held out an
uncertain hand and mumbled something like '*pinjeeshi*'. Cesare
clutched the shirt to his chest as if he had seen a snake. 'What did
he say?' he asked me, as if he suspected that he had been mor-
tally insulted; but it was a rhetorical question, for he recognized
(or guessed) Polish numbers much more quickly than I.

'You're mad,' he then stated categorically, pointing his index
finger at his temple and turning it like a drill. The public rumbled

with laughter, visibly siding with this preposterous foreigner who had come from the ends of the earth to perform wonders in their market squares. The Big Belly stood agape, rocking from foot to foot like a bear. '*Du fereek*,' continued Cesare pitilessly (he meant to say '*verrückt*'); then, to clarify, he added: '*du meschuge*.' A storm of savage laughter broke out; everyone had understood this. '*Meschuge*' is a Hebrew word which has survived in Yiddish, and as such is universally understood in all Central and Eastern Europe: it means 'mad', but it carries the additional idea of an empty, melancholic, doltish and lunar folly.

The Big Belly scratched his head and hitched up his trousers, full of embarrassment. '*Sto*,' he then said, trying to make peace: '*Sto zlotych*,' a hundred zloty.

The offer was interesting. Cesare, somewhat appeased, turned to Big Belly as man to man, with a persuasive voice, as if to convince him of some involuntary yet clumsy transgression of his. He spoke to him at length, opening up his heart, with warmth and confidence, explaining to him: 'You see? You understand? Don't you agree?'

'*Sto zlotych*,' repeated the other obstinately.

'He is a *testa dura*, as stubborn as a mule,' Cesare said to me. Then, as if overcome by unexpected tiredness, and in a final attempt to reach agreement, he put a hand on his shoulder and said to him maternally: 'Listen. Listen, pal. You haven't understood me. Let's try it this way. You give me this much' (and with his fingers he traced 150 on his belly), 'you give me *Sto Pinjeeshi*, and it's all yours. Agreed?'

The Big Belly mumbled and shook his head negatively, staring at the ground; but Cesare's clinical eye had caught the sign of capitulation: an imperceptible movement of his hand towards the back pocket of his trousers.

'Come on. Shake out those shekels!' Cesare rushed on, striking while the iron was hot. The money was finally produced and the shirt changed hands. But immediately Cesare tore me from my ecstatic admiration.

'Come on, lad. Let's hop it, before he puts his hand through the hole.' So, fearful lest the client discover the hole too quickly, we hopped it, forgoing our attempt to get rid of the unsaleable chronometer. We walked at a slow dignified pace as far as the nearest corner, then we cut and ran as fast as our legs would carry us, and returned to the camp by devious routes.

6

Victory Day

Life in the camp of Bogucice, the surgery and the market, rudimentary human relations with Russians, Poles and others, rapid oscillations between hunger and a full belly, between hopes of return and disappointment, expectancy and uncertainty, barrack life and improvisations, almost a spurious form of military life in a temporary and foreign environment, aroused in me discomfort, nostalgia and, above all, boredom. On the other hand it agreed with Cesare's habits, character and aspirations.

At Bogucice, Cesare flourished visibly, day by day, like a tree nourished by the spring sap. At the market he now had a fixed place and an affectionate clientele, created from nothing by himself by virtue of nicknames: The Bearded Lady, Skin and Bones, Booby, as many as three Buttocks, The Street Walker, Frankenstein, a Junoesque girl whom he called the Old Bailey and many others. In the camp, he enjoyed unquestioned prestige: he had quarrelled with Giacomantonio, but many others entrusted him with goods to sell, without a contract, purely on trust, so that he was never short of money.

One evening he disappeared: he did not come back to camp for dinner, or to the dormitory to sleep. Naturally, we did not create complications; nevertheless, when his absence had lasted for three days and nights, even I, who by nature am not very apprehensive, and was even less so as regards Cesare, began to feel slightly uneasy.

Cesare returned at dawn of the fourth day, as dishevelled and bristly as a cat returning from a roof-top jamboree. He had bags under his eyes, but they still shone with a proud light. 'Leave me alone,' he said as soon as he entered, although no one had asked him anything, and most of us were still snoring. He threw himself on his bunk with an air of extreme exhaustion; but after a few minutes, unable to contain the great secret pent up inside him, he came over to me just as I was waking up. In a hoarse voice, with a grim expression on his face as if he had been at a witches' sabbath for the past three nights, he told me: 'I've made it at last. I've got a *panienca*.'

The news did not sound particularly thrilling to me. He was certainly not the first to manage it; other Italians, particularly soldiers, had got themselves a girl in the city; for '*panienca*' is the exact equivalent of '*segnorina*', with an equally distorted sound.*

It was not a very difficult undertaking, since men were scarce in Poland; in fact, many Italians had 'established' themselves, impelled not merely by the national amatory myth, but also because they felt a deeper and more serious need, a nostalgia for a home and for affection. As a result, the dead or distant husband had been replaced not only in the woman's heart and bed, but in some cases in all his duties: Italians could be seen going to work in the coalfields together with Poles in order to carry their wages 'home', or serving behind the counter in a store, while strange families were to be seen on Sundays, walking decorously along the boulevards, the Italian arm in arm with a Polish girl, holding an excessively blond child by the hand.

---

* 'Segnorina', a distortion of 'Signorina' (young lady), became current in Italy to describe the Allied soldiers' girlfriends, near-prostitutes.

But, Cesare explained to me, his case was different (all cases are always different, I thought, yawning). His *panienca* was beautiful, unmarried, elegant, clean, in love with him and therefore inexpensive. Besides this, she was extremely experienced; her only defect was that she spoke Polish. So if I were his friend, I had to help him.

I was hardly in a position to help him very much, I wearily explained to him. In the first place, I did not know more than thirty words of Polish; in the second place, I was wholly lacking in the sentimental terminology he required; in the third place, I did not feel in the right mood to go with him. But Cesare refused to give up: perhaps the girl understood German. He had in mind a very clear plan; so would I kindly stop being obstructive, and tell him the German for this, that and the other.

Cesare overestimated my linguistic knowledge. The things he wanted to learn from me are not taught in any German language course, nor had I had the slightest occasion to learn them in Auschwitz; moreover, they were such subtle and idiomatic questions that I suspect that they do not exist in any language other than Italian and French.

I explained my doubts to him, but Cesare looked offended. He put on his shoes and left, mumbling curses at me. I was being subversive, that was clear; it was sheer envy. He came back in the afternoon, and threw in front of me a nice pocket Italian–German dictionary which he had bought for twenty zloty at the market. 'There is everything here,' he told me with an air that admitted of no further discussion or quibbling. Alas, there was not everything; in fact the essential things were missing, those things which a mysterious convention expurgates from the universe of printed paper; it was money thrown away. Cesare went away again, disillusioned with culture, with friendship, indeed with printed paper itself.

From then on he paid only rare visits to the camp; his

panienca provided generously for all his needs. At the end of April he disappeared for a whole week. Now, that was not the end of just any April; it was the memorable one of 1945.

Unfortunately we were not able to understand the Polish newspapers; but the size of the headlines which increased day by day, the names we could read on them, the very air we breathed in the streets and at the Kommandantur, made us understand that victory was near. We read 'Vienna', 'Koblenz', 'Rhine'; then 'Bologna'; then, with emotion and joy, 'Turin' and 'Milan'. Finally, 'Mussolini', in enormous letters, followed by an awesome and indecipherable past participle; and at last, in red ink, covering half a page, the final, cryptic and exhilarating announcement; 'BERLIN UPADL!'

On 30 April Leonardo, I and a few other passholders were summoned by Captain Egorov; with a curiously reserved and embarrassed air, which was untypical of him, he told us through the interpreter that we should have to hand back the *propusk*; the following day we should receive another one. Naturally we did not believe him, but we still had to give back the card. The measure seemed to us absurd and slightly annoying, and increased our anxiety and expectancy; but the next day we understood the reason.

For the next day was 1 May; it was followed on the 3rd by some important Polish holiday; on the 8th the war ended. The news, although expected, exploded like a hurricane; for eight days the camp, the Kommandantur, Bogucice, Katowice and the whole of Poland and the entire Red Army burst out in a fit of delirious enthusiasm. The Soviet Union is a gigantic country, and harbours within its heart gigantic vigour, a Homeric capacity for joy and abandon, a primordial vitality, an uncontaminated pagan appetite for carousals, carnivals, massive revelry.

In a few hours the atmosphere turned tropical. There were Russians everywhere, like ants coming out of an anthill; they embraced each other as if they were all old friends, and sang and shouted; although generally unsteady on their legs, they danced with each other, and overwhelmed anyone they happened to meet with embraces. They fired shots in the air, and sometimes not in the air; a young baby-faced soldier was brought to us in the surgery, a parachutist, with a bullet shot passing from his abdomen through his back. Miraculously the shot had not harmed any vital organs; the boy-soldier stayed in bed for three days and peacefully submitted to medical care, looking at us with eyes as virgin as the sea; then one evening, as a festive band of his companions passed by in the street, he jumped out of his bed fully dressed, wearing his uniform and boots, and like the good parachutist he was, simply threw himself into the road from the first-floor window before the eyes of the other patients.

The already tenuous traces of military discipline vanished. On the evening of 1 May the sentry snored drunken and sprawling on the ground in front of the camp gate, with his sten-gun on his shoulder; then he was seen no more. It was useless to go to the Kommandantur for anything urgent; the person responsible was not there, or was in bed sleeping off his drunkenness, or was engaged in mysterious and feverish preparations in the school gymnasium. It was extremely fortunate that the kitchen and surgery were in Italian hands.

What these preparations were for we soon found out. They were organizing a great party for Victory Day; a theatrical performance, with choruses, dancing and recitation, offered by the Russians to us, the guests of the camp. To us Italians; because in the meantime, as the other nationalities had been moved off according to some complicated plan, we had remained as a large majority at Bogucice, in fact, almost alone with a few French and Greeks.

Cesare came back to us on one of these tumultuous days. He

was in an even worse condition than before; covered in mud from head to foot, in rags, haggard and suffering from a monstrously stiff neck. He had a bottle of Vodka in his hand brand new and full, and his first concern was to search around until he found another empty bottle; then, scowling and funereal, he created an ingenious funnel with a piece of cardboard, decanted the vodka, broke the bottle into small pieces, collected the fragments in a sheet of paper and with an air of secrecy went to bury them in a hole at the back of the camp.

He had been struck by misfortune. One evening, returning from the market to the girl's house, he had found a Russian there; he had seen his military greatcoat in the hall with its belt and holster, and a bottle. He had taken the bottle, as a partial indemnity, and had wisely gone away; but the Russian had apparently come after him, perhaps because of the bottle, or perhaps through retrospective jealousy.

Here his account became more obscure and less plausible. He had sought in vain to escape and had soon convinced himself that the whole Red Army was on his tracks. He had ended up at a funfair, but even there the hunt had continued, throughout the night. He had spent the last few hours lurking under the floor of the dance hall, while all Poland danced on his head; but he had not abandoned the bottle, because it represented all that was left to him of a week of love. He had destroyed the original container as a precaution, and insisted that the contents be consumed immediately by his closest friends. It was a melancholic and taciturn drinking bout.

The 8 May came: a day of exultation for the Russians, of diffident vigil for the Poles, of joy tinged with deep nostalgia for us. From that day, in fact, our homes were no longer forbidden us, no war front now separated us from them, no concrete obstacle, only red tape; we felt that our repatriation was now our due, and every hour spent in exile weighed on us like lead; but the total lack of news from Italy weighed on us even more. Nevertheless, we all went to the Russians' show, and we did well.

The theatre had been improvised in the school gymnasium: in fact, everything had been improvised, actors, seats, choir, programme, lights, curtain. The tails worn by the compere, Captain Egorov in person, were strikingly improvised.

Egorov appeared on the stage blind drunk, fitted up with an enormous pair of trousers which reached to his armpits, while his tails swept the floor. He was overcome by a desperate alcoholic despondency, and presented the various comic or patriotic numbers in the programme in a sepulchral voice, amid resounding sobs and fits of tears. His equilibrium was uncertain; at crucial moments he grabbed the microphone, and then the audience fell suddenly silent as when an acrobat leaps into space from his trapeze.

Everybody appeared on the stage: the whole Kommandantur. Marya directed the choir, which was excellent, as are all Russian choirs, and which sang *Moskva moya* ('My Moscow') with wonderful impetus and harmony and manifest good faith. Galina performed by herself, dressed in a Circassian costume and boots, in a giddy dance in which she revealed fantastic and unsuspected athletic talents; she was overwhelmed by applause, and thanked the audience with emotion, dropping innumerable eighteenth-century curtsies, her face as red as a tomato and her eyes glittering with tears. Dr Danchenko and the Mongol with moustaches were as good: although full of vodka, they performed as a pair one of those demoniac Russian dances in which one jumps in the air, crouches down, kicks out and pirouettes on one's heels like a spinning top.

There followed a remarkable imitation of Charlie Chaplin, personified by one of the robust girls from the Kommandantur, with an exuberant bust and bottom, but punctiliously faithful to her prototype as regards bowler hat, moustache, shoes and cane. And finally, announced by Egorov in a tearful voice, and greeted by all the Russians with a savage shout of approval, there appeared on the stage Vanka Vstanka.

Who Vanka Vstanka is, I cannot really say: perhaps a character from a popular Russian mime. In this instance, he was a timid, dim-witted, love-lorn little shepherd, who wanted to declare his passion for his mistress but did not dare. His mistress was the huge Vassilissa, the Valkyrie responsible for the canteen, as dark as a raven, and muscular, capable of flooring at a swipe an unruly diner or an unfortunate wooer (more than one Italian had tried); but who would have recognized her on the stage? Here her rôle had transformed her; the guileless Vanka Vstanka (off stage one of the lieutenants), his face coated with white and pink powder, courted her from afar, in an Arcadian manner, through twenty melodious strophes unfortunately incomprehensible to us, stretching supplicating and hesitant arms towards his beloved; she repulsed him with smiling but resolute grace, warbling equally sweet and teasing replies. But slowly the distance diminished, while the noise of the applause increased in proportion; after much skirmishing, the two shepherds exchanged chaste kisses on the cheek, and ended by rubbing their backs against each other vigorously and sensuously to the irrepressible enthusiasm of the audience.

We left the theatre slightly dazed, but almost moved. The performance had satisfied our deepest feelings; it had been improvised in a few days, and this was noticeable; it was a home-made performance, unpretentious, puritanical, often childish. Yet it presupposed something not improvised, but deep-rooted and robust; a youthful intense native capacity for joy and self-expression, a loving and friendly familiarity with the stage and with the audience a long way removed from empty exhibitionism or intellectual abstractions, from conventionality or tired imitations. Consequently, within its limits, it had been a warm, alive performance, not vulgar, not commonplace, but generously free and self-assertive.

The following day everything had returned to normal and, except for slight shadows under their eyes, the Russians had resumed their habitual appearance. I met Marya at the surgery, and told her that I had greatly enjoyed myself, and that all the Italians had much admired her and her colleagues' theatrical qualities; it was the simple truth. Marya was, normally and by nature, a not very methodical but extremely practical woman, solidly rooted in the tangible immediacies of her everyday experience, friendly to men of flesh and hostile to the haze of theories. But how many human minds are capable of resisting the slow, fierce, incessant, imperceptible driving force of indoctrination?

She replied with didactic seriousness. She thanked me formally for the praise, and assured me that she would communicate it to the whole Command; then she informed me with great gravity that dancing and singing, as well as recitation, form part of the scholastic curriculum in the Soviet Union; that it is the good citizen's duty to perfect his abilities or natural talents; that the theatre is one of the most precious instruments of collective education; and other pedagogic platitudes, which sounded absurd and vaguely irritating to my ear, still full of the great gust of vitality and comic force of the previous evening.

On the other hand, Marya herself ('old and mad', according to the eighteen-year-old Galina's description) seemed to possess a second personality, quite distinct from her official one; for she had been seen the evening before, after the theatre, drinking like a fish, and dancing like a Bacchante until late at night, exhausting innumerable partners, like some possessed cavalier riding horse after horse into the ground.

*

Victory and peace were also celebrated in a different manner which, indirectly, almost cost me very dearly. In the middle of May a football match took place between the Katowice team and a team of Italians.

It was in fact a return game; a first match had been played without particular solemnity two or three weeks before, and had been won comfortably by the Italians against an anonymous scratch team of Polish miners from the suburbs.

But for the return match the Poles took the field with a first-class team; word got about that some players, including the goalkeeper, had been brought for the occasion from no less a place than Warsaw, while the Italians, alas, were in no condition to do likewise.

The goalkeeper was a nightmare. He was a lamp-post of a man, blond, with an emaciated face, a concave chest and slouching movements like an Apache. He had none of the leap, the emphatic crouch and the nervous twitching of the professional; he stood in the goal with insolent condescension, leaning against one of the posts as if he was only watching the game, with an outraged but also outrageous air. Yet the few times the ball was kicked at the goal by the Italians, he was always in its path, as if by chance, without ever making an abrupt movement; he would stretch out one – only one – long arm, which seemed to emerge from his body like a snail's horn and to possess the same invertebrate and adhesive quality. The ball stuck there solidly, drained of all its momentum; it slid down his chest, then down his body and leg, to the ground. He never used the other hand; during the whole match he kept it ostentatiously in his pocket.

The game was played on a ground in the suburbs at some distance from Bogucice and the Russians had given passes for the occasion to the entire camp. The match was fiercely disputed, not only between the rival teams, but also between both of these and the referee; for the referee, who was the guest of honour, the occupant of the VIPs' box, the director of the match and the linesman all at once, was the NKVD captain, the unsubstantial inspector of the kitchens. Now, with his fracture perfectly healed, he seemed to follow the game with intense interest, but not of a sporting kind; with an interest of a mysterious nature, perhaps aesthetic, perhaps metaphysical. His behaviour was irritating, in fact debilitating, if judged by the criteria of the many experts among the spectators; on the other hand, it was exhilarating, and worthy of a high-class clown.

He interrupted the game continually, arbitrarily, with piercing blasts of his whistle and with a sadistic preference for the moments when the game was being fought at the goal's mouth; if the players did not listen to him (and they soon stopped listening to him, because the interruptions were so frequent), he leapt over the wall of his box with his long booted legs, threw himself into the mêlée whistling like a train, and would not let up until he had gained possession of the ball. Then sometimes, he would take it in his hand, turning it over and over with a suspicious air, as if it were an unexploded bomb; at other times, with imperious gestures, he would order it to be placed at a certain point on the field, then would go up to it, unsatisfied, and move it a few inches, walk around it thoughtfully for a long time and finally, as if convinced of heaven knows what, make a sign for the game to continue. At other times again, when he managed to get the ball at his feet, he would make everybody move away, and would kick it at the goal with all his strength; then he would turn radiantly to the public, which bellowed with anger, and salute it for a long time, clasping his hands above his head like a victorious boxer. He was, however, rigorously impartial.

In these conditions, the match (which was deservedly won by the Poles) dragged on for over two hours, until about six in the evening; probably it would have gone on until nightfall had it depended solely upon the captain, who was not in the least worried about the time, who behaved on the field as if he were the Lord's Anointed, and who seemed to derive a crazy and inexhaustible pleasure from his misinterpreted duties as director of the game. But as twilight came, the sky rapidly darkened, and when the first drops of rain fell he whistled the game to an end.

The rain soon turned into a deluge; Bogucice was far away, there was no shelter on the road and we returned to the camp soaked to the skin. The next day I felt ill; my illness remained mysterious for a long time.

I could no longer breathe freely. It felt as though there were a blockage somewhere in my lungs, an acute pain, a deep stabbing pang, which seemed to be located somewhere above my stomach, but behind, towards the back, and which impeded me from inhaling beyond a certain point. This point dropped, from day to day, from hour to hour; the ration of air it conceded me was reduced with a slow and constant progression that terrified me. On the third day I could no longer move; on the fourth, I lay on my bunk supine, immobile, with short frequent breaths like those of a panting dog.

7

The Dreamers

Although Leonardo tried to hide it from me, he could not understand, and was seriously worried by, my illness. It was difficult to discover its real nature, because his entire professional equipment consisted of one stethoscope; it seemed not only difficult, but hardly advisable, to obtain permission from the Russians to send me to the civilian hospital of Katowice; there was also little to be hoped for from Dr Danchenko.

So for some days I remained stretched out, immobile, drinking only a few spoonfuls of soup, for every time I tried to move, or to swallow some solid food, the pain started up savagely and cut short my breath. After a week of tortured immobility, Leonardo, by dint of tapping my back and chest, managed to discover a symptom: it was a dry pleurisy, nestling insidiously between the two lungs, encumbering the mediastinum and the diaphragm.

Then he did far more than is normally expected of a doctor. He turned himself into a clandestine merchant and drug-smuggler, sturdily assisted by Cesare, and walked miles through the city, from one address to another, searching for sulphonamides and calcium injections. He was not very successful as regards the drugs, because sulphonamides were extremely rare and could be found only on the black market at prices which were prohibitive to us. But he found something better. He discovered a mysterious colleague in Katowice, who possessed a not very legal, but well-equipped, surgery, a pharmaceutical stock, much money and free time, and who was also Italian (or almost).

In fact, everything relating to Dr Gottlieb was wrapped up in a thick cloud of mystery. He spoke Italian perfectly, but German, Polish, Hungarian and Russian equally well. He came from Fiume, Vienna, Zagreb and Auschwitz. He had been at Auschwitz, but he never stated in what quality or condition, nor was he a man to whom it was easy to put questions. It was difficult to understand how he had survived in Auschwitz, for he had an anchylosed arm; it was still more difficult to imagine by what secret paths, and in what fantastic manner he had managed to remain there, never separated from his brother and his equally mysterious brother-in-law, and then, within a few months of leaving the Lager, despite the Russians and the law, to become a wealthy man and the most esteemed doctor in Katowice.

He was a wonderfully equipped person. Intelligence and cunning emanated from him like energy from radium, with the same silent and penetrating continuity, without effort, without a pause, without a sign of exhaustion, in all directions at once. It was clear from the first that he was an excellent doctor. But I was never able to discover if his professional excellence was merely one aspect, one side of his high intellect, or if it was itself his instrument of penetration, his secret weapon to turn enemies into friends, to render prohibitions null, to change no into yes; this too formed part of the cloud in which he wrapped himself and which moved with him. It was an almost visible cloud, which made his looks and the lines of his face hard to decipher, and which led one to suspect, beneath every action of his, every phrase, every silence, the existence of a tactic and a technique, the pursuit of unperceivable ends, a continual shrewd labour of exploration, elaboration, penetration and possession.

Nevertheless, Dr Gottlieb's intelligence, aimed though it was at practical ends, was not inhuman. So abundant was his self-assurance, his expectancy of victory, his faith in himself, that a large portion remained to bestow on assisting his less gifted neighbours; and in particular on assisting us, for we had escaped like him from the mortal trap of the Lager, a circumstance about which he showed himself strangely sensitive.

Gottlieb restored my health like a thaumaturge. He came once to study the case, then on various other occasions to bring vials and syringes, and a last time, when he said to me: 'Rise and walk.' The pain had disappeared, my breathing was free; I was very weak and hungry, but I got up, and I could walk.

Nevertheless, I did not leave the room for another three weeks. I spent the interminable days lying down, avidly reading the odd assortment of books I managed to lay my hands on: an English grammar in Polish, *Marie Walewska, le tendre amour de Napoléon*, a textbook of elementary trigonometry, *Rouletabille à la rescousse*, *The Convicts of the Cayenne*, and a curious Nazi propaganda novel, *Die Grosse Heimkehr* ('The Great Repatriation'), which portrayed the tragic destiny of a Galician village of pure German race, oppressed, sacked and finally destroyed by the ferocious Poland of Marshal Beck.

It was sad to be confined within four walls, when outside the air was full of spring and victory, and the wind carried stimulating smells from the nearby woods of moss, fresh grass and mushrooms; and it was humiliating to be dependent on companions for even the most elementary needs, to collect my food from the canteen, and to get water, and in the early days even to change my position in bed.

There were about twenty others in my dormitory, including Leonardo and Cesare; but the most outstanding personality, of more than human stature, was the oldest among them, the Moor from Verona. He must have come from a stock tenaciously

attached to the soil, for his real name was Avesani, and he came
from Avesa, the launderers' quarter of Verona celebrated by
Berto Barbarani.* He was over seventy, and showed all his years;
he was a great gnarled old man with huge bones like a dinosaur,
tall and upright on his haunches, still as strong as a horse,
although age and fatigue had deprived his bony joints of their
suppleness. His bald cranium, nobly convex, was encircled at its
base with a crown of white hair; but his lean, wrinkled face was
of a jaundice-like colour, while his eyes, beneath enormous
brows like ferocious dogs lurking at the back of a den, flashed
yellow and bloodshot.

In the Moor's chest, skeletal yet powerful, a gigantic but indeterminate anger raged ceaselessly; a senseless anger against
everybody and everything, against the Russians and the Germans, against Italy and the Italians, against God and mankind,
against himself and us, against day when it was day, and against
night when it was night, against his destiny and all destinies,
against his trade, even though it was a trade that ran in his
blood. He was a bricklayer; for fifty years, in Italy, America,
France, then again in Italy, and finally in Germany, he had laid
bricks, and every brick had been cemented with curses. He
cursed continuously, but not mechanically; he cursed with
method and care, acrimoniously, pausing to find the right word,
frequently correcting himself and losing his temper when unable
to find the word he wanted; then he cursed the curse that would
not come.

It was quite clear that he was possessed by a desperate senile
madness; but there was a greatness in his madness, a force and
a barbaric dignity, the trampled dignity of beasts in a cage, the
dignity that redeemed Capaneus and Caliban.

The Moor hardly ever got up from his bunk. He lay there all

* A dialect poet of Verona of the 1920s.

day, his enormous, yellow, bony feet sticking out of the end of the bunk half-way across the room; next to him on the floor lay a large shapeless bundle, which none of us ever dared to touch. It contained apparently all his worldly possessions; a heavy woodcutter's axe hung from its outside. Normally, the Moor stared into the distance with bloodshot eyes and stayed silent; but the minimal stimulus was enough, a noise in the corridor, a question asked of him, an incautious brush against his obtrusive feet, an attack of rheumatism; then his deep chest rose up like the sea swelling in a storm, and the mechanism of abuse was once more set in motion.

We respected him, and feared him with a vaguely superstitious fear. Only Cesare approached him, with the impertinent familiarity of a bird scratching about on the craggy back of a rhinoceros, and he amused himself by rousing the Moor's anger with stupid and obscene questions.

Next to the Moor lived the inept Ferrari with his lice, the bottom of the class at the Loreto school. But he was not the only member of the San Vittore confraternity in our dormitory; it was also well represented by Trovati and Cravero.

Trovati, Ambrogia Trovati alias Dusk, was not more than thirty years old; he was of small stature, but muscular and extremely nimble. 'Dusk', he explained to us, was a stage name; he was proud of it, and it fitted him perfectly, for he was a man of a darkened mind, who lived on fanciful expedients in a mental state of perpetual frustrated rebellion. He had passed his adolescence and youth between prison and the stage, and it seemed as if the two institutions were not clearly distinguished in his confused mind. Imprisonment in Germany must finally have tilted the balance.

In his conversation, the true, the possible and the fantastic were intermingled in a varied and inextricable tangle. He spoke of prison and the law courts, as of a theatre, in which nobody is really himself, but everybody is acting, showing off his talents, imitating somebody else, reciting a part; and the theatre, in its turn, was a great obscure symbol, a dark instrument of perdition, the external manifestation of an underground sect, evil and ubiquitous, which rules at everybody's expense, and comes to your home, takes you, puts a mask on you, makes you become what you are not, and do what you do not want to do. This sect is Society; the great enemy, whom he, Dusk, had always fought: he had always been defeated, but had always heroically risen again.

It was Society who had come down to search for him, to challenge him. He used to live in innocence, in a terrestrial paradise; he had been a barber, and had owned his shop, at the time of the visitation. Two messengers had come to tempt him, to propose to him diabolically that he sell his shop and give himself to Art. How well they had known his weak spot; they had flattered him, they had praised the shape of his body, his voice, the expressiveness and mobility of his face. He had resisted twice, three times, then he had given way, and with the address of the film studio in his hand had begun to wander around Milan. But the address was false, they had sent him from door to door; until he had realized that it was a conspiracy. The two messengers had followed him in the background with a movie camera, they had stolen all his words and his gestures of disappointment, and so they had made him an actor without his realizing. They had stolen his image, his shadow, his soul. It was they who had made his sun set, and who had baptized him 'Dusk'.

This was the end for him. He was in their hands: his business sold, no contract, little money, a small part every now and again, a little theft to keep alive. Until his great epopee: fleshy homicide. He had met one of his seducers in a street, and had knifed him; he had become guilty of fleshy homicide, and for this crime had been dragged into court. But he had refused to retain a lawyer, because the whole world was against him, to the last man, and he knew it. Nevertheless, he had been so eloquent, and had presented his case so well, that the Court had acquitted him on the spot with a great ovation, and everyone had wept.

This legendary trial stood at the centre of Trovati's nebulous memory; he relived it at every moment of the day, he spoke of nothing else, and frequently, after dinner in the evening, he forced all of us to join him in enacting his trial as a sort of mystery play. He assigned a part to each of us: you the judge, you the prosecutor, you the jury, you the clerk, you the public – everybody was given his part peremptorily. But the accused, and at the same time the defence counsel, was always himself; and when the moment of his torrential harangue arrived, at every performance he explained first, in a rapid 'aside', that fleshy homicide occurs when somebody sticks a knife not into the chest or the stomach, but here, between the heart and the armpit, in the flesh; and it is less serious.*

He would speak without stopping, passionately, for a whole hour, wiping authentic sweat from his brow; then, throwing the folds of a non-existent toga over his left shoulder with a broad gesture, he would conclude: 'On, on, ye snakes, deposit your venom!'

The third former inmate of San Vittore, Cravero from Turin, was, by contrast, an accomplished rogue, uncontaminated, without refinements, one of those rare beings in whom the abstract criminal hypothesis of the penal code seemed to take flesh and human shape. He knew all the jails of Italy well, and had lived in Italy (he admitted it without reserve, in fact with

---

* The descriptive '*omicidio polposo*' ('fleshy homicide') is Trovati's distortion of the technical legal term '*omicidio colposo*' ('homicide without malice aforethought').

pride) as a thief, burglar and ponce. Possessing such qualities, he had found no difficulty in settling in Germany; he had worked for only one month for the Todt Organization at Berlin, then he had disappeared, ably blending himself into the murky background of the local underworld.

After two or three attempts, he had found the right sort of widow. He helped her with his experience, procured her clients, and took over the financial side of disputed cases, even including knifing; in return she looked after him. He felt himself perfectly at home in that house, despite the difficulties of language, and certain curious habits of his protégée.

When the Russians reached the gates of Berlin, Cravero, who did not like disturbances, weighed anchor, leaving the woman in the lurch, although she burst into tears. He had been overtaken, nevertheless, by the rapid advance and, shifting from camp to camp, had ended up at Katowice. He did not stay there long. In fact, he was the first of the Italians to decide to attempt repatriation by himself. Accustomed as he was to living outside the law, he was not particularly worried by the obstacle of the numerous frontiers he had to pass without documents and of the thousand miles he had to travel without money.

As he was going to Turin, he very courteously offered to take a letter to my home. I accepted, with a certain levity, as will be seen; I accepted because I was ill, because I have great and deep faith in my neighbour, because the Polish post did not work and because Marya Fyodorovna had paled and changed the subject when I asked her to write a letter on my behalf to be sent to the west.

Cravero left Katowice in the middle of May, and reached Turin in the record time of one month, slipping like an eel through innumerable check-points. He traced my mother, gave her the letter (it was my only sign of life in nine months to reach its destination) and confidentially described to her my extremely worrying state of health; naturally I had not written this in my letter, but I was alone, ill, abandoned, without money, in urgent need of help; in his opinion, I had to be provided for immediately. Certainly it was no easy undertaking; but he, Cravero, my bosom friend, was there to help. If my mother gave him 200,000 lire, he would bring me home to safety in two or three weeks. In fact, if the young lady (my sister, who was listening to the conversation) wanted to accompany him ...

It is to my mother's and my sister's credit that they were not wholly taken in by the messenger. They sent him away, asking him to call again in a few days, as they did not have the sum of money available. Cravero went downstairs, stole my sister's bicycle, which was in front of the house, and disappeared. Two years later, at Christmas, he sent me an affectionate greetings card from prison in Turin.

The evenings when Dusk exempted us from rehearsing his trial, Mr Unverdorben took the stage. This strange and attractive name belonged to a mild touchy little old man from Trieste. Mr Unverdorben, who would not reply to anybody who did not call him 'Mr' and who insisted on being addressed with respect, had lived a long adventurous double existence, and like the Moor and Dusk was the prisoner of a dream, in fact of two dreams.

Inexplicably he had survived the Birkenau Lager, and emerged from it with a terrible phlegmon on one foot, and could not walk; so he was the most assiduous and obsequious of those who offered me company and help during my illness. He was also very loquacious, and if he had not repeated himself so frequently, as old men do, his confidences would be enough to make a novel. He was a musician, a great misunderstood musician, a composer and conductor; he had composed a lyric opera, *The Queen of Navarre*, which had been praised by Toscanini; but the manuscript lay unpublished in a drawer, because his enemies had examined his music with such indecent application that in the end they had discovered four consecutive bars in his score which were identical with four in *I Pagliacci*. His good faith was obvious, crystal clear, but the law does not joke about such matters. Three bars yes, four no. Four bars are plagiarism. Mr Unverdorben had been too much of a gentleman to dirty his hands with lawyers and law-suits; in a virile manner, he had said good-bye to art, and had created a new existence for himself as a chef on board transatlantic liners.

He had travelled a lot, and had seen things which no one else had seen. Above all, he had seen extraordinary animals and plants, and many secrets of nature. He had seen the crocodiles of the River Ganges, which have a single rigid bone running from the tip of the nose to the tail, and which are extremely ferocious and race like the wind; but, because of this singular bone structure, they can only move backwards and forwards like a train on railway lines, and all you have to do to be safe is to place yourself by their side, at a slight angle from their axis.

He had seen the jackals of the Nile, which drink while they run so as not to be bitten by the fish; at night their eyes shine like lanterns, and they sing with raucous human voices. He had also seen Malaysian cabbages which are like our cabbages, but much bigger; if you merely touch their leaves with a finger, you cannot free yourself again; the hand, and then the arm, and then the rash person's entire body is drawn inwards slowly but irresistibly, into the monstrous sticky heart of the carnivorous plant, and digested little by little. The only remedy, which almost nobody knows, is fire, but you have to act quickly; it is enough to light a match under the leaf that has seized its prey, and the plant's grip slowly relaxes. In this way, thanks to his promptness and knowledge of natural history, Mr Unverdorben had saved the captain of his boat from sure death. Then there are certain little black snakes which live buried in the squalid sands of

Australia, and which dart out at a man from afar, in the air, like bullets; one bite of theirs is enough to knock out a bull. But everything in nature is balanced, there is no offence without a defence, every poison has its antidote; it is enough to know what it is. The bite of these reptiles is promptly cured if treated with human saliva; but not the saliva of the person who has been attacked. This is why no one ever travels alone in those parts.

In the long Polish evenings, the air in the dormitory, heavy with tobacco and human smells, was saturated with senseless dreams. This is the most immediate fruit of exile, of uprooting: the prevalence of the unreal over the real. Everyone dreamed past and future dreams, of slavery and redemption, of improbable paradises, of equally mythical and improbable enemies; cosmic enemies, perverse and subtle, who pervade everything like the air. Everyone, except perhaps Cravero, and certainly D'Agata.

D'Agata had no time to dream, because he was obsessed by the fear of bugs. Of course, nobody liked these unpleasant companions; but in the end we had all grown accustomed to them. They were not few and scattered, but a compact army, which invaded all our pallets at springtime; during the day they nestled in the chinks of the walls and in the wooden bunks, and as soon as the confusion of the day died down, they sallied forth. We would willingly have ceded them a small portion of our blood; it was less easy to accustom ourselves to feel them running furtively over our faces and bodies, under our clothes. The only people to sleep peacefully were those who were fortunate enough to be heavy sleepers, and who managed to fall into unconsciousness before the bugs woke up.

D'Agata, who was a minute, sober, reserved and extremely clean Sicilian bricklayer, was forced to sleep by day, and spent the nights perching on his bed, staring around, his eyes dilated with horror, insomnia and spasmodic concentration. He clutched a rudimentary tool in his hand, which he had constructed from a stick and a piece of wire grating, and the wall next to him was covered with a lurid constellation of bloody spots.

At first, these habits of his had been derided; was his skin thinner than ours? But then compassion had prevailed, mixed with a trace of envy; because, of all of us, D'Agata was the only one whose enemy was concrete, present, tangible, capable of being fought, beaten, crushed against the wall.

8

Southwards

I had been walking for hours in the marvellous morning air, drawing it deeply into my battered lungs like medicine. I was not very steady on my feet, but I felt an imperious need to take possession of my body again, to re-establish a contact, by now broken for almost two years, with trees and grass, with the heavy brown soil in which one could feel the seeds chafing, with the ocean of air wafting the pollen from the fir trees, wave upon wave, from the Carpathians to the black streets of the mining city.

I had been wandering around like this for a week now, exploring the environs of Katowice. The pleasant weakness of convalescence ran through my veins. At the same time, powerful doses of insulin also ran through my veins, prescribed, found, bought and injected in agreement by Leonardo and Gottlieb. While I walked, the insulin carried out its prodigious work in silence; it ran through my blood searching for sugar, took care of its diligent combustion and conversion into energy, and distracted it from other less proper destinies. But there was not much sugar available; suddenly, dramatically, almost always at the same time, the supplies ran out; then my legs folded under me, everything grew black and I was forced to sit on the ground wherever I was, frozen and overwhelmed by an attack of ferocious hunger. At this point, the labours and gifts of my third protector, Marya Fyodorovna Prima, came to my aid; I took a packet of glucose from my pocket and swallowed it greedily. After a few minutes, light returned, the sun grew warm once more and I could begin my walk again.

When I returned to the camp that morning, I came on an unusual scene. In the middle of the square stood Captain Egorov, surrounded by a dense crowd of Italians. He was holding a large revolver, which, however, he only used to emphasize the salient parts of the discourse he was making with broad gestures. Very little of his speech could be understood. Basically only two words, because he repeated them frequently; but these two words were heavenly messengers: '*Ripatriatsiya*' and '*Odyessa*'.

So, we were to be repatriated via Odessa; we were to return home. The whole camp instantly ran wild. Captain Egorov was lifted from the ground, revolver and all, and carried precariously in triumph. People bellowed in the corridors: 'Home! home!'; others turned to their luggage, making as much noise as possible, and throwing rags, waste paper, broken shoes and all sorts of rubbish out of the window. In a few hours the whole camp emptied, under the Olympian eyes of the Russians; some were going to the city to take leave of their girls, others quite simply to paint the town red, others still to spend their last zloty on provisions for the journey or in other more futile ways.

Cesare and I also went to Katowice, with this last programme in mind, carrying our savings and those of five or six comrades in our pockets. For what could we hope to find at the frontier? We did not know, but we had seen enough of the Russians and their ways so far, as to make it seem unlikely that we should find a money exchange at the frontier. So common sense, as well as our euphoric state, counselled us to spend the not excessively large sum we possessed to the very last zloty; to use it all up, for example, in organizing a large Italian-style

dinner, based on spaghetti *al burro* which we had not eaten for
so long a time.

We walked into a grocery store, placed all our money on the
counter, and explained our intentions to the shopkeeper as best
we could. I told her, as usual, that I spoke German but was not
German; that we were Italians about to leave, and that we
wanted to buy spaghetti, butter, salt, eggs, strawberries and
sugar in the most opportune proportions for a total of exactly
sixty-three zloty, not one more nor one less.

The shopkeeper was a wrinkled old woman, with a shrewish
and diffident air. She looked at us closely through her tortoise-
shell glasses, then stated flatly, in excellent German, that
according to her we were not Italians at all. First of all, we
spoke German, albeit somewhat badly; then; and above all,
Italians had black hair and passionate eyes, while we possessed
neither. At the most, she would concede that we were Croats; in
fact, now that she thought about it, she had met some Croats
who resembled us. We were, quite indisputably, Croats.

I was quite annoyed, and told her abruptly that we were
Italians, whether she liked it or not; Italian Jews, one from
Rome, and one from Turin, who came from Auschwitz and
were going home, and we wanted to buy and spend, and not
waste time in futile discussion.

Jews from Auschwitz? The old woman's look mellowed, even
her lines seemed to soften. That was another matter. She took us
into the back room, made us sit down, offered us two glasses of
real beer, and at once poured forth her legendary story with
pride, her epopee, near in time but already amply transformed
into a *chanson de geste*, refined and polished by innumerable
repetitions.

She was aware of Auschwitz, and everything relating to
Auschwitz interested her, because she had run the risk of going
there. She was not Polish, but German; formerly, she had owned

a shop in Berlin, with her husband. They had never liked Hitler, and perhaps they had been too incautious in allowing these singular opinions of theirs to leak out in the neighbourhood; in 1935 her husband had been taken away by the Gestapo, and she had never heard of him again. It had been a terrible blow, but one has to live, and she had continued her business till 1938, when Hitler, '*der Lump*', had made his famous speech on the radio in which he declared he wanted to start a war.

Then she had grown angry and had written to him. She had written to him personally, 'To Mr Adolf Hitler, Chancellor of the Reich, Berlin', sending him a long letter in which she advised him strongly not to wage war because too many people would be killed, and pointed out to him that if he did he would lose, because Germany could not win against the whole world; even a child could understand that. She had signed the letter with her name, surname and address; then she had settled down to wait.

Five days later the brown-shirts arrived and, on the pretext of carrying out a search, had sacked and turned her house and shop upside down. What did they find? Nothing. She had never meddled in politics; there was only the draft of the letter. Two weeks later they called her to the Gestapo. She thought they would beat her up and send her to the Lager; instead they treated her with loutish contempt, told her they should hang her, but that they were convinced she was only '*eine alte blöde Ziege*', a stupid old goat, and that the rope would be wasted on her. However, they had withdrawn her trading licence and had expelled her from Berlin.

She had lived from hand to mouth in Silesia on the black market and other expedients, until, as she had foreseen, the Germans had lost the war. Then, since the whole neighbourhood knew what she had done, the Polish authorities had created no difficulties about granting her a licence for a grocery store. So now she lived in peace, fortified by the thought of how much better the world would be if the rulers of this earth had followed her advice.

At the moment of the departure, Leonardo and I gave back the keys of the surgery and said good-bye to Marya Fyodorovna and Dr Danchenko. Marya appeared silent and sad; I asked her why she did not come to Italy with us, at which she blushed as if I had made a dishonourable proposal. Danchenko intervened; he was carrying a bottle of alcohol and two sheets of paper. At first we thought the alcohol was his personal contribution to the stock of medicaments for the journey, but no, it was for a farewell toast, which was dutifully drunk.

And the sheets of paper? We were amazed to learn that the Command expected from us two declarations of thanks for the humanity and correctness with which we had been treated at Katowice; Danchenko also begged us to mention his name and work explicitly, and to sign the papers, adding the title 'Doctor of Medicine' to our names. This Leonardo was able to do and did; but in my case it was false. I was perplexed, and sought to make Danchenko understand this; but he had no time for formalism such as mine, and rapping his finger on the paper told me angrily not to create difficulties. I signed as he wanted; who was I to deprive him of a little help in his career?

But the ceremony was not yet over. Danchenko in turn took out two testimonials written in a beautiful hand on two sheets of lined paper, evidently torn from an exercise book. My testimonial declared with unconstrained generosity that 'Primo Levi, doctor of medicine, of Turin, has given able and assiduous help to the Surgery of this Command for four months, and in this manner has merited the gratitude of all the workers of the world.'

*

The following day our perpetual dream became reality. A train was waiting for us at Katowice station; a long train of goods trucks, which we Italians (about eight hundred) took possession of with cries of delight. First, Odessa; then a fantastic journey by sea through the gates of the Orient; and then Italy.

The prospect of travelling some hundreds of miles in those dilapidated trucks, sleeping on the bare floor, did not worry us at all; nor were we worried by the derisory food supplies provided by the Russians: a little bread, and a packet of soya-bean margarine for each truck. It was a margarine of American origin, heavily salted and as hard as Parmesan cheese; evidently destined for tropical climates, it had finally come into our hands by a series of unimaginable accidents. The rest of our supplies, the Russians assured us with their habitual nonchalance, would be distributed during the journey.

The train, with its cargo of hope, left in the middle of June 1945. There was no escort, no Russian on board; Dr Gottlieb was responsible for the convoy, for he had attached himself spontaneously to us, and had taken on himself the cumulative duties of interpreter, doctor and consul for the itinerant community. We felt in good hands, remote from all doubt or uncertainty; at Odessa the ship was waiting for us.

The journey lasted six days, and if in the course of it we were not forced by hunger to turn beggars or bandits, and in fact reached the end in a reasonably healthy condition, the credit was exclusively Dr Gottlieb's. It became clear immediately after our departure that the Russians of Katowice had sent us on our journey blindly, without making any arrangements with their colleagues at Odessa or at the intermediate stages. When our train stopped at a station (it stopped frequently and for long periods, because regular trains and military transports had precedence), no one knew what to do with us. The stationmasters and the military commanders watched us arrive with doleful surprise, only anxious to rid themselves in turn of our inconvenient presence.

But Gottlieb was there, as sharp as a knife; there was no bureaucratic complication, no barrier of negligence, no official obstinacy which he was unable to remove in a few minutes, each time in a different way. Every difficulty dissolved into mist in the face of his effrontery, his soaring fantasy, his rapier-like quickness. He came back from each encounter with the monster of a thousand faces, which lives wherever official forms and circulars gather, radiant with victory like St George after his duel with the dragon, and recounted the rapid exchange, too conscious of his superiority to glory in it.

The local stationmaster, for example, had demanded our travel warrant, which notoriously did not exist; Gottlieb told him that he was going to pick it up, and entered the telegraph office nearby, where he fabricated one in a few moments, written in the most convincing of official jargon, on some scrap of paper which he so plastered with stamps, seals and illegible signatures as to make it as holy and venerable as an authentic emanation from the Top. Another time he had gone to the Quartermaster's office of a Kommandantur and had respectfully informed him that eight hundred Italians had arrived in the station with nothing to eat. The Quartermaster replied '*nichevò*', his stores were empty, he needed an authorization, he would see to it tomorrow; and he clumsily tried to throw him out, like some importunate mendicant; but Gottlieb smiled, and said to him: 'Comrade, you haven't understood me. These Italians *must* be fed, and today, because this is what Stalin wants'; provisions arrived in a flash.

But for me the journey became a boundless torment. I must have recovered from my pleurisy, but my body was in open rebellion, and seemed to scoff at the doctors and their medicines. Every night, during my sleep, fever swept treacherously through me; an intense fever of unknown nature, which reached its peak near dawn. I used to wake up prostrate, only semi-conscious and with a wrist, an elbow or a knee numbed by stabbing pains. Then I was only capable of lying on the floor of the truck or on the platform, a prey to delirium and pain until about midday; after which, within a few hours, everything returned to normal, and towards evening I felt almost well. Leonardo and Gottlieb looked at me perplexed and helpless.

The train ran through endless fields, sombre towns and villages, dense wild forests which I thought had disappeared thousands of years before from the heart of Europe; the conifers and birches were so thick that they were forced desperately upwards, competing for the light of the sun in an oppressive verticality. The train forced its way as if in a tunnel, in green-black gloom, amid bare smooth trunks, under the high continuous roof of thickly intertwined branches. Rzeszów, Przemyśl with its grim fortifications, Lemberg (Lov).

At Lemberg, a skeleton city, destroyed by bombardment and the war, the train stopped for an entire night in a deluge of rain. The roof of our truck was not watertight; we had to get down and look for shelter. We and a few others could find nothing better than the service subway: dark, two inches of mud, with ferocious draughts. But as punctual as ever, my fever arrived in the middle of the night, like a merciful blow on the head, bringing me the ambiguous benefit of unconsciousness.

Ternopol, Proskurov. The train reached Proskurov at dusk, the engine was uncoupled, and Gottlieb assured us that we should not leave until the morning. So we prepared to sleep overnight in the station. The waiting-room was very large; Cesare, Leonardo, Daniele and I took possession of one corner, Cesare left for the village in his capacity as purveyor, and returned soon afterwards with eggs, lettuce and a packet of tea.

We lit a fire on the floor (we were not the only ones, nor the first; the room was covered with the remains of the innumerable bivouacs of people who had preceded us, and the ceiling and walls were black with smoke, as in an old kitchen). Cesare cooked the eggs, and prepared plenty of well-sugared tea.

Now, either that tea was far more robust than the sort we were used to, or Cesare had mistaken the quantity; because in a short time we lost every trace of sleep and tiredness, and felt ourselves kindled into an unusual mood – tense and alert, hilarious, lucid and sensitive. As a result, every act and every word of that night has remained impressed on my memory, and I can recall it as if it were yesterday.

Daylight disappeared with extreme slowness, at first pink, then violet, then grey, followed by the silvery splendour of a warm moonlit night. While we were smoking and talking gaily, two young girls, dressed in black, were sitting next to us on a wooden box. They were speaking together; not in Russian, but in Yiddish.

'Do you understand what they're saying?' asked Cesare.

'A few words.'

'Up and at 'em, then. See if they'll play.'

That night everything seemed easy to me, even understanding Yiddish. With unaccustomed boldness, I turned to the girls, greeted them and, trying to imitate their pronunciation, asked them in German if they were Jewish, and declared that we four were also Jewish. The girls (they were perhaps sixteen or eighteen years old) burst out laughing. '*Ihr sprecht keyn Jiddisch; ihr seyd ja keyne Jiden!*' 'You do not speak Yiddish; so you cannot be Jews!' In their language, the phrase amounted to rigorous logic.

Yet we really were Jews, I explained. Italian Jews: Jews in Italy, and in all Western Europe, do not speak Yiddish.

This was a great novelty for them, a comic oddity, as if

someone had affirmed that there are Frenchmen who do not speak French. I tried to recite to them the beginning of the *Shema*, the basic Hebrew prayer; their incredulity grew weaker, but their merriment increased. Who had ever heard Hebrew pronounced in so ridiculous a way?

The elder one's name was Sore; she had a small, sharp, mischievous face, rotund and full of asymmetrical dimples; our difficult, halting conversation seemed to cause her piquant amusement, and stimulated her like tickling.

But if we were Jews, then so were all those others, she said to me, pointing with a circular gesture to the eight hundred Italians who filled the room. What difference was there between us and them? The same language, the same faces, the same clothing. No, I explained to her; they were Christians, they came from Genoa, Naples, Sicily; perhaps some of them had Arab blood in their veins. Sore looked around perplexed; this was extremely confusing. In her country things were much clearer: a Jew was a Jew, and a Russian was a Russian, there were no two ways about it.

They were two refugees, she explained to me. They came from Minsk, in White Russia; when the Germans had drawn near, their family had asked to be transferred to the interior of the Soviet Union, to escape the slaughter of the Einsatzkommandos of Eichmann. Their request had been carried out to the letter; they had all been sent three thousand miles from their town, to Samarkand in Uzbekistan, near the Roof of the World, in sight of mountains twenty thousand feet high. She and her sister were still children at the time; then their mother had died, and their father had been mobilized for service on a frontier. The two of them had learnt Uzbek, and many other fundamental things: how to live from day to day, how to travel across continents with a small suitcase between the two of them, in fact how to live like the fowls of the air, who labour not, neither do they spin, and who take no thought for the morrow.

Such were Sore and her silent sister. Like us, they were returning home. They had left Samarkand in March, and had set out on the journey like feathers abandoning themselves to the wind. They had travelled, partly in trucks and partly on foot, across the Kara-kum, the Desert of the Black Sand; they had arrived at Krasnovodsk on the Caspian Sea by train, and there they had waited until a fishing boat took them to Baku. From Baku they had continued by any means they happened to find, for they had no money, only an unlimited faith in the future and in their neighbour, and a natural virgin love of life.

Everybody around was sleeping; Cesare listened to the conversation restlessly, occasionally asking me if the preliminaries were over and if we were getting down to brass tacks; then, disappointed, he went outside in search of more concrete adventures.

At about midnight the quiet of the waiting-room, and the girls' story, were abruptly interrupted. A door, connecting the large room by a small corridor to another smaller one, reserved for soldiers in transit, flew open violently, as if blown by a gust of wind. On the threshold appeared a Russian soldier, almost a boy, drunk; he looked around with absent eyes, then started forward, head lowered, lurching fearfully, as if the floor had suddenly tilted under him. Three Soviet officers were standing in the corridor, engaged in conversation. The boy soldier braked as he reached them, drew himself stiffly to attention, and gave a military salute, which the three returned with dignity. Then off he started again, moving in semicircles like a skater, cleared the outside door miraculously, and could be heard vomiting and gulping noisily on the platform. He came back with a slightly less uncertain step, once more saluted the impassive officers and disappeared. After a quarter of an hour, the identical scene was repeated, as if in a nightmare: dramatic entrance, pause, salute, hasty crooked journey across the sleepers' legs towards the open air, evacuation, return, salute; and so on for an infinite number of times, at regular intervals, without the three ever giving him more than a distrait glance and a correct salute.

So that memorable night passed until my fever conquered me once more; then I lay on the ground, shivering silently. Gottlieb came, and brought with him an unusual medicine: half a litre of raw vodka, illicitly distilled, which he had bought from some peasants; it tasted of must, vinegar and fire. 'Drink it,' he told me, 'drink it all. It will do you good, and in any case we have nothing else here for your illness.'

I drank the infernal philtre not without an effort, burning my mouth and throat, and in a short time fell into a state of nothingness. When I woke up the following morning, I felt oppressed by a heavy weight; but it was not the fever, nor a bad dream. I lay buried under a layer of other sleepers, in a sort of human incubator of people who had arrived during the night and who could find room only on top of those already lying on the floor.

I was thirsty; thanks to the combined action of the vodka and animal warmth, I must have lost pints of sweat. The singular cure was wholly successful; the fever and pains had definitely disappeared, and returned no more.

The train left, and in a few hours we reached Zhmerinka, a railway junction two hundred miles from Odessa. Here a great surprise and fierce disappointment awaited us. Gottlieb, who had conferred there with the military Command, went along the train, truck by truck, and informed us that we should all have to get off: the train was going no farther.

Why was it going no farther? And how and when would we reach Odessa? 'I don't know,' replied Gottlieb, embarrassed: 'nobody knows. I only know that we have to get off the train, settle ourselves somehow on the platform, and await orders.' He was very pale and visibly disturbed.

We got down, and spent the night in the station; Gottlieb's defeat, the first one, seemed to us a bad omen. The next morning our guide, together with his inseparable brother and brother-in-law, had disappeared. They had vanished into emptiness, with all their conspicuous luggage; somebody said he had seen them talking to Russian railwaymen, and in the night climbing on to a military train going back from Odessa to the Polish border.

We stayed at Zhmerinka for three days, oppressed by a sense of uneasiness, frustration or terror, according to our temperaments and the scraps of information we managed to extort from the Russians there. They manifested no surprise at our fate and our enforced stop, and replied to our questions in the most disconcerting of ways. One Russian told us that it was true, that various ships had left Odessa with English or American soldiers who were being repatriated, and that we also would embark sooner or later; we had food to eat, Hitler was no more, so why were we complaining? Another one told us that the previous week a trainload of Frenchmen, travelling to Odessa, had been stopped at Zhmerinka and directed towards the north 'because the railway lines were cut'. A third one informed us that he had personally seen a trainload of German prisoners travelling towards the Far East; the matter was clear, according to him, for were we not also allies of the Germans? All right then, they were sending us as well to dig trenches on the Japanese front.

To complicate matters another trainload of Italians coming from Rumania arrived at Zhmerinka on the third day. They looked totally different from us; there were about six hundred men and women, well dressed, with suitcases and trunks, some with cameras slung round their necks – almost tourists. They looked down on us, like poor relations; so far they had travelled in a regular train of passenger coaches, paying for their tickets, and were in order as regards their passports, money, travel documents and collective permit for Italy via Odessa. If only we could gain permission from the Russians to join up with them, then we too should reach Odessa.

With much condescension, they gave us to understand that they were persons of consequence; they were civilian and military officials from the Italian Legation at Bucharest, as well as certain other persons who, after the ARMIR* had been dissolved, had stayed in Rumania with various duties, or to fish in troubled waters. There were whole family groups among them, husbands with lawfully-wedded Rumanian wives and numerous children.

But the Russians, in contrast to the Germans, possess little talent for subtle distinctions and classifications. A few days later we were all travelling together towards the north, towards an unknown goal, at all events towards a new exile. Italian-Rumanians and Italian-Italians, all in the same cattle-trucks, all sick at heart, all in the hands of the inscrutable Soviet bureaucracy, an obscure and gigantic power, not ill-intentioned towards us, but suspicious, negligent, stupid, contradictory and in effect as blind as the forces of nature.

* Italian Army in Russia.

9

Northwards

In the few days we spent at Zhmerinka we were reduced to penury; this, in those conditions, was in itself not particularly tragic, compared with the far more serious prospect of an imminent departure for an unknown destination. Lacking the shelter provided by Gottlieb's talent for improvisation, we had undergone the full impact of the 'Rumanians'' superior economic power; they could pay five, ten times as much as we could for any goods, and did so, because they too had exhausted their food supplies, and they too foresaw that we should be leaving for a place where money would count for little, and where it would be difficult to keep it.

We had encamped at the station, and often made expeditions to the village, which consisted of low, unequal houses, built with a curious and amusing contempt for geometry and uniformity: nearly aligned façades, near vertical walls, near right angles; but here and there a pillar was to be found, resembling a column, with a pretentious capital and volutes. Thick thatched roofs covered smoky, gloomy interiors, where one could glimpse the enormous central stove with straw mattresses for sleeping, and the black icons in a corner. At a crossroad a gigantic, white-haired, barefoot story-teller recited; he stared at the sky with his blind eyes, and at intervals bent his head and made the sign of the cross on his forehead with his thumb.

In the main street, fixed on two stakes driven into the muddy soil, stood a wooden plaque with a map of Europe painted on it, now fading from the sun and rains of many a summer. It must have been used to follow the war bulletins, but it had been painted from memory, as if seen from a great distance; France was decidedly a coffee pot, the Iberian Peninsula a head in profile, with the nose sticking out from Portugal, and Italy a genuine boot, just a trifle oblique, with the sole and heel smooth and straightlined. Only four cities were shown in Italy: Rome, Venice, Naples and Dronero.

Zhmerinka was a large agricultural village, formerly a market town, as could be deduced from the huge central square, of trodden earth, with numerous parallel rows of iron bars to which beasts could be tethered. It was now wholly empty; but in a corner, in the shade of an oak tree, a tribe of nomads had encamped, a vision stemming from distant millennia.

Both men and women were dressed in goatskins, tied to their limbs with leather thongs; on their feet they wore slippers made from the bark of birch trees. There were several families, about twenty people, and their home was an enormous cart, as massive as some instrument of war, constructed of beams crudely squared and mortised, resting on heavy wheels of solid wood; the four shaggy carthorses to be seen grazing nearby must have had a hard time dragging it. Who were they, where did they come from and where were they going? We did not know; but in those days we felt that they were singularly close to us, blown like us by the wind, dependent like us on the fickleness of a distant, unknown, erratic will, symbolized in the wheels dragging us and them, in the stupid perfection of the circle which has neither beginning nor end.

Not far from the square, near the railway, we came across another apparition heavy with foreboding. We saw a depot of logs, massive and rough like everything in that country where the subtle and refined have no place; among the logs, beaten to the ground by the sun, cooked by the sun, lay a dozen German prisoners, like unattended cattle. No one guarded them, no one commanded them or looked after them; as far as we could see, they had been forgotten, simply abandoned to their fate.

They were dressed in rags, which were faded but still recognizable as the proud uniforms of the Wehrmacht. They had pinched, dazed, wild faces; accustomed to live, act and fight within the iron bounds of Authority, their support and sustenance, they found themselves impotent and inanimate when Authority itself ceased. These good subjects, good executors of all commands, good instruments of power, did not possess even a particle of power in themselves; they were emptied and inert, like barren leaves piled up by the wind in sheltered corners; they had not even sought safety in flight.

They saw us, and some of them moved towards us with the uncertain steps of automata. They asked for bread; not in their own language, but in Russian. We refused, because our bread was precious. But Daniele did not refuse; Daniele, whose strong wife, whose brother, parents and no fewer than thirty relatives had been killed by the Germans; Daniele, who was the sole survivor of the raid on the Venice ghetto, and who from the day of the liberation had fed on grief, took out a piece of bread, showed it to these phantoms and placed it on the ground. But he insisted that they come to get it dragging themselves on all fours; which they did, docilely.

It must have been true that groups of Allied ex-prisoners had embarked at Odessa months before, as some Russians had told us, for the station of Zhmerinka, our temporary and scarcely intimate residence, still bore the signs: a triumphal arch made of branches, now withered, bearing the words 'Long live the United Nations'; enormous ghastly portraits of Stalin, Roosevelt and Churchill, with phrases extolling the victory against the common enemy. But the brief season of concord between the three great allies must now have been drawing to its end, for the paintings were discoloured and faded by the weather, and were taken down during our stay. A painter arrived; he put up scaffolding along the wall of the station, and covered the slogan 'Workers of the world, unite!' with a coating of whitewash; in its place we saw, with a subtle sense of chill, another quite different slogan appear, letter by letter: '*V pered na Zapàd*', 'On towards the west'.

The repatriation of Allied soldiers had now finished, but other trains arrived and left for the south before our eyes. These were also Russian trains but quite distinct from the military ones, glorious and homely, which we had seen passing through Katowice. They were trainloads of Ukrainian women returning from Germany; only women, because the men had gone off as soldiers or partisans, or else had been killed by the Germans.

Their exile had been different from ours, and from that of the prisoners of war. Not all of them, but the majority, had abandoned their homes 'spontaneously'. A coerced, black-mailed spontaneity, distorted by subtle and heavy Nazi lies and propaganda, both threatening and enticing, blaring out from the radio, newspapers, posters; nevertheless, a demonstration of free will, an assent. Women aged sixteen to forty, hundreds of thousands of them, peasant women, students, factory workers, had left the devastated fields, the closed schools and bombarded factories for the invaders' bread. Not a few were mothers, who had left to earn bread for their children. In Germany they had found bread, barbed wire, hard work, German order, servitude and shame; now under the weight of their shame they were being repatriated, without joy and without hope.

Victorious Russia had no forgiveness for them. They

returned home in roofless cattle-trucks, which were divided horizontally by boards so as to exploit the space better: sixty, eighty women to a truck. They had no luggage, only the worn-out discoloured clothes they were wearing. If their young bodies were still solid and healthy, their closed and bitter faces, their evasive eyes, displayed a disturbing, animal-like humiliation and resignation; not a voice emerged from those coils of limbs, which sluggishly untangled themselves when the train stopped at the station. No one was waiting for them, no one seemed aware of them. Their inertia, their fugitive shyness, their painful lack of pudency, was that of humiliated and tame beasts. We alone watched their passage, with compassion and sadness, a new testimony to, and a new aspect of, the pestilence which had prostrated Europe.

We left Zhmerinka at the end of June, oppressed by a deep anguish born of disillusionment and uncertainty about our destiny which had found an obscure echo and confirmation in the scenes we had witnessed.

We were fourteen hundred Italians, including the 'Rumanians'. We were loaded on to about thirty goods trucks, which were tacked on to a northbound train. At Zhmerinka nobody knew or was prepared to tell us our destination; but we were going northwards, away from the sea, away from Italy, towards exile, solitude, gloom, winter. Despite this, we thought it a good sign that provisions were not distributed for the journey; perhaps it would not be a long one.

In fact we only travelled for two days and one night, with very few stops, through a majestic and monotonous scenery of desert steppes, forests, forlorn villages and wide slow rivers. It was uncomfortable, crushed in the goods trucks; on the first evening, taking advantage of a halt, Cesare and I got out to stretch our legs and find some more satisfactory arrangement.

At the head of the train we saw several passenger carriages, and a hospital car; it seemed empty. 'Why don't we climb in?' proposed Cesare. 'It's not allowed,' I replied foolishly. Why in fact should it be forbidden, and by whom? In any case, on various occasions we had noticed already that the Western religion (German in particular) of differential prohibitions has no deep roots in Russia.

The hospital car was not only empty, but offered sybaritic refinements. Washbasins which worked, with water and soap; first-rate suspension to absorb the jarring of the wheels; wonderful bunks resting on adjustable springs, complete with white sheets and warm blankets. At the head of the bed I chose, I even found, as an additional gift of the gods, a book in Italian: *I Ragazzi di Via Paal*, which I had never read as a child. While our companions were already declaring us lost, we enjoyed a heavenly night.

The train crossed the River Beresina at the end of the second day, as the sun, garnet red, sank obliquely between the tree trunks with bewitching slowness, casting a blood-red glow on the waters, the woods and the battle-strewn plain. The journey ended a few hours later, in the middle of the night, at the height of a violent storm. We had to climb down in a deluge, in total darkness, lit momentarily by flashes of lightning. We walked for half an hour in single file through the grass and mud, each of us like a blind man, holding on to the man in front, while heaven knows whom the leader of the column followed; finally, soaked to the skin, we emerged at a huge dark edifice, half destroyed by bombardment. The rain continued, the floor was muddy and wet and more water came through the holes in the roof; we waited for day in a state of exhaustion and passive drowsiness.

The dawn arose in splendour. We went outside, and only then could we see that we had spent the night in the pit of a theatre, in the middle of a large Soviet military camp which had been destroyed and abandoned. All the buildings had been subjected to a Teutonically methodical devastation and plundering; the German armies in flight had carried away everything that could be carried: locks, bars, railings, the entire lighting and heating plant, the water pipes, even the fence-posts. Not a nail had been left in the walls. The tracks and sleepers of a near-by railway junction had been torn up: with a special machine, the Russians told us.

In short, it was more than a sack: it was the genius of destruction, of anti-creation, here as at Auschwitz; it was the mystique of barrenness, beyond all demands of war or impulse for booty.

But they had not been able to carry away the unforgettable frescoes which covered the inside walls: the work, naïve, forceful and crude, of some anonymous soldier-poet. Three gigantic horsemen, armed with swords, helmets and clubs, stood on a hill, turning their eyes towards an endless horizon of virgin lands to be conquered. Stalin, Lenin, Molotov, reproduced with reverent affection in intent, with sacrilegious audacity in effect, and really only recognizable by their respective moustache, pointed beard and spectacles. Then there was an enormous spider, at the centre of a web as large as the wall, with a lock of black hair across one eye, a swastika on its rump and written underneath: 'Death to Hitler's invaders.' A Soviet soldier in chains, tall and blond, raised a handcuffed arm to judge his judges; these, hundreds of them all against one, huddled on the benches of the amphitheatre-court, like so many repellent men-insects, with yellow and grey faces, twisted, distorted, as macabre as skulls, cringing against each other, like lemurs fleeing the light, driven back into nothingness by the prophetic gesture of the prisoner-hero.

In these spectral barracks, and spilling outside over the vast courtyards overgrown with grass, thousands of foreigners bivouacked, in transit like us, belonging to all the nations of Europe.

The generous warmth of the sun began to penetrate the damp soil, and mist arose from everything. I walked a few hundred yards away from the theatre, entering an overgrown meadow where I intended to strip and dry myself in the sun; and in the middle of the meadow, as if he were waiting for me, whom should I see but Mordo Nahum, my Greek, almost unrecognizable in his opulent fatness and the quasi-Soviet uniform he was wearing; he looked at me with his pale owlish eyes, lost in his round, rosy, red-bearded face.

He greeted me with fraternal cordiality, disregarding a spiteful question of mine about the United Nations who had taken so little care of him and his Greeks. He asked me how I was; did I need anything? Food? Clothes? Yes, I could not deny it, I had need of many things. 'It will be seen to,' he replied mysteriously and magnanimously; 'here I count for something.' He paused briefly, and added, 'Do you need a woman?'

I looked at him dumbfounded; I was afraid I had not understood him. But the Greek, with a broad gesture, swept three-quarters of the horizon with his hand: and then I saw that in the middle of the tall grass, idly stretched out in the sun, far and near, lay some twenty huge sleepy girls. They were blonde and rosy creatures, with powerful backs, massive frames and placid bovine faces, dressed in various primitive and incongruous styles. 'They come from Bessarabia,' the Greek explained to me: 'they are all employees of mine. The Russians like them like this, white and substantial. There was a great *pagaille*, a great muddle here before I arrived but since I have taken over, everything has been running smoothly: cleanliness, choice, discretion and no quarrels about money. It's also a good business: and sometimes, *moi aussi j'y prends mon plaisir*.'

I now recalled, in a new light, the episode of the hard-boiled egg, and the indignant challenge of the Greek: 'Come on, tell me an article I have never dealt in!' No. I had no need of a woman, or at least not in that sense. After a cordial conversation, we went our ways; and since then, with the subsiding of the whirl-wind which had upturned this old Europe, dragging it into a savage quadrille of separations and encounters, I have never again seen my Greek master, nor have I ever heard further of him.

10

The Little Hen

The assembly camp where I had so unexpectedly found Mordo Nahum was called Slutsk. Anyone searching for the village bearing this name on a good map of the Soviet Union could find it with a little care, in White Russia, about sixty miles south of Minsk. But the village called Starye Dorogi, our final destination, is not to be found on any map.

In July 1945, about ten thousand persons were resident at Slutsk; I say persons, because any more restrictive term would be inappropriate. There were men, but also a good number of women and children. There were Catholics, Jews, Orthodox Christians and Muslims; there were people with white and with yellow skins and Negroes in American uniform; Germans, Poles, French, Greeks, Dutch, Italians and others; and in addition, Germans pretending to be Austrians, Austrians declaring themselves Swiss, Russians stating that they were Italians, a woman dressed as a man and finally, conspicuous in the midst of this ragged crowd, a Magyar general in full uniform, as quarrelsome, motley and stupid as a cock.

Slutsk was comfortable. It was hot, excessively so; we slept on the ground, but there was no work to be done and there was food for everybody. In fact, the canteen was wonderful; the Russians entrusted it, for one week in rotation, to each of the principal nationalities represented in the camp. We ate in a huge room, clean and full of light; each table was laid for eight; all one had to do was to arrive at the correct time and sit down, without controls or shifts or queues, and the procession of voluntary cooks arrived at once, with surprising foods, bread and tea. During our brief stay the Hungarians were in office: they made fiery goulashes, and enormous portions of spaghetti with parsley, overcooked and crazily sugared. Moreover, faithful to their national idols, they had instituted a gypsy orchestra; six peasant musicians, in corduroy trousers and embroidered leather doublets, majestic and sweating, began with the Soviet national anthem, then the Hungarian and the *Hatikva* (in honour of the large nucleus of Hungarian Jews), and continued with interminable frivolous Tziganes until the last diner had laid down his fork.

The camp was not fenced. It consisted of broken-down buildings, of one or two storeys, aligned along the four sides of a vast grassy square, probably the old parade ground. Under the burning sun of the hot Russian summer, the square was filled with clusters of people sleeping or intent on delousing themselves, mending their clothes or cooking on improvised fires; the scene was animated by more energetic groups, playing football or ninepins. An enormous wooden hut, low and square, with three entrances all on the same side, dominated the centre. On the three architraves, an uncertain hand had painted in large Cyrillic characters, three words: *Mushskaya*, *Shenskaya*, *Ofitserskaya*, 'For men', 'For women', 'For officers'. It was the camp latrine, and at the same time its most salient feature. On the inside, there was only a floor with loose planks, and a hundred square holes, ten by ten, like a gigantic Rabelaisian multiplication table. There were no sub-divisions between the sections allotted to the three sexes; or if there once had been, they had disappeared.

The Russian administration took no care at all of the camp, so that one wondered if it really existed; but it must have existed, since we ate every day. In other words, it was a good administration.

We spent ten days at Slutsk. They were empty days, without encounters, without events to anchor the memory. One day we tried to leave the rectangle of barracks, and enter the plain to collect herbs to eat; but after half an hour's walk we found ourselves as if in the middle of the sea, at the centre of the horizon, without a tree, a hill, a house to choose as goal. The immense, heroic space of Russia gave a sense of giddiness to us Italians, accustomed as we were to a landscape of mountains and hills and a plain alive with the presence of man, and weighed down our hearts with painful memories. Later we tried to cook the herbs we had collected, but we got very little from them.

In an attic, I had found a textbook on obstetrics, in German, with good coloured illustrations, in two heavy volumes; and as printed paper is a vice of mine, and I had abstained for more than a year, I passed my time reading desultorily, or else sleeping in the sun amid the wild grass.

One morning, the news spread among us, with mysterious and lightning speed, that we should have to leave Slutsk, on foot, to settle at Starye Dorogi, forty-five miles away, in a camp for Italians only. The Germans, in analogous circumstances, would have covered the walls with bilingual placards, beautifully printed, specifying the hour of departure, the prescribed equipment, the timetable, and threatening deserters with the death penalty. The Russians, in contrast, allowed the ordinance to spread by itself, and the march to the other camp to organize itself.

The news provoked something of an uproar. In ten more or less comfortable days, we had settled down at Slutsk, and above all we feared leaving the extravagant abundance of the Slutsk kitchens for some unknown miserable condition. Moreover, forty-five miles are a lot; none of us was trained for so long a march, and few possessed suitable shoes. We tried in vain to obtain more precise information from the Russian Command; all we managed to find out was that we should have to leave on the morning of 20 July, and that a real Russian Command apparently did not exist.

On the morning of 20 July we collected in the main square, like an immense band of gypsies. At the last moment, it had emerged that Slutsk and Starye Dorogi were linked by rail; however, only the women and children, as well as the usual protégés, and the no less usual fast operators were allowed to travel by train. In fact, it did not need exceptional cunning to get round the tenuous bureaucracy ruling our fate; but not many of us were aware of this at the time.

The order to leave was given at about ten o'clock, followed immediately by a counter-order. After this, numerous other false departures followed, so that we began to move only about midday, without eating.

A large motorway runs from Slutsk to Starye Dorogi, the same one connecting Warsaw to Moscow. At that time it was wholly abandoned; it consisted of two lateral carriageways, of bare earth, meant for horses, and a central carriageway, formerly asphalted but ruined by explosions and the tracks of armoured vehicles, and consequently little different from the other two. It ran across an endless plain, almost without villages, and as a result it consisted of enormously long straight stretches; between Slutsk and Starye Dorogi there was only one curve, barely perceptible.

We had set out in a rather carefree mood; the weather was magnificent, we were quite well fed and the idea of a long walk in the heart of this legendary area, the Pripet marshes, had a certain fascination in itself. But we soon changed our minds.

In no other part of Europe, I think, can you walk for ten hours, and always remain at the same place, as if in a nightmare:

always with the same straight road in front of you, stretching to the horizon, always the same steppe and forests on both sides, and behind your back yet more road stretching to the other horizon, like a ship's wake; not a village, or a house, or smoke, or a milestone to show in some way that a bit of space had been conquered; not a living creature to meet, except for flights of crows and an occasional hawk cruising idly in the wind.

After a few hours' march, our column, initially compact, stretched for one or two miles. A Russian military cart brought up the rear drawn by two horses and driven by a hideous scowling NCO; he had lost both lips in battle, and his face was a terrifying skull from nose to chin. I think his duty was to pick up anyone exhausted; instead, he was diligently engaged in picking up the luggage gradually dropped by the wayside by people too weary to carry it any farther. For a while we deluded ourselves that he would give it back on arrival; but the first person who tried to stop and wait for the cart was greeted with shouts, cracks of the whip and inarticulate threats. This was how my two volumes of obstetrics ended, for they constituted far and away the heaviest part of my personal luggage.

By dusk, our group was now walking alone. Besides myself, there was the mild and patient Leonardo; Daniele, limping and furious from thirst and tiredness; Mr Unverdorben, with a Triestine friend of his; and, naturally, Cesare.

We stopped for a rest at the only curve breaking the relentless monotony of the road; there was a roofless hut, perhaps the only visible remains of a village swept away by the war. Behind it, we discovered a well, where we quenched our thirst greedily. We were tired, with swollen blistered feet. I had lost my archiepiscopal shoes long before, and had inherited, heaven knows from whom, a pair of cyclist's plimsolls, as light as a feather; but they were tight, and I was forced to take them off at intervals and walk barefoot.

We held a brief council: what if he made us walk all night? It would be hardly surprising; at Katowice once, the Russians had made us unload boots from a train for twenty-four hours on end, and they had also worked with us. Why not desert and hide in the forest? We would reach Starye Dorogi the next day at our leisure, the NCO certainly had no roll-call, the night was warm, there was water and between the six of us we had something for dinner, although not very much. The hut was in ruins, but there was still a bit of roof to shelter us from the dew.

'Excellent,' said Cesare, 'I'm all for it. I'm going to have roast chicken this evening.' So we hid in the wood until the cart with the skeleton had passed by, waited for the last laggers to leave the well, and took possession of our bivouac for the night. We spread our blankets on the ground, opened our sacks, lit a fire, and began to prepare dinner, with bread, *kasha* of millet and a tin of peas.

'To hell with your dinner!' said Cesare; 'to hell with your peas! Now get this: I want to hold a party this evening, and I'm going to have roast chicken.'

Cesare is an untameable man; I had already realized this from wandering around the markets of Katowice with him. It was useless to point out to him what a senseless idea it was searching for a chicken at night, in the middle of the Pripet marshes, without knowing Russian and without money to pay for it. It was useless to offer him a double ration of *kasha* to shut him up. 'You stay here with your bloody *kasha*; I'm going to look for my chicken by myself, and that's the last you'll see of me. So good-bye to you and the Russians and the hut; I'm off, and returning to Italy by myself. Perhaps via Japan.'

At that point I offered to accompany him. Not because of the chicken or the threats; but because I am fond of Cesare, and I enjoy watching him at work.

'Bravo, Lapè,' cried Cesare. Lapè is me; so Cesare baptized

me long ago and so he still calls me, for the following reason. Our hair was, of course, shaved off in the Lager; at the liberation, after a year of cropping, everybody's hair, and mine in particular, had regrown curiously smooth and soft; at that time my hair was still very short, and Cesare maintained that it reminded him of a rabbit's skin. Now 'rabbit', or rather 'rabbit skin', in the merchant's jargon which Cesare knew well, is called Lapè. Daniele, on the other hand, the bearded, hirsute, heavy-browed Daniele, as ardent for vengeance and justice as a prophet of old, was called Coralli; because, said Cesare, if corallines (glass beads) were to rain down, they would all be spiked in his hair.

'Bravo, Lapè,' he said to me; and then he explained his plan. Cesare, in fact, was a man of crazy designs, which he then pursued with much practical sense. He had not dreamt up the chicken; he had seen a well-beaten, and hence recent, path leading north from the hut. It probably led to a village; and if there was a village, there were also chickens. He went out into the open; it was now almost dark, and Cesare was right. On the brow of a barely perceptible rise in the ground, perhaps a mile and a half away, we could see a light shining between the tree trunks. So we left, stumbling over roots, pursued by swarms of voracious mosquitoes; we were carrying with us the only commodity our group had finally agreed to part with: our six plates, ordinary earthenware plates which the Russians had previously distributed as our equipment.

We walked in the dark, taking care not to lose the path, and shouting at intervals. No one replied in the village. When we were about a hundred yards away, Cesare stopped, drew in his breath and shouted: 'Hi! Russkies! We are friends. Italiansky. Have you got a chicken to sell?' This time the reply came: a flash in the dark, a sharp crack and the whistling of a bullet, some feet above our heads. I flattened myself on the ground, cautiously so as not to break the plates; but Cesare was furious, and stayed on his feet: 'Blast you! We're friends, I told you! We're as straight as they come – see for yourselves. We only want a chicken. We're not bandits, we're not Deutschky; we are Italiansky!'

There were no further shots, and already we could see human profiles on the brow of the hill. We approached cautiously, Cesare first, continuing his persuasive speech, and I behind, ready to throw myself on the ground a second time.

Finally we reached the village. There were no more than five or six wooden houses grouped around a minute square, and on the square, waiting for us, stood the entire population, about thirty people, for the most part old women, then children and dogs, all visibly alarmed. From the little crowd a grand bearded old man emerged, the one who had fired; he still held the firearm in his hand.

Cesare now considered that he had done his part, the strategic part, and called on me to do my duty. 'Now it's your turn. What are you waiting for? Explain to him that we are Italians, that we don't want to harm anybody and that we want to buy a chicken to roast.'

The people were considering us with diffident curiosity. They seemed satisfied that, although dressed like two convicts, we could not be dangerous. The old women had stopped cackling, and the dogs had also quietened down. The old man with the gun asked us questions which we did not understand; I knew only about a hundred words of Russian, and none of these was suited to the situation, except for '*Italiansky*'. So I repeated '*Italiansky*' frequently, until the old man in his turn began to say '*Italiansky*' for the benefit of the bystanders.

In the meantime Cesare, more down to earth, had taken the plates out of the sack, had placed five of them well in view on the ground as if at the market and held the sixth in his hand, tapping it on the edge with his nail to show it gave the right sound. The peasant women looked on, amused and curious. '*Tarelki*,' said one. '*Tarelki, da!*' I replied, delighted at learning the name of the merchandise we were offering; at which one of them stretched a hesitant hand towards the plate which Cesare was displaying. 'Hey there, what do you take me for?' he said, withdrawing it quickly: 'We're not giving them away!' And he turned to me waspishly: Well, what was I waiting for? Why didn't I ask for the chicken in exchange? What use were all my studies?

I was in a pickle. Russian, they say, is an Indo-European language, and chickens must have been known to our common ancestors in an epoch certainly previous to their subdivision into the various modern ethnic families. '*His fretus*', that is to say, on these fine foundations, I tried to say 'chicken' and 'bird' in all the ways known to me, but without any visible result.

Cesare was also perplexed. Cesare, deep down, had never really accepted that Germans speak German, and Russians Russian, except out of gross malice; then, in his heart of hearts, he was persuaded that they only pretended not to understand Italian through some refinement of the same malice. Malice, or extreme and scandalous ignorance: clear barbarism. There could be no other explanation. So his perplexity rapidly changed to anger.

He grumbled and swore. Was it possible that it was so difficult to understand what a chicken is, and that we wanted it in exchange for six plates? A chicken, one of those beasts that go around pecking, scratching and saying 'coccode-e-eh'; and rather half-heartedly, glowering and sullen, he put on a very second-rate imitation of the habits of the chicken, crouching on the ground, scraping first with one foot and then with the other and pecking here and there with his hands shaped like a wedge. Between one oath and the other, he also cried 'coccode-e-eh'; but this rendering of the chicken's cry is of course highly conventional; it is only to be heard in Italy and has no currency elsewhere.

So the result was negative. They goggled at us with amazement, and certainly took us for madmen. Why, for what conceivable reason, had we come from the ends of the earth to play the fool on their square? Hopping mad by now, Cesare even tried to lay an egg, pouring far-fetched insults on them all the while, so rendering the meaning of his performance even more obscure. At this improper spectacle, the housewives' chattering rose by an octave, and turned into the buzz of a disturbed wasps' nest.

When I noticed one of the old women approaching the old man, and speaking to him, looking nervously at us meanwhile, I realized that the situation was getting out of hand. I made Cesare get out of his unnatural posture, calmed him and approached the man together with him. 'Excuse me,' I said to the man and led him near a window, where a lamp lit up a piece of ground quite well. Here, painfully aware of the many suspicious glances, I drew a chicken on the ground, complete in all its attributes, including an egg behind it, to avoid all ambiguity.

Then I got up and said: 'You – plates. We – eat.'

A brief consultation followed; then an old woman sprang out of the hut, her eyes alight with joy and comprehension; she stepped forward a couple of paces, and in a shrill voice pronounced: '*Kura! Kuritsa!*'

She was very proud and happy that she had been the one to resolve the enigma. From all sides laughter and applause broke out and voices cried '*Kuritsa, Kuritsa!*'; and we also clapped our hands, caught up in the game and in the general enthusiasm. The old woman curtsied, like an actress at the end of her performance; she disappeared and re-emerged after a few minutes holding a hen already plucked. She dangled it comically under

Cesare's nose, as a double check; and when she saw that he reacted positively, she loosened her hold, collected the plates and carried them off.

Cesare, who understood these matters because he had once had a stall at Porta Portese market, assured me that the '*kurizetta*', the little hen, was fat enough, and worth our six plates. We took it back to the hut, woke up our companions who had already fallen asleep, relit the fire, cooked the chicken and ate it with our fingers because we no longer had any plates.

11

Old Roads

The hen, and the night spent in the open, were as good as a medicine for us. After a sound sleep, which wholly revived us, although we had slept on the bare ground, we woke up in the morning in excellent humour and health. We were contented, because of the sun, because we felt free, because of the good smell coming from the earth and also a little because a couple of miles away there were people not hostile to us, in fact cheerful and ready to laugh; it was true that they had shot at us, but they had afterwards welcomed us and had even sold us a chicken. We were contented because that day (we did not know about the next; but what happens tomorrow is not always important) we could do things which we had not done for too long; drink water from a well, stretch out in the sun in the middle of tall robust grass, smell the summer air, light a fire and cook, go into the woods in search of strawberries and mushrooms, smoke a cigarette looking at the high sky swept clean by the wind.

We could do these things and we did them, with puerile joy. But our resources were coming to an end; we could not live on strawberries and mushrooms, and none of us (not even Cesare, a townsman and Roman citizen 'since Nero's time') was morally and technically equipped for a precarious life of vagabondage and rural thefts. The choice was clear: either to rejoin at once the ranks of civilization, or to go hungry. Twenty miles of a dizzily straight road, however, still separated us from civilization, represented by the mysterious camp of Starye Dorogi. If we managed to cover them in one go, perhaps we should arrive in time for the evening meal; otherwise, we should have to camp once more on the road, in liberty, but on an empty stomach.

A rapid census of our possessions was carried out. They were not much; eight rubles in all. It was difficult to calculate their purchasing power, at that moment and in that place; our previous monetary experiences with the Russians had been incoherent and absurd. Some of them accepted money from any country without difficulty, even German or Polish money; others were suspicious, afraid of being cheated, and only accepted exchanges in kind or in metal coinage. Indeed the most improbable coinage was circulating: coins from Tsarist times, brought out of ancestral hiding places; guineas, Scandinavian crowns, even old coins of the Austro-Hungarian Empire. In contrast, at Zhmerinka we had seen the walls of one of the station latrines studded with German marks, meticulously stuck to the wall one by one with an unmentionable material.

In any case, eight rubles were not much; the price of one or two eggs. It was decided corporately that Cesare and I, now accredited as ambassadors, should go back to the village, and see on the spot what could best be bought with eight rubles.

We set off, and as we walked an idea occurred to us; not goods, but services. The best investment would be to ask our friends for the hire of a horse and cart as far as Starye Dorogi. Perhaps the money was too little, but we could try offering an item of clothing: it was hot enough anyway. So we arrived at the square, welcomed by friendly greetings and sly understanding smiles from the old women and furious barks from the dogs. When silence had been re-established, remembering my Michael Strogov and other books read long ago, I said '*Telega. Starye Dorogi*,' and showed my eight rubles.

A confused murmuring followed: strange to say, no one had understood. Nevertheless, my task looked like being less arduous than it had been on the previous evening; in a corner of the yard, under a roof, I had seen a four-wheeled farm cart, long and narrow, with sides like a 'V'; in short, a telega. I touched it, a little impatient at the obtuseness of these people: was this not a telega?

'*Tyelyega!*' the old man corrected me, with paternal severity, scandalized at my barbaric pronunciation.

'*Da. Tyelyega na Starye Dorogi*. We pay. Eight rubles.'

The offer was derisory: the equivalent of two eggs against twenty plus twenty miles of road, twelve hours' travel. Instead, the old man pocketed the rubles, disappeared into the stable, returned with a mule, harnessed it, signed to us to climb on, loaded a few sacks, still in silence, and drove off towards the main road. Cesare went to call the others, in front of whom we naturally showed off like peacocks. We were to enjoy an extremely comfortable journey in a *telega* or rather in a *tyelyega*, and a triumphal entry at Starye Dorogi, all for eight rubles; that is what a knowledge of languages and diplomatic ability means.

In reality, we soon realized (so, unfortunately, did our companions) that the eight rubles had been virtually wasted: the old man had to go to Starye Dorogi in any case, on some business of his own, and would perhaps even have taken us free of charge.

We set out about midday, lying down on the old man's not very soft sacks. However, it was still much better than travelling on foot; we could also enjoy the countryside in comfort.

For us the countryside was unusual and stupendous. The plain, which the day before had oppressed us with its solemn emptiness, was no longer rigorously flat. It rippled in light, barely perceptible undulations, perhaps the remains of ancient dunes, not more than a few feet high, but enough to break the monotony, rest the eyes and create a rhythm, a measure. Pools and marshes, large and small, stretched between one undulation and the next. The open ground was sandy, and here and there bristled with wild clumps of shrubs; elsewhere there were tall trees, but these were few and isolated. On both sides of the road lay shapeless rusty relics, guns, tanks, barbed wire, helmets, drums; the remnants of two armies which had confronted each other in these parts for so many months. We had entered the region of the Pripet marshes.

The road and countryside were deserted, but a little before dusk we noticed that someone was coming after us: a man, black against the white of the dust, was walking vigorously in our direction. Slowly but steadily he gained ground; soon he was within hailing distance, and we recognized the Moor, Avesani of Avesa, the grand old man. He too had spent the night in some hiding place, and was now striding towards Starye Dorogi with the impetus of a tempest, his white hair in the wind, his bloodshot eyes staring ahead of him. He moved forward regularly and powerfully like a steam locomotive; he had tied his famous, weighty bundle on his back and hanging from this his axe flashed, like the Scythe of Kronos.

He prepared to pass us as if he had not seen us or did not recognize us. Cesare called to him and invited him to climb on with us. 'Desecration of the world! Dirty inhuman swine!' the Moor replied promptly, giving voice to the blasphemous litany which perpetually filled his mind. He overtook us, and continued his epic march towards the horizon opposite.

Mr Unverdorben knew much more than we did about the Moor; we now learnt from him that the Moor was not (or was not only) an old lunatic. The bundle had its reason, as did the old man's wandering life. A widower for many years, he had a daughter, only one, now almost fifty, and paralysed in bed; she would never recover. The Moor lived for his daughter; every week he wrote her letters destined never to reach her; for her alone he had worked all his life, and had turned as dark as oak and as hard as stone. For her alone, wandering around the world as a migrant, the Moor pocketed everything that came his way, any object that presented even the smallest potentiality for use or for exchange.

We met no other living creature until we came to Starye Dorogi.

Starye Dorogi was a surprise. It was not a village; or rather, there was a minute village, in the middle of the wood, a little way off the road; but we learnt about this later, as we also learnt that its name meant 'Old Roads'. The cantonment assigned to us fourteen hundred Italians, however, was a single gigantic building, isolated on the edge of the road in the middle of uncultivated fields, on the fringe of the forest. Its name was 'Krasny Dom', the Red House, and in fact it was unstintingly red, both inside and out.

It was a truly singular building, which had grown without order in all directions like a volcanic flow; it was difficult to tell whether it was the work of many architects at loggerheads, or of a single one who was mad. The nucleus, now overwhelmed and suffocated by wings and extensions added confusedly later on, consisted of a three-storey block divided into small rooms, perhaps formerly used as military or administrative offices. But around this kernel there was everything: a room for lectures or meetings, a series of classrooms, kitchens, washrooms, a theatre to seat at least a thousand, a surgery, a gymnasium; and next to the main door, a little storeroom with mysterious brackets, which we took to be a ski deposit. But here too, as at Slutsk, nothing or almost nothing remained of the furniture and fittings; not only was there no water, but even the pipes had been carried away, as had the kitchen stoves, the theatre seats, the classroom benches, the banisters of the staircases. The most obsessive feature of the Red House was its staircases. They were to be found in abundance in the interminable building: emphatic and prolix staircases leading to absurd attics full of dust and rubbish; other narrow irregular staircases, blocked half-way by a column heaved up amateurishly to support a collapsing ceiling; fragments of warped, forked, anomalous staircases, linking floors of different levels in adjacent buildings. Memorable even among all these, along one of the façades ran a Cyclopean staircase, which climbed fifty feet up from a grass-covered courtyard, by steps three yards wide, and led nowhere.

Around the Red House there was no fence, not even a symbolical one as at Katowice. Nor were we under any regularly constituted surveillance; at the entrance there was often a Russian soldier, usually a boy, but he had no instructions about us Italians. His duty was solely to prevent other Russians coming at night to molest the Italian women in their quarters.

The Russians, officers and soldiers, lived in a wooden hut nearby, and other Russians, in transit along the road, occasionally stopped there; but they rarely bothered about us. The people who did bother about us were a small group of Italian officers, ex-prisoners of war, somewhat arrogant and uncivil; they were heavily conscious of their status as soldiers, they showed contempt and indifference towards us civilians, and – which somewhat surprised us – they maintained excellent relations with their Soviet counterparts in the hut next door. In fact, they enjoyed a privileged position not only in comparison with us, but also in comparison with the Soviet soldiers; they ate in the Russian officers' mess, they were given new Soviet uniforms (without badges of rank) and good military boots, and slept in camp beds with sheets and blankets.

Not, however, that the rest of us had any reason to complain.

We were treated exactly like the Russian soldiers as regards food and lodgings, and were not subjected to any particular regulation or discipline. Only a few Italians worked and these had offered spontaneously to run the kitchens, the baths and the generating plant. In addition, Leonardo acted as a doctor, and I as a nurse; but now, with the good weather, there were very few patients, and our offices were sinecures.

Anyone who wanted to could leave. Several did so, some from sheer boredom or from a spirit of adventure, others in an attempt to pass the frontiers and return to Italy; but they all returned, after a few weeks or months of vagabondage; for, although the camp was neither guarded nor fenced, the distant frontiers were, and strongly so.

On the Russian side there were no attempts to exert ideological pressure, in fact, no attempt to discriminate between us. Our community was too complicated; whether we were ex-soldiers of the ARMIR, ex-partisans, ex-Häftlinge from Auschwitz, ex-workers from the Todt Organization, ex-criminals or prostitutes from Milan jail, Communists, Monarchists or Fascists, the Russians displayed the most impartial indifference towards us. We were Italians, and that was enough; the rest was '*vsyo ravno*', all the same.

We slept on wooden planks covered with straw sacks: two feet per man. At first we protested, because it seemed too little, but the Russian Command pointed out courteously that our complaint was unfounded. At the head of the planks, scribbled in pencil, we could still read the names of Soviet soldiers who had occupied these places before us; we could judge for ourselves – there was one name per eighteen inches.

The same could be said, and was, about the food. We received two pounds of bread a day: rye bread, scarcely leavened, damp and sour; but it was a large ration and it was their bread. And the daily '*kasha*' was their '*kasha*': a compact block of lard, millet, beans, meat and spices, nourishing but ferociously indigestible, which we only learnt to render edible after several days of experiments by boiling it for some hours.

Three or four times a week, fish, 'ribba', was also distributed. It was river fish, of doubtful freshness, full of bones, heavy, raw, unsalted. What could we do with it? Few of us were ready to eat it as it was (as did many Russians); to cook it, we needed pots, seasoning, salt and skill. We soon concluded that the best thing was to sell it to the Russians themselves, to peasants at the village or to soldiers passing along the road; a new business for Cesare, who in a short time carried it to a high degree of technical perfection.

On the morning of the fish days, Cesare went around the dormitories, carrying a piece of wire. He collected the 'ribba', stuck the wire through its eyes, slung the stinking garland round his shoulders and disappeared. He returned after many hours, sometimes not until the evening, and distributed equitably among his contractors' rubles, cheese, quarters of chickens and eggs, to everybody's advantage, and above all to his own.

With the first profits of his trade he bought a balance, which noticeably increased his professional prestige. But to put a plan of his into effect he also needed another instrument of less obvious utility: a syringe. There was no hope of finding one at the Russian village, and so he came to me in the surgery, and asked if I could lend him one.

'What do you want to do with it?' I asked him.

'It's none of your business. I want a syringe; you have plenty here.'

'What size?'

'The biggest you have. It doesn't matter even if it's a little the worse for wear.'

In fact there was one, with a capacity of one fluid ounce,

cracked and practically useless. Cesare examined it with care, and declared that it was what he needed.

'But what are you going to do with it?' I asked again. Cesare looked at me sullenly, hurt by my lack of tact. He told me that it was his affair, his own bloody business, an experiment which might end well or badly and that in any case I was a fine friend sticking my nose into what had nothing to do with me. He wrapped up the syringe carefully and went off like an offended prince.

However, the secret of the syringe did not last long: life at Starye Dorogi was too idle for gossip and curiosity not to proliferate. In the following days, Cesare was seen by Signora Letizia going to fetch water in a bucket and carrying it to the woods; he was seen by Stellina in the woods, sitting on the ground with the bucket in the middle of a garland of fish, which 'he seemed to be feeding'; and finally he was met in the village by Rovati, his rival; he was without his bucket and selling fish, but they were strange fish, fat, firm and round, and not flat and limp like those we were given.

As happens with many scientific discoveries, the idea of the syringe had originated in a failure and in a fortuitous observation. A few days before, Cesare had exchanged fish at the village for a live chicken. He had returned to the Red House convinced that he had struck a good bargain; in return for only two fish they had given him a fine chicken, admittedly not young and with rather a melancholic air, but extraordinarily large and plump. Only after he had killed and plucked it had he realized that something was wrong; the chicken was unsymmetrical: its stomach was all on one side, and to touch it gave an impression of something hard, mobile and elastic. It was not the egg: it was a large watery cyst.

Naturally Cesare had to recoup his losses: he had managed to sell the animal immediately to no less a person than Mr Rovi, and had even made a profit; but then, like a Stendhalian hero, he had thought about it. Why not imitate nature? Why not try with the fish?

At first he had tried to fill them with water through their mouths by means of a tube, but the water all poured out again. Then he had thought of the syringe. With the syringe he noted a certain progress in many cases, but this was clearly dependent on the point at which the injection was made: sometimes the water came out again, immediately or soon after, at other times it stayed in indefinitely. Cesare had then dissected several fish with a knife, and managed to ascertain that, for a permanent effect, the injection needed to be made in the swimming bladder.

As a result the fish, which Cesare sold by weight, yielded from twenty to thirty per cent more than normal, besides having a far more attractive appearance. Certainly, the '*ribba*' treated like this could not be sold twice to the same client; but it could be sold extremely well to demobilized Russian soldiers passing along the road towards the east, who would only discover the trick some miles farther on.

But one day Cesare returned black in the face; he was without fish, money or goods: 'I've been bamboozled.' For two days it was impossible to speak to him; he lay on the straw hunched up, as bristly as a porcupine, and only came down for meals. Things had not gone as usual.

He recounted his adventure to me much later, one long warm evening, making me swear not to spread it around, because, if it was known, his commercial honour would suffer. In fact, the fish had not been torn from him violently by a furious Russian, as at first he had tried to pretend; the truth was quite different. He had given the fish away, he confessed to me, full of shame.

He had gone to the village, and, to avoid clients who had already been had, he kept off the main road and took a path leading through the woods; after a few hundred yards he saw an isolated cottage, or rather a ramshackle hut built of un-cemented bricks and corrugated iron. A skinny woman dressed in black and three pale children were sitting on the threshold. He approached, and offered her the fish, and she made him understand that she would have liked the fish, but had nothing to give in exchange; in fact, she and the children had not eaten for two days. She also made him enter the hut, and there was nothing inside, only piles of straw as in a kennel.

At this point the children had looked at him with such eyes that Cesare had thrown down the fish and run away like a thief.

12

The Wood and the Path

We stayed at Starye Dorogi, in that Red House full of mystery and pitfalls like a fairy castle, for two long months: from 15 July to 15 September 1945.

They were months of idleness and relative comfort, and full, therefore, of penetrating nostalgia. Nostalgia is a fragile and tender anguish, basically different, more intimate, more human than the other pains we had endured till then – beatings, cold, hunger, terror, destitution, disease. Nostalgia is a limpid and clean pain, but demanding; it permeates every minute of the day, permits no other thoughts and induces a need for escape.

Perhaps because of this, the forest around the camp exercised a deep attraction upon us. Perhaps it offered the inestimable gift of solitude to all who sought it; we had been deprived of this for so long! Perhaps because it reminded us of other woods, other solitudes of our previous existence; or perhaps, on the other hand, because it was solemn and austere and untouched like no other scenery known to us.

To the north of the Red House, beyond the road, there was a varied zone of thickets, glades and pine woods, broken by marshes and strips of fine white sand; you came across winding, barely discernible paths, leading to distant farms. But to the south, only a few hundred yards from the Red House, every human trace disappeared. So did every sign of animal life, except for the occasional fawn-coloured flash of a squirrel, or the sinister steady eye of a water snake, wrapped round a rotting trunk. There were no paths, no traces of woodsmen, nothing: only silence, desolation and tree trunks in all directions, pale birches, red-brown conifers, shooting vertically towards the invisible sky; the ground was equally invisible, covered by a thick layer of dead leaves and pine needles, and by clumps of wild waist-high undergrowth.

The first time I penetrated it, I learnt to my cost, with surprise and fear, that the risk of 'losing oneself in a wood' existed not only in fairy tales. I had been walking for about an hour, orientating myself as best I could by the sun, which was visible occasionally, where the branches were less thick; but then the sky clouded over, threatening rain, and when I wanted to return I realized that I had lost the north. Moss on the tree trunks? It covered them on all sides. I set out in what seemed the correct direction; but after a long and painful walk through the brambles and undergrowth I found myself in as unrecognizable a spot as that from which I had started.

I walked on for hours, increasingly tired and uneasy, almost until dusk; and I was already beginning to think that even if my companions came to search for me, they would not find me, or would only find me days later, exhausted by hunger, perhaps already dead. As daylight began to fade, swarms of large hungry mosquitoes rose up, as well as other unclassifiable insects, as large and hard as bullets, which darted blindly among the tree trunks, smashing into my face. Then I decided to set off straight ahead, generally speaking towards the north (that is, leaving on my left a slightly more luminous bit of sky, which should have corresponded to the west), and to walk without stopping until I met the main road, or in any case a path or a track. So I continued in the prolonged twilight of the northern summer, until it was almost night, a prey now to utter panic, to the age-old fear of the dark, the forest and the unknown. Despite my weariness, I felt a violent impulse to rush headlong in any direction, and to continue running so long as my strength and breath lasted.

Suddenly I heard the whistle of a train: this meant the railway was to my right, when, according to my calculations, it should have been far away to the left. So I had been going in the wrong direction. Following the noise of the train, I arrived at the railway before nightfall; then I kept to the glinting railway lines, moving in the direction of the Little Bear which had reappeared amid the clouds, and reached safety, first at Starye Dorogi, then at the Red House.

But there were some who had moved to the forest, and lived there; the first had been Cantarella, one of the 'Rumanians', who had discovered his vocation as a hermit. Cantarella was a Calabrian sailor, tall and ascetically thin, taciturn and misanthropic. He had built a hut from tree trunks and branches, half an hour's walk from the camp, and here he lived in wild solitude, dressed only in a loin-cloth. He was a contemplative, but not an idler; he exercised a curious priestly activity.

He possessed a hammer and a sort of roughly cast anvil, which he had salvaged from some war scrap and fixed in a tree stump; with these tools, and with empty food tins, he produced pots and pans with great skill and religious diligence.

He produced them on order, for the new couples. When, in our heterogeneous community, a man and woman decided to live together, and hence felt the need for a minimum of utensils to set up house, they went to Cantarella, holding hands. Without asking questions, he set to work, and in little more than an hour, with expert blows of the hammer, bent and twisted the tin-plate into the forms that the couple desired. He did not ask for payment, but accepted gifts in kind, such as bread, cheese, eggs.

In this manner, the marriage was celebrated, and in this manner Cantarella lived.

There were also other inhabitants of the wood; I realized this one day, when I chanced across a path that ran westwards, straight and clearly visible, which previously I had not noticed. It led to a particularly thick region of the wood, where it threaded its way along an old trench, and ended at the entrance to a casemate of trunks, almost totally underground: only the roof and the chimney projected above the surface. I pushed at the door, which yielded; there was nobody inside but the place was clearly inhabited. On the bare soil forming the floor (which was swept and clean) there was a stove, plates, an army bowl; in the corner, a pile of hay; hung on the walls, feminine clothing and photographs of men.

I returned to the camp, and discovered that I was the only one not to know about it: it was common knowledge that two German women lived in the casemate. They were two auxiliaries of the Wehrmacht, who had not managed to follow the Germans in defeat, and had remained isolated in the Russian wastes. They were afraid of the Russians, and had not given themselves up; for months they had lived precariously, by small thefts, by gathering herbs and by occasional furtive prostitution to Englishmen and Frenchmen who had occupied the Red House before us – until the arrival of the Italians had brought them prosperity and safety.

In our colony, women were few, not more than two hundred, and almost all had soon reached a stable arrangement: they were no longer available. So, to go to 'the girls in the wood' had become a habit for an indefinite number of Italians, and the only alternative to celibacy. An alternative which was rich with a complex fascination; because the matter was secret and vaguely dangerous (much more for the women than for them); because the girls were foreigners and had grown half savage;

because they were in need, and so gave one the ennobling feeling of 'protecting' them; and because of the exotic, fairy-tale scenery of the meetings.

Not only Cantarella, but the Velletrano as well had found his personality in the woods. The experiment of transplanting a 'savage' into civilization has been tried many times, often with excellent results, to demonstrate the fundamental unity of the human species; with the Velletrano the opposite was accomplished, for, a native of the Jewish quarter of Rome, he had been transformed back into a 'savage' with admirable ease.

In fact, he could never have been very civilized. The Velletrano was a Jew of about thirty, a survivor of Auschwitz. He must have created a problem for the Lager official responsible for tattoos, because both his muscular forearms were already thickly covered with them: Cesare, who had known him for some time, explained to me that they were the names of his women; he also pointed out that the Velletrano's real name was not Velletrano, nor had he been born at Velletri, but had been sent out there to wet-nurse.

He rarely spent the night at the Red House; he lived in the forest, barefoot and half naked. He lived like our progenitors; he laid traps for hares and foxes, climbed up trees after nests, brought down turtle doves with stones and was not above raiding the chicken runs of the most distant farms; he collected mushrooms and berries generally held to be inedible, and in the evening one often met him near the camp, crouching on his heels in front of a large fire, roasting the day's prey and singing uncouthly. Afterwards, he would go to sleep on the bare ground, lying near the embers. But, as he was still born of man, in his own way he pursued virtue and knowledge, and day by day perfected his art and his instruments; he fabricated a knife, then a spear and an axe, and had he had the time, without doubt he would have rediscovered agriculture and pasturage.

When he had had a good day, he became sociable and affable; through Cesare, who willingly presented him like a freak at a fair, and who recounted his earlier legendary adventures, he invited everybody to Homeric feasts of roast meats; if anyone refused, he turned nasty and pulled out his knife.

After a few days of rain, followed by sun and wind, the mushrooms and bilberries in the wood grew with such abundance as to become of interest no longer from a purely bucolic or sporting point of view, but from a strictly utilitarian one. After taking appropriate measures to avoid losing the way, everybody spent whole days collecting them. The bilberries, which grew in much taller thickets than in Mediterranean countries, were almost as large as nuts, and very tasty; we took them back to camp by the pound, and even tried (in vain) to ferment their juice into wine. As for the mushrooms, there were two varieties: there were the normal brown mushrooms, savoury and certainly edible; and another type, similar to the former in shape and smell, but larger and tougher with slightly different colours.

None of us was certain if these latter were edible; on the other hand, could they be left to rot in the wood? They could not: we were all badly under-nourished, and, even more important, our memory of the hunger of Auschwitz was still too recent, and had changed into a violent mental stimulus, which obliged us to fill our stomachs to the utmost and imperiously forbade us to renounce any opportunity of eating. Cesare collected a fair quantity, and boiled them according to a recipe unknown to me, adding to the stew vodka and garlic bought in the village, because they 'kill all poisons'. Then he himself ate some, not much, and offered a little to many of us, so as to limit the risk and collect abundant evidence for the day after. The following day he walked around the dormitories and had never been so polite and solicitous: 'How are you, Signora Elvira? How are you, Don Vincenzo? Did you sleep well? Did you have a good night?' And meanwhile he examined their faces with a clinical eye. They were all well, the strange mushrooms could be eaten.

For the laziest and richest, there was no need to go to the wood to find extra provisions. Commercial contacts between the village of Starye Dorogi and the occupants of the Red House had soon become intensive. Every day peasant women arrived with baskets and pails; they sat on the ground, and stayed there for hours, without moving, waiting for clients. If a rain cloud burst, they did not leave, but merely pulled their skirts over their heads. Two or three times the Russians tried to drive them away, and stuck up bilingual edicts, which threatened both parties with punishments of crazy severity; then, as normally occurred, they lost interest in the matter, and the exchanges continued undisturbed.

There were old and young peasant women; the former were dressed in the traditional manner, with quilted blouses and skirts and handkerchiefs tied over their heads; the latter, in light cotton garments, went about for the most part barefoot and were frank, bold and ready to laugh, but not brazen. In addition to mushrooms, bilberries and raspberries, they sold milk, cheese, eggs, chickens, lettuce and fruit, and in exchange accepted fish, bread, tobacco and any piece of clothing or fabric, however torn and threadbare; naturally rubles could be used by those who still possessed them.

In a short time Cesare knew all the women, especially the young ones. I often went with him to these peasants, to listen to their interesting bargaining. I do not intend to deny the utility of speaking the same language in business affairs, but I can affirm from experience that it is not strictly necessary; each of the two knows exactly what the other wants, and although initially he does not know the intensity of the desire to buy or sell respectively, he can deduce it with excellent approximation from the expression on the other's face, from his gestures and from the number of his replies.

Let us look at Cesare, who is going to the market early in the morning with a fish. He looks for and finds Irina, his friend, his contemporary, whose sympathies he has conquered some time before by baptizing her 'Greta Garbo' and giving her a pencil; Irina has a cow and sells milk, *moloko*; in fact, in the evening, returning from the pasturage, she often stops in front of the Red House and milks the cow directly into her clients' receptacles. The problem today is to agree how much milk Cesare's fish is worth; Cesare is carrying a half-gallon pail (it is one of Cantarella's, which Cesare had picked up cheaply from a '*ménage*' which had broken down through incompatibility), and with his hand flat, palm down, indicates that he wants it full. Irina laughs, and replies with quick harmonious words, probably insults; she slaps away Cesare's hand, and with two fingers points half-way up the side of the pail.

Now it is Cesare's turn to grow angry; he brandishes the fish ('untreated'), dangles it in the air by its tail with an enormous effort, as if it weighed a hundredweight, and says: 'Look at the size!', then runs its entire length under Irina's nose, and while doing this closes his eyes and draws in his breath deeply, as if inebriated with the fragrance of the fish. Irina takes advantage of the second in which Cesare's eyes are closed to snatch the fish from him as quickly as a cat, to bite off its head cleanly with her white teeth, and to slap the flaccid mutilated corpse in Cesare's face, with all her considerable strength. Then, so as not to ruin their friendship and the bargaining, she touches the pail at the three-quarter mark: three pints. Half stunned by the blow, Cesare mutters a string of obscene gallantries which he judges fit to restore his virile honour; then, however, he accepts Irina's last offer, and leaves her the fish, which she devours on the spot.

We were to meet the voracious Irina later, several times, in a context which to us Latins seemed somewhat embarrassing, but which was perfectly natural to her.

In a glade in the wood, half-way between the village and the camp, was the public bath, to be found in every Russian village, and which at Starye Dorogi functioned on alternate days for the Russians and for us. It was a wooden hut, with two long stone benches inside, and zinc wash tubs of various sizes scattered about. On the wall there were taps with abundant hot and cold water. The soap, on the other hand, was not abundant: it was distributed with great parsimony in the dressing-room. The official responsible for the distribution of the soap was Irina.

She sat at a table with a small block of smelly greyish soap on it, and held a knife in her hand. We undressed, handed in our clothes for disinfection and lined up completely nude in front of Irina's table. The girl was extremely serious and incorruptible when carrying out her duties as a public official; she frowned with attention and stuck her tongue between her teeth like a child, as she cut a small slice of soap for everyone aspiring to a bath; a little thinner for skinny people, a little thicker for fat people, either because she had been ordered to do so, or because she was moved by an unconscious desire for a just distribution. Not a muscle of her face moved at the impertinences of her more foul-mouthed customers.

After the bath, we had to recover our clothes from the disinfection room; this was another surprise of the Starye Dorogi regime. The room was heated at 250° F.: the first time they told us we had to enter it personally to get our clothing, we looked at each other, perplexed; Russians are made of iron, as we had seen many times, but we were not, and we should certainly be roasted. Then someone tried, and we saw that the exploit was not so terrible as it seemed, so long as one observed the following precautions: to enter while still wet; to know the number of one's clothes hanger in advance; to take a deep breath before passing through the door and then not to breathe again and not to touch any metal object; above all, to hurry.

The disinfected clothing presented interesting phenomena; corpses of exploded lice, strangely deformed; plastic pens, forgotten in a pocket by some plutocrat, distorted and with the cover sealed up; melted candle ends soaked up by the cloth; an egg, left in a pocket as an experiment, cracked open and dried out into a horny mass, but still edible. But the two Russian attendants walked in and out of the furnace with indifference, like the legendary salamander.

So the days at Starye Dorogi passed by, in an interminable indolence, as sleepy and salubrious as a long holiday, only broken at intervals by the painful thought of a distant home and by the enchantment of our rediscovery of nature. It was useless to go to the Russians of the Command to ask why we were not returning, when we should return, by what road, what future awaited us; they knew no more than we did, or else, with polite candour, they proffered fantastic or terrifying or senseless answers: that there were no trains; or that war against America was about to start; that soon we should be sent to work in the *kolkhoz*; that they were waiting to exchange us for Russian prisoners in Italy. They told us these and other enormities without hatred or derision, in fact with an almost affectionate solicitude, as if they were speaking to children who asked too many questions, to quieten them.

They simply could not understand our haste to return home: were we not given food and beds? What did we lack at Starye Dorogi? We did not even have to work; did they, soldiers of the Red Army, who had fought four years, and had won the war, complain about not being sent home?

In fact they were returning home haphazardly, slowly and, to judge from appearance, in extreme disorder. The spectacle of the

Russian demobilization, which we had already admired at the station of Katowice, now continued in a different form before our eyes, day by day; groups of the victorious army passed by, no longer by rail, but along the road in front of the Red House, moving from west to east, in tight or straggling bands, at all hours of the day and night. Men passed by on foot, often bare-foot, with their shoes hanging from their shoulders to save the soles, because the march was long; with or without uniforms, armed or unarmed, some singing lustily, others grey-faced and exhausted. Some carried sacks or suitcases on their shoulders; others, the most varied of possessions, an easy chair, a standard lamp, copper pots, a radio, a pendulum clock.

Others passed by on carts, or on horseback; yet others, droves of them, on motor-cycles, driven at intoxicating speed, with an infernal noise. American Dodge trucks passed by, packed with men clinging even to the bonnet and mudguards; other trucks were towing equally packed trailers. We saw one of these trailers travelling on three wheels; a pine-trunk had been fixed as well as possible in place of the fourth wheel at an angle, so that one extremity rested and dragged along the ground. As it was slowly consumed by friction, the tree-trunk was pushed gradually farther down, so as to maintain the vehicle's equilibrium. Almost in front of the Red House one of the three remaining tyres deflated; the occupants, about twenty, got down, overturned the trailer to clear the road and again packed into the already overloaded truck, which left in a cloud of dust, while everybody cheered.

Other unusual vehicles also passed, always crammed: agri-cultural tractors, postal vans, German buses formerly used for city transport and still bearing the names of the Berlin terminals; some already broken down, and dragged by other vehicles or by horses.

About the beginning of August, this multiple migration

imperceptibly changed character. Horses slowly began to prevail over vehicles; after a week, one could only see the former, the road belonged to them. There must have been all the horses of occupied Germany, tens of thousands passing through each day; they moved by endlessly, tired, sweating, starving, accompanied by clouds of horse-flies and by sharp animal smells; they were goaded and urged on with cries and blows of the whip by girls, one to every hundred or more animals, who rode on horseback, without a saddle, bare-legged, sunburnt and dishevelled. In the evening, they drove the horses off the road into the fields and woods, so that they could graze in liberty and rest till dawn. There were carthorses, thoroughbreds, mules, mares with foals still sucking, rheumatic old hacks, asses; we soon realized not only that they were not counted, but also that their drovers took no interest at all in the animals which dropped out because they were tired or ill or limping, or in those which were lost during the. night. The horses were so many, what did it matter if one more or less reached its destination?

But for us, almost wholly deprived of meat for eighteen months, one horse more or less could make all the difference. The person to begin the hunt was, naturally, the Velletrano; he came to wake us one morning, covered in blood from head to foot, still clasping the primordial tool he had used, a splinter of an artillery shell tied with leather thongs to a forked stick.

From the investigation we carried out (because the Velletrano was not very good at explaining himself in words) it emerged that he had given the *coup de grâce* to a horse probably already on its last legs; the poor animal had a highly equivocal look, its stomach so swollen that it sounded like a drum, and froth on its mouth; it must have been kicking all night, as it lay on its side in its death agony, because with its hooves it had dug two deep brown semicircles out of the grass. But we ate it all the same.

After this beginning, several pairs of specialized hunter-

knackers were formed, who were no longer satisfied with felling
sick or stray horses, but chose the fattest ones, enticed them out
of the herd and then killed them in the wood. They preferred to
work in the first light of dawn; one covered the animal's eyes
with a cloth, while the other dealt the (not always) mortal blow
on its neck.

It was a period of absurd abundance; there was horsemeat for
everybody, without stint, gratis; the maximum the hunters would
ask for a dead horse was two or three rations of tobacco. In every
corner of the wood, and when it was raining even in the corridors and under the staircases in the Red House, men and women
were to be seen busily cooking enormous horse steaks with
mushrooms; it was thanks to these that we survivors of Auschwitz did not need many more months to regain our strength.

The Russians of the Command did not pay the slightest attention even to this plundering. Only once did they intervene, and
only once did they inflict a punishment: towards the end of the
migration, when horsemeat was already growing scarce and
the price was beginning to rise, one of the ex-jailbirds had the
impudence to open a real slaughterhouse, in one of the many
garrets of the Red House. The Russians frowned on this enterprise, though it was not clear whether on hygienic or moral
grounds; the culprit was publicly censured, declared a 'chort
(devil), *parazìt, spyekulànt*' and shut up in a cell.

It was not a very severe punishment: in the cell, for obscure
reasons – perhaps through a bureaucratic atavism which looked
back to a time when prisoners must long have been three to a
cell – one was given three rations of food a day. It made no difference whether the prisoners were nine, or one, or none; the
rations were always three. So the illegal butcher left his cell at
the end of his punishment, after ten days of overeating, as fat as
a pig and full of *joie de vivre*.

13

Holidays

As always happens, the end of our hunger laid bare and perceptible in us a much deeper hunger. Not only desire for our homes, which in a sense was discounted and projected into the future; but a more immediate and urgent need for human contacts, for mental and physical work, for novelty and variety.

Life at Starye Dorogi, which would have been little less than perfect if it had been felt to be a holiday interlude in a workaday existence, began to weigh on us because of the very idleness it forced upon us. In these conditions, several people left to seek life and adventures elsewhere. It would be inaccurate to speak of a flight, because the camp was not fenced or guarded, and the Russians did not count us, or did not count us carefully; quite simply, they said good-bye to their friends and took off. They got what they were searching for: they saw countries and peoples, they went far afield, some as far as Odessa or Moscow, others as far as the frontiers; they experienced the lock-ups of isolated villages, the biblical hospitality of the peasants, vague love-affairs, stupid interrogations by duty-bound police, more hunger and solitude. Almost all returned to Starye Dorogi, because, even if there was not a trace of barbed wire around the Red House, when they tried to force the legendary frontier towards the west they found it severely barred.

They returned, and resigned themselves to our regime of limbo. The days of the Nordic summer were very long; it was already light at three in the morning, and the dusk dragged on tirelessly until nine or ten in the evening. The excursions into the woods, meals, sleep, risky bathes in the marshes, ever-repeated conversations, plans for the future, were not enough to shorten the time of our expectation, or to lighten its weight, which increased day by day.

We tried to approach the Russians, but with little success. The most sophisticated ones (who spoke German or English) acted in a courteous but diffident manner towards us, and often brusquely interrupted a conversation, as if they felt guilty or spied on. With the most simple-minded ones, the seventeen-year-old soldiers of the Command and the peasants of the neighbourhood, the difficulties of language reduced us to stunted and primordial relationships.

It is six in the morning, but the light of day has long since banished sleep. I am walking towards a thicket where there is a stream, with a pot of potatoes organized by Cesare; it is our favourite place for cooking operations because there is water and wood, and today it is my turn to wash the plates and cook. I light a fire between three stones; and to my surprise, I see a Russian not far away, small but sturdy, with thick Asiatic features, intent on preparations similar to mine. He has no matches; he approaches me, and as far as I can judge is asking me for a light. He is stripped to the waist, wearing only his army trousers, and his air is not very reassuring. He wears a bayonet at his waist.

I offer him a lighted stick; the Russian takes it, but stands there looking at me with suspicious curiosity. Is he thinking that my potatoes are stolen? Or is he meditating whether to take them away from me? Or has he mistaken me for someone he does not like?

No, something else is worrying him. He has realized that I do not speak Russian, and this vexes him. The fact that a man, adult and normal, cannot speak Russian, which means he cannot speak, seems to him to smack of insolent arrogance, as if I had flatly refused to reply to him. He is not ill-intentioned, in fact, he is prepared to give me a hand, to raise me from my guilty condition of ignorance; Russian is so easy, everybody speaks it, even children who have not yet started to walk. He sits beside me; I continue to be anxious for my potatoes, and watch him carefully; but, to judge by his appearance, he has nothing else on his mind except a desire to help me recover lost time. He does not understand, he does not admit my attitude of refusal; he wants to teach me his tongue.

Alas, as a teacher he is not worth much; he lacks method and patience, and, even worse, works on the mistaken assumption that I can follow his explanations and comments. So long as it is simply a question of terms, everything goes quite well, and in fact I quite enjoy the game. He points to a potato, and says: '*Kartòfel*'; then he grips my shoulder with his mighty paw, pushes his index finger in my face, listens intently like a deaf man and waits. I repeat: '*Kartòfel*.' He puts on a disgusted expression; my pronunciation is wrong: I do not even know how to pronounce! He tries two or three times more, then he gets bored and tries a new word. '*Ogón*,' he says, pointing to the fire; that is better, apparently my repetition satisfies him. He looks around searching for other pedagogic objects, then stares at me with intensity, slowly rising to his feet as he does so, as if he wished to hypnotize me; then, in a flash, he whips his bayonet out of its scabbard and flourishes it in the air.

I jump to my feet and make off, towards the Red House: too bad about the potatoes. But after a few steps I hear an ogrish laugh echoing behind my back: his joke has been successful.

'*Britva*,' he says to me, making the blade flash in the sun; and

I repeat the word, feeling somewhat uneasy. With a slash worthy of a paladin, he slices a branch clean off a tree; he shows it to me, and says: '*Dèrevo.*' I repeat: '*Dèrevo.*'

'*Ya russky soldàt.*' I repeat, as best I can: '*Ya russky soldàt.*' Another laugh, which seems to me contemptuous: *he* is a Russian soldier, I am not, and that makes quite a difference. He explains this to me in a confused manner, with a torrent of words, pointing first at my chest, and then at his, and nodding yes and no with his head. Clearly he regards me as a worthless pupil, a desperate case of obtuseness; to my relief, he returns to his fire and abandons me to my barbarism.

On another day, but at the same time and in the same place, I come across an unaccustomed spectacle. A group of Italians surround a boyish Russian sailor, tall, with rapid agile movements. He is 'narrating' an episode of war; and because he knows that his language is not understood, he expresses himself as best he can, in a manner which for him is nearly as spontaneous as, if not more so than, words: he expresses himself with all his muscles, with the precocious furrows on his face, with flashing eyes and teeth, with leaps and gestures; and from this is born a *pas seul*, full of fascination and force.

It is night, '*noch*': palms down, he moves his hands slowly around him. Everything is silent: he pronounces a long 'ssh' with his index finger parallel to his nose. He narrows his eyes and points to the horizon: there, far away, are the Germans, '*niemtzy*'. How many? Five, he indicates with his fingers; '*finef*', he adds in Yiddish for greater clarity. With his hand he digs a small round hole in the sand, and lays five twigs flat in it, these are the Germans; then a sixth twig pointing sideways, the '*mashina*', the machine-gun. What are the Germans doing? Here his eyes light up with savage mirth: '*spats*', they are sleeping (and for a moment he himself snores); they are sleeping, the fools, and they do not know what is coming to them.

What did he do? This is what he did: he approached, cautiously, against the wind, like a leopard. Then, with a leap, he jumped into the nest pulling out his knife; and now he repeats his former actions, wholly lost in a dramatic ecstasy. The ambush, and the sudden atrocious scuffle, are repeated before our eyes; the man, his face transfigured by a tense sinister grin, turns into a whirlwind; he jumps forwards and backwards, striking in front of him, to his side, high up and low down, in an explosion of deadly energy; but it is a lucid fury, his weapon (which exists, a long knife which he has taken out of his boot) penetrates, slashes, rips open with ferocity, but at the same time with tremendous skill, a foot away from our faces.

Suddenly the sailor stops, slowly rises; his knife drops from his hand; he is panting, his eyes grow vacuous. He looks at the ground, as if amazed not to see the corpses and blood there; he looks around bewildered, emptied; he becomes aware of us, and gives us a childish timid smile. '*Koniechno*,' he says: it is over; he walks slowly away.

Quite different, and just as mysterious then as it seems now, was the case of the Lieutenant. The Lieutenant (we were never able to learn his name, perhaps not by chance) was a young lean sallow Russian, perpetually frowning. He spoke Italian perfectly, with so slight a Russian accent that it could be mistaken for some Italian dialectal cadence; but, in contrast to all the other Russians of the Command, he showed little cordiality or sympathy towards us. He was the only person we were able to question. How was it he spoke Italian? Why was he with us? Why did they keep us in Russia four months after the end of the war? Were we hostages? Had we been forgotten? Why could we not write to Italy? When would we return? ... But the Lieutenant replied to all these questions, which weighed as heavy as lead, in a curt, elusive manner, showing a self-confidence and authority which ill accorded with his not very elevated rank. We noticed that even his superiors treated him with a strange deference, as if they were afraid of him.

He kept the same surly aloofness from the Russians as from us. He never smiled, he did not drink, he would not accept invitations, or cigarettes; he spoke little, with cautious words which he seemed to weigh one by one. At his first appearances, we had naturally thought of him as our interpreter and delegate at the Russian Command, but we soon saw that his duties (if he had any, and if his behaviour was not merely a complicated manner of boosting his own importance) must have been different, and we preferred to stay silent in his presence. From a few reticent remarks of his we realized that he had a good knowledge of the topography of Turin and Milan. Had he been to Italy? 'No,' he replied curtly, and gave no other explanations.

Public health was excellent, and the patients at the surgery were few and always the same, with boils, the usual imaginary illnesses, a little scabies, a touch of colitis. One day a woman came, complaining of vague disturbances: nausea, backache, giddiness, attacks of sweating. Leonardo examined her; she had bruises almost everywhere, but told us not to pay attention to them, she had fallen down the stairs. A detailed diagnosis was not very easy with so few instruments available, but, by a process of elimination and by deduction from the numerous precedents among our women, Leonardo declared to his patient that she was probably in her third month of pregnancy. The woman showed no joy, anguish, surprise or indignation; she accepted the diagnosis, thanked him, but did not go away. She went back to sit on the bench in the corridor, silent and tranquil, as if she were waiting for someone.

She was a small, dark-haired girl, about twenty-five years old, with a homely air, submissive and absent; her face, which was not very attractive, nor very expressive, did not seem new to me, nor did her way of speaking, with gentle Tuscan inflections.

I had certainly met her somewhere, but not at Starye Dorogi. I felt an evanescent sensation of an overlap, of a transposition, of a marked inversion of relationships, which however I was unable to define. In a vague but insistent manner, I linked this feminine image to a knot of intense feelings: of a humble and distant admiration, of gratitude, frustration, fear, even of abstract desire, but above all of a deep and indeterminate anguish.

As she continued to sit on the bench, quiet and still, with no signs of impatience, I asked her if she wanted something, if she still had need of us; surgery was over, there were no other patients, it was time to close. 'No, no,' she replied; 'I don't need anything. I shall go now.'

Flora! The nebulous memory abruptly took shape, coagulated into a precise, definite picture, rich in retrospective details of time and place, colours, states of mind, atmosphere, smells. She was Flora: the Italian from the Buna cellars, the woman from the Lager, the object of Alberto's and my dreams for over a month, unwitting symbol of a lost and by then unhoped-for liberty. Flora, last seen only a year ago, and it seemed a century.

Flora was a small-time prostitute, who had ended in Germany with the Todt Organization. She did not know German and had learnt no trade, so she had been set to sweep the floors of the Buna factory. She swept all day, wearily, exchanging not a word with anyone, never raising her eyes from her broom and her endless work. Nobody seemed to bother about her, while for her part she hardly climbed to the upper floors, almost as if she feared the light of day; she swept the cellars interminably, from top to bottom, and then began again, like a sleepwalker.

She was the only woman we had seen for months, and she

spoke our language, but we Häftlinge were forbidden to talk to her. To Alberto and myself she seemed beautiful, mysterious, incorporeal. Despite the prohibition, which in a sense multiplied the enchantment of our meetings by adding to them the pungent flavour of the illicit, we exchanged a few furtive phrases with Flora; we declared ourselves Italians, and asked her for bread. We asked her this reluctantly, only too aware that we were demeaning ourselves and the quality of this delicate human contact; but hunger, which rarely compromises, obliged us not to waste the occasion.

Flora often brought us bread, and gave it to us with a bewildered air, in the dark corners of the basement, sniffing back her tears. She was sorry for us, and would have liked to help us in other ways as well, but did not know how to and was afraid. Afraid of everything, like a defenceless animal; perhaps even of us, not directly, but in so far as we formed part of that foreign and incomprehensible world which had torn her from her country, had forced a broom into her hand and had relegated her beneath the earth, to sweep floors already swept a hundred times.

For our part, we were upset, grateful and full of shame. We suddenly became aware of our miserable appearance and suffered because of it. Alberto, who used to wander around all day with his eyes fixed to the ground like a bloodhound, and so found the most curious oddments, picked up a comb somewhere, and solemnly gave it to Flora, who still possessed her hair; after that we felt tied to her by a gentle unsullied tie, and we dreamt of her at night. Consequently we felt acute discomfort, an absurd and impotent mixture of jealousy and disillusionment, when we were forced by the evidence to realize, to admit to ourselves, that Flora had meetings with other men. Where and how and with whom? In the least attractive place and manner; not far away, in the hay, in a clandestine warren organized in a basement by a co-operative of German and Polish Kapos. Little was needed: a wink, an imperious nod of the head, and Flora laid down her broom and docilely followed the man of the moment. After a few minutes she returned alone; she adjusted her clothes and began to sweep again without looking us in the face. After this squalid discovery, Flora's bread was bitter to our taste, not that this stopped us from accepting and eating it.

I did not identify myself to Flora, through charity towards her and towards myself. Faced with these phantasms, of my Buna self, of the woman of my memories and of this reincarnation, I felt changed, intensely 'different', like a butterfly before a caterpillar. In the limbo of Starye Dorogi I felt dirty, ragged, tired, burdened, exhausted by expectation, yet young and full of vigour, looking towards the future; but Flora had not changed. Now she lived with a cobbler from Bergamo, not as a wife, but as a slave. She washed and cooked for him, and followed him with humble subdued eyes; the man, bull-like and apish, watched every step of hers, and beat her savagely at every trace of suspicion. Hence the bruises all over her, she had come to the surgery stealthily, and was now afraid to go out to meet her master's anger.

At Starye Dorogi no one demanded anything of us, no one importuned us, no pressure was placed on us, we did not have to defend ourselves from anything; we felt as inert and settled as an alluvial sediment. In this sluggish uneventful life of ours, the arrival of a Soviet military film truck marked a memorable date. It must have been a travelling unit, formerly in service with the troops at the front or in the supply lines, and now itself on its way home; it included a projector, a generating plant, a supply of films and the personnel to run it. It stopped at Starye Dorogi for three days, and gave a performance each evening.

The shows took place in the theatre hall; it was very spacious, and the seats carried off by the Germans had been replaced by rustic benches of unstable equilibrium on the floor which rose from the screen towards the gallery. The gallery, which also sloped, had been reduced to a narrow strip; the highest part had been divided in a moment of caprice by the mysterious and whimsical architects of the Red House into a series of small rooms without air or light, whose doors opened towards the stage. The unattached women of our colony lived there.

On the first evening an old Austrian film was shown, in itself mediocre, and of little interest to the Russians, but full of emotional charge for us Italians. It was a silent film about war and spying, with sub-titles in German: more exactly, it was about an episode of the First World War on the Italian front. The same candour and rhetorical equipment appeared as in analogous films of Allied production: military honour, sacred frontiers, soldiers of great heroism who nevertheless burst into tears as easily as virgins, bayonet attacks carried out with improbable enthusiasm. Only it was all turned upside down: the Austro-Hungarians, officers and soldiers, were noble and sturdy characters, valiant and chivalrous, with the spiritual sensitive faces of stoic warriors, the rough and honest faces of peasants, inspiring sympathy at the first glance. The Italians, all of them, were a crowd of vulgar numbskulls, all marked by striking and laughable physical defects: they were cross-eyed, obese, with narrow shoulders, bandy legs and low sloping foreheads. They were cowardly and ferocious, brutal and dimwitted; the officers had faces like effete dandies, crushed under the incongruous weight of kettle-like hats familiar to us from portraits of the generals Cadorna and Diaz; the soldiers had porcine or apish faces, accentuated by the helmets of our fathers, worn aslant or pulled down over their eyes treacherously to hide their looks.

The arch-villain, an Italian spy at Vienna, was a strange chimera, half D'Annunzio and half Victor Emmanuel, of such

absurdly small stature that he was forced to look up at everybody; he wore a monocle and a bow-tie, and paced up and
down the screen with arrogant strides like a cockerel. When he
returned to the Italian lines, he coldly superintended the shooting of ten innocent Tyrolean civilians.

We Italians, so little accustomed to seeing ourselves cast as
the 'enemy', odious by definition, and so dismayed at being
hated by anybody, derived a complex pleasure from watching
the film – a pleasure not without disquiet, a source of salutary
meditations.

On the second evening a Soviet film was announced, and the
audience began to warm up; the Italians, because it was the first
one they saw; the Russians, because the title promised a war
film, full of movement and shooting. The word got round;
Russian soldiers arrived unexpectedly from nearby and distant
garrisons, and thronged outside the doors of the theatre. When
the doors opened, they burst inside like a river in flood, climbing noisily over the benches and jostling against each other with
much pushing and shoving.

The film was ingenuous and uncomplicated. A Soviet military
plane was forced to land in an unspecified mountainous area
near the frontier; it was a small two-seater plane, with only the
pilot on board. Just as he had repaired the engine and was about
to take off, a local notable advanced, a turbaned sheikh with an
extraordinarily suspicious air, who, with flattering bows and oriental obeisances, begged to be taken on board. Even an idiot
would have understood that he was a dangerous rogue, probably a smuggler, a dissident leader or a foreign agent; but as it
was, the pilot, with thoughtless generosity, gave way to his
prolix entreaties, and placed him in the back seat of the plane.

We were shown the take-off, and some magnificent pan-
oramic views of mountain ranges sparkling with glaciers (I think
it was the Caucasus); then the sheikh, with secret viperous

movements, took a revolver from under his cloak, pushed it in the pilot's back and ordered him to change course. The pilot, who did not even turn round, reacted with lightning decision; he reared the plane into a sharp loop. The sheikh collapsed in his seat, overwhelmed by fear and nausea; but instead of putting him out of action, the pilot tranquilly continued the flight towards his destination. After a few minutes, and more admirable mountain scenery, the bandit recovered; he dragged himself towards the pilot, once more raised his revolver and repeated the attempt. This time the plane went into a nose dive, and plunged down for some thousands of feet, towards an inferno of precipitous peaks and abysses; the sheikh fainted and the plane regained height. So the flight continued for more than an hour, with continually repeated aggressions by the Muslim, and ever new acrobatics by the pilot; until after a final attempt by the sheikh, who seemed to have nine lives like a cat, the plane went into a spin; clouds, mountains and glaciers whirled boldly round it, until finally it came down safely on its predetermined landing-field. The inanimate sheikh was handcuffed; the pilot, as fresh as a rose, was not subjected to an inquiry, but had his hand shaken by proud superiors, was promoted on the field and received a shy kiss from a girl who seemed to have been waiting for him for some time.

The Russian soldiers in the audience followed the clumsy plot with noisy passion, applauding the hero and insulting the traitor; but it was nothing compared to what happened on the third evening.

Hurricane was announced for the third evening, quite a good American film of the 'thirties. A Polynesian sailor, a modern version of the 'noble savage', a simple man, strong and mild, is vulgarly provoked in a bar by a group of drunken whites, and wounds one of them slightly. Reason is clearly on his side, but no one testifies in his favour; he is arrested, tried and, to his pathetic incomprehension, condemned to a month in prison. He holds out only for a few days; not only because of an almost animal-like need of liberty and intolerance of bondage, but above all because he feels, he knows, that not he but the whites have violated justice; if this is the law of the whites, then the law is unjust. He knocks down a guard and escapes amid a shower of bullets.

Now the mild sailor has become a real criminal. He is hunted all over the archipelago, but it is pointless searching so far; he has returned quietly to his village. He is taken again, and relegated to a distant island, condemned to hard labour, and endures toil and beatings. He escapes again, throws himself into the sea from a vertiginous cliff, steals a canoe and sails for days towards his homeland, without food or water; he reaches it exhausted, just as the hurricane promised by the title is threatening to break. The hurricane bursts out at once wildly, and the man, like a good American hero, fights alone against the elements, and saves not only his woman, but the church, the pastor and all the faithful who had thought they would find shelter in the church. Rehabilitated, with his girl at his side, he advances towards a happy future, under the sun which breaks through the disappearing clouds.

This story, typically individualistic, elementary and not badly told, aroused the Russians to seismic enthusiasm. An hour before the beginning, a tumultuous crowd (attracted by the poster, which portrayed a magnificent Polynesian girl, scantily dressed) was already pushing against the doors; they were almost all very young soldiers, armed. It was clear that there was not room for everybody in the large theatre, not even standing; for this very reason they fought doggedly with their elbows to gain entrance. One fell, was trampled on and came the next day to the surgery; we thought we should find him smashed up, but he only had a few bruises: a people of solid bones. Soon the doors were broken open, smashed to pieces and the pieces used as clubs; when the film started, the crowd which stood crushed inside the theatre was already highly excited and bellicose.

It seemed as if the people in the film were not shadows to them, but flesh and blood friends or enemies, near at hand. The sailor was acclaimed at every exploit, greeted by noisy cheers and sten-guns brandished perilously over their heads. The policemen and jailers were insulted with bloodthirsty cries, greeted with shouts of 'leave him alone', 'go away', 'I'll get you', 'kill them all'. After the first escape, when the exhausted and wounded fugitive was once more captured, and even worse, sneered at and derided by the sardonic asymmetrical mask of John Carradine, pandemonium broke out. The audience stood up shouting, in generous defence of the innocent man; a wave of avengers moved threateningly towards the screen, but were cursed at and checked in turn by less heated elements or by those who wanted to see the end. Stones, lumps of earth, splinters from the demolished doors, even a regulation boot flew against the screen, hurled with furious precision at the odious face of the great enemy, which shone forth oversize in the foreground.

When the long and vigorous scene of the hurricane was reached, a witches' sabbath ensued. One could hear the sharp cries of the few women who had remained trapped in the crowd; a pole appeared, then another one, passed from hand to hand above our heads, amid deafening shouts. At first we could not understand what they were meant for, then the design became clear; it had probably been planned by the excluded Russians, who were creating an uproar outside. They were attempting an escalade of the gynaeceum-gallery.

The poles were raised and rested against the balcony, and various enthusiasts took off their boots and began to clamber up, as they do with greasy poles at a village fair. From this moment the spectacle of the escalade distracted all attention from the other spectacle which continued on the screen. As soon as one of the aspirants managed to climb above the tide of heads, he was pulled down by his feet and dragged back to the ground by ten or twenty hands. Groups of supporters and adversaries formed; one bold man managed to free himself from the crowd and pull himself up by his arms, followed by another one on the same pole. When they had almost reached the height of the balcony they fought among themselves for a few minutes, the lower one grabbing the other one's heels, the latter defending himself by kicking out blindly. At the same time, on the balcony, one could see the heads of a group of Italians, who had hastily climbed up the tortuous stairs of the Red House to protect the besieged women; the pole, pushed back by the defenders, oscillated, balanced for a long moment in a vertical position, then crashed among the crowd like a pine tree cut down by woodsmen, with the two men clinging to it. At this point, whether by chance or through a wise intervention of the authorities, the projector lamp went out, everything plunged into darkness, the noise of the pit reached a fearful intensity and everybody poured out into the moonlit night amid shouts, oaths and acclamations.

To everyone's regret, the cinema troupe left the next morning. The following evening a renewed and bold Russian attempt to invade the feminine quarters occurred, this time across the roofs and gutters; after this, a night patrol of Italian volunteers was set up. Furthermore, the women in the gallery decamped as an extra precaution, and joined the larger part of the feminine population, in a collective dormitory; a less intimate but securer arrangement.

14

The Theatre

About the middle of August a meeting ground with the Russians was found. Despite professional secrecy, the whole camp soon knew that the 'Rumanians' were organizing a revue, with the agreement and approval of the authorities; auditions took place in the theatre, whose doors had been restored as well as possible, and which was guarded by pickets who refused entry to all outsiders. Among the acts in the revue, there was a tap-dance: the specialist, an extremely conscientious sailor, practised every evening, among a small circle of experts and consultants. Now, tap-dancing is noisy by its very nature; the Lieutenant passed nearby, heard the rhythmic noise, forced the picket, in which he was clearly exceeding his authority, and entered. He watched two or three sessions, to the discomfort of the bystanders, without emerging from his habitual reserve and without relaxing his hermetic mask; then, unexpectedly, he informed the organizing committee that he was a passionate fan of tap-dancing in his spare time, and that he had long wanted to learn exactly how to tap-dance; so the dancer was invited, indeed ordered, to give him a series of lessons.

The spectacle of these lessons so interested me that I found a way of watching, slipping through the back ways of the Red House and hiding myself in a dark corner. The Lieutenant was the best pupil imaginable: very serious, willing, tenacious and physically gifted. He danced in his uniform, with boots, for exactly one hour a day, without allowing his teacher or himself a moment's rest. He made very rapid progress.

When the revue opened, a week later, the tap-dance number was a surprise to everybody; teacher and pupil danced, faultlessly, with impeccable parallelism and synchronism; the teacher, winking and smiling, dressed in an extravagant gypsy costume created by the women; the Lieutenant, funereal, with his nose in the air and his eyes fixed on the ground, as if he was performing a sacrificial dance. Naturally, he was in uniform with his medals on his chest and his holster on his belt dancing with him.

They were applauded; equally applauded were several other not very original numbers (a few Neapolitan songs from the classical repertory: *I Pompieri di Viggiu*,* a sketch in which a lover conquers his girl's heart with a bunch not of flowers, but of *ribba*, our stinking daily fish; the *Montanara** sung in chorus, with Mr Unverdorben leading the choir). But two rather unusual numbers gained an enthusiastic, and well-merited, success.

A large fat person came on the stage, with hesitant steps, and legs wide apart, masked, muffled and bundled up, like the famous Michelin man. He greeted the public like an athlete, with his hands clasped above his head; meantime, two assistants, with great effort, rolled alongside him an enormous piece of equipment consisting of a bar and two wheels, like those used by weight-lifters.

He bent down, gripped the bar, tensed all his muscles; nothing happened, the bar did not move. Then he took off his cloak, folded it meticulously, placed it on the ground and prepared for another attempt. When the weight again did not move from the ground, he took off a second cloak, placing it next to the first;

* Popular songs, originating in the Second World War.

and so on with various cloaks, civilian and military cloaks, rain-coats, cassocks, greatcoats. The athlete diminished in volume visibly, the stage filled up with garments and the weight seemed to have grown roots in the ground.

When he had finished with the cloaks, he began to take off jackets of all kinds (among them a Häftling striped jacket, in honour of our minority), then shirts in abundance, always trying to lift the instrument with punctilious solemnity after each piece of clothing had been removed, and renouncing the attempt without the least sign of impatience or surprise. However, when he took off his fourth or fifth shirt, he suddenly stopped. He looked at the shirt with attention, first at arm's length, then close up; he searched the collar and seams with agile monkey-like movements, and then with his thumb and forefinger pulled out an imaginary louse. He examined it, his eyes dilated with horror, placed it delicately on the ground, drew a circle around it with chalk, turned back, with a single hand snatched the bar from the ground, which for the occasion had become as light as a feather, and crushed the louse with one clean blow.

After this rapid parenthesis, he continued taking off shirts, trousers, socks and body-belts with gravity and composure, trying in vain to lift the weight. In the end, he stood in his pants, in the middle of a mountain of clothing; he took off his mask, and the public recognized in him the sympathetic and popular cook Gridacucco, small, dry, hopping and bustling, aptly nick-named 'Scannagrillo' (Cricket Butcher) by Cesare. Applause burst out: Scannagrillo looked around bewildered, then, as if seized by sudden stage-fright, picked up his weight, which was probably made of cardboard, put it under his arm and scampered off.

The other great success was the 'Three-Cornered Hat'. It is a song totally lacking in sense, which consists of a single, continually repeated quatrain ('My hat has got three corners – three corners has my hat – if it did not have three corners – it would not be my hat'), and is sung to a tune so trite and custom-worn that its origin is now unknown. However, its characteristic is that, at every repeat, one of the words of the quatrain is omitted, and replaced by a gesture: a concave hand on the head for 'hat', a fist touching the chest for 'my', fingers drawn together as they rise, to represent the surface of a cone, for 'corners'; and so on, until, with the final elimination, the strophe is reduced to a stunted stuttering of articles and conjunctions which cannot be expressed by signs, or, according to another version, by total silence scanned by rhythmic gestures.

In the heterogeneous group of the 'Rumanians' there must have been someone who had the theatre in his blood; in their interpretation, this infantile whimsicality turned into a sinister, obscurely allegorical pantomime, full of symbolic and disquieting echoes.

A small orchestra, whose instruments had been provided by the Russians, began the tired motif, in low muted tones. Slowly swaying to the rhythm, three nightmare figures came on to the stage; they were wrapped up in black cloaks, with black hoods on their heads, and from the hoods emerged three faces, of corpse-like, decrepit pallor, marked by deep livid lines. They entered with a hesitant dance step, holding three long unlighted candles in their hands. When they reached the centre of the stage, always in time to the rhythm, they bowed towards the public with senile difficulty, slowly bending their stiff joints, with small worrying wrenches; they took two full minutes to bend down and rise again, minutes which were full of anguish for all the spectators. They painfully regained an erect position, the orchestra stopped and the three phantoms began to sing the stupid strophe in a tremulous broken voice. They sang; and at every repeat, with the accumulation of gaps replaced by uncertain gestures, it seemed as if life, as well as voice, would drain from them. With the rhythm accentuated by the hypnotic pulsation of a single muted drum, the paralysis proceeded slowly and ineluctably. The final repetition, with absolute silence from orchestra, singers and public, was an excruciating agony, a death throe.

When the song ended, the orchestra began again lugubriously; the three figures, with a final effort, trembling in every limb, repeated their bow. Unbelievably they once more managed to straighten themselves, and with their candles wavering, with a horrible and macabre hesitation, but always in time to the rhythm, they disappeared for ever behind the scenes.

The 'Three-Cornered Hat' number took away one's breath, and every evening was greeted with a silence more eloquent than applause. Why? Perhaps because, under the grotesque appearance, one perceived the heavy breath of a collective dream, of the dream emanating from exile and idleness, when work and troubles have ceased, and nothing acts as a screen between a man and himself; perhaps because we saw the impotence and nullity of our life and of life itself, and the hunch-backed crooked profiles of the monsters generated by the sleep of reason.

More innocuous, indeed puerile and burlesque, was the allegory of the next programme to be arranged. It was already obvious from the title, *The Shipwreck of the Spiritless*; we were the spiritless, we Italians lost on our way home, grown used to an existence of inertia and boredom; the desert island was Starye Dorogi; and the cannibals were ostentatiously the worthy Russians of the Command. One hundred per cent cannibals; they appeared on the stage naked and tattooed, prattled in some primitive and unintelligible jargon, fed on raw and bloody human meat. Their leader lived in a hut made of branches, he had a white slave permanently on all fours as a seat, and on his chest hung a large alarm clock which he consulted, not to tell the time, but to read the omens for governmental decisions. Comrade Colonel, in charge of our camp, must have been a man of wit, or extremely forbearing, or else just dim, to have authorized so harsh a caricature of his person and office; or perhaps, once more, it was a question of the age-old beneficent Russian insouciance, of that Oblomovian negligence, which was to be found at all levels at that happy moment of their history.

In truth, once at least the suspicion crossed our minds that the Command had not digested the satire, or that it regretted its decision. After the first performance of *The Shipwreck*, all hell broke loose in the Red House in the middle of the night; yells in the dormitories, kicks at the doors, commands in Russian, Italian and bad German. Those of us who had come from Katowice, and had already witnessed a similar upheaval, were only half frightened; the others lost their heads (the 'Rumanians' in particular, who were responsible for the script); rumour of a Russian reprisal immediately went round, and the most apprehensive were already thinking of Siberia.

The Lieutenant acted as intermediary, and on this occasion seemed even more gloomy and sullen than usual; through him, the Russians made us all get up and dress hastily, and line up in one of the winding passages of the building. Half an hour, an hour passed and nothing happened; at the end of the queue, where I was in one of the last places, nobody knew where the head began, nor did the line move forward a step. Beside the possibility of a reprisal for the *Spiritless*, the rashest of hypotheses ran through the line: the Russians had decided to search out the Fascists; they were looking for the two girls in the wood; they were subjecting us to an examination for VD; they were recruiting people to work in the *kolkhoz*; they were looking for specialists, like the Germans. Then we saw an Italian pass by beaming cheerfully. He said: 'They're giving out money!' and shook a wad of rubles in his hand. No one believed him; but a second, then a third one passed and they all confirmed the information. The incident was never clearly understood (but then, who ever fully understood why we were at Starye Dorogi, and what we were doing there?); according to the most sensible interpretation, it seems probable that we had been equated with prisoners of war, at least by some Soviet departments, and so were owed compensation for the days of work we had carried out. But what criterion was used to compute these days (hardly any of us had ever worked for the Russians, either at Starye Dorogi or before); why they also paid the children, and above all, why the ceremony had to occur so tumultuously between two and six in the morning – all this is destined to remain obscure.

The Russians distributed salaries varying from thirty to eighty rubles a head, either following inscrutable criteria, or haphazardly. They were not huge sums, but they pleased everyone; they were equivalent to luxuries for a few days. At dawn we returned to bed, commenting on the event in different ways; no one understood that it was a good omen, a prelude to repatriation.

But from that day, even without an official announcement, the signs multiplied. Tenuous, uncertain, timid signs; but enough to spread the sensation that something was finally moving, something was about to happen. A patrol of young Russian soldiers arrived, baby-faced and lost; they told us that they had come from Austria, and would soon have to leave again to escort a convoy of foreigners; but they did not know where. The Command, after months of useless petitions, distributed shoes to all in need of them. Finally, the Lieutenant disappeared, as if he had been assumed into Heaven.

It was all extremely vague, and not a little ambiguous. Even granting that a departure was imminent, what assurance was there that it was a repatriation, and not another transfer to heaven knows where? The long experience we had by now acquired of Russian methods counselled us to temper our hopes

with a salutary coefficient of doubt. The season also contributed
to our disquiet; in the first weeks of September the sun and sky
clouded over, the air became cold and damp and the first rain
fell to remind us of the precariousness of our situation.

The road, meadows and fields changed into a desolate marsh.
Water leaked through the roofs of the Red House in abundance,
dripping pitilessly on the bunks at night; yet more water entered
through the glassless windows. None of us had heavy clothes.
In the village we saw peasants coming back from the wood with
carts of faggots and branches; others were patching up their
houses, adjusting the thatched roofs; all of them, even the
women, wore boots. The wind carried a new alarming smell
from their homes; the bitter smoke of damp wood burning, the
smell of approaching winter. Another winter, the third one – and
what a winter!

But finally the announcement came: the announcement of our
return, of our salvation, of the conclusion of our lengthy wanderings. It came in two novel unusual ways, from two different
sides, and was convincing and open and dissipated all anxiety.
It came in the theatre and through the theatre, and it came along
the muddy road, carried by a strange and illustrious messenger.

It was night, it was raining, and in the crowded theatre (what
else could one do in the evening, before slipping between the
damp sheets?) there was a repeat performance of *The Shipwreck
of the Spiritless*, perhaps the ninth or tenth. This *Shipwreck*
made a shapeless but savoury dish, enlivened by its sharp and
good-natured allusions to our everyday life; we had all followed
it, every line of it, and by now we knew it by heart, and at every
performance we were less inclined to laugh at the scene in which
a Cantarella even more savage than the original built a huge
metal pot to order for the Russian cannibals, who intended to
cook the leading Dispirited bigwigs in it; and every time the final
scene, when the ship arrived, cut deeper.

Because there was, and clearly had to be, a scene in which a sail appeared on the horizon, and all the castaways ran laughing and crying on to the inhospitable beach. Now, just as the doyen among them, white-haired and by now bowed from the interminable wait, pointed his finger towards the sea and shouted: 'A sail!' and just as all of us, with a lump in our throats, got ready for the traditional happy ending of the final scene, and for our retirement once more to our bunks, we heard a sudden thud, and saw the cannibal chief, a veritable *Deus ex machina*, fall vertically on to the stage, as if from the sky. He tore the alarm clock from his neck, the ring from his nose and the band of feathers from his head, and shouted in a thunderous voice: 'Tomorrow we leave!'

We were taken by surprise, and at first did not understand. Perhaps it was a joke? But the savage pursued: 'I am telling the truth, this is not theatre, this time it's real! The telegram has arrived, tomorrow we are all going home!' This time it was we Italians, spectators, actors and stagehands, who immediately overwhelmed the terrified Russians, who had understood nothing of this scene, which was not in the script. We emerged from the hall in disorder, and at first there was an anxious exchange of questions without answers; but then we saw the Colonel, surrounded by Italians, nodding assent, and we understood that the hour had come. We lit fires in the woods, and no one slept; we spent the rest of the night singing and dancing, recalling past adventures and remembering our lost companions – for it is not given to man to enjoy uncontaminated happiness.

The next morning, while the Red House was already buzzing and humming like a beehive whose swarm is about to leave, we saw a small car approach along the road. Very few passed by, so our curiosity was aroused, especially as it was not a military car. It slowed down in front of the camp, turned and entered, bouncing on the rough surface in front of the bizarre façade. Then we saw that it was a car all of us knew well, a Fiat 500A, a *Topo-lino*, rusty and decrepit, with the suspension piteously deformed.

It stopped in front of the entrance, and was at once surrounded by a crowd of inquisitive people. An extraordinary figure emerged, with great effort. It went on and on emerging; it was a very tall, corpulent, rubicund man, in a uniform we had never seen before: a Soviet General, a Generalissimo, a Marshal. When all of him had finally emerged from the door, the minute bodywork rose a good six inches, and the springs seemed to breathe more freely. The man was literally larger than the car, and it was incomprehensible how he had got inside. His conspicuous dimensions were further increased and accentuated, when he took a black object from the car, and unfolded it. It was a cloak, which hung down to the ground from two long wooden epaulettes; with an easy gesture, which gave evidence of his familiarity with the garment, he swung it over his back and fastened it to his shoulders, with the result that his outline, which had appeared plump, became angular. Seen from behind, the man was a monumental black rectangle one yard by two, who strode with majestic symmetry towards the Red House, amid two rows of perplexed people over whom he towered by a full head. How would he get through the door, as wide as he was? But he bent the two epaulettes backwards, like two wings, and entered.

This celestial messenger, who travelled alone through the mud in a cheap ancient ramshackle car, was Marshal Timoshenko in person, Semyòn Konstantinovich Timoshenko, the hero of the Bolshevik revolution, of Karelia and Stalingrad. After his reception by the local Russians, which was singularly sober and lasted only a few minutes, he emerged once more from the building and chatted unaffectedly with us Italians, like the rough Kutuzov in *War and Peace*, on the meadow, in the middle of the pots with fish on the boil and the washing hung out to dry. He spoke Rumanian fluently with the 'Rumanians' (because he was, in fact is, a native of Bessarabia), and even knew a little Italian. The damp wind ruffled his grey hair, which contrasted with his ruddy suntanned complexion, that of a soldier, an eater and a drinker; he told us that it was really true; we were to leave soon, very soon; 'War over, everybody home'; the escort was ready, the supplies for the journey as well, the papers were in order. Within a few days the train would be waiting for us at Starye Dorogi station.

15

From Starye Dorogi to Iasi

Nobody was really surprised that the departure was not to be expected 'tomorrow' in a literal sense, as the savage had said in the theatre. On various occasions already we had been able to verify that the corresponding Russian term, by one of these semantic lapses which never occur without a reason, had come to mean something far less definite and peremptory than our 'tomorrow' and, in harmony with Russian habits, meant rather 'one of the following days', 'sometime or other', 'in the near future'; in short, the rigorous temporal determinant is softly blurred. We were not surprised, nor were we particularly aggrieved. Once our departure was certain, we became aware, to our own amazement, that this endless land, these fields and woods which had witnessed the battle to which we owed our salvation, these virgin primordial horizons, this vigorous people full of the love of life, had entered our hearts, had penetrated into us and would remain there for a long time, glorious and living images of a unique season of our existence.

So not 'tomorrow', but a few days after the announcement, on 15 September 1945, we left the Red House in a troupe and reached the station of Starye Dorogi in a festive mood. The train was there, it was waiting for us, it was not an illusion of our senses; there was coal and water, and the engine, enormous and majestic like a monument of itself, stood at the right end. We hastened to touch its side: alas, it was cold. There were sixty trucks, goods trucks, somewhat the worse for wear, standing in a siding. We invaded them with jubilant fury, and without quarrels; there were fourteen hundred of us, or twenty to twenty-five persons to a truck, which, in comparison with our many previous railway experiences, meant travelling comfortably and restfully.

The train did not leave at once, in fact, not until the following day; and it was clearly useless interrogating the head of the minute station, for he knew nothing. Only two or three trains passed during this time, and none stopped, none even slowed down. When one of them approached, the stationmaster waited for it on the platform, holding up a garland of branches with a sack hanging from it; the engine-driver leant out of the engine as it rushed by, with his right arm hooked. He seized the garland, and immediately threw a similar one to the ground, also with a sack; this was the postal service, Starye Dorogi's only contact with the rest of the world.

Apart from this, everything was immobile and quiet. Around the station, which was on a slight elevation, the prairies extended interminably, delimited only to the west by the black line of the woods and cut by the giddy ribbon of the railway line. Cattle grazed in herds, few and scattered at wide intervals; this was all there was to break the uniformity of the plain. During the long evening of our vigil, we could hear the songs of the shepherds, tenuous and modulated; one began, a second replied some miles away, then another and yet another, from every side of the horizon, until it seemed as if the very earth were singing.

We prepared for the night. After so many months and displacements, we now formed an organized community; consequently, we had not distributed ourselves casually in the trucks, but according to spontaneous nuclei of cohabitation.

The 'Rumanians' occupied about ten trucks; three belonged to the San Vittore thieves, who did not want anybody and whom nobody wanted; another three were for the single women; four or five were taken by the couples, legitimate or otherwise; two, divided into two floors by a horizontal partition, and conspicuous because of the laundry hanging out to dry, belonged to families with children. The most striking of all was the orchestra-car: the entire theatrical company resided there, with all their instruments (including a piano), kindly donated by the Russians at the moment of departure. On Leonardo's initiative, our truck had been designated the hospital-car; a presumptuous and hopeful title as Leonardo possessed only a syringe and a stethoscope, while the wooden floor was as hard as that of the other trucks; however, there was not even one sick person in the whole train, nor did a single patient present himself during the entire journey. There were about twenty of us, among whom were, naturally, Cesare and Daniele, and, less naturally, the Moor, Mr Unverdorben, Giacomantonio and the Velletrano; besides these, there were about fifteen ex-POWs.

We spent the night drowsing restlessly on the bare floor of the truck. Day came; the engine was smoking, the driver was at his post, waiting with Olympian calm for the boiler to build up pressure. In the middle of the morning the engine roared, with a marvellous, deep metallic voice; it shook, vomited black smoke, the stay rods tightened and the wheels began to turn. We looked at each other, almost bewildered. We had resisted, after all; we had won. After the year of Lager, of anguish and patience, after the wave of death that followed the liberation, after the cold and hunger, the contempt and the haughty company of the Greek, after the illness and misery of Katowice, after the senseless journeys which had made us feel condemned to orbit for eternity in Russian space, like useless spent stars, after the idleness and bitter nostalgia of Starye Dorogi, we were rising once more, travelling upwards, on the journey home. Time, after two years of paralysis, had regained vigour and value, was once more working for us, and this put an end to the torpor of the long summer, to the threat of the approaching winter, and made us impatient, hungry for the days and miles ahead.

But soon, from the very first hours of the journey, we were to realize that the hour of impatience had not yet sounded; the happy journey promised to be long and laborious and not without surprises; a small railroad Odyssey within our greater Odyssey. Patience was still needed, in unforeseeable doses; yet more patience.

Our train was over five hundred yards long; the trucks were in a poor condition, the track also, the velocity derisory, not more than twenty to thirty miles an hour. The railway line was single tracked; the stations with a siding sufficiently long to permit halts were few: the train often had to be uncoupled into two or three parts and pushed on to side lines with complicated and sluggish manoeuvres, so as to allow other trains to pass through.

There were no authorities on board, except for the engine-driver and the escort, which consisted of the seven eighteen-year-old soldiers who had come from Austria to pick us up. Although they were armed to the teeth, they were plain, well-mannered creatures, gentle and naïve, as cheerful and happy-go-lucky as schoolboys on holiday, and totally lacking in authority and practical sense. Every time the train stopped, we saw them walking up and down the platform, with their weapons slung from their shoulders and a proud officious air. They paraded their importance as though they were escorting a convoy of dangerous criminals, but it was all on the surface; we soon realized that their inspection concentrated increasingly on the two family trucks, half-way down the train. They were not attracted by the young wives, but by the vaguely domestic atmosphere which emanated from those itinerant gypsy-like dwellings, and which reminded them perhaps of their distant homes and their recent childhood; but above all they were allured by the children, so much so that, after the first halt, they chose the family trucks as their daily domicile, and returned to the truck reserved for them only at night. They were courteous and obliging; they willingly helped the mothers, went to get water and chop wood for the stoves. They struck up a curious and one-sided friendship with the Italian children. They learnt various games from them, including that of the circuit: this is a game played with marbles rolled along a complicated path. In Italy it is supposed to be related to the *Giro**; so the enthusiasm with which these young Russians assimilated it seemed strange to us, as there are few bicycles in Russia, and cycle races do not exist. At all events, for them it was a discovery: it was not unusual to see the seven Russians leave their sleeping-truck at the first stop in the morning, run to the family trucks, open the door authoritatively and pick up the still sleepy children and put them on the ground. Then they cheerfully dug out the circuit in the ground with their bayonets, and plunged into the game in great haste, on all fours with their weapons on their backs, anxious not to lose even a moment before the engine whistled.

On the evening of the 16th we reached Bobruisk, on the evening of the 17th Ovruch; and we realized that we were repeating the course of our last journey north, which had taken us from Zhmerinka to Slutsk and to Starye Dorogi, but in the opposite direction. We spent the interminable days partly sleeping, partly chatting or watching the majestic deserted steppe unfolding before our eyes. From the first days, our optimism lost a little of its shine; this journey of ours, which all appearances

* Annual cycle race around the country.

led us to hope would be the last, had been organized by the Russians in the vaguest and most careless of ways; or rather, it seemed as if it had not been organized at all, but decided by heaven knows whom, heaven knows where, with a simple stroke of the pen. In the whole train there were only two or three maps, disputed endlessly, on which we traced our problematic progress with difficulty; it was quite clear that we were travelling south, but with an exasperating slowness and irregularity, with incomprehensible deviations and stops, sometimes travelling only a few dozen miles in twenty-four hours. We often went to interrogate the engine-driver (there was no point in talking to the escort; they seemed happy merely to be travelling in a train, and it was of no importance to them to know where they were or where they were going); but the engine-driver, who emerged like a god of the underworld from his fiery cabin, spread out his arms, shrugged his shoulders, swept his hand in a semicircle from east to west and replied every time: 'Where are we going tomorrow? I don't know, dear friends, I don't know. We are going where we find railway tracks.'

The person who endured the uncertainty and enforced idleness worst of all of us was Cesare. He sat in a corner of the truck, hypochondriacal and bristling, like a sick animal, and did not judge the countryside outside, or us inside the truck, worthy of a single glance. But his was a specious inertia; people in need of activity find opportunities everywhere. As we ran through a district covered with small villages, between Ovruch and Zhitomir, his attention was attracted by a brass ring worn by Giacomantonio, his shifty ex-partner from the Katowice market.

'Will you sell it to me?' he asked him.

'No,' Giacomantonio replied laconically, just as a start.

'I'll give you two rubles.'

'I want eight.'

The bargaining continued for a long time; it seemed clear that both found it a diversion, an agreeable mental exercise, and that the ring was only a pretext, an excuse for a sort of friendly game, a practice bargain so as not to lose their skill. But it was not so; Cesare, as always, had conceived an exact plan.

To everybody's amazement, he yielded quickly, and acquired the ring, which he seemed to prize enormously, for four rubles, a figure grossly disproportionate to the value of the object. Then he withdrew into his corner, and dedicated the rest of the afternoon to mysterious exercises, driving away with angry snarls all inquisitive people who asked him questions (the most insistent was Giacomantonio). He had taken pieces of different quality cloth from his pockets, and diligently polished the ring, inside and out, breathing on it every now and again. Then he took out a packet of cigarette paper, and carefully continued his work with it, with extreme delicacy, no longer touching the metal with his fingers; occasionally, he would lift the ring up to the light of the window, and study it, turning it round slowly as if it were a diamond.

Finally, what Cesare had been waiting for occurred; the train slowed down and stopped at a village station, not too large and not too small; the halt looked like being a short one, as the train remained on the main line in one section. Cesare got down, and began to walk up and down the platform. He held the ring half hidden against his chest, under his jacket. He approached the Russian peasants who were waiting, one by one, with a conspiratorial air, half showed it to them, and whispered nervously: '*Tovarishch, zèloto, zèloto!*' ('gold').

At first the Russians did not listen to him. Then an old man looked closely at the ring, and asked the price; Cesare, without hesitating, said: '*Sto*' ('one hundred'); a modest enough price for a gold ring, a criminal one for a brass ring. The old man offered forty. Cesare pretended to be indignant and turned to somebody else. He continued like this with various clients, protracting matters and looking for the person who offered most; mean-

time, he kept an ear open for the engine whistle, in order to conclude the business and jump on to the train as it was leaving.

While Cesare was showing the ring to various people, we
could see others discussing in small groups, suspicious and
excited. At that moment the engine whistled; Cesare yielded the
ring to the last bidder, pocketed about fifty rubles and rapidly
climbed on to the train, which was already moving. The train
ran for one, two, ten yards; then it slowed down again, and
stopped with a great screeching of brakes.

Cesare had closed the running doors and was peering out of
the gap, at first triumphant, then worried, finally terrified. The
man with the ring was showing his acquisition to the other peasants; these passed it from hand to hand, turned it over on all
sides and shook their heads with an air of doubt and disap-
proval. Then we saw the incautious purchaser, evidently
repentant, raise his head and march resolutely along the train,
in search of Cesare's refuge; an easy search, as ours was the only
truck with its doors closed.

The matter was taking a decidedly bad turn; the Russian,
who was clearly no genius, perhaps would not have managed to
identify the truck by himself, but two or three of his colleagues
were already pointing with energy in the right direction. Cesare
suddenly jumped back from his spy hole, and had recourse to an
extreme measure; he crouched in a corner of the truck, and
made us conceal him hastily under all the available coverings. In
a short time he disappeared under an enormous mass of blankets, eiderdowns, sacks and jackets; from which, listening
carefully, I seemed to hear, muted and faint, and blasphemous
in that context, words of prayer emerge.

We could already hear the Russians shouting in front of the
truck, and banging against the doors, when the train moved off
again with a violent jerk. Cesare re-emerged, as white as death,
but recovered immediately: 'Now let them look for me!'

The following morning, under a radiant sun, the train stopped at Kazàtin. The name did not seem new to me; where had I read or heard it? Perhaps in war bulletins? But I had the impression of a nearer, more immediate recollection, as if someone had spoken to me about it at length recently; after, and not before, the Auschwitz caesura, which snapped in two the chain of my memories.

Suddenly, standing on the platform, immediately in front of our truck, I saw my nebulous recollection personified: Galina, the girl from Katowice, the translator-dancer-typist of the Kommandantur, Galina of Kazàtin. I got down to greet her, full of joy and amazement at so improbable a meeting: to find my only Russian friend in this boundless land!

She had not changed very much; she was a little better dressed, and sheltered from the sun under a pretentious parasol. Nor had I changed much, at least externally; a little less puny and under-nourished than before, though just as ragged; but rich with a new wealth, the train standing behind me, the slow but sure engine, Italy nearer every day. She wished me a happy return; we exchanged a few hurried and embarrassed words, in a language which was neither hers nor mine, in the cold language of the invader, and we separated immediately, as the train was leaving. In the truck, which was jolting towards the frontier, I sat and smelt the cheap perfume which her hand had left on mine, happy that I had seen her again, sad at the memory of the hours spent in her company, of things unsaid, of opportunities unseized.

We passed through Zhmerinka once more, with suspicion, remembering the days of anguish we had spent there a few months before; but the train proceeded without difficulties, and on the evening of 19 September, after crossing Bessarabia rapidly, we were on the Pruth, at the border. In the deep gloom, as a sort of dismal farewell, the Soviet frontier police carried out a tumultuous and disorderly inspection of the train, searching (so they told us) for rubles, which it was forbidden to export; not that it mattered, as we had spent them all. We crossed the bridge, and slept on the other side, in the stationary train, anxious for the light of day to reveal Rumanian soil to us.

It was in fact a dramatic sight. When we threw open the doors in the early morning, a surprisingly domestic scene opened out before our eyes; no longer a deserted, geological steppe, but the green hills of Moldavia, with farms, haystacks and rows of vines; no longer enigmatic Cyrillic signs, but, right in front of our truck, a decrepit hovel, blue-green with verdigris, with clear writing on it, curiously similar to the Italian words: '*Paine, Lapte, Vin, Carnaciuri de Purcel*', bread, milk, wine, pork sausages. And in fact, in front of the hovel there was a woman, who was pulling an enormously long sausage out of a basket at her feet, and measuring it by lengths like string.

We saw peasants like our own, with broiled faces and pale foreheads, dressed in black, with jackets and waistcoats and watch-chains over their bellies; girls on foot or on bicycles, dressed almost like ours, whom we could have mistaken for Venetian or Abruzzese peasant girls. There were goats, sheep, cows, pigs, chickens. But, standing at a railway crossing, to act as a check to any precocious illusion of home, was a camel, driving us back into another world; a worn-out, grey, woolly camel, laden with sacks, exhaling haughtiness and stupid solemnity from his prehistoric leporine muzzle. The language of the place sounded equally mixed to our ears; well-known roots and terminations, but entangled and contaminated in a millenary common growth, could be heard alongside others, of a strange wild sound; a speech familiar in its music, hermetic in its sense.

At the frontier took place the complicated and difficult ceremony of transference from the ramshackle trucks of Soviet-gauge lines to others, equally ramshackle, with a western gauge;

and soon after we entered the station of Iasi, where the train was laboriously broken up into three parts; a sign that the halt would last for many hours.

At Iasi two notable things occurred; the two German women from the woods appeared from nowhere, and all the married 'Rumanians' disappeared. The smuggling of the two Germans across the Soviet border must have been organized with great audacity and ability by a group of Italian soldiers; we never learnt the exact details, but rumour had it that the two girls had spent the critical night of the passage across the frontier hidden under the floor of the truck, secreted between the rods and the suspension. We saw them walking on the platform the next morning, offhand and arrogant, bundled up in Soviet military clothes and covered in mud and grease. Now they felt safe.

Simultaneously, we saw violent family conflicts explode in the trucks of the 'Rumanians'. Many of them, who had formerly belonged to the diplomatic corps or had been demobilized themselves from the ARMIR, had settled in Rumania and had married Rumanian women. At the end of the war, almost all of them had opted for repatriation, and the Russians had organized a train for them which should have taken them to Odessa, to embark there; but at Zhmerinka they had been attached to our luckless train, and had followed our fate; we never knew if this had happened through design or negligence. The Rumanian wives were furious with their Italian husbands; they had had enough of surprises and adventures and journeys and encampments. Now they had re-entered Rumanian territory, they were at home, they wanted to stay there and they would not listen to reason; some argued and wept, others tried to drag their husbands on to the platform, the wildest hurled their luggage and household possessions out of the trucks, while their children, terrified, ran screaming all around. The Russians of the escort had run to the scene, but they understood nothing and stood and looked on, inert and undecided.

As the halt at Iasi threatened to last all day, we left the station and wandered through the deserted streets, between low mud-coloured houses. A single, minute, archaic tram ran from one end of the city to the other; the ticket collector stood at a terminal; he spoke Yiddish, he was a Jew. With some effort we managed to understand each other. He informed me that other trainloads of ex-prisoners had passed through Iasi, of all races, French, English, Greek, Italian, Dutch, American. In many of these there had been Jews in need of assistance; so the local Jewish community had formed a relief centre. If we had one or two hours to spare, he counselled us to go as a delegation to the centre; we should be given advice and help. In fact, as his tram was about to leave, he told us to climb on, he would put us down at the right stop and would take care of the tickets.

Leonardo, Mr Unverdorben and I went; we crossed the dead city and reached a squalid, crumbling building, with temporary boarding in place of the doors and windows. Two old patriarchs, with a scarcely more opulent or flourishing air than ours, received us in a gloomy, dusty office; but they were full of affectionate kindness and good intentions, they made us sit on the only three chairs, overwhelmed us with attention and precipitately recounted to us, in Yiddish and French, the terrible trials which they and a few others had survived. They were prone to tears and laughter; at the moment of departure, they invited us peremptorily to drink a toast with terrible rectified alcohol, and gave us a basket of grapes to distribute among the Jews on the train. They also emptied all the drawers and their own pockets, and raked together a sum of *lei* which on the spot seemed to us astronomical; but, later, after we had divided it, and taken into account the inflation, we realized that its value was principally symbolic.

16

From Iasi to the Line

For several days we continued to travel towards the south, by small stages, across a countryside still enjoying summer, past towns and villages with barbaric, resounding names (Ciurea, Scantea, Vaslui, Piscu, Bràila, Pogoanele); on the night of 23 September we saw the fires of the petroleum wells of Ploesti blazing; then our mysterious pilot turned west, and the following day we realized from the position of the sun that our course had been inverted; we were once more navigating towards the north. Without recognizing them, we admired the castles of Sinaia, a royal residence.

By now our truckload had exhausted all its ready money, and had sold or exchanged everything, however small, which was thought to possess commercial value. Consequently, apart from occasional strokes of luck or lawless exploits, our only source of food was what the Russians gave us; the situation was not dramatic, but confused and enervating.

It never became clear who was responsible for the victualling; most probably the Russians of the escort, who drew at random the most ill-assorted, or perhaps the only available, rations from every military or civilian depot within reach. Whenever the train stopped and was uncoupled, each truck sent two delegates to the Russians' truck, which was slowly transformed into a chaotic travelling bazaar; the Russians, with no regard for rules, distributed to these delegates provisions for their respective trucks. It was a daily game of chance; as regards quantity, the rations were sometimes scarce, sometimes Gargantuan, sometimes non-existent; and as regards quality, as unforeseeable as all things Russian. We received carrots, and yet more carrots, and yet still more carrots, for days on end; then the carrots disappeared, and the beans arrived. They were dry beans, as hard as pebbles; to cook them, we had to soak them for hours in whatever vessel we could lay our hands on, bowls, tins, pots, which we then hung from the roof of the truck; at night, when the train braked abruptly, this hanging forest oscillated violently, water and beans poured down on the sleepers, and scuffles, mirth and upheavals resulted in the dark. Potatoes came, then *kasha*, then gherkins, but without oil; then oil, half a bowl a person, when the gherkins were finished; then sunflower seeds, an exercise in patience. One day we received bread and sausage in abundance, and everybody breathed again; then grain for a week on end, as if we were chickens.

Only the family-trucks had stoves on board; the rest of us managed to cook on the ground on camp fires which we lit in haste as soon as the train stopped, and put out half-way through the cooking, amid quarrels and oaths, when the train set off again. We cooked intensely, furiously, listening for the whistle of the engine, with one eye on the starving vagrants, who emerged at once in crowds from the countryside, attracted by the smoke, like bloodhounds by a scent. We cooked like our forefathers, on three stones; and as stones could not always be found, every truck ended by possessing its own. Spits and ingenious devices appeared; Cantarella's pots re-emerged.

The problem of wood and water became urgent and compelling. Necessity simplifies: private woodpiles were raided in a flash; snow barriers, which in those countries were piled up alongside the rail tracks in the summer months, were stolen;

fences, railway sleepers, once (for want of anything better) an entire goods truck abandoned after an accident, were demolished; in our truck the presence of the Moor and his famous axe was providential. As for water, in the first place we needed suitable vessels, which meant that every truck had to procure a bucket, by barter, theft or purchase. Our bucket, legitimately bought, revealed a leak at the first experiment; we repaired it with a piece of plaster from the surgery, and it miraculously withstood the cooking as far as the Brenner, when it peeled off.

Normally it was impossible to collect a supply of water at the stations; an endless queue formed in front of the fountain (when there was one) in a few seconds, and only a few buckets could be filled. Some people crept stealthily to the tender which held the water for the engine; but if the driver saw them, he would fly into a rage, and bombard these rash persons with oaths and burning coal. Nevertheless, we sometimes managed to tap hot water from the belly of the engine itself; it was slimy, rusty water, unsuitable for cooking but quite useful for washing.

The best sources were country wells. The train often stopped in the fields, at a red signal; it was impossible to foresee whether the halt would last a few seconds or hours. So we all hastily unbuckled our trouser belts to knot together and form a long rope; then the nimblest person in the truck rushed off, with the rope and bucket, in search of a well. I was the nimblest person in my truck, and I often succeeded in the enterprise; but once I ran a serious risk of losing the train. I had already dropped the bucket into the well and was lifting it laboriously, when I heard the engine whistle. If I lost the bucket and belts, our precious common property, I should dishonour myself for ever; so I pulled up the bucket with all my strength, got hold of it, poured the water on the ground and ran off, hampered by the knotted belts, towards the train, which was already moving. A second's delay could mean a month's delay; I ran without stopping, for my life, jumped over two hedges and the fence and rushed over the slippery gravel of the rail-bed as the train slid past me. My truck had already gone by; charitable hands from other trucks stretched out towards me, gripped the belts and the bucket, while yet more hands grabbed my hair, shoulders, clothing, and hoisted me on to the floor of the last truck, where I lay semi-conscious for a long time.

The train continued to move north; it entered an increasingly narrow valley, crossed the Transylvanian Alps through the Predal Pass on 24 September, amid austere naked mountains, in bitter cold, and descended on Brasov. Here the engine was detached, guarantee of a long halt and the customary ceremonial began to take place; people with a furtive ferocious air, with hatchets in their hands, wandered round the station and outside; others with buckets quarrelled over the little water; others still stole hay from the haystacks, or transacted business with the local inhabitants; children wandered around in search of trouble or small opportunities to steal; women washed clothing or themselves in public, exchanged visits and passed on news from truck to truck, rekindled ill-digested quarrels and sparked off new ones. The fires were immediately lit, and we began to cook.

Next to our train stood a Soviet military convoy, full of lorries, armoured cars and fuel tankers. It was guarded by two robust female soldiers, in boots and helmets, with guns on their shoulders and fixed bayonets; they were of indefinable age and of gnarled, unprepossessing appearance. When they saw fires being lit just in front of the petrol tankers, they grew rightly indignant at our irresponsibility and, shouting 'nelzya nelzya', ordered them to be put out immediately.

Everybody obeyed, cursing; everybody, except a handful from the Alpine Brigade, hardboiled types, veterans of the Russian campaign, who had rustled up a goose and were roasting it.

They held council with sober words, while the two women ful-
minated at their backs; then two of them, nominated by the
majority, got up, with the severe and resolute faces of men about
to sacrifice themselves conscientiously for the common good.
They advanced on the women soldiers face to face and spoke to
them in a low voice. The negotiations were surprisingly short;
the women put down their helmets and arms, then the four, serious and composed, left the station, took a narrow path and
disappeared from our view. They returned a quarter of an hour
later, the women in front, a little less gnarled and with slightly
congested faces, the men behind, dignified and calm. The goose
was nearly ready; the four squatted on the ground with the
others, the goose was carved up and divided in pieces, then,
after the brief truce, the Russian women resumed their weapons
and their duties.

From Brasov our route once more turned to the west,
towards the Hungarian frontier. Rain began to fall steadily and
worsened the situation; it was difficult to light the fires, we were
wearing our only set of clothing, mud soaked in everywhere.
The roof of our truck was not watertight; only a few square
yards of the floor remained inhabitable, as water dripped down
pitilessly on the rest. Quarrels and disputes broke out endlessly
when it was time to go to bed.

It is an age-old observation that in every human group there
is a predestined victim; one who inspires contempt, whom all
mock, about whom stupid malignant gossip grows, on whom,
by some mysterious agreement, all unload their bad tempers and
their desire to hurt. The victim of our truck was the Carabiniere.
It would be difficult to establish the reason why, if a reason
existed; the Carabiniere was a young Abruzzese, polite, mild,
helpful, with a pleasant appearance. He was not even particularly obtuse, in fact he was rather touchy and sensitive, and
consequently suffered acutely from the persecution to which he

was subjected by the other soldiers in the truck. But there it was, he was a Carabiniere; and it is well known that there is little love lost between the Force (so called by antonomasia) and the other armed forces. Carabinieri are reproved, perversely, for their excessive discipline, seriousness, chastity, honesty, their lack of humour, their indiscriminate obedience, their habits, their uniform. Fantastic, grotesque, inept legends circulate about them, and are handed down in barracks from generation to generation: the legend of the hammer, the legend of the oath. I shall say nothing of the first, which is too infamous; as regards the latter, the version I heard was that the young recruit to the Force is obliged to swear a secret, loathsome, infernal oath, in which, among other things, he solemnly pledges 'to kill his father and mother'; and that every Carabiniere either has killed them or will kill them, otherwise he will fail to win promotion. Our poor little wretch could not even open his mouth: 'You keep quiet, you who've killed father and mother.' But he never rebelled; he accepted this and a hundred other insults with the adamantine patience of a saint. One day he took me aside, as a neutral observer, and assured me 'that the business of the oath was not true'.

For three days, virtually without stopping, we travelled in the rain, which made us bad-tempered and mean, only halting once for a few hours at a village full of mud, with the glorious name of Alba Julia. On the evening of 26 September, after travelling more than five hundred miles on Rumanian soil, we reached the Hungarian frontier, near Arad, at a village called Curtici.

I am convinced that the inhabitants of Curtici still remember the scourge of our passage; in all probability it has now become one of the local legends, and will be talked of round the fire for generations, as elsewhere they will still speak of Attila and Tamburlane. This detail of our journey is also destined to remain obscure; according to all the evidence, the Rumanian military or railway authorities no longer wanted us or had already 'off-loaded' us, while the Hungarian authorities did not want to accept us, or had not 'taken over the consignment'; as a result, we remained riveted to Curtici, we and the train and the escort, for seven exhausting days, and we devastated the place.

Curtici was an agricultural village with perhaps a thousand inhabitants, and possessed very little; we were fourteen hundred, and had need of everything. In the seven days we emptied all the wells, exhausted the supplies of wood and caused grave damage to everything in the station that could be burnt; as for the station latrines, it is better not to speak of them. We provoked a fearful increase in the price of milk, bread, maize, poultry; after which, once our purchasing power had been reduced to zero, thefts occurred by night, and later also by day. Geese, which as far as we could see constituted the main local wealth, and initially circulated freely along the muddy paths in solemn well-ordered flotillas, disappeared completely, partly captured, partly shut up in their coops.

Every morning we opened our doors with the absurd hope that the train might have moved without our realizing, while we were asleep; but nothing had changed, the sky was always black and rainy, the muddy houses always facing us, the train as inert and impotent as a stranded ship. We bent down to examine the wheels, those wheels which were supposed to take us home; but no, they had not moved an inch, they seemed soldered to the tracks, and the rain was turning them rusty. We were cold and hungry, and we felt abandoned and forgotten.

On the sixth day, enervated and envenomed more than the rest of us, Cesare abandoned us. He declared that he had had enough of Curtici, of the Russians, of the train and of us; that he did not want to go mad, or to die of hunger, or be cut to pieces by the locals; that when a man was on his toes he got along better by himself. He added that, if we wanted, we could always follow him; but his terms were clear: he was fed up with living in want, he was ready to take risks, but he wanted to cut it short, make money rapidly, and return to Rome by plane. None of us felt up to following him, and Cesare left; he took a train for Bucharest, had many adventures, and succeeded in his intention, that is, he returned to Rome by air, although later than us; but that is another story, a story '*de haulte graisse*', which I shall not recount, or shall recount elsewhere, only if and when Cesare gives me permission.

If in Rumania I had enjoyed a delicate philological pleasure at such names as Galati, Alba Julia, Turnu Severin, immediately we entered Hungary I was confronted with Békéscsaba, followed by Hódmezövasárhely and Kiskunfélegyháza. The Hungarian plain had turned into a marsh, the sky was a leaden colour, but we were saddened above all by Cesare's absence. He had left a painful emptiness among us; in his absence, nobody knew what to speak of, nobody managed any longer to conquer the boredom of the interminable journey, the fatigue of the nineteen days of rail-travel which weighed upon us. We looked at each other with a vague sense of guilt; why had we allowed him to leave? But in Hungary, despite the impossible names, we now felt ourselves in Europe, protected by a civilization which was ours, sheltered from alarming apparitions such as that of the camel in Moldavia. The train moved towards Budapest, but did not enter it; on 6 October it stopped more than once at Ujpest and other suburban stations, leaving us with ghostly visions of ruins, temporary huts and deserted roads; then it moved into the plain once more, in gusts of rain and a film of autumn mist.

It stopped at Szób on market day; we all got down to stretch our legs and spend the little money we possessed. I no longer had anything; but I was hungry, and bartered my Auschwitz jacket, which I had jealously preserved until then, for a noble mixture of fermented cheese and onions, whose acute aroma had conquered me. When the engine whistled, and we climbed into the truck, we counted ourselves and found that we were two more than before.

One was Vincenzo, and no one was surprised. Vincenzo was a difficult boy; a Calabrian shepherd of sixteen, who had somehow ended up in Germany. He was as wild as the Velletrano, but of different temperament: as timid, reserved and contemplative as the latter was violent and bloodthirsty. He had wonderful blue eyes, almost feminine, and a fine, expressive, dreamy face; he hardly ever spoke. He was a nomad at heart, restless, attracted by the woods at Starye Dorogi as if by invisible demons; on the train, too, he had no stable residence in any one truck, but wandered through all of them. We understood the reason for his instability immediately; no sooner had the train left Szób than Vincenzo collapsed to the ground with the whites of his eyes showing and his jaws clenched like a vice. He roared like a beast, and fought, stronger than the four soldiers who held him down: an epileptic fit. He had certainly had others, at Starye Dorogi and before; but every time he had felt the warning signs, urged on by his fierce pride, he had taken refuge in the forest, so that no one should know of his illness; or, perhaps, he fled in the face of the illness, like birds before a storm. During the long journey, as he could not stay on the ground, he changed truck when he felt the attack approaching. He stayed with us only a few days, then disappeared; we found him roosting on the roof of another truck. Why? He replied that he could see the countryside better up there.

The other new guest, for different reasons, also presented a difficult case. Nobody knew him; he was a robust youth, barefoot, dressed in a Red Army jacket and trousers. He spoke only Hungarian and none of us were able to understand him. The

Carabiniere told us that the boy had approached him while he was eating some bread at the village, and had stretched out his hand; he had given him half his food, and from then on had not managed to shake him off; the boy must have followed him without anyone noticing, while we were all climbing hurriedly into the truck.

He was well received; one mouth more to feed was not a worry. He was an intelligent, cheerful boy; as soon as the train started, he introduced himself with great dignity. His name was Pista and he was fourteen. Father and mother? Here it was more difficult to understand each other; I found a pencil stub and a piece of paper, and drew a man, a woman and a child between them; I pointed to the child and said 'Pista'; then I waited. Pista turned grave, and then sketched a drawing which was all too painfully obvious: a house, an aeroplane, a falling bomb. Then he cancelled the house, and drew a large smoking heap beside it. But he was not in a mood for sad things; he screwed up the sheet, asked for another and drew a cask, with remarkable precision: the bottom and all the visible staves in the right perspective; then the hoops, and the hole with the tap. We looked at each other puzzled; what did the message mean? Pista laughed happily; then he drew himself next to it, with a hammer in one hand and a saw in the other. Hadn't we understood yet? This was his trade, he was a cooper.

Everybody liked him immediately; moreover, he tried to be useful; he swept the floor every morning, enthusiastically washed the bowls, went to fetch water and was happy when we sent him 'shopping' to his compatriots at the various halts. He could already make himself understood in Italian by the time we reached the Brenner; he sang beautiful songs of his country, which no one understood, and then sought to explain them with gestures, making us all laugh wholeheartedly, himself first of all. He was as fond of the *Carabiniere* as a younger brother, and slowly cleansed him of his original sin: true, the *Carabiniere* had killed his father and mother, but, all told, he must be a good boy, since Pista followed him. He filled up the gap left by Cesare. We asked him why he had come with us, what brought him to Italy; but we were unable to understand, partly because of the difficulty of conversing, but above all because he himself did not know. He had wandered round stations like a stray dog for months; he had followed the first human creature who had looked at him with pity.

We had hoped to cross from Hungary into Austria without further frontier complications, but it was not so easy; on the morning of 7 October, the twenty-second day of our journey, we reached Bratislava in Slovakia, in sight of the Beskidy, the same mountains which had closed the lugubrious horizon of Auschwitz. Another language, another coinage, another route; would we now complete the circle? Katowice was 120 miles away; would we begin another vain, exhausting circuit of Europe? But we entered German territory in the evening; on the 8th we were stranded at the goods depot of Leopoldau, a suburban station of Vienna, and we felt almost at home.

The suburbs of Vienna were ugly and casual like those we knew at Milan and Turin and, like the last visions we recalled of those cities, were reduced to rubble by bombardment. Passers-by were few: women, children, old people, not a single man. Paradoxically, their language also sounded familiar to me; some even understood Italian. We changed what money we possessed at random for local money, but it was useless; as at Cracow in March, all the shops were closed, or sold only rationed goods. 'But what can one buy at Vienna without a ration card?' I asked a little girl no more than twelve years old. She was dressed in rags, but wore shoes with high heels and was heavily made up: '*Uberhaupt nichts*,' she replied contemptuously.

We returned to the train to sleep; during the night we

travelled a few miles, with much jolting and screeching, and found ourselves transferred to another station, Vienna-Jedlersdorf. Next to us another train emerged from the fog, or rather the corpse of a train: the engine was standing on end, absurdly, its muzzle pointing to the sky as if it meant to climb there; all the trucks were charred. We approached, driven by an instinct for plunder and by a curiosity tinged with mockery; we promised ourselves a malignant satisfaction in laying hands on the ruins of these German objects. But derision was answered by derision: one truck contained odd scraps of metal which must have belonged to musical instruments that had been burnt, and hundreds of earthenware ocarinas, the only things to survive; another truck was full of regulation pistols, melted and rusted; the third held a tangle of curved sabres, which the fire and rain had soldered into their scabbards for all eternity: vanity of vanities, and the cold taste of perdition.

We walked away, and wandered round until we found ourselves on the banks of the Danube. The river was in flood, turbid, yellow and threateningly swollen; at that point its course is almost straight, and we could see, one behind the other, in a misty nightmare perspective, seven bridges, all smashed exactly at the centre, all with their broken segments plunging into the eddying water. As we returned to our itinerant dwelling, we were startled by the clanging noise of a tram, the sole sign of life. It was running crazily on the loose rails, along the deserted avenues, without halting at the stops. We saw the driver at his post, as pale as a ghost; behind him, delirious with enthusiasm, stood the seven Russians of our escort, and not another passenger: it was the first tram they had ever travelled in. Some hung out of the windows and cheered, while others incited and threatened the driver into increasing his speed.

There was a market on a big square; once again a spontaneous and illegal market, but far more wretched and furtive than the Polish ones I had frequented with the Greek and Cesare; in fact, it reminded me strongly of another scene, the Exchange at the Lager, indelible in our memories. There were no stalls, but people on their feet, shivering and restless, in little cliques, ready to run away, with their bags and suitcases in their hands and their pockets swollen; they exchanged minute trifles, potatoes, slices of bread, loose cigarettes, small items of worn-out rubbish from their homes.

We climbed into our trucks with heavy hearts. We had felt no joy in seeing Vienna undone and the Germans broken, but rather anguish: not compassion, but a larger anguish, which was mixed up with our own misery, with the heavy, threatening sensation of an irreparable and definitive evil which was present everywhere, nestling like gangrene in the guts of Europe and the world, the seed of future harm.

The train seemed unable to tear itself away from Vienna; after three days of halts and manoeuvres, on 10 October, hungry, drenched and wretched, we found ourselves at Nussdorf, another suburb. But on the morning of the 11th, as if it had suddenly picked up a lost scent, the train moved decisively towards the west; with unaccustomed speed it passed through St Polten, Loosdorf and Amstetten, and in the evening a sign appeared on the road which ran parallel to the railway, as portentous to our eyes as the birds which tell navigators of land nearby. It was a vehicle unknown to us: a squat, graceless, military vehicle, as flat as a tin can with a white, and not a red, star painted on its side: in short, a jeep. A Negro was driving it; one of the occupants waved his arms at us, and shouted in Neapolitan dialect: 'You're going home, you bums!'

Clearly the demarcation line was nearby; we reached it at St Valentin, a few miles from Linz. Here we had to get down; we said good-bye to the young barbarians of the escort and to our excellent engine-driver, and passed into American hands.

Almost by definition, it can be said of transit camps that the shorter the average stay, the worse the organization. At St Valentin one stopped only for a few hours, a day at the most, and consequently it was an extremely dirty and primitive camp. There was no lighting, no heating, no beds: we slept on the bare wooden floor, in frightfully decrepit huts, in the middle of ankle-deep mud. The only efficient equipment was in the baths and the disinfection room; the West took possession of us by this form of purification and exorcism.

A few gigantic, taciturn GIs, unarmed, but embellished with a myriad of gadgets whose significance and use escaped us, were responsible for this ritual task. Everything went well with the bath; there were about twenty wooden cabins, with luke-warm showers and bath wraps, a luxury never seen again. After the bath, they took us to a vast brick room, divided in two by a cable on which ten curious implements were hanging, vaguely similar to pneumatic drills; we could hear an air compressor pulsating outside. All fourteen hundred, that is all of us, were crammed to one side of the division, men and women together; and at this point ten officials appeared on the scene, with a science-fiction attire, wrapped up in white overalls, with helmets and gas masks. They seized the first of the flock, and without wasting time stuck the tubes of the hanging instruments into all the openings of their clothes in turn: under collars and belts, into pockets, up trouser legs, under skirts. They were a sort of pneumatic blower, which blew out insecticide: the insecticide was DDT, an absolute novelty to us, like the jeeps, penicillin and the atomic bomb, which we learnt about soon afterwards.

Everybody accommodated himself to the treatment, swearing or laughing from the tickling, until it came to the turn of a naval officer and his beautiful fiancée. When the hooded men laid chaste but rough hands on her, the officer placed himself decisively in between. He was a robust and resolute young man: woe betide anyone who touched his woman.

The perfect mechanism stopped abruptly; the hoods consulted briefly, with inarticulate nasal sounds, then one of them took off his mask and overalls and planted himself in front of the officer with his fists at the ready for a fight. The others formed an orderly circle, and a regular boxing match began. After a few minutes of silent and gentlemanly combat, the officer fell to the ground with a bleeding nose; the girl, shaken and pale, was dusted all over according to the regulations, but without anger or vengefulness, and everything re-established itself in American order.

17

The Awakening

Austria borders on Italy, and St Valentin is only 180 miles from Tarvisio; but on 15 October, the thirty-first day of our journey, we crossed a new frontier and entered Munich, prey to a disconsolate railway tiredness, a permanent loathing for trains, for snatches of sleep on wooden floors, for jolting and for stations; so that familiar smells, common to all the railways of the world, the sharp smell of impregnated sleepers, hot brakes, burning fuel, inspired in us a deep disgust. We were tired of everything, tired in particular of perforating useless frontiers.

But from another point of view, the fact of feeling a piece of Germany under our feet for the first time, not a piece of Upper Silesia or of Austria, but of Germany itself, overlaid our tiredness with a complex attitude composed of intolerance, frustration and tension. We felt we had something to say, enormous things to say, to every single German, and we felt that every German should have something to say to us; we felt an urgent need to settle our accounts, to ask, explain and comment, like chess players at the end of a game. Did 'they' know about Auschwitz, about the silent daily massacre, a step away from their doors? If they did, how could they walk about, return home and look at their children, cross the threshold of a church? If they did not, they ought, as a sacred duty, to listen, to learn everything, immediately, from us, from me; I felt the tattooed number on my arm burning like a sore.

As I wandered around the streets of Munich, full of ruins, near the station where our train lay stranded once more, I felt I was moving among throngs of insolvent debtors, as if everybody owed me something, and refused to pay. I was among them, in the enemy camp, among the *Herrenvolk*; but the men were few, many were mutilated, many dressed in rags like us. I felt that everybody should interrogate us, read in our faces who we were, and listen to our tale in humility. But no one looked us in the eyes, no one accepted the challenge; they were deaf, blind and dumb, imprisoned in their ruins, as in a fortress of wilful ignorance, still strong, still capable of hatred and contempt, still prisoners of their old tangle of pride and guilt.

I found myself searching among them, among that anonymous crowd of sealed faces, for other faces, clearly stamped in my memory, many bearing a name: the name of someone who could not but know, remember, reply; who had commanded and obeyed, killed, humiliated, corrupted. A vain and foolish search; because not they, but others, the few just ones, would reply for them.

If we had taken one guest on board at Szób, after Munich we realized that we had taken on board an entire contingent: our train consisted no longer of sixty, but of sixty-one trucks. A new truck was travelling with us towards Italy at the end of our train, crammed with young Jews, boys and girls, coming from all the countries of Eastern Europe. None of them seemed more than twenty years old, but they were extremely self-confident and resolute people; they were young Zionists on their way to Israel, travelling where they were able to, and finding a path where they could. A ship was waiting for them at Bari; they had purchased their truck, and it had proved the simplest thing in the world to attach it to our train: they had not asked anybody's permission, but had hooked it on, and that was that. I was amazed, but they laughed at my amazement: 'Hitler's dead, isn't he?' replied their leader, with his intense hawk-like glance. They felt immensely free and strong, lords of the world and of their destinies.

We passed through Garmisch-Partenkirchen and in the evening reached the fantastically disordered transit camp of Mittenwald, in the mountains, on the Austrian border. We spent the night there, and it was our last night of cold. The following day the train ran down to Innsbruck, where it filled up with Italian smugglers, who brought us the greetings of our homeland, in the absence of official authorities, and generously distributed chocolate, grappa and tobacco.

As the train, more tired than us, climbed towards the Italian frontier it snapped in two like an overtaut cable; there were several injuries, but this was the last adventure. Late at night we crossed the Brenner, which we had passed in our exile twenty months before; our less tired companions celebrated with a cheerful uproar; Leonardo and I remained lost in a silence crowded with memories. Of 650, our number when we had left, three of us were returning. And how much had we lost, in those twenty months? What should we find at home? How much of ourselves had been eroded, extinguished? Were we returning richer or poorer, stronger or emptier? We did not know; but we knew that on the thresholds of our homes, for good or ill, a trial awaited us, and we anticipated it with fear. We felt in our veins the poison of Auschwitz, flowing together with our thin blood; where should we find the strength to begin our lives again, to break down the barriers, the brushwood which grows up spontaneously in all absences, around every deserted house, every empty refuge? Soon, tomorrow, we should have to give battle, against enemies still unknown, outside ourselves and inside;

with what weapons, what energies, what willpower? We felt the weight of centuries on our shoulders, we felt oppressed by a year of ferocious memories; we felt emptied and defenceless. The months just past, although hard, of wandering on the margins of civilization now seemed to us like a truce, a parenthesis of unlimited availability, a providential but unrepeatable gift of fate.

With these thoughts, which kept us from sleep, we passed our first night in Italy, as the train slowly descended the deserted, dark Adige Valley. On 17 October, we reached the camp of Pescantina, near Verona, and here we split up, everyone following his own destiny; but no train left in the direction of Turin until the evening of the following day. In the confused vortex of thousands of refugees and displaced persons, we glimpsed Pista, who had already found his path; he wore the white and yellow armband of the Pontifical Organization of Assistance, and collaborated briskly and cheerfully in the life of the camp. And then we saw advance towards us a figure, a well-known face, a full head higher than the crowd, the Moor of Verona. He had come to say good-bye to us, to Leonardo and me; he had reached his home, the first of all of us, for Avesa, his village, was only a few miles away. And he blessed us, the old blasphemer: he raised two enormous knobbly fingers, and blessed us with the solemn gesture of a Pontiff, wishing us a good return and a happy future.

I reached Turin on 19 October, after thirty-five days of travel; my house was still standing, all my family was alive, no one was expecting me. I was swollen, bearded and in rags, and had difficulty in making myself recognized. I found my friends full of life, the warmth of secure meals, the solidity of daily work, the liberating joy of recounting my story. I found a large clean bed, which in the evening (a moment of terror) yielded softly under my weight. But only after many months did I lose the habit of walking with my glance fixed to the ground, as if searching for something to eat or to pocket hastily or to sell for bread; and a dream full of horror has still not ceased to visit me, at sometimes frequent, sometimes longer, intervals.

It is a dream within a dream, varied in detail, one in substance. I am sitting at a table with my family, or with friends, or at work, or in the green countryside; in short, in a peaceful relaxed environment, apparently without tension or affliction; yet I feel a deep and subtle anguish, the definite sensation, of an impending threat. And in fact, as the dream proceeds, slowly or brutally, each time in a different way, everything collapses and disintegrates around me, the scenery, the walls, the people, while the anguish becomes more intense and more precise. Now everything has changed to chaos; I am alone in the centre of a grey and turbid nothing, and now, I *know* what this thing means, and I also know that I have always known it; I am in the Lager once more, and nothing is true outside the Lager. All the rest was a brief pause, a deception of the senses, a dream; my family, nature in flower, my home. Now this inner dream, this dream of peace, is over, and in the outer dream, which continues, gelid, a well-known voice resounds: a single word, not imperious, but brief and subdued. It is the dawn command of Auschwitz, a foreign word, feared and expected: get up, '*Wstawàch*'.

Turin, December 1961–November 1962.

Postscript:
The Author's Answers to His
Readers' Questions

Someone a long time ago wrote that books too, like human beings, have their destiny: unpredictable, different from what is desired and expected. The first of these two books also has a strange destiny. Its birth certificate is distant: it can be found where one reads that 'I write what I would never dare tell anyone.' My need to tell the story was so strong in the Camp that I had begun describing my experiences there, on the spot, in that German laboratory laden with freezing cold, the war, and vigilant eyes; and yet I knew that I would not be able under any circumstances to hold on to those haphazardly scribbled notes, and that I must throw them away immediately because if they were found they would be considered an act of espionage and would cost me my life.

Nevertheless, those memories burned so intensely inside me that I felt compelled to write as soon as I returned to Italy, and within a few months I wrote *If This is a Man*. The manuscript was turned down by a number of important publishers; it was accepted in 1947 by a small publisher who printed only 2,500 copies and then folded. So this first book of mine fell into oblivion for many years: perhaps also because in all of Europe those were difficult times of mourning and reconstruction and the public did not want to return in memory to the painful years of the war that had just ended. It achieved a new life only in 1958, when it was republished by Einaudi, and from then on the interest of the public has never flagged. In Italy the book has sold more than 500,000 copies; it has been translated into eight languages and adapted for radio and theatre. This belated success encouraged me to write *The Truce*, the natural continuation of its older brother, which, unlike it, immediately met with an excellent reception from the public and critics.

In the course of the years, I have been asked to comment on the two books hundreds of times, before the most diverse audiences: young and adult, uneducated and cultivated, in Italy and abroad. On the occasion of these encounters, I have had to answer many questions: naïve, acute, highly emotional, superficial, at times provocative. I soon realized that some of these questions recurred constantly; indeed, never failed to be asked: they must therefore spring from a thoughtful curiosity, to which in some way the text of the book did not give a satisfactory reply. I propose to reply to these questions here.

1. *In these books there are no expressions of hate for the Germans, no desire for revenge. Have you forgiven them?*

My personal temperament is not inclined to hatred. I regard it as bestial, crude, and prefer on the contrary that my actions and thoughts, as far as possible, should be the product of reason; therefore I have never cultivated within myself hatred as a desire for revenge, or as a desire to inflict suffering on my real or presumed enemy, or as a private vendetta. Even less do I accept hatred as directed collectively at an ethnic group, for example, all the Germans; if I accepted it, I would feel that I was following the precepts of Nazism, which was founded precisely on national and racial hatred.

I must admit that if I had in front of me one of our persecutors of those days, certain known faces, certain old lies, I would be tempted to hate, and with violence too; but exactly because I am not a Fascist or a Nazi, I refuse to give way to this temptation. I believe in reason and in discussion as supreme instruments of progress, and therefore I repress hatred even within myself: I prefer justice. Precisely for this reason, when describing the tragic world of Auschwitz, I have deliberately assumed the calm, sober language of the witness, neither the lamenting tones of the victim nor the irate voice of someone who seeks revenge. I thought that my account would be all the more credible and useful the more it appeared objective and the less it sounded overly emotional; only in this way does a witness in matters of justice perform his task, which is that of preparing the ground for the judge. The judges are my readers.

All the same I would not want my abstaining from explicit judgement to be confused with an indiscriminate pardon. No, I have not forgiven any of the culprits, nor am I willing to forgive a single one of them, unless he has shown (with deeds, not words, and not too long afterward) that he has become conscious of the crimes and errors of Italian and foreign Fascism and is determined to condemn them, uproot them, from his conscience and from that of others. Only in this case am I, a non-Christian, prepared to follow the Jewish and Christian precept of forgiving my enemy, because an enemy who sees the error of his ways ceases to be an enemy.

2. Did the Germans know what was happening?

How is it possible that the extermination of millions of human beings could have been carried out in the heart of Europe without anyone's knowledge?

The world in which we Westerners live has grave faults and dangers, but when compared to the countries in which democracy is smothered, and to the times during which it has been smothered, our world has a tremendous advantage: everyone can know everything about everything. Information today is the 'fourth estate': at least in theory the reporter, the journalist and the news photographer have free access everywhere; nobody has the right to stop them or send them away. Everything is easy: if you wish you can receive radio or television broadcasts from your own country or from any other country. You can go the newsstand and choose the newspaper you prefer, national or foreign, of any political tendency – even that of a country with which your country is at odds. You can buy and read any books you want and usually do not risk being incriminated for 'anti-national activity' or bring down on your house a search by the political police. Certainly it is not easy to avoid all biases, but at least you can pick the bias you prefer.

In an authoritarian state it is not like this. There is only one Truth, proclaimed from above; the newspapers are all alike, they all repeat the same one Truth. So do the radio stations, and you cannot listen to those of other countries. In the first place, since this is a crime, you risk ending up in prison. In the second place, the radio stations in your country send out jamming signals, on the appropriate wavelengths, that superimpose themselves on the foreign messages and prevent your hearing them. As for books, only those that please the State are published and translated. You must seek any others on the outside and introduce them into your country at your own risk because they are considered more dangerous than drugs and explosives, and if they are found in your possession at the border, they are confiscated and you are punished. Books not in favour, or no longer in favour, are burned in public bonfires in town squares. This went on in Italy between 1924 and 1945; it went on in National Socialist Germany; it is going on right now in many countries, among which it is sad to have to number the Soviet Union, which fought heroically against Fascism. In an authoritarian State it is considered permissible to alter the truth; to rewrite history retrospectively; to distort the news, suppress the true, add the false. Propaganda is substituted for information. In fact, in such a country you are not a citizen possessor of rights but a subject, and as such you owe to the State (and to the dictator who represents it) fanatical loyalty and supine obedience.

It is clear that under these conditions it becomes possible (though not always easy; it is never easy to deeply violate human nature) to erase great chunks of reality. In Fascist Italy the undertaking to assassinate the Socialist deputy Matteotti was quite successful, and after a few months it was locked in silence. Hitler and his Minister of Propaganda, Joseph Goebbels, showed themselves to be far superior to Mussolini at this work of controlling and masking truth.

However, it was not possible to hide the existence of the enormous concentration camp apparatus from the German people. What's more, it was not (from the Nazi point of view) even desirable. Creating and maintaining an atmosphere of undefined terror in the country was part of the aims of Nazism. It was just as well for the people to know that opposing Hitler was extremely dangerous. In fact, hundreds of thousands of Germans were confined in the camps from the very first months of Nazism: Communists, Social Democrats, Liberals, Jews, Protestants, Catholics; the whole country knew it and knew that in the camps people were suffering and dying.

Nevertheless, it is true that the great mass of Germans remained unaware of the most atrocious details of what happened later on in the camps: the methodical industrialized extermination on a scale of millions, the gas chambers, the cremation furnaces, the vile despoiling of corpses, all this was not supposed to be known, and in effect few did know it up to the end of the war. Among other precautions, in order to keep the secret, in official language only cautious and cynical euphemisms were employed: one did not write 'extermination' but 'final solution,' not 'deportation' but 'transfer,' not 'killing by gas' but 'special treatment,' and so on. Not without reason, Hitler feared that this horrendous news, if it were divulged, would compromise the blind faith which the country had in him, as well as the morale of the fighting troops. Besides, it would have become known to the Allies and would have been exploited as propaganda material This actually did happen but because of their very enormity, the horrors of the camps, described many times by the Allied radio, were not generally believed.

The most convincing summing-up of the German situation at that time that I have found is in the book *DER SS STAAT* (*The Theory and Practice of Hell*) by Eugene Kogon, a former Buchenwald prisoner, later Professor of Political Science at the University of Munich:

> What did the Germans know about the concentration camps? Outside the concrete fact of their existence, almost nothing. Even today they know little. Indubitably, the method of rigorously keeping the details of the terrorist system secret, thereby making the anguish undefined, and hence that much more profound, proved very efficacious.
>
> As I have said elsewhere, even many Gestapo functionaries did not know what was happening in the camps to which they were sending prisoners. The greater majority of the prisoners themselves had a very imprecise idea of how their camps functioned and of the methods employed there. How could the German people have known? Anyone who entered the camps found himself confronted by an unfathomable universe, totally new to him. This is the best demonstration of the power and efficacy of secrecy.
>
> And yet ... and yet, there wasn't even one German who did not know of the camps' existence or who believed they were sanatoriums. There were very few Germans who did not

have a relative or an acquaintance in a camp, or who did not know, at least, that such a one or such another had been sent to a camp. All the Germans had been witnesses to the multi-form anti-Semitic barbarity. Millions of them had been present – with indifference or with curiosity, with contempt or with downright malign joy – at the burning of synagogues or humiliation of Jews and Jewesses forced to kneel in the street mud. Many Germans knew from the foreign radio broadcasts, and a number had contact with prisoners who worked outside the camps. A good many Germans had had the experience of encountering miserable lines of prisoners in the streets or at the railroad stations. In a circular dated November 9, 1941, and addressed by the head of the Police and the Security Services to all ... Police officials and camp commandants, one reads: 'In particular, it must be noted that during the transfers on foot, for example from the station to the camp, a considerable number of prisoners collapse along the way, fainting or dying from exhaustion ... It is impossible to keep the population from knowing about such happenings.'

Not a single German could have been unaware of the fact that the prisons were full to overflowing, and that executions were taking place continually all over the country. Thousands of magistrates and police functionaries, lawyers, priests and social workers knew genetically that the situation was very grave. Many businessmen who dealt with the camp SS men as suppliers, the industrialists who asked the administrative and economic offices of the SS for slave-labourers, the clerks in those offices, all knew perfectly well that many of the big firms were exploiting slave labour. Quite a few workers performed their tasks near concentration camps or actually inside them. Various university professors collaborated with the medical research centres instituted by Himmler, and various State doctors and doctors connected with private institutes collaborated with the professional murderers. A good many members of military aviation had been transferred to SS jurisdiction and must have known what went on there. Many high-ranking army officers knew about the mass murders of the Russian prisoners of war in the camps, and even more soldiers and members of the Military Police must have known exactly what terrifying horrors were being perpetrated in the camps, the ghettos, the cities, and the countrysides of the occupied Eastern territories. Can you say that even one of these statements is false?

In my opinion, none of these statements is false, but one other must be added to complete the picture: in spite of the varied possibilities for information, most Germans didn't know because they didn't want to know. Because, indeed, they wanted *not* to know. It is certainly true that State terrorism is a very strong weapon, very difficult to resist. But it is also true that the German people, as a whole, did not even try to resist. In Hitler's Germany a particular code was widespread: those who knew did not talk; those who did not know did not ask questions; those who did ask questions received no answers. In this way the typical German citizen won and defended his ignorance, which seemed to him sufficient justification of his adherence to Nazism. Shutting his mouth, his eyes and his ears, he built for himself the illusion of not knowing, hence not being an accomplice to the things taking place in front of his very door.

Knowing and making things known was one way (basically then not all that dangerous) of keeping one's distance from Nazism. I think the German people, on the whole, did not seek this recourse, and I hold them fully culpable of this deliberate omission.

*

3. Were there prisoners who escaped from the camps? How is it that there were no large-scale revolts?

These are among the questions most frequently put to me by young readers. They must, therefore, spring from some particularly important curiosity or need. My interpretation is optimistic: today's young people feel that freedom is a privilege that one cannot do without, no matter what. Consequently, for them, the idea of prison is immediately linked to the idea of escape or revolt. Besides, it is true that according to the military codes of many countries, the prisoner of war is required to attempt escape, in any way possible, in order to resume his place as a combatant, and that according to The Hague Convention, such an attempt would not be punished. The concept of escape as a moral obligation is constantly reinforced by romantic literature (remember the Count of Montecristo?), by popular literature, and by the cinema, in which the hero, unjustly (or even justly) imprisoned, always tries to escape, even in the least likely circumstances, the attempt being invariably crowned with success.

Perhaps it is good that the prisoner's condition, not-liberty, is felt to be something improper, abnormal – like an illness, in short – that has to be cured by escape or rebellion. Unfortunately, however, this picture hardly resembles the true one of the concentration camps.

For instance, only a few hundred prisoners tried to escape from Auschwitz, and of those perhaps a few score succeeded. Escape was difficult and extremely dangerous. The prisoners were debilitated, in addition to being demoralized, by hunger and ill-treatment. Their heads were shaved, their striped clothing was immediately recognizable, and their wooden clogs made silent and rapid walking impossible. They had no money and, in general, did not speak Polish, which was the local language, nor did they have contacts in the area, whose geography they did not know, either. On top of all that, fierce reprisals were employed to discourage escape attempts. Anyone caught trying to escape was publicly hanged – often after cruel torture – in the square where the roll-calls took place. When an escape was discovered, the friends of the fugitive were considered accomplices and were starved to death in cells; all the other prisoners were forced to remain standing for twenty-four hours, and sometimes the parents of the 'guilty' one were arrested and deported to camps.

The SS guards who killed a prisoner in the course of an escape attempt were granted special leaves. As a result, it often happened that an SS guard fired at a prisoner who had no intention of trying to escape, solely in order to qualify for leave. This fact artificially swells the official number of escape attempts recorded in the statistics. As I have indicated, the actual number was very small, made up almost exclusively of a few Aryan (that is, non-Jewish, to use the terminology of that time) Polish prisoners who lived not far from the camp and had, consequently, a goal towards which to proceed and the assurance that they would be protected by the population. In the other camps things occurred in a similar way.

As for the lack of rebellion, the story is somewhat different. First of all, it is necessary to remember that uprisings did actually take place in certain camps: Treblinka, Sobibor, even Birkenau, one of the Auschwitz dependencies. They did not have much numerical weight; like the analogous Warsaw Ghetto uprising they represented, rather, examples of extraordinary moral force. In every instance they were planned and led by prisoners who were privileged in some way and, consequently, in better physical and spiritual condition than the average camp prisoner. This is not all that surprising: only at first glance does it seem paradoxical that people who rebel are those who suffer the least. Even outside the camps, struggles are rarely waged by *Lumpenproletariat*. People in rags do not revolt.

In the camps for political prisoners, or where political prisoners were in the majority, the conspiratory experience of these people proved valuable and often resulted in quite effective defensive activities, rather than in open revolt. Depending upon the camps and the times, prisoners succeeded, for example, in blackmailing or corrupting the SS, curbing their indiscriminate power; in sabotaging the work for the German war industries; in organizing escapes; in communicating via the radio with the Allies, furnishing them with accounts of the horrendous conditions in the camps; in improving the treatment of the sick, substituting prisoner doctors for the SS ones; in 'guiding' the selections, sending spies and traitors to death and saving prisoners whose survival had, for one reason or another, some special importance; preparing, even in military ways, to resist in case the Nazis decided, with the Front coming closer (as in fact they often did decide), to liquidate the camps entirely.

In camps with a majority of Jews, like those in the Auschwitz area, an active or passive defence was particularly difficult. Here the prisoners were, for the most part, devoid of any kind of organizational or military experience. They came from every country in Europe, spoke different languages and, as a result, could not understand one another. They were more starved, weaker and more exhausted than the others because their living conditions were harsher and because they often had a long history of hunger, persecution and humiliation in the ghettos. The final consequences of this were that the length of their stays in the camps was tragically brief. They were, in short, a fluctuating population, continually decimated by death and renewed by the never-ending arrivals of new convoys. It is understandable that the seed of revolt did not easily take root in a human fabric that was in such a state of deterioration and so unstable.

You may wonder why the prisoners who had just got off the

trains did not revolt, waiting as they did for hours (sometimes for days!) to enter the gas chambers. In addition to what I have already said, I must add here that the Germans had perfected a diabolically clever and versatile system of collective death. In most cases the new arrivals did not know what awaited them. They were received with cold efficiency but without brutality, invited to undress 'for the showers'. Sometimes they were handed soap and towels and were promised hot coffee after their showers. The gas chambers were, in fact, camouflaged as shower rooms, with pipes, taps, dressing rooms, clothes hooks, benches and so forth. When, instead, prisoners showed the smallest sign of knowing or suspecting their imminent fate, the SS and their collaborators used surprise tactics, intervening with extreme brutality, with shouts, threats, kicks, shots, loosing their dogs, which were trained to tear prisoners to pieces, against people who were confused, desperate, weakened by five or ten days of travelling in sealed railway carriages.

Such being the case, the statement that has sometimes been formulated – that the Jews didn't revolt out of cowardice – appears absurd and insulting. No one rebelled. Let it suffice to remember that the gas chambers at Auschwitz were tested on a group of three hundred Russian prisoners of war, young, army-trained, politically indoctrinated, and not hampered by the presence of women and children, and even they did not revolt.

I would like to add one final thought. The deeply rooted consciousness that one must not consent to oppression but resist it instead was not widespread in Fascist Europe, and it was particularly weak in Italy. It was the patrimony of a narrow circle of political activists, but Fascism and Nazism had isolated, expelled, terrorized or destroyed them outright. You must not forget that the first victims of the German camps, by the hundreds of thousands, were, in fact, the cadres of the anti-Nazi political parties. Without their contribution, the popular will to resist, to organize for the purpose of resisting, sprang up again much later, thanks, above all, to the contribution of the European Communist parties that hurled themselves into the struggle against Nazism after Germany, in 1941, had unexpectedly attacked the Soviet Union, breaking the Ribbentrop–Molotov pact of September 1939. To conclude, reproaching the prisoners for not rebelling represents, above all, an error in historical perspective, expecting from them a political consciousness which is today an almost common heritage but which belonged at that time only to an elite.

4. Did you return to Auschwitz after the liberation?

I returned to Auschwitz twice, in 1965 and in 1982. As I have indicated in my books, the concentration camp empire of Auschwitz did not consist of only one camp but rather of some forty camps. Auschwitz central was constructed on the outskirts of the town of the same name (Oswiecim, in Polish). It had a capacity of about 20,000 prisoners and was, so to speak, the administrative capital of the complex. Then there was the camp (or, to be more precise, the group of camps – from three to five, depending on the period) of Birkenau, which grew to contain about 60,000 prisoners, of which about 40,000 were women, and in which the gas chambers and cremation furnaces functioned. In addition, there was a constantly varying number of work camps, as far away as hundreds of kilometres from the 'capital.' My camp, called Monowitz, was the largest of these, containing, finally, about 12,000 prisoners. It was situated about seven kilometres to the east of Auschwitz. The whole area is now Polish territory.

I didn't feel anything much when I visited the central Camp. The Polish government has transformed it into a kind of national monument. The huts have been cleaned and painted, trees have been planted and flowerbeds laid out. There is a museum in which pitiful relics are displayed: tons of human hair, hundreds of thousands of pairs of spectacles, combs, shaving brushes, dolls, baby shoes, but it remains just a museum – something static, rearranged, contrived. To me, the entire camp seemed a museum. As for my own Camp, it no longer exists. The rubber factory to which it was annexed, now in Polish hands, has grown so that it occupies the whole area.

I did, however, experience a feeling of violent anguish when I entered Birkenau Camp, which I had never seen as a prisoner. Here nothing has changed. There was mud, and there is still mud, or suffocating summer dust. The blocks of huts (those that weren't burned when the Front reached and passed this area) have remained as they were, low, dirty, with draughty wooden sides and beaten earth floors. There are no bunks but bare planks, all the way to the ceiling. Here nothing has been prettied up. With me was a woman friend of mine, Giuliana Tedeschi, a survivor of Birkenau. She pointed out to me that on every plank, 1.8. by 2 metres, up to nine women slept. She showed me that from the tiny window you could see the ruins of the cremation furnace. In her day, you could see the flames issuing from the chimney. She had asked the older women: 'What is that fire?' And they had replied: 'It is we who are burning.'

Face to face with the sad evocative power of those places, each of us survivors behaves in a different manner, but it is possible to describe two typical categories. Those who refuse to go back, or even to discuss the matter, belong to the first category, as do those who would like to forget but do not succeed in doing so and are tormented by nightmares; and the second group who have, instead, forgotten, have dismissed everything, and have begun again to live, starting from zero. I have noticed that the first group are individuals who ended in the camps through bad luck, not because of a political commitment. For them the suffering was traumatic but devoid of meaning, like a misfortune or an illness. For them the memory is extraneous, a painful object which intruded into their lives and which they have sought – or still seek – to eliminate. The second category is composed, instead, of ex-political prisoners, or those who possessed at least a measure of political preparation, or religious conviction, or a strong moral consciousness. For these survivors, remembering is a duty. They do not want to forget, and above all they do not want the world to forget, because they understand that their experiences were not meaningless, that the camps were not an accident, an unforeseen historical happening.

The Nazi camps were the apex, the culmination of Fascism in Europe, its most monstrous manifestation, but Fascism existed before Hitler and Mussolini, and it survived, in open or masked forms, up to the defeat of the Second World War. In every part of the world, wherever you begin by denying the fundamental liberties of mankind, and equality among people, you move towards the concentration camp system, and it is a road on which it is difficult to halt. I know many ex-prisoners who understand very well what a terrible lesson their experience contains and who return every year to 'their' Camp, guiding pilgrimages of young people. I would do it myself, gladly, if time permitted, and if I did not know that I reached the same goal by writing books and by agreeing to talk about them to my readers.

5. Why do you speak only about German camps and not the Russian ones as well?

As I have already written in my reply to the first question, I prefer the role of witness to that of judge. I can bear witness only to the things which I myself endured and saw. My books are not history books. In writing them I have limited myself strictly to reporting facts of which I had direct experience, excluding those I learned later from books or newspapers. For example, you will note that I have not quoted the number of those massacred at Auschwitz, nor have I described details of the gas chambers and crematoriums. This is because I did not, in fact, know these data when I was in the Camp. I only learned them afterward, when the whole world learned them.

For the same reason I do not generally speak about the Russian camps. Fortunately I was never in them, and I could repeat only the things I have read, which would be the same things known to everyone interested in the subject. Clearly, however, I do not want to, nor can I, evade the duty which every man has, that of making a judgement and formulating an opinion. Besides the obvious similarities, I think I can perceive substantial differences.

The principal difference lies in the finality. The German camps constitute something unique in the history of humanity, bloody as it is. To the ancient aim of eliminating or terrifying political adversaries, they set a monstrous modern goal, that of erasing entire peoples and cultures from the world. Starting roughly in 1941, they became gigantic death-machines. Gas chambers and crematoriums were deliberately planned to destroy lives and human bodies on a scale of millions. The horrendous record belongs to Auschwitz, with 24,000 dead in a single day, in August 1944. Certainly the Soviet camps were not and are not pleasant places to be, but in them the death of prisoners was not expressly sought – even in the darkest years of Stalinism. It was a very frequent occurrence, tolerated with brutal indifference, but basically not intended. Death was a byproduct of hunger, cold, infections, hard labour. In this lugubrious comparison between two models of hell, I must also add the fact that one entered the German camps, in general never to emerge. Death was the only foreseen outcome. In the Soviet camps, however, a possible limit to incarceration has always existed. In Stalin's day the 'guilty' were sometimes given terribly long sentences (as much as fifteen or twenty years) with frightening disregard, but a hope – however faint – of eventual freedom remained.

From this fundamental difference, the others arise. The relationships between guards and prisoners are less inhuman in the Soviet Union. They all belong to the same nation, speak the same language, are not labelled 'Supermen' and 'Non-men' as they were under Nazism. The sick are treated, though all too inadequately. Confronted with overly hard work, an individual or collective protest is not unthinkable. Corporal punishment is rare and not too cruel. It is possible to receive letters and packages with foodstuffs. Human personality, in short, is not denied and is not totally lost. As a general consequence, the mortality figures are very different under the two systems. In the Soviet Union, it seems that in the harshest periods mortality hovered around 30 per cent of those who entered. This is certainly an intolerably high figure, but in the German camps mortality mounted to between 90 and 98 per cent.

I find very serious the recent Soviet innovation, that of summarily declaring certain dissenting intellectuals insane, shutting them into psychiatric institutions, and subjecting them to treatments that not only cause cruel suffering but distort and weaken their mental functioning. This shows how greatly dissent is feared. It is no longer punished but there is an effort to destroy it with drugs (or with the threat of drugs). Perhaps this technique is not very widespread (it appears that in 1985 these political 'patients' do not exceed a hundred) but it is odious because it constitutes a despicable use of science and an unpardonable prostitution on the part of the doctors who lend themselves so slavishly to abetting the wishes of the authorities. It reveals extreme contempt for democratic confrontation and civil liberties.

On the other hand, and as far as the precisely quantitative

aspect is concerned, one must note that in the Soviet Union the camp phenomenon appears to be on the decline, actually. It seems that around 1950, political prisoners were numbered in the millions. According to the data of Amnesty International they would number about ten thousand today.

To conclude, the Soviet camps remain anyway a deplorable manifestation of illegality and inhumanity. They have nothing to do with Socialism; indeed, they stand out as an ugly stain on Soviet Socialism. They should, rather, be regarded as a barbaric legacy from Tzarist absolutism from which the Soviet rulers have been unable or have not wished to liberate themselves. Anyone who reads *Memories of a Dead House*, written by Dostoievski in 1862, will have no difficulty recognizing the same prison 'features' described by Solzhenitsyn a hundred years later. But it is possible, even easy, to picture a Socialism without prison camps. A Nazism without concentration camps is, instead, unimaginable.

6. *Which of the characters in* If This is a Man *and* The Truce *have you seen again since the liberation?*

Most of the people who appear in these pages must, unfortunately, be considered to have died during their days in the Camp or in the course of the huge evacuation march mentioned in the last chapter of the second book. Others died later from illnesses contracted during their imprisonment. I have been unable to find a trace of still others. Some few survive and I have been able to maintain or reestablish contact with them.

Jean, the 'Pikolo' of the Canto of Ulysses, is alive and well. His family had been wiped out, but he married after his return and now has two children and leads a very peaceful life as a pharmacist in a small town in the French provinces. We get together occasionally in Italy, where he vacations. At other times I have gone to join him. Strange as it may seem, he has forgotten much of his year in Monowitz. The atrocious memories of the evacuation march loom larger for him. In the course of it, he saw all his friends (Alberto among them) die of exhaustion.

I also quite often see the person I called Piero Sonnino, the man who appears as Cesare in *The Truce*. He too, after a difficult period of 're-entry', found work and built a family. He lives in Rome. He recounts willingly and with great liveliness the vicissitudes he lived through in Camp and during the long journey home, but in his narratives, which often become almost theatrical monologues, he tends to emphasize the adventurous happenings of which he was the protagonist rather than those tragic ones at which he was passively present.

I have also seen Charles again. He had been taken prisoner only in November 1944 in the hills of the Vosges near his house, where he was a partisan, and he had been in the Camp for only a month. But that month of suffering, and the terrible things which he witnessed, marked him deeply, robbing him of the joy of living and the desire to build a future. Repatriated after a journey much like the one I described in *The Truce*, he resumed his profession of elementary school teacher in the tiny school in his village, where he also taught the children how to raise bees and how to cultivate a nursery for firs and pine trees. He retired quite a few years ago and recently married a no-longer-young colleague. Together they built a new house, small but comfortable and charming. I have gone to visit him twice, in 1951 and 1974. On this last occasion he told me about Arthur, who lives in a village not far from him. Arthur is old and ill, and does not wish to receive visits that might reawaken old anguish.

Dramatic, unforeseen, and full of joy for both of us was refolding Mendi, the 'modernist rabbi' mentioned briefly. He recognized himself in 1965 while casually reading the German translation of *If This is a Man*, remembered me, and wrote me a long letter, addressing it in care of the Jewish Community of

Turin. We subsequently wrote to each other at length, each informing the other about the fates of our common friends. In 1967 I went to see him in Dortmund, in the German Republic, where he was rabbi at the time. He has remained as he was, 'steadfast, courageous, and keen,' and extraordinarily cultivated besides. He married an Auschwitz survivor and has three children, now grown up. The whole family intends to move to Israel.

I never saw Dr Pannwitz again. He was the chemist who subjected me to a chilling 'State examination.' But I heard about him from that Dr Muller to whom I dedicated the chapter 'Vanadium' in my book *The Periodic Table*. When the arrival of the Red Army at the Buna factory was imminent, he conducted himself like a bully and a coward. He ordered his civilian collaborators to resist to the bitter end, forbade them to climb aboard the train leaving for the zones behind the Front, but jumped on himself at the last moment, profiting from the confusion. He died in 1946 of a brain tumour.

I have lost contact with almost all the characters in *The Truce*, with the exception of Cesare (of whom I have spoken before) and Leonardo. Dr Leonardo De Benedetti, a native of Turin like myself, had lost his dearly beloved wife at Auschwitz. After returning to our city, he resumed his profession with courage and commitment and was a precious friend, wise and serene, for many years. Besides his patients, innumerable others turned to him for help and advice and were never disappointed. He died in 1983 at the age of eighty-five, without suffering.

7. How can the Nazis' fanatical hatred of the Jews be explained?

It can be said that anti-Semitism is one particular case of intolerance; that for centuries it had a prevailingly religious character; that in the Third Reich it was exacerbated by the nationalistic and military predisposition of the German people and by the 'differentness' of the Jewish people; that it was easily disseminated in all of Germany – and in a good part of Europe – thanks to the efficiency of the Fascist and Nazi propaganda which needed a scapegoat on which to load all guilts and all resentments; and that the phenomenon was heightened to paroxysm by Hitler, a maniacal dictator.

However, I must admit that these commonly accepted explanations do not satisfy me. They are reductive; not commensurate with, nor proportionate to, the facts that need explaining. In rereading the chronicles of Nazism, from its murky beginnings to its convulsed end, I cannot avoid the impression of a general atmosphere of uncontrolled madness that seems to me to be unique in history. This collective madness, this 'running off the rails,' is usually explained by postulating the combination of many diverse factors, insufficient if considered singly, and the greatest of these factors is Hitler's personality itself and its profound interaction with the German people. It is certain that his personal obsessions, his capacity for hatred, his preaching of violence, found unbridled echoes in the frustration of the German people, and for this reason came back to him multiplied, confirming his delirious conviction that he himself was the Hero prophesied by Nietzsche, the Superman redeemer of Germany.

Much has been written about the origin of his hatred of the Jews. It is said that Hitler poured out upon the Jews his hatred of the entire human race; that he recognized in the Jews some of his own defects, and that in hating the Jews he was hating himself; that the violence of his aversion arose from the fear that he might have 'Jewish blood' in his veins.

Again, these explanations do not seem adequate to me. I do not find it permissible to explain a historical phenomenon by piling all the blame on a single individual (those who carry out horrendous orders are not innocent!). Besides, it is always difficult to interpret the deep-seated motivations of an individual. The hypotheses that have been proposed justify the facts only up to a point, explain the quality but not the quantity. I must admit that I prefer the humility with which some of the most serious historians (among them Bullock, Schramm, Bracher) confess to *not understanding* the furious anti-Semitism of Hitler and of Germany behind him.

Perhaps one cannot, what is more one must not, understand what happened, because to understand is almost to justify. Let me explain: 'understanding' a proposal or human behaviour means to 'contain' it, contain its author, put oneself in his place, identify with him. Now, no normal human being will ever be able to identify with Hitler, Himmler, Goebbels, Eichmann, and endless others. This dismays us, and at the same time gives us a sense of relief, because perhaps it is desirable that their words (and also, unfortunately, their deeds) cannot be comprehensible to us. They are non-human words and deeds, really counter-human, without historic precedents, with difficulty comparable to the crudest events of the biological struggle for existence. The war can be related to this struggle, but Auschwitz has nothing to do with war; it is neither an episode in it nor an extreme form of it. War is always a terrible fact, to be deprecated, but it is in us, it has its rationality, we 'understand' it.

But there is no rationality in the Nazi hatred: it is a hate that is not in us; it is outside man, it is a poison fruit sprung from the deadly trunk of Fascism, but it is outside and beyond Fascism itself. We cannot understand it, but we can and must understand from where it springs, and we must be on our guard. If understanding is impossible, knowing is imperative, because what happened could happen again. Conscience can be seduced and obscured again – even our consciences.

For this reason, it is everyone's duty to reflect on what happened. Everybody must know, or remember, that when Hitler and Mussolini spoke in public, they were believed, applauded, admired, adored like gods. They were 'charismatic leaders'; they possessed a secret power of seduction that did not proceed from the credibility or the soundness of the things they said but from the suggestive way in which they said them, from their eloquence, from their histrionic art, perhaps instinctive, perhaps patiently learned and practised. The ideas they proclaimed were not always the same and were, in general, aberrant or silly or cruel. And yet they were acclaimed with hosannahs and followed to the death by millions of the faithful. We must remember that these faithful followers, among them the diligent executors of inhuman orders, were not born torturers, were not (with a few exceptions) monsters: they were ordinary men. Monsters exist, but they are too few in number to be truly dangerous. More dangerous are the common men, the functionaries ready to believe and to act without asking questions, like Eichmann; like Höss, the commandant of Auschwitz; like Stangl, commandant of Treblinka; like the French military of twenty years later, slaughterers in Algeria; like the Khmer Rouge of the late seventies, slaughterers in Cambodia.

It is, therefore, necessary to be suspicious of those who seek to convince us with means other than reason, and of charismatic leaders: we must be cautious about delegating to others our judgement and our will. Since it is difficult to distinguish true prophets from false, it is as well to regard all prophets with suspicion. It is better to renounce revealed truths, even if they exalt us by their splendour or if we find them convenient because we can acquire them gratis. It is better to content oneself with other more modest and less exciting truths, those one acquires painfully, little by little and without shortcuts, with study, discussion, and reasoning, those that can be verified and demonstrated.

It is clear that this formula is too simple to suffice in every case. A new Fascism, with its trail of intolerance, of abuse, and of servitude, can be born outside our country and be imported into it, walking on tiptoe and calling itself by other names, or it can loose itself from within with such violence that it routs all defences. At that point, wise counsel no longer serves, and one must find the strength to resist. Even in this contingency, the memory of what happened in the heart of Europe, not very long ago, can serve as support and warning.

8. What would you be today if you had not been a prisoner in the Camp? What do you feel, remembering that period? To what factors do you attribute your survival?

Strictly speaking, I do not and cannot know what I would be today if I had not been in the Camp. No man knows his future, and this would be, precisely, a case of describing a future that never took place. Hazarding guesses (extremely rough ones, for that matter) about the behaviour of a population has some meaning. It is, however, almost impossible to foresee the behaviour of an individual, even on a day-to-day basis. In the same way, the physicist can prognosticate with great exactitude the time a gram of radium will need to halve its activity but is totally unable to say when a single atom of that same radium will disintegrate. If a man sets out towards a crossroad and does not take the left-hand path, it is obvious that he will take the one on the right, but almost never are our choices between only two alternatives. Then, every choice is followed by others, all multiple, and so on, *ad infinitum*. Last of all, our future depends heavily on external factors, wholly extraneous to our deliberate choices, and on internal factors as well, of which we are, however, not aware. For these well-known reasons, one does not know his future or that of his neighbour. For the same reason no one can say what his past would have been like 'if.'

I can, however, formulate a certain assertion and it is this: if

I had not lived the Auschwitz experience, I probably would never have written anything. I would not have had the motivation, the incentive, to write. I had been a mediocre student in Italian and had had bad grades in history. Physics and chemistry interested me most, and I had chosen a profession, that of chemist, which had nothing in common with the world of the written word. It was the experience of the Camp and the long journey home that forced me to write. I did not have to struggle with laziness, problems of style seemed ridiculous to me, and miraculously I found the time to write without taking even one hour away from my daily professional work. It seemed as if those books were all there, ready in my head, and I had only to let them come out and pour on to paper.

Now many years have passed. The two books, above all the first, have had many adventures and have interposed themselves, in a curious way, like an artificial memory, but also like a defensive barrier, between my very normal present and the dramatic past. I say this with some hesitation, because I would not want to pass for a cynic: when I remember the Camp today, I no longer feel any violent or dolorous emotions. On the contrary, on to my brief and tragic experience as a deportee has been overlaid that much longer and complex experience of writer-witness, and the sum total is clearly positive: in its totality, this past has made me richer and surer. A friend of mine, who was deported to the women's Camp of Ravensbrück, says that the camp was her university. I think I can say the same thing, that is, by living and then writing about and pondering those events, I have learned many things about man and about the world.

I must hasten to say, however, that this positive outcome was a kind of good fortune granted to very few. Of the Italian deportees, for example, only about 5 per cent returned, and many of these lost families, friends, property, heath, equilibrium, youth. The fact that I survived and returned unharmed is due, in my opinion, chiefly to good luck. Pre-existing factors played only a small part: for instance, my training as a mountaineer and my profession of chemist, which won me some privileges in the last months of imprisonment. Perhaps I was helped too by my interest, which has never flagged, in the human spirit and by the will not only to survive (which was common to many) but to survive with the precise purpose of recounting the things we had witnessed and endured. And, finally, I was also helped by the determination, which I stubbornly preserved, to recognize always, even in the darkest days, in my companions and in myself, men, not things, and thus to avoid that total humiliation and demoralization which led so many to spiritual shipwreck.

TRANSLATED BY RUTH FELDMAN

Afterword:
Saving the Scaffolding

PAUL BAILEY

In 1943 Primo Levi, a young chemist from Turin, helped to form a partisan band which he and his comrades hoped would eventually be affiliated with the Resistance movement 'Justice and Liberty'. At the end of the year he was captured by the Fascist militia and sent to a detention camp at Fossoli. He stayed there a few weeks. On 21 February 1944 it was announced that all the Jews in the camp would be leaving the following day for an unknown destination. They were told to prepare themselves for a fortnight of travel. On the train the next morning – 650 'pieces' crammed into twelve goods wagons – they found out where they were going: Auschwitz. 'A name without significance for us at that time, but it at least implied some place on this earth.'

On arrival the children, the old men and most of the women were 'swallowed up by the night'. Ninety-six men and twenty-nine women entered the respective camps of Monowitz-Buna and Birkenau: the rest went to the gas chamber. Of the 125 people sent to the camps only three made the return journey to Italy after the liberation. One of them was Primo Levi. Some years later, when he had adjusted himself to normal life once more, he sat down and wrote about the twenty months he spent in hell. Two short books, *If This is a Man* and *The Truce*,

contain the recollections that came to him in that uneasy tranquillity.

Two books, but they should be read as one. Although a crude
over-simplification, it is nevertheless essentially true that *If This
is a Man* is about the descent into, and *The Truce* about the
flight away from, hell. The statement is crude because the first
book, despite its appalling subject, is not dispiriting. Levi does
not flinch from setting down the unbelievable details of that cru-
elty born of the 'mystique of barrenness', but then neither does
he paint them in lurid colours to press his point home. The facts
are surely enough. Paradoxically, what finally emerges from the
book is a sense of Man's worth, of dignity fought for and maintained against all the odds:

> Then for the first time we became aware that our language
> lacks words to express this offence, the demolition of a man.
> In a moment, with almost prophetic intuition, the reality was
> revealed to us: we had reached the bottom. It is not possible
> to sink lower than this; no human condition is more miser-
> able than this, nor could it conceivably be so. Nothing
> belongs to us any more; they have taken away our clothes,
> our shoes, even our hair; if we speak, they will not listen to
> us, and if they listen, they will not understand. They will even
> take away our name: and if we want to keep it, we will have
> to find in ourselves the strength to do so, to manage somehow
> so that behind the name something of us, of us as we were,
> still remains. '

Häftling* 174517 – 'We have been baptized, we will carry the
tattoo on our left arm until we die' – found the strength in himself to retain something of Primo Levi. But, at the beginning of

* Prisoner

his internment especially, it wasn't easy; he was shocked into
finding it by the example of others:

> ... after only one week of prison, the instinct for cleanliness
> completely disappeared in me. I wander aimlessly around the
> washroom when I suddenly see Steinlauf, my friend aged
> almost fifty, with nude torso, scrub his neck and shoulders
> with little success (he has no soap) but great energy. Steinlauf
> sees me and greets me, and without preamble asks me
> severely why I do not wash. Why should I wash? Would I be
> better off than I am? Would I please someone more? Would
> I live a day, an hour longer? I would probably live a shorter
> time because to wash is an effort, a waste of energy and
> warmth ... We will all die, we are all about to die ... Stein-
> lauf interrupts me. He has finished washing and is now
> drying himself with his cloth jacket which he was holding
> before wrapped up between his knees and which he will soon
> put on. And without interrupting the operation he adminis-
> ters me a complete lesson ... This was the sense, not
> forgotten either then or later: that precisely because the
> Lager was a great machine to reduce us to beasts, we must
> not become beasts; that even in this place one can survive,
> and therefore one must want to survive, to tell the story, to
> bear witness; and that to survive we must force ourselves to
> save at least the skeleton, the scaffolding, the form of civi-
> lization ... We must walk erect, without dragging our feet,
> not in homage to Prussian discipline but to remain alive, not
> to begin to die.

Levi does not say how Steinlauf died – presumably he disappeared in one of the many 'selections'. Nor did he take all of the
older man's advice literally: many months of freedom passed
before he lost the habit of walking with his eyes fixed to the

ground, as if searching for bread or something to sell or exchange for it.

If This is a Man and its sequel are books about a man among men: there are no saints and no heroes in the accepted sense. Indeed, what Levi says of his friend Leonardo in *The Truce* could with equal justice apply to himself:

> Besides good fortune, he also possessed another virtue essential for those places: an unlimited capacity for endurance, a silent courage, not innate, not religious, not transcendent, but deliberate and willed hour by hour, a virile patience, which sustained him miraculously to the very edge of collapse.

And Levi did have good fortune, though the phrase is an obscenity when one thinks of the horrors that he and Leonardo and the other survivors were forced to combat. But he was not 'selected' and by some miracle he was ill with scarlet fever when the Germans fled from Auschwitz in January 1945, taking all the healthy prisoners with them. The healthy, who numbered almost 20,000, vanished on the march. A few of the sick survived, surrounded by corpses and tormented by the groans of dying men. 'The living are more demanding; the dead can wait. We began to work as on every day.' The work by this time was the work of healing, of finding and sharing food with the helpless, not the humiliating drudgery imposed upon them by the SS (a sign at the entrance to the camp read *Arbeit Macht Frei*, 'Work Gives Freedom'). It is on this note of hope that *If This is a Man* ends: with the Häftlinge, tired and hungry, creeping out of the shadows and slowly becoming men again.

Still, the book is not all blackness, though the tone of the narrative is elegiac and those millions of accusing ghosts haunt its every sentence. Levi does not omit from his story the faint glimmers of light that came on rare occasions to shine briefly out of the evil murk. There is the story of Lorenzo, for instance:

> In concrete terms it amounts to little: an Italian civilian worker brought me a piece of bread and the remainder of his ration every day for six months; he gave me a vest of his, full of patches; he wrote a postcard on my behalf to Italy and brought me the reply. For all this he neither asked nor accepted any reward, because he was good and simple and did not think that one did good for a reward ... His humanity was pure and uncontaminated, he was outside this world of negation. Thanks to Lorenzo, I managed not to forget that I myself was a man.

But *The Truce* is almost all light. It tells of Levi's journey home to his native Turin, and the quiet, hesitant note of hope and renewal that ends the first book is transformed into something like a trumpet blast in its pages. The reader's eyes open with Levi's as he becomes aware of the abundant life about him. Like the great novels he devoured as a youth ('printed paper is a vice of mine'), it is a celebration of other men's uniqueness. In Auschwitz he had learned a new morality, one that had made him more tolerant of the failings of others, and he draws a clear line in *The Truce* between the good thieves and the bad, the genuinely strong man and the vicious bully. There are unforgettable portraits of the people he met or who shared his journey with him: Cesare, from the Roman slums, making fish fatter with the aid of a syringe and selling them to gullible Russian peasants; the resourceful Greek, Mordo Nahum; Mr Unverdorben, the composer of a fantasy opera, *The Queen of Navarre*, praised by a fantasy Toscanini and never performed because of four consecutive bars which were identical with four in *I Pagliacci*; the ministering angel, Dr

Gottlieb; the stately Moor of Verona, warding off friendship
with obscenities. But the self-styled Colonel Rovi is perhaps the
most incredible character of them all – an official interpreter at
Katowice camp who cannot speak a word of German or
Russian, dressed in a uniform composed of Soviet boots, a
Polish railwayman's cap and a jacket and a pair of trousers
from an unknown source.

What is chastening about Levi's writing is its freedom from
self-indulgence. There isn't even a hint of hysterical recrimina-
tion. How easy, and how understandable, it would have been
for him to have adopted such a tone. He chose to build instead:
out of the mud, the blows dealt without anger, out of that
unique humiliation he has constructed two incomparable works
of art, written in a careful, weighted and serenely beautiful prose
(the quality of which Stuart Woolf has captured in his exem-
plary translations). In Italy they are rightly regarded as classics,
but not – as yet – of the safe kind. I hope they will one day be
so regarded in Britain and America. They should be required
reading for the decriers of the merely human, the dazed pursuers
of the Maharishis, and the armchair Jeremiahs who make a
profitable business out of the dissemination of gloom. But, most
of all, I hope they find their way into the hands of the practi-
tioners of the new sentimentality – those who try to persuade us,
with increasing shrillness, that Man is vile: the artists who use
the terrible fact of the camps for emotional and aesthetic effect,
and the critics who compare their grimmer brand of kitsch to
King Lear and the paintings of Goya's last years. Levi, who has
confronted the unendurable, could not be persuaded that our
short time on earth is just a matter of waste disposal. He has
heard songs other than those of the crow. His books remind us
that the scaffolding is worth saving. We who weren't interned
should endeavour to build things that are worthy of its support.

*

This preceeding article was written in the 1970s for a series published in the *New Statesman* about forgotten writers. The literary editor Anthony Thwaite had invited several novelists and critics to choose a book or books they considered shamefully neglected. At that time, Primo Levi wasn't so much forgotten in Britain as totally unknown. *If This is a Man* had been out of print for seventeen years; *The Truce* for fifteen. It was my seriously pleasurable task to bring them to the attention of a new generation of readers. I was asked to produce an enthusiastic piece, and that is what I did. If I were invited to write about Levi today, my tone would be more measured and thoughtful, in the light of his suicide. But I was younger then and he was vibrantly alive, yet one thing remains constant – the fact that *If This is a Man* (its rightful, sceptical title, not the simplistic *Survival in Auschwitz*, as it's known in America) is destined to live for ever.

Paul Bailey
April 2013